£35.00
2 C90

D1460467

94

G

95

Health, Happiness, and Security

Health, Happiness, and Security
The creation of the National Health Service

Frank Honigsbaum

ROUTLEDGE
London and New York

First published 1989 by Routledge
11 New Fetter Lane, London EC4P 4EE

© 1989 Frank Honigsbaum

Phototypeset in 10pt Times by
Mews Photosetting, Beckenham, Kent
Printed and bound in Great Britain by
Billings & Sons Limited, Worcester

British Library Cataloguing in Publication Data

Honigsbaum, Frank
    Health happiness and security: the creation
    of the National Health Service.
    1. Great Britain. National Health Services,
    1940–1950
    I.Title
    362.1′0941

ISBN 0-415-01739-4

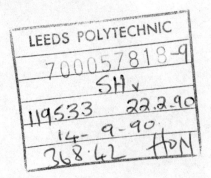

To Naomi, Mark, and Claire

I have always been deeply concerned about social reform and I am quite convinced that the National Insurance Act, which we have already passed, and this Bill, if it is passed, will prove by far the greatest social reforms which have been passed by Parliament and that they will bring a health and happiness and security to millions in a way which no previous Acts of Parliament ever have done.

Archbishop of York, the Most Reverend and Right Honourable Cyril Foster Garbett, during the debate on the National Health Service Bill in the House of Lords, 8 October 1946, volume 143, column 35

Contents

1989

Preface   xi

Abbreviations   xiv

Introduction   xv

Part 1 Prelude to Planning, 1911 to 1936

1 Failure of reform   3
2 Ministry rejects takeover of voluntary hospitals   13
3 Ministry intent to create a hospital service   22

Part 2 GP Service

4 A salaried service under municipal control   33
5 Doctors reject municipal control   51
6 Resistance to compromise   64
7 Doctors reject White Paper   72
8 Retreat to the panel system   86
9 Bevan the pragmatist   94

Part 3 Moran's Consultant Service

10 Moran organizes consultants   113
11 Who is a consultant? Who should decide?   127
12 The struggle for regional control   133
13 Bevan's concessions — more to consultants or GPs?   143

Part 4 National Hospital Service

14 No charge for hospital care   157
15 Deadlock in negotiations   165
16 The hospitals are nationalized   172

Contents

Part 5 Free and Complete Care for All

17 Financial constraints   187
18 Beveridge pressure   192
19 NHS costs   197
20 Medical movement towards universal coverage   204

Part 6 Assessment

21 Civil servants and doctors: their influence compared   213

Appendix The crisis in NHS negotiations, April 1948   219

Notes   222

Bibliography   265

Name index   273

Subject index   278

Preface

This study traces the part played by the civil service in the creation of the National Health Service. The ultimate decisions were made by ministers, but this book shows how they were influenced by the staff who serviced them.

During the course of the study, it became apparent that the wishes of the medical profession could not be ignored. Indeed, when it came to the planning of the consultant service, the task was delegated to a semi-official committee headed by Lord Moran, president of the Royal College of Physicians. This study also reveals the extent to which the doctors influenced policy.

In 1979 I published a book, *The Division in British Medicine*, which covered this subject from the standpoint of general practice. John Pater, a civil servant at the Ministry of Health during the 1940s, followed with a work that dealt with the NHS as a whole. In it, he noted that the ministry records on which his study was based were out of order and incomplete. This prompted the Departmental Record Officer, J. Worsfold (since retired), to put the matter right. The Public Record Office at Kew is now filled with volume after volume in the MH 80 (and other) series containing documents that were not available before. For the first time, it is possible to obtain a fairly complete picture of what went on within the portals of government.

The same applies to the debates that raged within the medical profession, only parts of which were published in the medical press. File after file will be found in the registry section of the library of the British Medical Association, while Lord Moran left behind a large number of boxes in the library of the Royal College of Physicians. Another huge depository is available in the library of the Royal College of Obstetricians and Gynaecologists. Still other data dealing with the work of the London County Council and King Edward's Hospital Fund for London can be seen at the Greater London Record Office.

Within the consultant world, only the internal debates that took place in the Royal College of Surgeons remain obscure. Despite repeated requests, I was unable to secure access to that source. However, a former president of the college, Sir Reginald Murley, kindly supplied a verbatim account of a crucial meeting of fellows held in April 1948. From this and other sources it was possible to obtain some sense of the role played by the college and its president, Sir Alfred (later

Lord) Webb-Johnson. I am grateful to Dr George Rettie for help in this process, as well as for insights into the organization on whose executive he served — the Fellowship for Freedom in Medicine founded by Lord Horder.

All of this has been supplemented by an exhaustive study of the medical press — notably, the *British Medical Journal* and *The Lancet* — as well as interviews and correspondence with key figures. I am particularly indebted to three former civil servants who took part in the planning process and who let me question them at length — John Pater, Sir George Godber, Sir Alan Marre. Bevan's parliamentary private secretary — Donald Bruce, now Baron Bruce of Donnington — also answered many queries and I learned much from an interview with the BMA's secretary in the 1940s, Charles Hill, now Baron Hill of Luton.

Bevan's biographer, Michael Foot, has produced a detailed account of NHS negotiations based on interviews with Lord Moran and other key figures, all of whom are now deceased. In it, Foot recreates a conversation between Bevan and Moran which suggests that Moran had much to do with Bevan's key decision to nationalize the hospital service. Pater, on the other hand, gives a fellow civil servant credit for the idea — Mr (later Sir) John Hawton. No documents exist to support either claim. Indeed, Foot believes the idea may have come from Bevan himself, and Godber, as well as Bruce, raised the same thought. It has not been possible to resolve this issue.

My interest in the NHS began in 1957 and over the years I have learned much from interviews with leading figures involved in its development. Most relevant for this study were meetings with Sir Wilson Jameson, Sir Guy Dain, Sir Allen Daley, Dr Harvey Flack, Mr Somerville Hastings and Dr David Stark Murray. All are now deceased, but I gained many insights from the conversations we had. However, it should be made clear that I am solely responsible for the judgements made in this book. Not all the people interviewed would agree with the way I have interpreted the events of the 1940s.

Most of the research was carried out in the Public Record Office and the libraries of the British Medical Association, Royal College of Physicians, and Royal College of Obstetricians and Gynaecologists. To the staffs of each I am grateful for their assistance as well as for permission to cite the papers examined. The same applies to the archivist of the British Library of Political and Economic Science, London School of Economics, for access to the papers of Sir William (later Lord) Beveridge, Political and Economic Planning, and the British Hospitals Association; to the archivist at Churchill College, Cambridge, for access to the papers of Sir Henry Willink; to the archivist at Nuffield College, Oxford, for access to the papers of Sir Norman Chester and the Fabian Society; to the archivist at the Brynmor Jones Library at the University of Hull for access to the papers of Somerville Hastings and the Socialist Medical Association; to the staff at the headquarters of the Trades Union Congress and the Labour Party for access to their papers dealing with social insurance and health subjects. I also wish to thank the Controller of Her Majesty's Stationery Office for permission to reproduce Crown copyright material.

Funding for this study has come from my own sources and for this I owe everything to my late father; no one could have been more generous or understanding. I wish to thank Mrs Gertrude Howard for providing an office as well as living space while my own house was undergoing repair; without her aid this book would have taken much longer to complete. The title was the result of a suggestion made by Phillip Knightley after reading the epigraph. Taken from the words of the Archbishop of York, it succinctly expresses what the health service means to the British public.

I am deeply grateful to Gill Davies of Routledge for arranging the publication of this work, as well as to the colleagues who processed the manuscript – Heather Gibson, Louise Clairmonte, David Symes, Kate Fraser, and Julia Foguel. Two friends – Betty Bostetter and Ruth Richardson – also made valuable suggestions with regard to publication.

Finally, as always, I am grateful to my wife, Naomi, for her support and criticism, and to my children, Mark and Claire, for their years of forbearance.

Abbreviations

Abbreviations used in the text are as follows:

AMC	Association of Municipal Corporations
BHA	British Hospitals Association
BMA	British Medical Association
BMJ	*British Medical Journal*
CCA	County Councils Association
CHSC	Central Health Services Council
CMAC	Central Medical Academic Council
CMB	Central Medical Board
CMO	chief medical officer of Ministry of Health
CMSC	Central Medical Services Council
GMC	General Medical Council
GP	general practitioner of medicine
HMC	hospital management committee
LCC	London County Council
MOH	medical officer of health
MPA	Medical Policy Association
MPU	Medical Practitioners' Union
NHI	National Health Insurance
NHS	National Health Service
PEP	Political and Economic Planning
RCOG	Royal College of Obstetricians and Gynaecologists
RCP	Royal College of Physicians
RCS	Royal College of Surgeons
RHB	regional hospital board
SMA	Socialist Medical Association
TUC	Trades Union Congress
UGC	University Grants Committee

Introduction

The creation of the NHS was the result of many forces and it has been necessary to treat each of its main parts separately to clarify their development. After describing the movements that preceded the start of planning in 1936, we shall see how Ministry officials proceeded sporadically until 1941 when outside pressure forced them to step up the pace. At first they intended to concentrate on the hospital sector, but since that had to await the outcome of a survey they turned to the GP service, where demands for reform were building up fast. We shall follow that movement to its completion in 1948 and then retrace our steps to do the same for the consultant and hospital services. In the midst of these negotiations, the concept of a comprehensive service open to all gradually emerged and we shall examine that movement from beginning to end. Finally, we shall conclude with an assessment of the relative influence exerted by civil servants and doctors.

Attention is focused on planning in England and Wales; proposals for Scotland and Northern Ireland are cited only where they had relevance to negotiations in England and Wales. The study concentrates on medical and hospital services, not other forms of treatment. For the most part, the form taken by the NHS was determined by the arrangements made with doctors and hospitals in England and Wales and that is where our study will centre.

Part 1
Prelude to Planning, 1911 to 1936

A perfect service is something we have to work up to, but I know we have not the means in the course of the next year or two, or three to set it up, but I also know that once we start no Chancellor of the Exchequer can stop. He has got to go on, and what I think is important is that we should set it on the right lines at first.

David Lloyd George, Chancellor of the Exchequer, addressing the Medical Advisory Committee of the English National Insurance Commission, 2 October 1912. Full text on file in the Treasury section of the Public Record Office, T 172/62, page 10

Chapter one

Failure of reform

The NHS is the most comprehensive in the world and the civil service had the immense task of planning its creation. This study describes how the work was carried out and the extent to which the civil service influenced the structure that emerged.

But the movement which led to the creation of the NHS did not start with the civil service, nor was the civil service the only force involved in its development. Many outside government contributed to the process, and it is necessary to understand their role if the part played by the civil service is to be seen in its proper perspective. This chapter describes the many attempts made to expand public provision before 1936, when the civil service took its first hesitant steps towards a process which led to the creation of the service in 1948.

National Insurance Act of 1911

Public provision of health care in Britain began with the Poor Law.[1] Throughout the nineteenth century, boards of guardians offered free services to those who could pass a means test. However, because of the stigma and limited number of persons involved, that is not the proper starting point for understanding the emergence of a service which embraced the nation as a whole. Rather, we must look to the medical provisions of the 1911 Insurance Act which, before they were replaced by the NHS in 1948, covered half the population.

By modern standards, the 1911 Act was a modest measure.[2] It provided only GP and drug care for employed members of the working class, not their dependants or the unemployed. Some black-coated workers and self-employed persons with modest incomes were covered, but for the most part the Act did not apply to the middle and upper classes. They were left to their own devices, and the same applied to insured persons whenever they needed hospital and specialist treatment. Only sanatorium care for TB sufferers was offered under NHI and that became more widely available in 1921 when responsibility for its provision passed to local authorities.

Otherwise, if insured persons could not afford to pay privately for hospital care, they had to resort to charity or the Poor Law; only patients with infectious disease could count on free care in municipal isolation hospitals. Some local authorities had begun to make wider provision, directing their efforts mainly at mothers and children in an attempt to reduce high maternal and infant mortality rates, but over the country as a whole, voluntary hospitals and similar charities were all that stood between private practice and the Poor Law.

Despite its limitations, the Insurance Act represented an enormous advance. Before 1911, only the elite of the working class — some 4 to 5 million artisans — could afford free GP care through membership of friendly societies or other bodies that offered contract practice. After 1911, the entire employed working class was covered, and that meant some 15 million persons, or roughly one-third of the nation.

Moreover, the author of the Insurance Bill — David Lloyd George, Chancellor of the Exchequer — did not intend to stop there. He planted the seeds of the NHS in his 1911 measure, hoping in time to merge insurance services with those of local authorities, and expanding care to the point where it gave nearly everyone all that medical science had to offer. First would come 'dependants and specialists'; the panel system (as NHI's medical benefit came to be called) would be extended to cover the dependants of insured persons and it would be enlarged to embrace specialist as well as GP treatment. After that, hospital care would be added, and as costs rose, more and more of the middle class might participate. Such was the vision Lloyd George held out to the doctors who helped him start the panel system in 1912 but who were dissatisfied with its restricted range[3] (see the quotation on page 1).

Dawson Report

The first attempt at extension came with the creation of the Ministry of Health in 1919. Dr Christopher (later Lord) Addison, the medical Minister, made a vigorous effort to expand the system beyond the slender foundations which he helped to lay in 1911. He asked his medical advisory committee to set forth the direction in which health services should move, and the committee — chaired by Sir Bertrand (later Lord) Dawson, the leading physician of the day — produced a report which called for the development of an elaborate network of hospitals and health centres in which all three branches of the profession — GPs, consultants, municipal public health officers — would work together.[4] It was hoped that a start could be made by extending the range and cover of NHI services, while linking them closer with the municipal sector, but the move collapsed with the onset of the long depression in 1921.[5]

Additional benefits under NHI

Thereafter, the only way to expand the panel system seemed to be through the surplus funds of approved societies, the semi-autonomous bodies that administered the cash benefits, covering sickness and maternity, that were provided under the

Act. These funds could be utilized every five years if the benefits paid by the societies to their members fell below expectations and enabled profits to be made. Societies with healthy workers produced them; those with sick ones did not. Following the first valuation that started in 1918, societies with surplus funds began to provide additional benefits in 1921, but since they were administered directly by the societies, none fell in the medical sphere. This was because the doctors wanted nothing to do with the societies, an antipathy inherited from the bitter battles they had fought with the friendly societies between 1895 and 1910. In 1911 the profession had managed to wrest control of medical benefit from the approved societies (which were friendly and other societies with a different name), entrusting administration to insurance committees instead. In medical eyes, it was bad enough that the societies had a 60 per cent majority on these committees, but the profession was not going to tolerate a situation in which management was solely under society control as it had been in the days of club practice. Additional benefits, since they came from the surplus funds of approved societies and thus could be said to be directly financed by them, were administered in this way.

So under NHI the doctors made sure that any additional benefits in the nature of medical care would never come into operation. Dependant coverage was allowed until 1928, while specialist services were permitted thereafter, but neither was ever provided.[6] As a result, the most widely offered additional benefits were in the dental and optical sphere. Insured persons could still secure specialist medical care free or without great cost, but to do it they had to endure long waits in the outpatient departments of voluntary hospitals.

Pooling surplus funds for specialist services

The civil servants at the Ministry of Health were not happy with this arrangement; they did not like the way the range of GP care had been narrowed under NHI. The panel system left practitioners as independent entrepreneurs in their own surgeries and paid mainly in a way (by capitation, or so much per patient, whether they saw the patient or not) that offered no incentive to extend the range of service. Advances in medical science, together with the separation of many GPs from the hospital world, produced a relentless contraction of panel care. And in the process, it was widely believed, quality fell.

Ministry officials saw the solution in the provision of specialist services.[7] At one stroke that would both widen range and raise standards. The Royal Commission on NHI, which reported in 1926, agreed; it called for the pooling of half of society surplus funds so that specialist services might be offered to all insured persons through insurance committees (or their successors) as the doctors desired.[8] Unfortunately, only the poorer societies from the trade union world agreed; the other approved societies rejected all thought of sharing their wealth, the strongest opposition coming from the dominant friendly society and industrial assurance sectors.[9]

5

National maternity service

That seemed to end all prospect of reform, but the maternal mortality rate was too high to ignore. Politicians from all parties felt they had to attack the problem, and that applied particularly to the Prime Minister, Stanley Baldwin, and his Minister of Health, Neville Chamberlain, both of whom had experienced personal tragedies with childbirth. (Baldwin's birth had left his mother an invalid for life, and his wife suffered much pain while delivering six children.[10] Chamberlain's mother died in childbirth.[11]) If a way could be found to finance the development of maternity services without heavy calls on the exchequer, there was reason to expect government support, no matter which party was in power.

Fred (later Lord) Kershaw, a union approved society leader, devised a method. In 1927 he proposed a cut in NHI's maternity benefit (from £2 to £1) so as to free funds for municipal development.[12] Despite some misgivings, the Consultative Council on Approved Societies Work (set up by the Ministry of Health to gauge approved society opinion) secretly endorsed the proposal. However, Kershaw's plan struck at the heart of industrial assurance interest in NHI. The cash payments made on the birth of children could be used to purchase assurance policies, and the industry opposed any reduction in maternity benefit. Chamberlain succumbed to this pressure, but Baldwin did not. In the 1929 election, Baldwin not only promised to add a service element under municipal administration but wanted the approved societies to give up the cash benefit.[13]

Labour thus came to power in June 1929 with wide backing for local authority development. Arthur Greenwood, the Minister of Health, was determined to act; he even had hopes of going beyond maternity care and creating a salaried service that would cover everyone for everything.[14] However, difficulties arose which delayed legislation, the most formidable coming from the doctors. They had long been alarmed by the spread of local authority clinics, fearing that such development would lead to a salaried service with little room for private practice. In the summer of 1929 the British Medical Association (BMA) struck back with a plan of its own, calling for fewer clinics, more domiciliary deliveries and greater GP participation in local authority work.[15]

This provoked a counter-scheme from the assurance offices, who criticized severely GP work in ante-natal care. It was far better, they argued, to leave the service to municipal specialists, and they threw their weight behind local authority development but at a pace slow enough as not to require a cut in maternity benefit. Rather, they suggested, let exchequer or rate finance be used to support a modest development of clinic services.[16]

As a result, a strange alliance emerged. Had they felt free to speak, medical officers of health (MOHs) would have applauded the stand taken by the assurance offices, and so would have many socialists and leaders of women's organizations who had long been alarmed by the high rate of maternal mortality. From the time Sidney and Beatrice Webb launched their campaign to reform the Poor Law in 1909, these groups had been allied in a movement to expand the municipal sector on a salaried basis. They deeply resented the way the panel system had deflected their aims — but they were also critical of the manner in which assurance agents diverted the payment of maternity benefits. The leaders of the assurance industry cleverly exploited this opening. By directing their attacks on panel practitioners, they placated the municipal movement and managed to stave off a cut in maternity benefit.[17]

This and other divisions forced Greenwood to delay legislation, with the result that he lost office in August 1931, before he could act.[18] The financial crisis which arose in that year ruled out Exchequer aid for maternity services and thereafter the assurance offices found it possible to turn the approved society world against Kershaw's plan to raise funds by a cut in maternity benefit.[19]

Municipal development

However, the movement for reform did not die. Not even in the depths of the depression could the government — now National — ignore the maternal mortality rate. Rising unemployment deprived many working women of NHI aid and an Act passed in 1932 threw out thousands more in an attempt to restore insurance principles to health care.[20] This, together with the long-standing needs of dependants who had been excluded from NHI, generated public pressure for extended state service and the government responded in the way the assurance offices desired — by subsidizing the development of municipal clinics.[21]

Local authorities had long had power to expand services for mothers and children under two acts passed in 1918 — the Education Act and the Maternity and Child Welfare Act. These services had grown steadily throughout the 1920s, and in the 1930s the Ministry channelled efforts in two directions. In the eighteen towns with the blackest records it started a full-scale campaign to lower the mortality rate; there, every facet of maternal care was provided.[22] Elsewhere, efforts were largely confined to the ante-natal period. During the 1930s the number of ante-natal clinics rose by a third from 1,000 to 1,500, so that by 1938 they covered 61 per cent of births.[23]

This movement was accompanied by a wider one, initiated by the Local Government Act of 1929, which abolished boards of guardians and gave local authorities responsibility for administering the Poor Law. Some enlightened authorities began the slow process of upgrading pauper hospitals and developing a full municipal service. But the powers provided under this Act, as well as the two in 1918, were permissive and that resulted in the most uneven development. A few authorities, like the London County Council (LCC), did much; many others did little.[24]

Furthermore, the BMA had managed to insert a ban in the 1918 Acts which barred local authorities from creating a general domiciliary service — which meant that their efforts were confined almost entirely to the hospital and clinic sphere.[25] It was true that this did not apply in Scotland where municipal development was governed by a different statute passed in 1915,[26] but since medical opposition

7

was as strong there as in England, not many local authorities dared to exercise the greater powers they possessed.

Only Poor Law provision was wider, offering a corps of district medical officers to render domiciliary care, but, despite the fact that local authorities now administered it, few people wished to make use of the service because of the harsh means test involved.[27] Nor was access to other municipal services free from difficulty. Though provided outside the Poor Law, local authorities were instructed under the 1929 Act to impose charges on all who could afford to pay. The only exception applied to TB and other forms of infectious disease.[28]

Despite these restrictions, the growth of municipal services became a cause of increasing medical concern, particularly in 1936 when an Act was passed which made midwives salaried employees of local authorities. Though the maternity services provided were not free, the doctors had good reason to wonder whether they might soon be. And with that development might come wider provision for all dependants, leading in time to the creation of a comprehensive municipal service employing doctors on a salaried basis. [29]

In 1929 the BMA had tried to meet this threat not only with a national maternity policy but also with a general medical plan that would protect the profession from wider encroachment.[30] Under it, the panel system would be extended to cover 'dependants and specialists', thereby enabling independent practitioners to absorb the work of municipal clinics. Specialist provision, because of its lower cost, held out more hope of implementation, and the rising tide of disablement claims under the Insurance Act stirred approved society interest in this direction. Discussions began in 1935 and dragged on for three years with the expectation that the societies could at last be persuaded to let go of their surplus funds. But the talks collapsed when the BMA tried to extend the number of GPs who would be allowed to act as specialists. If the societies were to finance the proposal, they wanted the work done by fully-qualified consultants. In 1938, the Council of the BMA decided (but only by one vote) to forget specialist services until dependants could be added as well.[31]

One medical leader was relieved by this decision — Sir Henry Brackenbury, a GP of immense public spirit who dominated the making of BMA policy between the wars. His interest lay in the development of general practice along community lines and he feared that the addition of specialist services would steer GPs in a hospital direction. He wanted dependant coverage to come first since that would bring whole families under GP care and stimulate interest in the social and psychological components of illness.[32]

Beyond that, he and other medical leaders saw in dependant coverage a way of reducing approved society influence on the panel system. The wider the population covered by NHI, the more difficult it would be to retain the insurance principle and that, as the Royal Commission on NHI had noted in 1926, led logically to a general scheme administered by local authorities.[33] In the process, the profession might trade society for municipal influence but Brackenbury, from his long experience in local government, hoped it would be possible to develop a satisfactory relationship with local authorities and their MOHs.[34] For him, that seemed preferable to the continued involvement of approved societies in medical work. Conflict had been endemic since the system began, and though tension had eased by the 1930s, the societies still could not resist the temptation to interfere in medical matters — as became evident during the course of a pay dispute in 1937.[35]

Earlier, the friendly societies had been the main source of medical irritation, but after the exchange over maternity policy in 1929 it was the assurance offices which the profession disliked. Few GPs could forgive the offices for the aspersions they had cast on ante-natal work. Ideally, what the doctors wanted was an extended panel system without the approved societies. To achieve that and to secure a place for GPs in public health clinics, they thought they might have to accept links with local authorities, but they were willing to do so only if safeguards were provided that would protect them from municipal control. Under no conditions did the doctors wish to place themselves under MOH supervision. They therefore had to steer a delicate course between panel practice and a salaried service.[36]

BMA–TUC alliance

In their concern about the insurance industry's influence on social policy, the doctors were not alone. They had an ally from the approved society world — the trade unions, who had seen their membership growth stunted and their extended benefit plans shattered by assurance office resistance.[37] And it was not only within NHI that the unions had cause to complain of insurance industry practices; even worse were the abuses the insurance companies (and employers) had committed in the field of workmen's compensation.[38] By the 1930s, coal-miners and other workers exposed to the risks of industrial accidents wanted the insurance industry out of social insurance.

From this convergence of interests, a surprising alliance emerged; in 1937 the BMA and the Trades Union Congress (TUC) formed a joint committee to promote common interests. Thereafter, the doctors did all they could to further union policy on workmen's compensation — while the unions, to the horror of their colleagues in the labour movement, did the same for the doctors on maternity plans.[39] Just as workmen's compensation became the focal point of the union attack on social insurance, so maternity benefit became the centre of medical pressure on NHI since it was in these areas that insurance principles came most in conflict with social policy. And just as the unions, because of labour preference for municipal administration, left it to the doctors to resist local authority encroachment, so the doctors, because of their fear of alienating the NHI world and opening the door to a salaried service, left it to the unions to attack the inequalities inherent in the approved society system.

Union and medical interests also converged on the Poor Law. The unions sought to soften its administration and to protect as many members as possible from the indignity of a means test — while the doctors strove to prevent Poor Law medical services from developing on a salaried basis, pressing local authorities to employ local GPs on the free choice principle.[40] However, few authorities relented and as unemployment deepened due to the depression, more and more insured persons found themselves exposed to the means test. A special bill had to be enacted in 1935 to reverse the damage done in 1932 when 200,000 insured persons exhausted their right to NHI and were, as one friendly society critic put it, 'crucified on the cross of the insurance principle'.[41] Once again, it seemed to the doctors as well as the unions, social insurance policy was being dictated by the insurance industry.

Revival of reform

All these pressures mounted throughout the 1930s, their effects becoming most evident in that section of the British Isles most affected by the depression — Scotland. There, in 1933, a strong movement arose for the extension of public health services to protect the thousands of unemployed who had lost their right to NHI's medical benefit under the 1932 Act. This led to the creation of an official committee charged with the task of finding some way to reconcile divergent medical and municipal interests so as to produce the long-awaited enlargement of public provision.[42] The committee chairman was Edward P. Cathcart, Regius Professor of Physiology at Glasgow University, and the secretary was Niven S. McNicholl, a civil servant at the Scottish Office.[43]

The committee reported in June 1936, while the English Midwives Bill was wending its way through Parliament. That Bill showed a preference to a salaried service under municipal control, but the doctors hoped the Cathcart Committee would find otherwise. They were not disappointed. Though the report was riven by dissenting opinions, the majority did tend to endorse the BMA view, calling for the extension of the panel to dependants, and rejecting the idea of a salaried service. However, the committee did feel the need to raise the standard of panel care and sought to do so by imposing restrictions on the freedom the profession had enjoyed under NHI. Not only were doctors to lose the right of unfettered entry to panel practice, but they were to be subject to tighter disciplinary control than had applied in the past. And, though the exact form of administration was left undefined, the whole system was to be subject to municipal oversight. The committee thus showed its concern for 'unification' as well as 'extension' — that is, with the need to find some way of absorbing NHI services within a municipal framework so as to secure unified development.[44]

When the time came in 1937 for Scotland to implement its own maternity policy, Cathcart influence was evident. Instead of following the English example, the Scottish Department made room for GPs. Though local authorities had the right to form a salaried service, they were encouraged to use self-employed doctors working alongside midwives. Here was the way the Secretary of State for Scotland, Dr (later Sir) Walter Elliot, justified the decision: 'the Government thought it right, at any rate in the initial stages, that GPs should be given a chance to show that the confidence placed in them was justifiable'.[45]

One member of the Cathcart Committee did not share this view and he had much influence in the public health world. This was Dr (later Sir) Alexander Macgregor, MOH of Glasgow. Unlike their colleagues in the rest of Scotland, GPs in that city did not undertake much midwifery, and Macgregor felt free to opt for a salaried service, a preference he had shown in his dissent from the Cathcart Report.[46] But he failed to reckon on medical opposition and the Second World War began before he could exercise his preference.[47] Scotland as a whole proceeded to give GPs the chance Elliot intended.

The experiment had implications far beyond the bounds of midwifery; it was designed to test 'the validity of founding public medicine upon a private contract basis'. [48] For the first time, GPs were given a statutory place in a municipal service. But they were on trial: if they performed well, they could expect to win MOH support for an extended panel system; if not, then they might be faced with the threat of a salaried service. It was no wonder that in 1937 the chairman of the Council of the BMA, Dr (later Sir) Kaye le Fleming, saw the whole future of general practice bound up in the experiment.[49]

How well did the profession perform? In a word — badly. The maternal mortality rate fell as sharply in Scotland as it did in England, but the doctors could take no credit. It was due to the discovery in 1935 of a new wonder drug, prontosil, which heralded the start of the sulphonamide revolution. This slashed the mortality rate and made it less hazardous to use GPs, but it did not change their predilection for vaginal exams and forceps, practices that had become 'almost an obstetrical crime' to specialists.[50] Looking back in 1950, Professor James Young, one of the leading obstetricians of the day, gave his judgement on the experiment: 'This saving in life was in no sense due to an improvement in the standards of midwifery. There was as much puerperal infection due to the same cause as before, but this infection and these causes were concealed by the life-saving properties of the new drugs.'[51]

Nor was that all. One-fourth of the profession refused to work the Act in Scotland because the fees were too low.[52] As for the rest, it was found that 'doctors sometimes complete forms for examinations that they have not given'.[53] Despite the difference in the two systems, only a few more deliveries were carried out by practitioners in Scotland than in England.[54]

It soon became clear that all of the other professions and organizations involved in maternity work wanted nothing more to do with GPs.[55] Nearly all these groups came out for a salaried service, and, surprisingly, so did some GPs. The cry came particularly from Scotland where a number of doctors felt that 'they were required to sacrifice too much for the GP principle'.[56] Behind their demand was a belief in the need for new methods of practice. Only in that way, they felt, could they secure the competence required for maternity and other work.

We thus see the fight over midwifery merging with the larger struggle on health policy that raged throughout the 1930s. It was in the midst of this ferment, in the autumn of 1936, that the civil servants at the Ministry of Health began to lay plans for the creation of a new — and wider — national service.

Chapter two

Ministry rejects takeover of voluntary hospitals

Following the Cathcart Report in June 1936, the Ministry of Health began to plan the extension of NHI's medical benefit by way of merger with municipal services. The first document in this file is dated 7 November 1936, but the first formal planning meeting was not held until 7 February 1938.[1] According to Sir Arthur MacNalty, the department's CMO at the time, the Minister, Sir Kingsley Wood, asked him in 1937 to prepare a report on the feasibility of a national health service,[2] and even outside the department it was believed that the government intended to start a comprehensive system before its term of office expired.[3]

Extension combined with unification

The move within the department was initiated by Arthur W. Neville, an Assistant Secretary who had been engaged in NHI work since 1914.[4] For some time he had harboured a plan to put insurance committees under local authority control, and he mentioned it to the Minister (Wood) as well as to the Permanent Secretary, Sir George Chrystal. Wood asked Neville to elaborate his thoughts with the hope of finding some way to satisfy the growing demand for the addition of specialist services to the panel system.

Neville saw unification as the way because specialist services were already provided by local authorities in their hospitals and clinics. He also thought suffic- ient time had elapsed since 1929 (when the Local Government Act imposed heavy burdens) to enable local authorities to absorb new duties. Though the doctors and approved societies had previously opposed the move, Neville hoped their resistance could be overcome by the prospect of specialist provision. Both parties would receive representation on a newly formed health committee, but unlike the insurance committee, which had 60 per cent of its members from approved societies, this one would have a bare majority of municipal appointees.[5]

The move was strongly supported by the doctors' ally in the approved society world, the trade unions, and this led Robert Spear (later Lord) Hudson to take it up in January 1937, a few months after he had become Parliamentary Secretary to the Ministry. What prompted Hudson was the concern felt by the unions at the rising tide of disablement claims under NHI. During the 1930s many of the unemployed had turned to it in desperation after they had exhausted their right to unemployment insurance. Though the amount of benefit was small — 7s. per week for men between 1920 and 1942, 5s. or 6s. for women after 1933 — it continued as long as incapacity lasted before the normal pension age (65 for men, or 60 for women after 1940). It was the only social insurance payment free from a work condition.[6] Hudson was well aware of its importance since, before moving to the Ministry of Health, he had been Parliamentary Secretary at the Ministry of Labour (1931–5) and Minister of Pensions (1935–6).[7] He also could expect the Permanent Secretary to be sympathetic since Chrystal had been Secretary of the Ministry of Pensions for sixteen years before he moved to the Health Department in September 1935.[8]

In a move unusual for a politician, Hudson prepared a long statement on the need for extended health services to tackle the disability benefit problem. Early diagnosis, combined with specialist care, was seen as the way to curb costs but, unlike Neville, Hudson warned against the extension of NHI services until the issue of local authority control was resolved. Insurance committees had had their day; in the interest of economy, they ought to go. And he believed that both the doctors and the approved societies would accept the loss if they could be assured of representation on the new municipal committees. Though local authorities had traditionally been opposed to representation by interest groups, he thought they would accept it if it were made clear that 'the ultimate aim is to place under their control the organisation of a comprehensive health service'.[9]

Due to the depression and the unemployment difficulties it caused, Hudson recognized that the extension of the panel to dependants was then more popular than specialist provision, but he ruled it out on grounds of cost. To reduce expenditure further, he envisaged charges for those who were not insured. Though everyone would be entitled to receive specialist care from local authorities, only insured persons would secure it as of right; the rest would have to pay or pass a means test. The time, he urged, had come to make an advance. Action on treatment for cancer was then pending (an act appeared in 1939) and Hudson saw it as the moment to add the full range of specialist services.

MacNalty was slow to react. Hudson asked him to prepare a memorandum on 10 December 1936, but MacNalty did not do so until 15 March.[10] What deterred him was belief in municipal provision and the fear that the addition of specialist services under NHI would spur its development outside the hospital world — that is, in the privately-owned surgeries of panel practitioners. Local authorities had developed a wide range of specialist services over the years, particularly in the hospitals that had been upgraded since the 1929 Act, and MacNalty thought it better to base specialist services there since, as experience with TB treatment had shown, it would be possible to cover the whole population and not just insured persons. Furthermore, he argued, it was no good offering specialist advice without hospital care.

In any case, he doubted if public opinion was ready for the abolition of insurance committees. Unification would eventually come, but all that could be done now was build a halfway house, letting insurance committees pay local authorities for specialist services as they had done for TB treatment before 1921 (when responsibility for TB care passed wholly to local authorities). A special grant could be made to local authorities for the first five years to stimulate development. If the BMA and local authorities agreed to this plan, MacNalty wanted to proceed immediately with the full range of specialist care; otherwise he thought provision should be restricted to cancer treatment.

Nothing more was done until early 1938. Then, stimulated by expected Scottish action on the Cathcart Report, as well as by a report by Political and Economic Planning (PEP) surveying the whole field of health care,[11] the department held its first office policy conference to set long-term improvements. At the outset, it was clear that MacNalty's view had prevailed. Though some consideration had been given to the BMA's plan for the addition of specialist care to NHI, Chrystal stressed that 'the policy of the Ministry had always been development of public health [i.e. municipal] services'.[12]

At this meeting the possibility of dependant coverage also arose. Juveniles (those aged 14 to 16) had been added to NHI in 1937, and the Cathcart Committee as well as PEP had seen provision for dependants as a way to improve maternity services.[13] But the costs were high — some £12 million was needed, of which £2 million would fall on the Exchequer — and that made implementation difficult.[14] Nevertheless, Kingsley Wood did not rule it out. Before the second office conference in April 1938 he told Chrystal that he wanted to introduce cancer proposals in the autumn and 'further developments of the health services were not excluded'.[15]

However, only specialist provision was seriously considered, and its addition to NHI was rejected on the same grounds as before. Yet if dependants were ever included, then departmental feeling ran strongly in favour of municipal administration. The Deputy Secretary, Sir John Maude, stressed this view in order to secure greater control over the panel system and an improvement in GP care. The CMO agreed, 'and it was thought a strong moh might be a powerful influence in this direction'.[16] There was even felt to be a case for exploring the cost of a salaried service if the capitation fee for dependants had to be set too high. Only one lone voice challenged this view — Hervey (later Sir Angus) de Montmorency, known as 'Demo' within the department, an Assistant Secretary who had been engaged in NHI administration since the panel system began.[17] He doubted whether the doctors would be willing to accept any more stringent control than had been exercised through NHI's disciplinary procedure.

This whole process ended on 27 June 1938. Then it was agreed to proceed only with cancer treatment as the Treasury was likely to oppose more general provision of specialist care.[18] Hudson, who had been the driving force behind the extension movement, had left the Ministry in 1937 and Kingsley Wood followed in May 1938. This brought Walter Elliot into the department from Scotland where, as Secretary of State, he had piloted the Scottish Maternity Act through Parliament. Elliot was the first doctor to become Minister of Health since Christopher Addison was forced out in 1921.[19]

Financial difficulties of London hospitals

Hospital services did not figure in these early discussions except in relation to specialist care, and under MacNalty's lead the department was content to leave the subject with local authorities. Until the Emergency Medical Service (EMS) began in 1938–9, the Ministry had little to do with hospitals. Under the 1929 Local Government Act, its role was limited to a review of major projects; once a local authority appropriated a Poor Law institution and ran it as a municipal hospital under section 131 of the 1875 Public Health Act, it could act on its own, free from central interference.[20] No one in the department even knew the extent of municipal development.[21]

As for voluntary hospitals, their only contact with the state came through local authorities, and that was mainly in connection with the payments they received for providing cancer, TB, and VD treatment.[22] Those engaged in medical education as teaching hospitals also received state aid, but that was channelled through the University Grants Committee (UGC), not the Ministry of Health.

Hospital planning did not arise on its own until the London teaching hospitals ran into financial trouble in 1938. On 10 March Sir Frederick Menzies, the London County Council's chief medical officer, wrote confidentially to the Minister of Health about the plight of London's twelve teaching hospitals. The reason was due to the rising cost of medical education, but another problem arose from the growing demand for pay from hospital doctors who had traditionally given their services free. This led to a deficit in 1937 of some £300,000 for London's voluntary hospitals. Of the twelve teaching hospitals, five were in trouble, the most serious being King's College Hospital. It had approached the LCC for aid to avoid the closure of beds. Since London's teaching hospitals were national institutions, Menzies suggested the creation of a royal commission to solve the problem.[23]

This led to a series of meetings between Ministry and hospital spokesmen which eventually produced a major conference on 27 January 1939.[24] By this time it was clear that the Ministry wanted the LCC to bear the burden itself. In that way the LCC could apply pressure on the voluntary sector and facilitate co-operation with municipal hospitals, perhaps even force the closure of inefficient units. Throughout the country as a whole, similar problems had arisen. In large provincial cities, voluntary hospitals were also in serious financial trouble, and the Ministry did not see how aid could be confined to London alone. Nor did it want to single out teaching hospitals for special attention since it was felt that London had too many medical schools.[25]

However, the LCC was not disposed to help. Menzies had indicated a willingness to aid the teaching hospitals but not the voluntary sector as a whole, since some units were inefficient. Herbert Morrison, Labour leader of the LCC, expressed this view at the conference. Speaking for himself and not the Council as a whole (which had not been consulted), he agreed that the teaching hospitals rendered a national service and that nursing education needed aid, but he ruled out a block grant out of fear that charitable donations would dry up: 'If they did [render aid] there would be no stop between that and the whole financing of voluntary hospitals from public funds.'[26] LCC payments to the voluntary sector already amounted to £160,000 a year and Morrison did not feel it wise to give more.

Creation of the Emergency Medical Service

This left the Ministry to sort out the problem, and most voluntary hospitals wanted it that way. Though one prominent consultant — Lord Dawson — preferred LCC aid to a state grant, the same could not be said of his colleagues in the teaching hospital world. As the department itself observed at the time, 'These hospitals trust and would be guided by the Ministry, but were apprehensive of undue control by the L.C.C.'[27]

This preference was verified once the EMS began, and the Ministry found itself compelled to make grants to voluntary hospitals. As the threat of war mounted in the 1930s, the need for such a service became apparent to deal with the many civilian casualties expected from bombing raids.[28] Planning began in earnest in June 1938, and the service was formally established in May 1939, only a few months before the Second World War began.

From the outset of the planning process, voluntary hospital leaders made sure they were protected from local authority control. Initially, hospital organization was based on the concept of casualty clearing stations relating to a base hospital, with local authorities (under the Air Raid Precautions Department of the Home Office) in charge of the former and the Ministry of Health of the latter. However, this distinction could not be maintained; any hospital might have to treat casualties and provide prolonged treatment. 'For this reason', Elliot explained to Parliament in March 1939, 'it was decided that the local authorities should be relieved of all their direct responsibility for the organization of hospital accommodation, and that the Government should undertake the whole of the service, with assistance from the authorities.'[29]

London was organized differently, but again without local authority control. Here, there were 50,000 beds, most of a first-class surgical type, but not all were needed for casualties, so a novel scheme developed. London was divided into ten sectors radiating from Charing Cross, each having a teaching hospital at the apex and with casualties evacuated outwards. As Elliot described them, 'The sectors are, in effect, 10 new synthetic cities.'[30]

This scheme was devised by a committee headed by Sir Charles McMoran Wilson (later Lord Moran), Dean of St Mary's Hospital Medical School.[31] It enabled the teaching hospitals to preserve their natural catchment areas — which radiated out from the centre of inner London to the home counties and the outer shires — but it did nothing to promote co-operation among themselves or with LCC hospitals. In the LCC's view, too many sectors were established north of the Thames, there was too much rigidity between them, there was no medium for settling disputes, too many beds were reserved for casualties in the voluntary hospitals and, as a result, many beds were left empty while the LCC's hospitals were over-crowded. Most painful of all, too many doctors were allotted to the voluntary hospitals and not enough to the municipal units.[32]

In 1939 the Ministry created a small body — known as the 'Chrystal Committee' — to meet these criticisms, and a triumvirate was established to settle disputes between sectors. But these remedies failed to satisfy Menzies or his successor Dr (later Sir) Allen Daley. They continued to co-operate only because they felt it a duty to make the scheme work.[33]

Ministry considers takeover of voluntary hospitals

Aside from these difficulties, it soon became apparent that the scheme had done more than equip 200,000–300,000 beds for air-raid casualties; it had brought the department into direct contact with the voluntary hospitals and altered the way they worked. These factors led Elliot to consider a national takeover of the voluntary hospitals after the war began in September 1939.[34] The idea had been proposed as early as June 1938 by a key figure involved in the formation of the EMS — Dr Leslie (later Lord) Haden Guest, a Labour MP loosely associated with the Socialist Medical Association (SMA) but flexible enough in his thinking to be acceptable to the BMA.[35] It gathered strength as the threat of war grew, because of the widespread feeling that a national service, embracing all kinds of care, might be needed to deal with evacuation and air-raid problems.

Within the Ministry, a retired civil servant was asked to consider the proposal. This was Sir Edward Forber who, as Deputy Secretary of the department from 1925 to 1930, had played an important role in the development of the 1929 Local Government Act. Forber rejected Elliot's suggestion mainly because he thought the doctors and the Cabinet would resist, but his attitude was also coloured by a desire to preserve the voluntary hospitals. Some restriction of the voluntary sector was desirable only if it resulted in the closure of cottage hospitals, where much bad surgery was performed, but that move would have to be part of the formation of a state medical service, and the moment was not opportune for that: 'My general view is that at the present time a national scheme is legislatively impracticable and administratively not worth while.'[36]

MacNalty was also asked to consider the proposal and he presented a more balanced appraisal, but agreed with Forber in the belief that 'most doctors would be bitterly opposed'.[37] For this reason, he favoured a more gradual approach, letting hospital doctors became accustomed to state involvement and seeking their aid when the time was ripe for national service. When that moment came, he was sure the profession would prefer national to municipal control.

On the 22 September, the day after this appraisal was prepared, MacNalty came down strongly against the proposal on the grounds that the Ministry did not have the staff to undertake the task.[38] In this he was supported (and perhaps abetted) by the civil servant in charge of EMS planning, Neville, who thought it wiser to proceed along the lines already set — that is, by encouraging voluntary and municipal hospitals to work together.[39] London, Neville recognized, presented a special problem because it had been almost impossible to persuade the LCC to co-operate with voluntary hospitals, or to induce voluntary hospitals to act jointly. But he was hopeful that sector organization would lead to greater co-ordination. Over the country as a whole, he suggested two innovations: compel the creation of joint hospital boards that would bring voluntary and municipal hospitals together, as had already been done in Manchester and Oxford on a voluntary basis; and force voluntary hospitals to work together by making financial aid conditional on regional grouping along the lines proposed by the Voluntary Hospitals Commission chaired by Lord Sankey in 1937.[40]

Maude also opposed a takeover of voluntary hospitals, but on different grounds; he feared their subscriptions would fall if they fell under state control. In his view the only feasible way of building a hospital service was on an insurance basis and that, he believed, was the position the Treasury would take. Therefore, nothing should be done to undermine the contributory schemes developed under voluntary hospital auspices. They could be used to cover persons not insured by NHI, while hospital benefit might be added to NHI so as to protect and secure funds from those included within the Act. What Maude most opposed was the local authority method of recovering charges after the event. That had not been effective and if it were relied upon, Maude was sure it 'would lead the insured population to think, with some justification, that they were paying contributions for something which others get for nothing'.[41]

Maude's conception also envisaged the inclusion of dependants under NHI's hospital benefit and that would pave the way for a new administration freed from approved society and insurance committee influence. Such a move might eventually produce the divorce of domiciliary care from NHI and, in Maude's view, that was long overdue, but he recognized the political difficulty standing in the way.

In the midst of all this, on 28 October, an article appeared which indicated that the Ministry may have misjudged the medical mood. A paper written by a special commissioner of *The Lancet* — who was in fact Dr Stephen (later Lord) Taylor, an assistant editor — called for the abolition of voluntary hospitals and the development of regional organization under the control of a public corporation in place of the Ministry of Health.[42] This was designed to appease doctors who were concerned about central as well as municipal control but who might be willing to accept a different form of organization under a body on which the profession as a whole could be represented.

However, within the department, Forber reacted angrily, defending Ministry administration and dismissing the idea of a public corporation. Nor, in Forber's view, did the author have the competence to make such suggestions:

In fact the writer is not a very instructed person. He evidently knows little about the local authorities' hospital service or about local government generally, and has no appreciation of the functions of Parliament or of what Parliament would stand. It is open to doubt whether he knows a great deal even about consulting practice. His article reads like that of a stickpit consultant, possibly one who is addicted to broadcasting.[43]

Yet whereas before Forber had seen no need for regional organization, now he gave it consideration because of the movement underway. The medical press had hailed the regionalization of the EMS as a portent of things to come and the British Hospitals Association (BHA) was working on a scheme that contemplated the creation of fifty or more regions. Forber criticized this plan because it ignored municipal boundaries, and he raised doubts about the need for regional govern-ment. But if it were regarded as inevitable, then he urged the department to start developing its own scheme before the idea was pre-empted by voluntary hospitals.[44]

MacNalty did not agree with Forber, objecting to any form of central control whether by a Ministry or otherwise. He reminded his colleagues that their policy since the 1929 Local Government Act had been to foster the growth of municipal hospitals, with the expectation that one day charity would dry up and destroy the voluntary sector. In place of Ministry control he came down strongly in favour of local authority rule, not least because it was necessary to link hospitals with other forms of treatment:

> Not only would Local Authorities much resent the control of municipal hospitals being taken out of their hands, but on medical grounds a number of considera-tions arise.
> A hospital by itself is only a building. To function effectively it must be based on health services both as a field for the hospital *clientele* and for obser-vation and after-care. The hospital is only one branch of the Local Govern-ment system of Health Services.[45]

Four months later, in May 1940, with the country facing the danger of invasion, Forber came out against long-range planning. The nation, he expected, would be faced with severe financial constraints once the war ended and voluntary hospitals in London would probably emerge in better shape than many anticipated. A complete takeover of the voluntary sector would be less likely after the war than before it. He urged the Ministry to concentrate on minor reforms and proceed with a regionalization plan that would promote co-operation between municipal and voluntary hospitals.[46]

With this view most civil servants agreed, and that ended all thought of a takeover of the voluntary sector. In 1943 an official Scottish committee headed by Sir Hector Hetherington called for the denationalization of seven EMS hospitals in Scotland, turning them over to municipal or voluntary hospital control.[47]

Underlying the department's rejection of the nationalization idea was the feeling, widely held within the civil service, that if voluntary hospitals were to be taken over, it ought to be done by local authorities rather than the Ministry of Health. A similar point of view, as we saw, applied to domiciliary care, and this meant that from the very beginning of the planning process, the department was heading towards a comprehensive service under municipal control. Yet it had done little to promote local authority development during the decade before, failing to use financial levers that were available under the 1929 Local Government Act (see Chapter 17, p. 187). As a Fabian Society report complained, the Ministry's CMO expressed admirable sentiments but he did not translate them into action. As a result, local authorities looked on the department as little more than a watchdog.[48]

Chapter three

Ministry intent to create a hospital service

During the first half of 1940, policymaking at the Ministry came to a halt. The main cause was the demands imposed by the threat of Nazi invasion, but the department was also paralysed by doubts about regional organization. MacNalty was the leading opponent, preferring to let municipal development take its toll of the voluntary hospital sector.

In October an important debate took place in Parliament which roused the Ministry from its lethargy. Rhys Davies, a trade union MP with long experience of approved society work, introduced a motion calling for the extension of medical provision under NHI. Citing a warning issued by the prominent physician, Lord Horder, he stressed the need to deal with the infectious and contagious diseases that were likely to arise from the devastation caused by war. An even greater challenge was lodged by the TUC's spokesman in Parliament, its medical adviser, Dr H.B.W. Morgan. He pleaded with the Minister — now Malcolm Macdonald — to deal with the nation as a whole and not just the insured:

> Will he not consider a real national health system by which every citizen is entitled in disease to the best medical attention available, irrespective of class, colour, economic status or anything else? I ask the right honourable Gentleman to have the vision to frame a policy which will make his name famous in the annals of his Department.[1]

Shortly after, Macdonald himself came under pressure to reorganize the hospital service and he pressed Maude to get on with the job.[2] In December an office committee was formed to deal with post-war hospital policy and it was said to have held weekly meetings.[3] Only a few records have survived, but it is clear that discussions went beyond hospital care and covered medical services generally. It was during this period — the last half of 1940 and the start of 1941 — that the Ministry vaguely developed the concept of a comprehensive service open to all, but with charges imposed on those not insured.

MacNalty did not long participate. He was not up to the task of planning a comprehensive health service and left office on 11 November 1940, having reached the normal retirement age of 60. His place was taken by Sir Wilson Jameson, the man whom Sir George Newman preferred as his successor in 1935.[4] Chrystal also reached retirement age (in August 1940) but at the suggestion of Kingsley Wood, now Chancellor of the Exchequer, he was appointed secretary of the new Reconstruction Problems Committee set up under Arthur (later Lord) Greenwood, Minister without portfolio, the body which gave birth to the famous Beveridge Report in 1942.[5] Chrystal made this move on 11 February 1941, and Maude, his deputy, succeeded him. Thereafter, Maude dominated policymaking within the department until July 1945, when he retired at 62 upon Labour's assumption of office.[6] Though he might have been asked to stay on, someone decided it was time for him to go.

Debate on regional organization

Three days after MacNalty retired, a debate on regional organization began within the department. E.D. Macgregor, an Assistant Secretary with strong municipal sympathies, endorsed MacNalty's view and opposed the idea *in toto*.[7] He was rebutted by John Pater, a principal concerned with hospital planning, who stressed the need to impose a duty on voluntary hospitals to co-operate with local authorities. At present, he argued, the voluntary hospitals evoke a spirit of 'splendid isolation' and think only of how local authorities can help them, not vice versa.[8]

One month later, on 18 December, Pater returned to the attack. He criticized those (like Forber) who opposed action during the war: 'In war-time the atmosphere is favourable for advance on a wide front, quite apart from the fact that it is a time when the normal order is disturbed in every sphere and is ripe for change.'[9] He had no patience with the proposal to form advisory boards; they, as the Manchester and Oxford experience had shown, were powerless bodies and had not done 'much more than touch the fringe of the hospital problem'.[10] What was needed were regional bodies with a majority of directly elected members and with power to cover more than the hospital sector. Eventually, even a salaried domiciliary service might be brought under their control. But in making this proposal, Pater warned against regional groups on the Sankey Commission model. Such bodies were confined to voluntary hospitals and created the danger of organized opposition to municipal effort. A movement in this direction had already been started by a new force in the hospital world — the Nuffield Provincial Hospitals Trust.

The opposite view was taken by Mr (later Sir) John Wrigley, Principal Assistant Secretary and Director of the housing and town planning division. He was devoted to the concept of local government and recoiled from infringement of its authority:

> In my own view it is more important that the general body of the people should be interested in these services, and themselves should be made responsible for the manner in which they are governed and in which these services are provided, than they should be provided from above with a mechanically perfect organisation for which they have no responsibility and in which they can take no interest.[11]

He thus saw democratic control as more important than efficient organization and would accept regional bodies only in an advisory mode. Perhaps at a later date, as confidence in regional bodies grew, they might acquire executive powers, but, meanwhile, Wrigley wanted direction to remain under the control of local authorities. They could be expected to develop hospital facilities gradually — though not so fast in Cornwall or Hereford as in London — but he did anticipate the spread of a salaried municipal GP service on a large scale.

Opinion within the department was thus divided on the question of regional powers, and there was a reluctance to resolve the issue. Those who had been involved in EMS administration (like Pater) tended to favour regional authority, while others in the public health and housing sections (like Wrigley) wished to preserve traditional ties with local authorities. In January 1941 Maude tried to force a clear choice, but produced only a pallid compromise.[12] An office conference came down on the side of municipal development, yet conceded some executive powers to regional bodies, if only to restrict the kind of surgical operations performed in cottage hospitals.[13]

Nor was the question of finance easier to resolve. Maude reiterated his call for an insurance basis, but now recognized the difficulty of using NHI because contributions would have to be raised too high to cover hospital care.[14] Yet, Jameson stressed the need to include NHI so as to divert part of the money for GP treatment to hospital services.[15]

In February, Mr (later Sir) Arthur Rucker, Maude's deputy, with a long record of devoted service to the department, summarized the principles agreed thus far.[16] The new service was to be made available to all, but charges were to be imposed on those who were not insured. All below a certain income limit (similar to the one set for NHI which, with dependants, covered over 80 per cent of the population) would be compulsorily insured, while the rest would have to secure their own insurance or be liable for payment after the event. The service was to be put under the oversight of directly elected regional bodies, but their relationship with local authorities was left open. Voluntary hospitals were to continue much as before, being dependent on regional bodies only for some finance.

Even the status of NHI was left undecided. On the medical side, continuation of the panel system offered a less radical break with the past, but it was expected that doctors in urban areas would shift to a salaried service, while the profession everywhere would be based on clinics (in effect, out-patient departments) that were linked with a network of hospitals. Only where administration was concerned was there a clear case (and opening) for radical reform. Cash benefits would be moved to the Ministry of Labour or a new Ministry of Insurance, while medical benefit would presumably be put in some way under local authorities. It was recognized that the scheme did not give doctors enough voice in administration but regional bodies could appoint medical advisory committees to guide them, particularly on the delicate question of hospital staffing.

Maude seeks other advice

With so much unresolved, Maude found it difficult to live with uncertainty. He was under pressure to establish a national system but he did not want the Ministry to act both as prosecutor and judge. He thought it wiser to let regional bodies assume the prosecuting role, leaving the department free to make final decisions. The major issue to be decided was the relationship between municipal and voluntary hospitals and, for the first time, Maude doubted whether the voluntary hospitals would be able to attract sufficient funds to survive. If not, they might have to turn themselves over to local authorities, thereby raising a number of delicate points.[17]

Maude thus seemed to be leaning in the direction of regional organization, but there remained the question of the area to be covered. Spokesmen for the Nuffield Trust were pressing for new boundaries, wider than those for civil defence, with the hope of diluting municipal influence.[18] Maude found this difficult to accept. Within the department, no departure from traditional local authority areas would be tolerated until local government itself was reformed, and that was a distant prospect. Rucker suggested a way out by placing a duty on local authorities to provide hospital treatment, leaving it to them to form their own regional bodies.[19] But Forber was swift to note that this might produce a reaction not only from the voluntary hospitals but also from some county councils, those that covered large areas (or populations) and saw no need for wider groupings.[20]

All of this left the department no nearer a solution than when the debate started and Maude turned to one of his most trusted colleagues for aid, de Montmorency. Because of his long service in the department, 'Demo's' advice was rated highly, not only on health matters but also on the social services and local government.[21] During 1940 he had moved on loan to St Anne's near Blackpool to help Sir Laurence Brock with his work in the mental health field as chairman of the Board of Control. Brock himself had earlier been in the Ministry, having served as secretary of the Cave Committee which tried to ease the finances of voluntary hospitals in 1921.[22] Brock and 'Demo' were a formidable team and in January 1941 Maude made 'Demo' a corresponding member of the office group on hospital policy, no doubt with the hope that he and Brock would suggest a way out of the department's dilemma.[23]

'Demo's' response was along the lines favoured by Maude. He suggested the creation of advisory councils on a regional basis, with the final decision left to the Minister. But he threw doubts on Maude's preference for insurance finance because 'you cannot compel people to insure for hospital treatment unless and until you can guarantee the beds'.[24] With the shortage of hospital stock, the country did not have enough beds to make any such guarantee.

Brock went further and questioned the wisdom of regional organization *per se* based on his experience with mental hospital boards (embracing several local authorities) in Lancashire and the West Riding. Their performance, Brock indicated, compares 'very unfavourably' with the average good local authority: 'The absence of any effective pressure from public opinion leads to a good deal of mediocrity in their administration with the result that a city like Manchester is far less well served than if it had the management of its own institution.'[25]

For the moment, this seems to have settled the issue; Maude returned to the traditional local authority role the department had favoured. On the 28 February he made this clear to Forber: 'I rather suspect that if and when the time for action comes we shall find that something based on the good old county and county borough system will hold the field.'[26]

In the midst of this debate, the future of the GP service constantly intruded, if for no other reason than to decide the method by which patients would be admitted to hospital. But it was also felt that the separate development of the panel system could no longer be tolerated; in any reorganization of the hospital service, GPs would have to be brought into closer contact than had prevailed before the war.[27]

The subject was raised with some force by Macgregor in January 1941. No matter how the hospital service was reorganized, he expected the bodies responsible to become concerned with general practice, and he saw the extension of NHI as the means of making the tie. The addition of dependants and specialist services would pave the way for a full state medical service 'and it seems worth while thinking whether we can't take the whole business at one gulp'.[28] Because of the growing pressure for equality in treatment, he doubted whether the public would stand much longer for the continuation of the panel system or the difference in additional benefits offered by the approved societies. He therefore urged consideration of GP reform now: 'It may be that the vested interests are too powerful, but I think the kite should be flown.'[29]

Maude did not take up the challenge. Overburdened with war duties, he and his colleagues had little time to resolve such issues and were content to let matters drift.[30] That was the situation until the middle of 1941.

Nuffield Trust forces statement on hospital policy

This neglect of policymaking was ended by the Nuffield Provincial Hospitals Trust. It had grown out of a movement started by Alderman William Hyde in Oxford in 1935. Hyde was a man of many parts; besides having a long record of service on the Oxford County Council, he had extensive experience of NHI, having been secretary of the National Federation of Rural Workers' Approved Society from 1913 to 1937. But that was not all; he had close ties with Lord Nuffield (whose automobile factory was in Oxford) and, with the aid of Mr (later Sir) William Goodenough, deputy chairman of Barclay's Bank, Hyde persuaded Nuffield to start the Hospitals Trust in December 1939.

The aim was to prevent a financial crisis in the provinces similar to the one that had threatened the voluntary hospitals in London. And the main method used was to promote regional co-operation along the lines pioneered by Hyde in Oxford and endorsed by the Sankey Commission in 1937.[31] The Sankey Report had called for the establishment of a central body to stimulate the movement and Sankey himself hoped the government would fund it. But the civil servants at the Ministry did not see this as a concern of state, believing (in accordance with the mandate implicit in the 1929 Local Government Act) that they should concentrate their efforts on the municipal side.[32] The Nuffield Trust filled the vacuum left by the department, and the regional movement was confined to voluntary hospitals.

However, in January 1941 the Nuffield Trust sought to enlarge its scope, bringing in municipal hospitals with Ministry aid. Goodenough approached Macdonald and the Minister responded favourably, possibly without consulting his civil servants.[33] Perhaps Macdonald was annoyed with local authorities because of the shortcomings they had displayed in the air-raid emergency service,[34] but whatever the reason, he gave his blessing to the Nuffield movement.

Within the department, Pater in December 1940 had warned about the threat to municipal effort posed by Nuffield,[35] but no action was taken until local authorities became alarmed. The LCC was the first to protest. On 12 August its chairman, Charles (later Lord) Latham, wrote a vitriolic article in the *Star*, denouncing 'the plotters' who were trying to bring municipal hospitals under voluntary hospital control through the device of national and joint boards: 'The Fifth Columnists against democracy are preparing to steal the people's municipal hospitals.'[36]

Ten days later another protest was registered by the Kent County Council,[37] and this was followed by one from the body which represented county councils as a whole, the County Councils Association (CCA).[38] Feeling within the local authority world cut across political boundaries; Conservatives as well as Liberals and socialists were alarmed by the activities of the Nuffield Trust.

Despite Pater's warning in December 1940, this took the Ministry by surprise. Macdonald had left the department in February to become High Commissioner in Canada, and he was replaced by Ernest Brown, no stranger to health politics. As Secretary for Scotland since May 1940, Brown had been involved in policy-making months before he arrived at the Ministry of Health. Yet he too endorsed the Nuffield movement, again without realizing its implications.[39] At that point (March 1941), Brown later indicated, he intended to defer a statement on hospital policy until the end of the year, but the municipal protest demanded immediate attention.[40]

Maude was so dilatory in preparing a policy that he did not do so until Chrystal (who was anxious to have something ready for the Reconstruction Problems Committee) prodded him in June.[41] Macgregor thought 'Demo' would be the right person to do it, and he had Chrystal convey this message to Maude. By August, at or about the time the municipal outburst occurred, Maude had some preliminary thoughts ready, and one reason for the Ministry's delay was the hope of reforming the GP service at the same time.[42] Where hospital organization was concerned, Maude was cautious; he suggested a weak form of co-ordination that would leave local authorities and voluntary hospitals in command of their resources. However, there was possibly a hint of voluntary hospital dominance

27

in the document because Maude stressed the need to follow the pattern set by the Cancer Act — and that statute, since it had been concerned mainly with expensive radium treatment, had tended to make teaching hospitals the centre around which organization proceeded. In making this suggestion, Maude may have been influenced by Forber who, like the Treasury, was anxious to do nothing to damage the voluntary hospitals or create a situation in which their finances might have to be assumed by the state.[43]

This policy implied that the voluntary hospitals would be able to attract sufficient funds to maintain independence, but Brock had doubts. Indeed, he expected their imminent absorption within a municipal framework as the Ministry had always anticipated. Brock's conception of regional organization thus leaned strongly towards local authority dominance. Only mental hospitals, he argued, should remain outside this framework because his experience had shown that direct municipal control produced better results. With some reservations, 'Demo' concurred.[44]

That finally seems to have settled the issue. Maude proceeded to draft a statement that came down firmly on the local authority side, ruling out direct Exchequer grants to voluntary hospitals. Any public money they received would have to go through local authorities. Here was the way Maude justified the policy to a civil servant in the Scottish Department:

> As I see the matter it is essential that the responsibility for public provision of hospitals should be placed fairly and squarely on one authority in each area, and I do not think it would be administratively practicable to divide the responsibility between the local authorities and the voluntary bodies. Moreover, apart from administrative difficulties such a system would perpetuate and accentuate the distinction between the two systems which already exists. It is, of course, a main feature of our policy to obliterate this distinction and unless we succeed in so doing I feel little doubt that the municipal hospitals will find themselves with a stigma not unlike that attaching to the old Poor Law.[45]

However, because of Treasury concern for the future of voluntary hospitals, Maude was not able to depart greatly from previous policy.[46] Therefore, the statement Brown made to Parliament on 9 October[47] left scope for private finance.

1 It announced the intent to create a comprehensive hospital service after the war, but it was not to be freely available. Insurance tests were envisaged, thus ensuring the future of contributory schemes.
2 For the first time, a duty was to be placed on the larger local authorities (counties and county boroughs) to organize the service. Previously, under the 1929 Local Government Act, they had only a permissive power. (This did not apply to Scotland; there a compulsory power did exist but, judging from the strength of the voluntary sector, it was probably little used.)
3 Voluntary hospital participation was envisaged but funds were to be

channelled through local authorities except in the case of the teaching hospitals which, it was later decided, would receive their money direct from the University Grants Committee (UGC).

Despite its municipal bias, Maude had good reason to expect the voluntary hospitals to endorse this policy. As early as March 1941 Maude was surprised to find that Goodenough was willing to accept municipal responsibility for hospital development.[48] And when the statement was finally prepared, all the leading organizations from the voluntary hospital world supported it, urging that it be announced without delay.[49] What no one seemed to realize was how swifty these attitudes would change once the financial basis of the voluntary hospital movement was eroded and the threat of municipal dominance appeared.

Nor was local authority support any more secure. Indeed, the first cries of discontent came from that source, and arose from the way the Ministry chose to conduct a hospital survey. This study began innocently enough; it was designed to ease LCC fears of regional organization on the EMS model. As Daley (who succeeded Menzies as MOH for the LCC in 1939) put it to the Ministry in March, 'There are too many sectors, sector boundaries impede proper distribution of medical and nursing staff, they are based on the geographical position of voluntary teaching hospitals and are run very largely with an eye to the interests of the voluntary hospitals.'[50] Menzies also could not resist making his views known to the Ministry. He thought the only way to save the hospital empire he had built was to develop dual organization, keeping the LCC's municipal hospitals separate from the voluntary sector.[51]

In September the LCC made it clear that it would not tolerate organization by a regional council; rather, it would only accept plans devised by the department and demanded that it undertake a hospital survey to prepare the way.[52] The Ministry duly complied, but then another area (from the northwest) requested a survey and this proved too difficult for the department to conduct alone.[53] The Nuffield Trust, which had already conducted surveys of its own, was asked to participate. Soon, the study was enlarged to cover the country as a whole, with the Nuffield Trust responsible for seven of the ten teams appointed.[54]

Though the Trust agreed to suspend its regionalization effort until the survey was completed, municipal fears mounted. Early in 1943, one of the leading figures from the MOH world — Dr J. J. Buchan of Bradford — threatened to boycott the survey because of Nuffield participation. Jameson pleaded for restraint: 'I dread the possibility of Bradford's refusal to co-operate being the starting point of an epidemic of similar resistance to our proposals.'[55]

In the event, the survey went ahead and the reports, originally meant to be confidential, were published in 1945. But throughout the period, local authority suspicions remained and this made the Ministry all that more anxious to placate municipal opinion when detailed planning began in 1942.

Part 2
GP Service

We are satisfied that the continuance of the arrangements under which the panel system is carried out — arrangements which represent a cross between private practice and a public service and in some respects exhibit the weaknesses of both systems — cannot be accepted.

From a paper by Sir John Maude, Permanent Secretary of the Ministry of Health, for Ministers on a proposed GP service, November 1942, MH 77/26 or 80/24 in the Public Record Office, page 5

Chapter four

A salaried service under municipal control

Planning did not start in earnest until 1942. Before then, the Ministry of Health had made periodic attempts but allowed itself to be defeated by obstacles in its path. First, in 1936, it tried to realize the long-awaited extension of GP services under NHI; then, in 1939, it turned to the development of a hospital policy that would secure closer co-ordination between the municipal and voluntary sectors. Neither effort succeeded, partly because the parties involved presented problems, but mainly because the department lacked the will to force the pace. Had support from the Treasury been anticipated, the Ministry might have roused itself, but the fear of imposing additional costs on the Exchequer prompted it to do nothing, and the pressure of war work provided a convenient excuse to avoid hard decisions.

The task of undertaking a hospital survey gave the Ministry another cause to procrastinate. There was reason to expect that the Ministry would start planning a hospital service immediately after the statement of intent was issued on 9 October 1941, but it did no such thing. When Chrystal sought information on the financial aspects of hospital policy, he was told by Neville (who in turn cited 'A.G.', probably Arthur Greenwood) that the department could not go into that until the hospital survey was completed.[1] Though all the detailed planning still had to be worked out, Maude as late as November 1942 thought it would be possible to 'secure a fair measure of agreement'.[2] All the Ministry felt able to do where hospital policy was concerned was create an inter-departmental committee to consider the organization of medical schools. This it did in March 1942, with Goodenough in charge.[3] Once again, it must have seemed to the municipal world, the Nuffield Trust was exerting an extraordinary influence on health policy.

However, reform on the GP side could not be so easily dismissed. Pressure here had been building up since the war began, with repeated attempts being made to widen the department's vision, particularly by extending NHI to dependants. Clement Attlee, leader of the Labour Party and Lord Privy Seal in Churchill's coalition government, tried to do so at the very first meeting of the Reconstruction Problems Committee on 6 March 1941.[4] The organization of the medical profession, he stressed, must be considered along with hospital policy. Others took up the theme in Parliament, but Brown resisted the effort, echoing Maude's view that the hospital question had to be settled first.[5]

Trade unions force Beveridge Report

This did not satisfy the doctors or the trade unions; for years they had been struggling to free themselves from the restrictions imposed on the panel system as well as from the extraordinary influence which the insurance industry seemed to exert on social policy. Though the alliance formed by the BMA and the TUC in 1937 had produced only meagre results by the time the war began, the parties did set forces in motion which led to the wide-ranging recommendations of the Beveridge Report in November 1942.[6]

The main pressure centred on workmen's compensation, and it was the unions that took the lead. In 1938, after years of resisting reform, the government decided to create a royal commission which would open the way to necessary change. However, hearings did not begin until 1939 and the outbreak of war in September gave the employers an excuse not to give evidence, with the result that the commission's proceedings were suspended in 1940. Though attempts were made to revive the process, they failed, and the commission never did progress to the point where it could issue a report.

That forced the unions to try a different tack, and they widened the target to include NHI as well as workmen's compensation. A TUC deputation to the Ministry of Health on 6 February 1941 pressed the point home. It demanded sweeping reform of health services as well as cash benefits, calling for an overhaul of the hospital system together with the long-awaited extension of the GP service: 'What is needed is a complete examination of Health Insurance, having in mind the development of other social services since the scheme started.'[7]

The Ministry responded cautiously, hoping to contain the inquiry within NHI bounds, but Greenwood — reflecting Labour concern within the government — pressed for wider action to include workmen's compensation. At the first meeting of the Reconstruction Problems Committee on 6 March, he demanded the reassembly of the royal commission so that it could produce conclusions without delay. Brown suggested an alternative if this were not possible; let Edgar Hackforth, a member of the royal commission (and recently retired as Controller of NHI), express views on how workmen's compensation might be unified with NHI and the contributory pensions scheme.[8]

Over the next month Greenwood made efforts to resurrect the commission, and when that failed he stressed the need for a larger study. On 10 April he wrote to Brown as follows:

> The kind of inquiry which I should propose to set up would be an inquiry to be held in private by a small Committee which would not take any formal evidence but would examine the questions referred to it in the light of information already available and any other information or advice it may obtain by way of informal consultation and inquiries.[9]

At that point, Greenwood thought the committee should be confined to civil servants from the departments concerned, although he did anticipate the possible inclusion of one or two independent experts like Sir Hector Hetherington, chairman of the Royal Commission on Workmen's Compensation. That suggestion had come from Mr (later Sir) Robert Bannatyne of the Home Office, who was anxious to provide continuity between the commission and the new committee.[10] But it was resisted by Ernest Bevin, the powerful trade union leader who had become Minister of Labour. He was mainly interested in the medical aspects of workmen's compensation and wanted the royal commission reactivated. Only when that again failed did Bevin accept the alternative of an inter-departmental inquiry. But he was certain that a committee 'consisting partly of civil servants and partly of outsiders would be no good'. The civil servants agreed. All but Bannatyne believed 'it should be a Departmental Committee with no outsiders'.[11]

Yet before the committee was formally constituted in June, an outsider was appointed and the man selected was not the one preferred by Bannatyne but an expert whose competence lay in the field of unemployment insurance — Sir William (later Lord) Beveridge. The choice was made by Greenwood alone and the civil servants resented it. Though Beveridge was working at the Ministry of Labour and had earlier spent many years in the civil service, he was regarded as an outsider by the conference of departmental representatives who met in May to decide the form the inquiry should take. As Bannatyne put it, Beveridge 'is now really in the position of an independent expert and his inclusion is inconsistent with the recommendations of the conference'.[12]

Nevertheless, it was accepted and Bevin himself agreed to the choice, apparently because he wanted an excuse to remove Beveridge from the Ministry of Labour.[13] Yet Bevin, along with his former colleagues at the TUC, never had reason to regret the appointment because Beveridge proceeded to produce a report which recommended nearly all that the unions desired. Above all, he called for the end of the approved society system and the exclusion of the insurance industry from workmen's compensation or the payment of any benefits provided by the state.[14]

Beveridge himself paid tribute to the TUC for its part in initiating the inquiry[15] and throughout the course of the proceedings, he took care to solicit union views, seeking advice on a formula that would exclude the insurance industry from state provision.[16] As soon as the report was issued, he appeared before the members of the General Council of the TUC and pointed out how closely his recommendations conformed with theirs.[17]

Even the wide-ranging nature of the report owed much to union pressure. Brown, in May 1941, had to hold out the prospect of a comprehensive survey in order to persuade the TUC to accept the limited improvements he proposed in NHI.[18] And before Bevin finally accepted the method of an inter-departmental committee, he tried to add burial insurance and rehabilitation to its remit.[19] At first, as a result of a conference of ministers, specific mention of industrial assurance was excluded,[20] and even then the Treasury feared publication of the terms of reference.[21] Later, in November 1941, Treasury officials became more concerned when they saw the direction in which Beveridge was heading. Kingsley

Wood tried to add two or three outsiders in the hope of curbing Beveridge, but Greenwood resisted,[22] and in order to free the civil servants on the committee from responsibility it was decided to let Beveridge sign the report alone.[23] Then and only then was it considered safe to bring industrial assurance within the terms of reference,[24] and Beveridge in his report called for its transformation into a public service. It was with some justification that one trade unionist in 1943 proudly described the TUC as 'the father of the Beveridge Report'.[25]

Medical pressure for reform

As for the question of health services, it was considered to be only half in the Beveridge remit and the representatives from the health departments (Hamilton Farrell for the Ministry of Health, Muriel Ritson for the Scottish Department) tried to exclude it at the Committee's first meeting on 8 July.[26] But Beveridge refused to accept the restriction, calling attention to the close relation between health insurance and health development. Though he agreed to leave the details of organization to others, he favoured a salaried service and could not resist the temptation to hint at its necessity to keep the costs of certification under control.[27] Nor could he confine his views on health services to health insurance alone. When the report appeared the creation of a comprehensive service covering everyone was one of its three key assumptions.[28] (For more on Beveridge's interest in health care, see page 192.)

While the unions concentrated their efforts on the Beveridge Committee, their ally — the doctors — were not idle. As early as August 1940 the BMA decided to form a Medical Planning Commission (MPC) to spell out how the health service should be organized.[29] By May 1942 the MPC — containing representatives from all branches of the profession including the prestigious consultant leaders of the royal colleges — had a draft interim report ready which called for a comprehensive system that would cover all but the wealthiest 10 per cent of the population.[30]

Not only did the doctors want hospital and specialist services added to the GP care already provided by the panel, but they thought general practice itself should be reorganized so that GPs would work in health centres. Group practice on the teamwork model proposed by the Dawson Report in 1920 was to be the order of the day, though without the hospital role for GPs which Dawson had envisaged. Much of this had been anticipated before by the BMA in its General Medical Service scheme, first published in 1929 and reissued with some changes in 1938.[31] But this time the plan had the sanction of consultants from the royal colleges as well as the mass of GPs and specialists who made up the BMA.

Maude found himself under pressure from Beveridge and the doctors long before their respective reports appeared. The MPC began to develop its policies in September 1941, and Ministry observers were present throughout, keeping the department informed of the direction in which the profession was heading.[32] In December, the deputy secretary of the BMA — Dr Charles (later Lord) Hill —

made sure Beveridge was notified as well. Writing unofficially to the secretary of the Beveridge Committee — D.N. (later Sir Norman) Chester — he stressed the doctors' probable neutrality on the insurance issue. The method of finance was likely to be left to others; what the profession did feel strongly about was the need to create a medical service for at least 90 per cent of the population. And when the service was extended, he indicated, most MPC members probably preferred it to be on the basis of NHI.[33]

What Hill implied was that the doctors wished to retain their independent contractor status as enshrined in the panel system but they would not object to the abandonment of insurance finance, particularly if that resulted in the abolition of the approved societies. Since Hill had the task of preparing the draft report, his judgement of MPC views could not be lightly dismissed.

Meanwhile, Beveridge was developing his own thoughts. On 1 December 1941 he prepared a document which set forth many of the recommendations that appeared in the final report. 'Health' occupied a notable place; it ranked first of the three key assumptions he made, instead of second (as in the final report), and called for a 'free universal medical service' financed mainly from taxation. However, he did add a contributory element for general practice in order to give the social security department a stake in the administration of health services. And he left scope for voluntary insurance on the hospital side so as to protect the contributory schemes considered vital for the preservation of voluntary hospitals. He did this by suggesting the need for 'hotel' charges for inpatient treatment.[34]

Though Beveridge recognized that the organization of health services lay outside his remit, he did not see how he could avoid the subject. On 2 February he sent Maude a document which touched on two delicate issues; not only did he favour the payment of GPs by salary to control certification of cash sickness benefits, but he suggested the need for local authority 'regrouping' in order to foster closer relations between municipal and voluntary hospitals.[35] A salaried method of payment was needed mainly because of the expected increase in disability benefits which had been held at a painfully low level under NHI.[36]

Maude plans GP service

Maude had been told that Beveridge was moving in this direction, and in collaboration with 'Demo' he felt compelled to develop a scheme for the GP service.[37] 'Demo' was the more reluctant, fearful of Treasury reaction to Beveridge's wide-ranging ideas, but though he considered the concept of a national health service to be less Utopian, he did not like the thought of taking health out of insurance and presented arguments for as well as against the panel system. On balance 'Demo' thought the scales were tilted slightly in favour of a salaried service and if that did come, he agreed that it should be managed by the same body 'which has the general responsibility for the hospital service, i.e. presumably the local authority'. But then, 'Demo' warned, that change 'is likely to be even less palatable to the B.M.A. than a single national service', and there was no chance of its acceptance unless the terms of service were set centrally.[38]

The general import of 'Demo's advice was to move slowly if at all, but Maude found this hard to accept:

> I agree with much of what you say, but I feel pretty sure that we must here work out some sort of scheme for a general medical service, if only for the reason that in its absence Beveridge, who is thirsting to do the job himself, will probably induce Greenwood to invite him to make a report on the subject.[39]

Early in February, Maude began to work in earnest on GP reform. This is when the detailed planning of the health service could be said to have started. Previously, Maude had assumed only that hospital reorganization would be necessary because of the changes wrought by war. Even though GP reform might be even more needed, he did not see it as inevitable.[40] But now, as a result of the pressure applied by Beveridge and the BMA, he altered his priorities and stressed the need to take advantage of the opportunity offered by the war to create a comprehensive and integrated service. Hospital planning might have to wait for the completion of the Ministry's survey, but GP reform could not be delayed; it had to come now or it might never come at all. If it were delayed, vested interests would harden and become more expensive to eradicate. There were thousands of young doctors in the armed forces with no ties to existing practices, but if they were given time to settle down the government would find it not only more difficult but more expensive to persuade the profession to enter public service. Every doctor who had sunk money into a practice would expect to be compensated for any loss he might suffer when the new system began.[41] Slowly but surely, Maude was transformed from a cautious civil servant into a radical social reformer.

The transformation began with a document Maude prepared in February, setting forth the problems presented by GP reform.[42] In it, he assumed (following Beveridge's lead) that the GP service would cover everyone and that as much as 95 per cent of the population would use it. Private practice would still be allowed, but though Maude thought the middle classes would find it difficult to tolerate the kind of treatment meted out under the panel, he did not expect them to show the same affinity for private medicine as they did for private education.

Middle class attitudes were thus an important part of Maude's concern, and he also had to take them into account when he considered the critical issue of the day: should a salaried service be substituted for the panel system? To cope with this problem, he set forth the salient features of the panel and then presented arguments for and against it. In defence of the panel he had little to say, noting briefly that its supporters claimed it promoted higher standards through competition, permitted greater free choice than was possible under a salaried service, preserved confidentiality, and left scope for doctors to form partnerships or employ assistants so that they would not have to practise alone.

On the other side, he provided a long list of grievances, drawing deeply on his long experience in the Ministry as a solicitor dealing with the disciplinary procedure. That procedure, he stressed, offered no real check over medical work since it depended on complaints from patients and they could not tell good treatment from bad. As a result, it was difficult to remove a delinquent doctor from the system. Had some means of selection been provided beforehand, the problem might have been eased, but, Maude stressed, every medical man had a right to join the panel and this inevitably meant that bad ones were there: 'It is notorious that there are some panel doctors who are unfit — by reason of age, infirmity, drink, etc. — to take part in a public service.'

Equally objectionable in Maude's view was the way practices were brought and sold. This forced young doctors to start their career with a load of debt and Maude noted that even supporters of the panel considered the situation to be 'something of a scandal'. Yet he did not see how the custom could be ended as long as free choice and the competitive system remained. An element of goodwill was bound to inflate the purchase price of a house and surgery sold by one doctor to another. For thirty years, he lamented, the authorities had tried to solve this problem but had failed and it would become much worse if all patients were on the panel.

Beyond that, Maude did not attach much value to competition. Not only did it lead doctors to provide too many drugs and sickness certificates, but it failed to promote teamwork. It also created the impression of a double standard of treatment; since nearly all doctors had panel as well as private patients, it was widely believed (though not proved) that they gave better treatment to those who paid.

Another problem which weighed heavily on Maude's mind was the amount of income GPs should receive if the panel were enlarged so that it all but eliminated private practice. If the capitation fee were kept at its present level, then — with a list size of 2,000 patients — the income of 90 per cent of doctors would be far too low — under £1,000 gross, or about £650 or £700 net per year. But if the fee were raised substantially, then it might lift GP incomes too high, raising the pay of newly qualified doctors to MOH level. In making both comparisons, Maude took care to relate GP remuneration to those in the public health service, not with consultants and others in the voluntary hospital world who were governed by different considerations. And that kind of comparison made it possible to contend that the pay issue for GPs raised 'a large question of social policy', one that could be solved only by switching to a salaried service.

The next question Maude considered was the cost of the service and how it should be met. Here he had to distinguish between hospital and GP care. The former had to retain the aid of contributory schemes if voluntary hospitals were to survive, and that was the main reason why the October 1941 statement of policy called for patient payments. But there was no similar need with GP care and Maude wanted to avoid any justification for the continuance of approved societies. Even if Beveridge had not called for their abolition, the department would have had to do something to secure greater uniformity of benefits.[43] Club and panel practice did have a contributory basis and Beveridge had suggested that a payment should be made to the health service from the social security fund in order to give those responsible for cash benefits a voice in medical care. But Maude wanted to make access to GPs as free as it had been under NHI, not merely to encourage early treatment but, more importantly, to ensure careful certification of sickness benefits.

He therefore thought it necessary to make a distinction between the two services in order to justify contributions to hospital but not GP care. A 'hotel' charge provided the means since it 'represents at least in part a saving to the patient'. The distinction was somewhat spurious and could not be sustained but it was difficult to think of any other rationale.

When it came to costs, Maude was able to offer a modest estimate — some £35 million — because only GP care was involved. For the health service as a whole, he gave Beveridge a figure of £185 million and he managed to cut that to £130 million by excluding mental illness and mental handicap hospitals from the national plan (see page 197). Maude had good cause to make this exclusion; not only had Brock stressed the need to reform the mental health law[44] but the mental health service hardly involved voluntary hospitals. They were content to leave care to local authorities who put the mentally ill in self-contained units far removed from population centres.[45] Few aside from the doctors and the LCC wanted to integrate them with the general hospital service.[46] Only costs presented a problem, since hospital stays were much longer for mental patients than for others. To finance the service, some local authorities had formed joint boards of their own and it was cheaper for the Ministry to let them run them than have the Exchequer bear half the cost.

But even with mental hospitals excluded, the hospital burden weighed heavily on Maud's mind, thereby giving additional reason to start with GP care. And in his estimate of costs, he dropped all pretence of holding open the option of a panel system; his figures were based solely on the assumption of a salaried service. The two scales he used — averaging £1,300 for the higher paid GP and £800 for the lower — fell neatly within the limits set for public health officers, thereby ensuring that no GP would earn more than the MOH who supervised him. Nor did Maude make any mention of compensation for existing practices. GPs were to enter the new service with only a pension in mind, and the cost estimate for that made no allowance for years in practice before the new health service began.

But that was not the only factor which kept the cost estimate low; Maude allowed only £10 per doctor for the equipment he would use. GPs, he envisaged, would work in groups of five or six at 'common clinics' (another term for health centres) provided by the state — yet Maude evidently thought £50 would be sufficient to promote 'the conception of team work which underlies modern medical and scientific practice'.[47]

He made no attempt to present a balanced appraisal of the panel system. His mind was made up — he strongly favoured a salaried service and he left

'Demo' in no doubt: 'Rightly or wrongly I have convinced myself that the panel system covering the population or even, say 90% of it is simply impracticable for the financial reasons set out.'[48] The main difficulty, he believed, would come from the inclusion of the middle and upper classes. Though they might welcome a public service because of post-war problems, he agreed with 'Demo' that they would not readily accept a salaried doctor, and a transitional period would be needed to give them and their medical men time to adjust. It would be possible to exclude such classes entirely, thus preserving a lucrative source of private practice, but this, Maude warned, would raise

> in an acute form the difficult question whether, and to what extent, doctors in the State service should be allowed to take private practice. Our general feeling here is strongly against a part-time system, and it cuts right across the conception which the CMO [Jameson] and others have of the State practice being for the most part carried on at communal clinics and supported at the public expense.[49]

Maude invited 'Demo's' comments and throughout their correspondence expressed a readiness to defer to his judgement: 'You are much more up-to-date than I in the intricacies of the panel system.'[50] But 'Demo' was not one to flout the feelings of the Permanent Secretary. Earlier, before Maude's position had hardened, 'Demo' had tried to present a balanced view of the panel system, finding much in its favour and doubting whether some criticisms were justified — such as the charge that GPs gave better care to private than to panel patients. But after reading Maude's paper, 'Demo' came down firmly on the Secretary's side: 'on grounds both of efficiency and finance, the new service ought to be salaried and not on a panel basis'.[51]

Diluting municipal control

Thereafter, only one major issue remained: who should administer the service? But this, as Maude recognized, was the most difficult of all:

> To work out a salaried scheme *on paper* is an amusing and by no means difficult job. The main problem, I believe, is whether and to what extent it should be a local government scheme. I can just imagine the profession accepting a national medical service; I cannot imagine them accepting, say, 150 local medical services.[52]

Yet, with some modifications, this is precisely what Maude proceeded to propose. Indeed, it was difficult for him to do otherwise, since the thrust of official policy had been in the direction of municipal control since the panel system began. There was a strong local government tradition in the department stemming from the ranks of the old Local Government Board which had been absorbed within the Ministry of Health when it was created in 1919. At least eight leading civil servants came from that Board: J.N. Beckett, Forber, H.H. George (who dealt with all questions of finance), G.H. Henderson of the Scottish Department, Macgregor, MacNalty, F.F. Marchbank, and Wrigley. Because their duties embraced housing as well as health, Ministry staff saw themselves as the main spokesmen for municipal interests in Whitehall and they did not believe local government could survive if health duties were removed.[53] Nor did they think it possible to unify the service without municipal control; GPs had to be linked with local authority care if the system was to function effectively. Added to this was the key question of finance; local authority control meant lower costs for the Exchequer and Maude was intent on presenting the Treasury with the smallest bill he could muster.

However, before Maude proceeded to develop a municipal plan, he made one last effort to deter Beveridge. At a meeting on 17 February 1942 Maude asked Beveridge not to mention local authorities and also to avoid any reference to medical treatment 'which would embarrass his Department in its present negotiations with various bodies'.[54] All Maude wanted Beveridge to say was that NHI's medical benefit should be replaced by a domiciliary system which was a part of the public health service. Beveridge refused, declaring that he not only intended to discuss medical care with the various bodies involved in NHI but also that he wanted to raise the possibility of a salaried service to control certification.

It seemed clear to Maude that Beveridge might deal with the details of medical treatment and he lost no time in developing the rest of his plan.[55] Following a discussion with Jameson and others, he fashioned an imaginative compromise which was designed to retain the basic element of municipal control but would give the doctors some of the rights they had enjoyed under the panel system.[56] The most important involved free entry. Every doctor had the right to practise under NHI and no one could stop him; all the authorities could do was remove him after he had committed some terrible offence, and that could be established only after a complaint from a patient had been upheld through a long and tortuous series of hearings.

Over the years there had been occasional cries to end the privilege of free entry[57] and 'Demo' did not see how it could be retained in a salaried service; at that point, some sort of selection would be needed. Maude's — or rather Jameson's — way of solving this problem was to let a Central Medical Board (CMB) composed mainly of doctors make the decision. Not only would the CMB determine who was fit to enter the service but it would regulate the intake into medical schools so that the profession did not become overcrowded. With nearly all of medical work being absorbed in a public service, Maude anticipated that the government would have to provide employment opportunities for those who underwent the long, costly, and specialized training required. But in exchange for this assurance, Maude thought the state had the right to expect higher standards of competence and character than had prevailed in the past.

After the entry process was completed, local authorities would take over. They would select doctors from the list kept by the CMB, which would be acting merely as an employment agency. Once in municipal employ, a doctor would be subject to the same MOH oversight as any public health officer. Only his salary and general conditions of service would be set centrally, as it had been under NHI. Maude also thought the CMB might have some control over promotions, or at least an advisory role.

Otherwise, municipal rule would be unfettered. Above all else, Maude was anxious to give the local authority power to terminate a doctor's contract after reasonable notice without going through the tortuous route of the complaint procedure. But that would result in dismissal only from the local authority involved. The discharged doctor would still be eligible to serve elsewhere unless the CMB, after due inquiry, ruled otherwise. And local authorities would be required to set up a committee, that would contain a number of doctors, for dealing with the public medical service.

Under this arrangement, the profession would have some means of expressing its views to a local authority — and the power of the authority itself would be limited. It would have control over a doctor only so long as he remained in its employ; after that, the CMB would do its best to find work elsewhere or, failing that, provide means of subsistence. But — and this would prove to be the critical omission — the doctors would not have the same place on local authorities as they enjoyed on insurance committees.

Maude recognized that this new system could not be introduced overnight. It would take time for doctors to adjust, particularly those who catered to middle class patients and had little experience of panel practice. Perhaps, he thought, it would be advisable to try salaried experiments like the one that was almost made at Bradford in 1912 when local doctors threatened to withhold their services from NHI.[58] But if it were decided to cover the whole population from the start, Maude did not see how a salaried service could be introduced in some areas and not in others. What he feared most was the creation of 'a new and very large vested interest' in the panel system if it were enlarged to include dependants and others. In that event, the selling value of practices would rise dramatically, thus making it doubtful whether the system could be ended. With this concern 'Demo' emphatically agreed.[59]

He also shared Maude's other fear — that the new service might somehow perpetuate the belief in a double standard of treatment that had plagued the panel. The only way to avoid it was to require whole-time service and not let doctors divide their day between public and private patients. Those with large private practices might choose to stay out of the service and, in that event, it might become necessary to exclude their fee-paying patients as well. A whole-time requirement thus seemed to exclude the possibility of universal coverage and it might not solve the 'double standard' danger either; patients in the public sector might again come to feel that the service they received was not as good as the one offered to those who paid outside. It was no wonder that Maude found the proposals he made inadequate; they were 'nothing more than a confession of failure to find a satisfactory solution'.[60] Eventually it was decided that the only way to meet it was to let existing doctors have the right to treat public and private patients when the new service began, but to deny the privilege to those just starting practice.[61]

The doctors' plan

Maude had not yet shown his paper on the GP service to his Minister (Brown), but that did not stop him from sending it to others beside 'Demo'. On 4 March he posted a copy to Beveridge[62] and on 5 March one went to a Mr Hogan (probably E.A. Hogan, Assistant Secretary of the Scottish Department) who, Maude assumed, had been invited to attend a meeting of the 'Beveridge group' at the Reform Club where the paper would be discussed.[63] Yet another copy was given to the Government Actuary, Sir George Epps, who warned Maude about his estimate of GP costs; not only were the salary levels set too low but far more than £10 per doctor would be needed for equipment in health centres.[64] However, neither this nor other advice from Epps made any effect on Ministry estimates; throughout the course of negotiations, the department held fast to its figure of £35 million for the GP service (see page 197).

But the person to whom Maude most wanted to show his paper was the secretary of the BMA, Dr George Anderson, and a copy was sent to him. In that way the Ministry hoped to influence the profession's plan before the MPC reported in May and indeed, when the report appeared, the department was delighted to note 'the extent of the ground common to both schemes'.[65]

Though the MPC rejected the idea of universal coverage, it went a long way towards it by reaffirming the BMA's long-standing call for the inclusion of dependants as well as employed persons within the income limits set by NHI. This would have brought some 90 per cent of the population into the public sector, and the BMA's policymaking representative body, meeting shortly thereafter in September, went further; by the narrow vote of ninety-four to ninety-two, it decided to cover everyone.[66]

Even more heartening was the way the doctors accepted the need for group practice in health centres to end the isolation of general practice and satisfy the demands of modern medicine. As early as 1920 the profession had endorsed the teamwork principle (though only among GPs, not with consultants) in the Dawson Report, and the BMA incorporated the idea in the 1929 edition of its General Medical Service scheme. But as the result of clashes between GPs and MOHs in the 1930s, health centres were expunged when the plan was reissued in 1938.[67]

The Commission's support of the concept thus seemed to represent a significant advance; that part of the report impressed the Ministry more than any other. To Maude it had become clear that 'these proposals, if finally accepted, would represent an enormous advance in medical opinion and go a long way in the direction of a complete Public Medical Service'.[68] Jameson, who had been promoting the health centre idea in department circles, was even more encouraged. He saw the MPC report as 'a realisation on the part of the medical profession that their continued existence as a series of isolated units is in the interests neither of themselves nor of the public they serve'.[69]

However, when it came to the way health centres would operate, considerable differences appeared between the Ministry's and the doctor's concepts. The profession wanted group practice run on co-operative lines with no supervision by MOHs or other public health officers. Only a 'committee of principals' elected by the doctors would guide the work of the health centre. The Ministry found this proposal hard to swallow and hoped the profession could be persuaded to accept some supervision, particularly if clinicians rather than medical administrators were given the task.

Maude was so concerned that he had Jameson seek advice from a doctor who could describe the operation of groups that had already been formed.[70] The response was not encouraging. Dr M.U. Wilson reported that GPs in group practice stood in the same relation to each other as consultants in voluntary hospitals; no one exercised overriding control. Customarily, a senior partner supplied some guidance but, Wilson warned, 'I know of no group practice where even a very junior partner would submit to the sort of check on his clinical activities which is exercised by a member of the Honorary Staff of a Hospital over his House Surgeon or House Physician.'[71]

Even more disturbing was the way the profession wanted doctors to be paid. The Ministry was intent on creating a salaried service, particularly in health centres, but the MPC held fast to the capitation system. Here, in the doctors' view, was the surest way to protect their independent status — yet the department did not see how that could be reconciled with a public service that would cover all, or nearly all, the population. The nation could not tolerate the waste of manpower that went on 'in ordinary professional life', and the authorities would have to make sure health centres were efficiently run.[72] Some doctors would inevitably be more popular than others and some means would be needed to even out their work and pay. This could only be done through a salaried service entailing restriction of free choice but, the Ministry stressed, the latter already applied under the panel system since limits were placed on list size.

Therefore the department found little merit in the profession's proposal to retain the competitive system: 'so far as "free choice" is concerned, it makes little difference.' And competition was bad not only because it encouraged lax certification and prescribing but because it would obstruct teamwork.[73] How, Maude and his colleagues asked, could we expect the spirit of co-operation to prevail in health centres if doctors had to compete for patients? Thus, in contrast with policy in Britain and America today, the Ministry in 1942 saw competition as the root of all evil.

Ministry misjudges issue of municipal control

Where administration was concerned, the Ministry deceived itself into thinking that its differences with the profession were not great. Though the doctors put forward a proposal for a 'corporate body' to oversee the service from the centre, they did indicate a willingness to accept departmental control provided they could exert influence through advisory bodies on the national as well as the local level. The Ministry seemed ready to accept this proposal, and it thought the doctors were particularly attracted to the CMB idea that Jameson had proposed.

Similarly, even though the profession wished to retain the same right of free entry as it enjoyed under the panel, the department appeared to think it could persuade the doctors to accept selection. And though nothing was said in the MPC report about the more difficult question of removal, the Ministry assumed the doctors would be willing to accept an arrangement whereby the CMB would make the decision about expulsion from the service as a whole.

However, the profession's main concern centred on the degree of municipal control and it was here that the department miscalculated. Ideally, the doctors did not want local authorities to have anything to do with health services. From their battles with friendly societies at the turn of the century, they had learned that greater medical power could be marshalled at the centre and it was there that they wanted policymaking concentrated. Only routine duties should be delegated to local bodies, particularly to those like insurance committees which had an overwhelming majority of laymen appointed by approved societies.

The MPC report envisaged a similar pattern of administration in the new service, with local authorities being substituted for insurance committees because of the need to merge GP and hospital services. But the doctors did not want to be tied to local authorities that were too small or too poor to make decent provision, and they called for the creation of regional bodies that would cover 500,000 people. These bodies might take the form of new directly elected authorities or, less radically, of councils that would contain representatives of local authorities lying within its bounds. But, however it was done, the doctors demanded a voice in administration on the NHI model. This meant that they wanted not only to form local medical advisory committees but have a place on the managing bodies, either on committees of the new regional authorities to whom administrative powers would be delegated or, if the other grouping method were used, on the regional councils.

The Ministry flatly rejected the idea of directly elected regional authorities: 'This would be a retrogade step, and it is fairly certain that electors would not trouble to go to the poll.'[74] In its view, the need for a wider regional body could be met simply by relying on the larger local authorities that already existed, county councils and municipal boroughs. If these were not large enough, then joint boards could be formed (as had been provided under the 1936 Public Health Act and the 1939 Cancer Act). Furthermore, by using 200,000 instead of 500,000 as a sufficient population, the department managed to cut sharply the instances in which joint boards would be needed — from fifty to eighteen counties, and from eighty to fifty-five municipal boroughs.

Unlike the profession, the Ministry was intent on making little change in local authority rule. Furthermore, its conception of joint boards provided no place for doctors or others; only local authorities were to be represented and, since they would bear half the cost of the new service, it could rely on them to resist demands for representation. The doctors and voluntary hospitals would be

46

forced to acquiese because there seemed no other way to unify the service.

However, in deference to medical wishes, the department did hope to break the exclusive mould of local government. This was to be done on the pattern established in the field of education — by requiring local authorities to create statutory committees on which outsiders would be represented. The Ministry thought it could obtain these concessions from local authorities and it believed this form of medical representation, together with advisory committees, would satisfy the doctors.

It was further encouraged by the way the profession opted for health centres to be provided by the statutory health authority rather than by groups of doctors in voluntary partnerships. Indeed, nothing seemed to hearten the department more than the profession's preference for this form of health centre. Although the Ministry may not have been aware of this, the proposal arose from the MPC's GP Committee and it was strongly influenced by an unsigned 'Note on health centres' submitted in September 1941 which contained many ideas that Maude later made his own.[75] Thus it suggested the need not only for statutory health centres but abolition of the sale of practices and medical appointments to vacancies in place of the right of free entry that had existed under NHI. Only where the method of remuneration was concerned did the note differ; it left open the possibility of the capitation system rather than the salaried method Maude preferred. If Charles Hill was the author — as seems likely — its shows how he was striving to carry the MPC in the department's direction.

But here as elsewhere the Ministry only succeeded in deceiving itself. The profession's choice was not what it appeared; the doctors wanted statutory health centres not because they preferred local authority rule but because that was the surest way to secure control of municipal clinics (which would also be located there).[76] And medical finances being as precarious as they were, the doctors did not see how they could afford to provide health centres or group practice facilities from their own resources.

Furthermore, where the larger question of administration was concerned, the doctors' conception still departed greatly from the department's. For despite the concessions it thought it might obtain, the Ministry intended to lodge more control in municipal hands than the doctors would have tolerated. Only the question of removal from the service was clearly to be placed elsewhere. And while salaries and other conditions of employment were to be set centrally, no one in the department expected local authorities to be divorced from the process. Something like the Burnham procedure that determined public health salaries was bound to apply in the GP sector, and MOHs would have the task of fitting GPs into the salary scale.[77]

Maude's view hardened in the months that followed, and he would not tolerate dissent. When Alan Barlow of the Treasury suggested in November that the Ministry might be too optimistic in assuming this degree of municipal control, Maude responded:

This is the most important point of all. I have myself been very tempted with the idea of a centralised service with a considerable intermixture of professional organisation and management. The trouble is that it seems quite impracticable and wrong to divorce a GP service from the Public Health and Hospital Services, and the idea of removing these from local government is not practical politics.[78]

In the paper he prepared in November for Brown and other ministers, Maude went further, dismissing entirely the doctors' desire for freedom from control which the panel system offered:

We are satisfied that the continuance of the arrangements under which the panel system is carried on — arrangements which represent a cross between private practice and a public service and in some respects exhibit the weaknesses of both systems — cannot be accepted. They are indeed incompatible with the organisation of publicly provided Health Centres envisaged in the B.M.A. Report. Moreover, it is tolerably certain that the local authorities would decline to accept responsibility for administering a system so lacking in control and organisation.[79]

The logic of this argument seemed so overwhelming that Maude could not imagine the doctors resisting it. By February 1943, just before negotiations began, he and his colleagues had dropped all thought of *ad hoc* regional authorities and were concentrating on the concept of joint boards. And, Maude and his colleagues believed, once the doctors recognised the degree of professional control provided in the department's plan, they would drop their demand for larger areas and accept units of population smaller than 500,000. Though the Ministry still hoped to base joint boards on the larger local authorities, it was ready to go below county council level if the smaller authorities insisted. As for the profession's demand for a direct place in administration, that was seen as a secondary issue — a mere matter of status. It was expected that the doctors themselves would attach little importance to the demand once they realized that medical representatives on administrative bodies might turn out to be more 'bureaucratic' than lay representatives.

Competition: the root problem

Maude expected the profession's main objection to come on the salaried method of .payment and it was there that he and his colleagues concentrated their arguments. The most forceful statement was prepared by McNicholl who condemned the capitation system out of hand:

The capitation fee has not even the virtue of piece-work payment, in which the workers rule out competition for the materials of their job. It cuts clean across the idea of team work, the development of which is the main object of grouping. Indeed, if the capitation method of payment were adopted it would be better not to group the doctors and not bring them together in health centres. *Commercial competition among doctors is at the root of most of the difficulties of private medical practice to-day.* Those difficulties are masked to some extent at present by the fact that the competing doctors conduct their rival businesses from different premises. They could not be masked if the rival doctors were compelled to work in groups from health centres — to conduct their rival businesses over the same counter as it were.[80]

Maude was so impressed with these words that he made them his own.[81] He and his colleagues also came down strongly in favour of whole-time service, a ban to be imposed on private practice for those doctors who chose to participate in the public sector. Some allowance might have to be made for those in practice at the start of the service, but under no conditions would new entrants be granted the privilege. If private practice were generally allowed, it would expose the service to the same belief in a double standard that had plagued NHI: 'This, above everything, is the one idea we have got to abandon for good.'[82] Under NHI, panel and private practice had to operate side by side since the system covered only half the population, but the new service would apply to the nation as a whole without regard to social class or ability to pay:

> The essence of the new service must be that it becomes, and is seen by all to be, a full health provision of first class lines for a fitter population; that it has no sort of taint of poor relief or social distinction; that the whole practice of medicine as a profession is gradually directed, as a vital national activity, to building up and protecting the whole national health through a really popular national health service.[83]

In making such statements, Maude and his colleagues sounded surprisingly radical, so much so that there was little to distinguish their plan from the one proposed by the ardent reformers who made up the SMA.[84] But Maude was no socialist; he was a dedicated public servant devoted to the pursuit of national health and, like many of his social class, anxious to free medicine from the taint of commerce. In his view, as in that of others who had been educated at Rugby and Oxford, it was degrading for doctors to act like businessmen; they were members of an honourable profession and should conduct themselves with the same public spirit that motivated civil servants and university teachers. Beveridge shared the same feelings.[85]

Maude was also encouraged by the views of medical leaders. In July, the Ministry's observer on the MPC — Sir Weldon Dalrymple-Champneys, deputy CMO since 1940 — had reported that the MPC chairman (the surgeon Henry Souttar) and its secretary (Hill) believed the proposals in the report 'would lead inevitably to a whole-time salaried medical service'.[86] A former secretary of the BMA, Dr Alfred Cox, reinforced the prophecy just before negotiations began. Though Cox still believed in the free choice principle, he thought it had been undermined by the movement to hospital care. Patients in municipal and voluntary hospitals generally had to accept whoever treated them and that had led to a change in public attitudes. Cox — who hoped that all, or nearly all, doctors would enter the public service — now thought it more important to remove practitioners who failed to perform satisfactorily.

These words were music to Maude's ears and he made them known to Brown.[87] They were contained in two letters Cox sent to a former civil servant in the Ministry, R.W. Harris, who forwarded them to Maude in January 1943.[88] The department thus entered discussions in March hopeful that the profession would endorse its salaried plan.

Chapter five

Doctors reject municipal control

By February 1943 the Ministry had completed work on the GP service and it started formal discussions with the profession in March. Talks began simultaneously with local authorities and voluntary hospitals, but these were confined mainly to administrative structure. The focus was almost entirely on the GP service because detailed planning of the hospital sector had not yet begun. The Ministry had to await not only the completion of the hospital survey but the reports of the Goodenough Committee on medical schools (not issued until May 1944) and the Hetherington Committee on Scottish hospitals (not issued until August 1943). Even more important was the need to obtain detailed data on the supply and distribution of consultants. The way that survey was conducted created difficulties (see page 127) which delayed meaningful planning until 1945.

Maude's stress on the GP service

Maude attached more importance to medical than hospital policy, and throughout the discussions displayed a willingness to make concessions to the doctors which he did not want to offer voluntary hospitals. In his view, 'Medical services are the foundation of the health service as a whole. Matters of hospital policy are much more limited in scope and, to some extent, overlap with medical policy.'[1]

When Maude discussed medical policy it was unsually GPs, not consultants, that he had in mind. This was not only because of the Ministry's past experience with the panel system and Maude's passionate conviction that it needed to be reformed, but because GPs outnumbered consultants and specialists by five to one — roughly 20,000 GPs to some 4,000 consultants and specialists. When Maude held talks with the profession, he was dealing with representatives who came mainly from the ranks of GPs. The GP service, in his view, was 'undoubtedly the hardest nut to crack',[2] and, if GPs could be won over, he was sure hospital doctors would follow. As Pater put it in September 1942: 'If general practitioners are salaried officers of local authorities, presumably consultants will also become part of the salaried service.'[3] The first tentative outline of consultant services was not prepared until April 1943, one month after discussions with the profession began.[4]

Nevertheless, there were compelling reasons for treating the hospital service first. Early in 1942 Pater had drawn attention to the fact that there was a basis for a salaried service in the hospital world but not in general practice.[5] Not only did local authorities pay hospital doctors by salary, but so did the Ministry in the hospitals — voluntary as well as municipal — that came under its EMS scheme. Doctors who worked in voluntary hospitals had long been dissatisfied with their honorary status and EMS payments made them accustomed to the salaried form. It might therefore be easier to persuade GPs to accept a salaried service if an example were set by their consultant colleagues, and the same applied to GP tolerance of municipal control.

But the difficulty with this strategy was that there were too few consultants; GPs might simply ignore the example set in the hospital world. Maude did not feel he could take the risk; the GP service had to be ready to meet the certification needs of the cash benefits proposed in the Beveridge Report — and if reform was to come, it had to be done before doctors released from the armed forces settled back in practice and resisted efforts to change their old ways.

In December 1942 Maude tried to impress Brown with the urgency of GP reform and the need to deal with the health service as a whole in one bill.[6] Until that point Brown had expected hospital legislation to come first, but Maude gave reasons for delaying the process until both could be treated together. Where the hospital service was concerned, he wished to reach agreement only on lay-out and areas, thus confining attention to the administrative structure. But the GP service had to be discussed as a whole. Not even the outline of a policy had been announced, and Maude was anxious to secure the profession's assent to a salaried service. If it were forthcoming, the Ministry could proceed to lay-out health centres and, since no major construction programmes could be expected in the aftermath of war, the department had to earmark buildings which might be used. Here Maude saw the need to adapt whatever could be found, citing EMS accommodation, wartime nurseries, rest centres, and other emergency quarters as possibilities.[7]

Maude's time-table for legislation was to proceed as follows. Discussions would begin in March and end in September, when a White Paper would be issued. A bill might follow early in 1944 and the service would start in 1945, some twelve to eighteen months after the expected end of the war — which was later defined to mean the war with Germany, not Japan. If demobilization began near the end of 1944, then the GP service might have to get underway sooner, so that new practice premises would be in place before doctors returned home.[8]

Maude expected the discussions to be conducted in confidence, without publicity, until the White Paper was presented to parliament; no other arrangement would satisfy the demands of legislative protocol or the expectations of MPs.[9] But Maude failed to anticipate how difficult it would be for medical leaders to follow this procedure; if they were to secure agreement, they had to make the details known to the profession at large, and not (as Maude expected) simply to doctors who acted in a representative capacity.[10] And since (at Maude's insistence) the spokesmen on the representative committee came from all sections of the medical world, this meant that reports had to be made to consultants, MOHs, and others, as well as GPs.[11] Yet this consideration was apparent from the start; the doctors who met Maude in March insisted on using the term 'discussions' rather than 'negotiations' to describe what was in reality a bargaining process.[12] They also insisted on preparing longer reports of their own as a safeguard against the shorter minutes kept by the Ministry.[13]

Maude took similar precautions; he did not want to rely on the profession's representative committee to test the medical reaction. He set up the Ministry's own medical advisory committee, hoping it would command as much authority as the one under Dawson in 1920. (That committee fell into abeyance in 1921, and though smaller advisory committees were formed in the 1930s, they did not function effectively.) Like the Dawson Committee, the new advisory body contained twenty members, among whom were BMA and Royal College leaders as well as others who served on the profession's representative committee.[14] But unlike the Dawson Committee, the new body had the CMO, Jameson, in charge. Maude did not want a rerun of 1920 when Dawson produced plans too expensive for department demands.[15]

However, the committee did not live up to Ministry expectations. Maude wanted help on health centre plans and a sub-committee serviced by Pater was set up for the purpose.[16] But no sooner did the parent advisory committee meet than cries arose from medical ranks for it to steer clear of NHS affairs; that, the doctors declared, should be left to the representative committee which had been formed by the BMA and over which they had command.[17]

Thereafter the advisory committee tended to confine its attention to specialized subjects like cancer, TB, and VD. Only after the White Paper appeared in February 1944 did it again stray into NHS territory and Dr (later Sir) Guy Dain, the GP leader who had taken Souttar's place on the advisory committee as well as at the head of the BMA's council and negotiating team, had to issue a fresh warning.[18] That still left the health centre sub-committee free to carry on its work and in May it declared bed provision essential for every GP, just as Dawson had done in 1920.[19] The advisory committee as a whole endorsed this principle,[20] but with the prospect of health centres fading by that time, nothing came of these plans[21] and the committee plodded on until 1948 in a perfunctory manner. After the NHS began it was replaced by a larger body with a wider membership, the Central Health Services Council (CHSC). But like the Dawson Committee of 1920, the Council never served the purpose the Ministry intended because on all essential matters the doctors insisted on speaking through a body on which they were directly represented and whose views they could command, not one whose members were appointed by the Minister.[22]

Doctors versus local authorities

At the start discussions with local authorities went smoothly. Their spokesmen were delighted with the plan since it gave them control over GP as well as hospital and clinic care.[23] The challenge was welcomed by representatives of the three major municipal groups involved, the Association of Municipal Corporations (AMC), CCA, and LCC. The only point at which they criticized the GP plan was on costs; since they were to assume a large portion, they did not think the £35 million allowed by the Ministry was enough. What disturbed them most was the £2,000 estimate for a health centre, of which there were to be 3,000 in all.[24] (For more on costs, see page 197.)

Otherwise, their concern centred on the innovation of joint boards. Maude was intent on welding town and country together for hospital administration, to repair the damage done by the 1929 Local Government Act. Whereas the two areas had previously been combined within the old Poor Law unions for hospital purposes, the 1929 Act separated them, substituting the test of 'ordinary residence' for the 'doctrine of settlement'.[25] This made it difficult for patients from counties to use the many hospitals in municipal boroughs; in some counties as many as half the patients were dependent on access to borough hospitals.[26] Maude hoped the joint board would remove the barrier, but all the local authorities could think of was the threat to their autonomy, particularly through the board's precepting power.[27] Of the funds needed for the GP service, half was to come from local authorities, and the same applied to the cost of hospital and clinic services.[28] Though the LCC was large enough to constitute a health authority on its own, its leaders also displayed financial anxiety.

Local authority objections, however, were nothing compared to those of the doctors. The Ministry hoped joint boards would dilute their distaste for municipal rule but at the very first meeting on 25 March they made their opposition known: 'They would prefer central control, working through regional bodies from the centre.'[29] This preference was dictated partly by distrust of local government and disrespect for the people involved. As two Scottish doctors put it, 'They did not wish to be controlled in their day-to-day work by the non-scientific layman. Local authority administration was affected by political influence. Moreover, the average councillor was inclined to look after his friends.'[30]

Such feelings, as McNicholl had anticipated, arose from 'objection to control by the local butcher or baker'. It was 'partly snobbish and partly a genuine reaction against control by people who are not merely uninformed but have not learned how to allow the expert to get on with his job'.[31] It was also strongly affected by the doubt that local authorities had the commitment, technical competence, or financial resources to run a complete health service.[32]

But most was all was the fear of the MOH or the new director of medical services to be employed by the joint board.[33] Such bureaucrats had been the cause of many disputes between the wars and that made the doctors realize it was not wise to have an administrator, armed with a medical qualification, too close to their place of work. As one Scottish doctor put it, 'The further away they were from control . . . the better. Give them better facilities but as far as possible leave them free to do their work in their own way.'[34]

It was true that the doctors had criticisms to make of central government. They were annoyed at the failure of the Ministry of Health to make progress with NHI between the wars, believing that its involvement with housing and other matters made it neglectful of medical care. For this and other reasons, they preferred to have a corporate body (like the British Broadcasting Corporation or the old National Insurance Commission), composed mainly of doctors, in charge of the service. Or if that were not constitutionally possible, they preferred to be ruled by a government department concerned with health alone.[35]

But these were minor demands not pressed at all strongly compared with those directed at local authorities. Under no conditions would the doctors accept municipal rule, whether diluted through joint boards or not, unless they were given the same rights as they had under NHI — direct representation on the health authority or its managing committee, together with advisory powers similar to the local medical committee.[36] Only two medical leaders, Dawson and Moran, were ready to accept solely an advisory role and they were consultants, not GPs.[37] (Moran changed his mind after he saw the angry reaction his views stirred in the hospital world: see page 121.)

The demand for advisory powers presented no problem; local authorities were willing to accept them[38] and Jameson offered the same prospect on the national level: 'the profession can . . . have as powerful an Advisory Committee as they think necessary'.[39] But the grant of direct representation was another matter; local authorities rejected that outright, the strongest reaction coming from the socialist leaders of the LCC who feared that 'outsiders' might upset the political balance in London. The most LCC spokesmen would concede was co-option to a managing committee and that only at the discretion of the local authority. Under no conditions would they consider nomination by an outside body; all the doctors could expect was the chance to recommend names for appointment.[40]

In the midst of this dispute, the voluntary hospitals added their weight to medical demands. The BHA found the administrative structure 'entirely unacceptable', and it threatened to advise its members to withhold co-operation if the Ministry proceeded with its plan.[41] This reaction had been predictable before discussions began. On 20 February a leading consultant, Dr Geoffrey Bourne, had unleashed a powerful attack on 'autocratic' public administration as represented by the EMS as well as the LCC. In its place he wanted to substitute the 'democratic' system of voluntary hospitals which left consultants free to go their own way.[42] Sir Ernest Pooley of the King's Fund brought these views forcefully to Maude's attention on 24 March, but Maude rejected them out of hand. To him, the voluntary hospital system appeared to be 'much more an example of syndicalism, that is of control over an undertaking by the workers themselves' — a system that could best be seen in the self-governing colleges of Oxford and Cambridge.[43] Maude had little respect for voluntary hospital administrators, believing that none could match the experience of the LCC's medical department or the Ministry's own EMS staff.[44]

G.H. Henderson of the Scottish Department proposed a compromise; give the doctors representation without voting powers.[45] Maude agreed, and so did the local authorities, but such rights, Maude warned, should be confined to doctors and voluntary hospitals, not others in the health world. He was fearful of extending the representation principle too far in the sphere of government.[46]

On the national level Maude tried to be equally generous to the doctors, offering them an administrative agency (CMB) and an advisory body, Central Medical Services Council (CMSC), composed mainly or entirely of doctors. Though the profession would not enjoy direct representation rights on the CMB, Maude did propose to grant it on the CMSC, along with the power to make reports and review regulations. The voluntary hospitals were expected to make similar demands but Maude offered them less, conceding only the possibility of an advisory body, to be called the Central Hospital Services Council, which might have the task of inspecting hospitals in order to alleviate voluntary hospital fears of municipal control.[47]

The doctors were thus to hold a privileged position in Maude's scheme, but that failed to satisfy them; they insisted on voting powers where local authorities were concerned and demanded stronger powers for the CMSC. Jameson wanted to satisfy the doctors on their CMSC demands but Maude resisted, fearful that the same privilege would have to be granted to others.[48]

Impasse in discussions

By the end of April discussions had reached an impasse and Maude met privately with the BMA's secretary, Anderson, and his deputy, Hill, to see if a compromise could be found. Though other issues had arisen, the BMA officials made it clear that the threat of municipal control was the main difficulty. The doctors found the Ministry's plan objectionable, even with the CMB safeguard, because it left too much discretion in local authority hands. They preferred to have central administration on EMS (or NHI) lines, leaving only health centres to be provided by local authorities or joint boards.

It was clear that this would be resented by local authorities; since they were given the duty of setting up health centres, they would insist on some review of medical work. Furthermore, the doctors' demand would create a split in administration — local authorities or joint boards being in control of hospitals while GPs fell under central direction. If this privilege were granted to GPs, it was feared that the medical officers already in municipal employ would make the same demands. As Maude told Brown, one cannot ignore 'the brutal and inescapable fact that the officer concerned in any service must submit to a certain amount of direction and control at the hands of those responsible for the service'.[49]

In Maude's view the only way out of this impasse was to give greater powers to the CMB. Joint boards would still supervise GP work in health centres but they would no longer have the sole right to hire and fire; rather, the CMB could order the employment of an unpopular doctor and it was to decide when service would be terminated. Maude had deliberately left a disciplinary procedure out of his original plan to avoid the need for a formal inquiry. He wanted termination to be decided by the ordinary rules of municipal administration, leaving the discharged doctor free to seek work elsewhere. He still hoped to preserve much of that arrangement, but he now suggested that CMB approval be required before the local decision was made, and the CMB was to decide whether a formal inquiry should be held.

In the hope of winning acceptance, Maude thought it better if the doctors proposed it, and he apparently made the suggeston to Anderson, but the BMA Secretary did not take it up.[50] Instead, on 12 May, he sent Maude an official letter rejecting the department's plan and demanding a royal commission to study the problem afresh.[51] Fearful that discussions were being hurried for certification purposes, the doctors urged the government to push ahead with the insurance (or cash benefit) side of the Beveridge Report, leaving health till later. Underlying this proposal was the hope of eliminating the approved societies so that the doctors could form a new administration on panel lines.

Maude was in no mood to delay the Ministry's plan. He and his Scottish colleagues ruled out a royal commission not only because it would mean a two year postponement but because it might breed bad feelings. If a commission were created — as at one point Maude seemed ready to do — the department, backed by the approved societies and others, would feel compelled to attack the panel system, and that would be deeply resented by the doctors.[52]

The exchange between the parties thus seemed to be going nowhere and with leaks appearing in the Beaverbook press,[53] BMA leaders felt the need to bring their case into public view. On 16 May Charles Hill delivered a blistering attack on the Ministry's plan before a mass meeting of London doctors.[54] The address was designed to appease the more militant members of the profession, but in Maude's view it violated the pledge of secrecy that had been made in March, under which it was agreed that neither party would go public before the White Paper was presented to Parliament. Yet according to Jameson's biographer, the CMO gave Hill permission to make this disclosure.[55]

Maude was furious and ready to resist public pressure,[56] but at a critical meeting with the doctors on 17 May Brown caved in. He agreed to start discussions afresh, putting his plan 'in the discard' if the doctors would drop their demand for a royal commission.[57] After due deliberation, the representative committee acquiesced and appointed a smaller body of eight doctors to continue the process.

Despite Brown's hasty retreat, Maude still had hopes of salvaging the Ministry plan, or at least a large part. He tried to persuade Anderson to alter the words 'in the discard' from the minutes of the meeting, using the more flexible term 'withdraw' instead.[58] But though Anderson refused and Brown's words were widely publicized, Maude persisted with the essentials of his plan. On 24 May he himself raised the proposal which he had hoped would come from the doctors, giving the CMB ultimate control over hiring and firing.[59]

However, he failed to make the concessions needed on private practice if his plan were to succeed. From the moment discussions began the doctors made it clear that they wanted an escape route if public service proved unbearable, and they stressed the point increasingly as the talks proceeded.[60] The lead was taken by Sir Alfred (later Lord) Webb-Johnson, president of the Royal College of Surgeons (RCS), the section of the profession that had most to gain from private practice (see page 139).

Maude did not respond; he was paralysed by fear of perpetuating the double standard of care that had plagued the panel. He held firmly to his intent to restrict severely the number of doctors who would be allowed to engage in private practice while participating in the public service. As he put it in an internal memorandum meant only for department eyes:

> The admission that the doctors themselves have any moral right to combine both kinds of practice is tantamount to saying that the public service in itself is either underpaid or for other reasons will not provide a satisfying career for a capable and vigorous man. To initiate a service on this assumption would be to invite failure.[61]

Turning point in policy

The doctors proved as intractable as ever at the next meeting on 3 June and a heated exchange erupted between Maude and Hill. The doctors, Hill emphasized, did not want the Ministry's plan but an extension of the panel system with only a few health centres tried on an experimental basis. This roused Maude to fury and he ruled out any arrangement which might pit the two systems side by side: 'the centres in contemplation would be expensive establishments, the staff other than doctors being provided by the health authority and it must be ensured that they are fully used and not in competition with another State provided service in the panel'. Dain wondered what was wrong with competition but it was this which worried Maude most of all: 'The Government could not agree to provide expensive premises and equipment and leave doctors to run it competitively.'[62]

Anderson, with whom Maude felt greater rapport, tried to forge a compromise, suggesting that an incentive be combined with a salaried service to lessen the need for administrative review. Reports by colleagues, refresher courses, and links with the hospital world were raised as possibilities and this persuaded Maude to look again at the method by which GPs would be paid.

That proved to be a turning point in Ministry policy. Thereafter, Maude showed a willingness to consider an alternative plan, allowing the panel to operate side by side with health centres until a full salaried service could be realized. Why did he change his mind? Certainly the heated opposition that arose in May and Brown's weak response were major factors. But Maude also may have seen how difficult it would be to sustain his argument against 'expensive' health centres when he allowed only £10 per doctor for equipment and £2,000 for the building itself.

Whatever the reason, Maude went to work on the reforms needed if the panel system were to continue.[63] Three changes were essential: controls had to be exercised over the location of doctors to secure a more even distribution; the sale of practices had to be abolished; and pensions had to be provided to facilitate retirement. All of this meant that the automatic right of entry which the profession had so highly prized under NHI would cease; doctors would still be generally free to enter the public service but they could not always practise where they liked. Otherwise, panel doctors would be subject to the same disciplinary procedure as in the past, but this might not be needed for those who worked on salary in health centres. Panel doctors would still have limits on list size, but a lower level — set at about two-thirds the normal maximum — would be imposed on those who chose to take private patients.[64]

The old fee-paying disputes that bedevilled the panel would not arise since the new service would cover everything and GPs could no longer charge for care that fell beyond the limited range of NHI. Capitation fees would have to be set at a level which would provide panel doctors with net incomes comparable to the £400 to £1,600 range of salaries that were to be paid to those in health centres. As an incentive for those on salary, postgraduate courses were considered, one being required every two years, with a formal examination after the eighth to qualify for an increase in scale.[65] Later it occurred to Maude that medical boards might be needed to control certification and rules might have to be applied over the employment of assistants.[66]

All of this was to provide only temporary respite for the panel system. Maude recognized that group practice was an untested idea and that GP isolation might be relieved simply by the addition of hospital and consultant services: 'The real advantage of the Health Centre system lies in an attitude of mind — the conception of the doctors as a scientific team primarily concerned with making a good job of their work.'[67] But he still believed in health centres and group practice — so much so that he wanted the government to state that system as its ultimate goal, with a target of 1,000 health centres to be built within three years of the end of the war. Though the concept had support in all quarters, it tended to be favoured most by those on the left, and Maude expected health centres to become a matter of party controversy.

Issue of local authority control still not resolved

Maude had reason to hope that this combination of systems might prove acceptable to the profession, but there still remained the issue of municipal control. The doctors might be willing to experiment with group practice in health centres, even perhaps with a salaried payment, but they did not want any part of the GP service under local authority direction. The concessions Maude had made on representation had not proved acceptable because they did not carry voting power. Nor was that all. The profession felt uneasy about the principle of universal coverage, and wanted an escape route no matter what sort of service was devised.

Matters were not made easier by the battle that had broken out between voluntary hospitals and local authorities. Like the doctors, the voluntary hospitals were trying to extricate themselves from municipal control and they wanted the same representation rights as the profession, with the two groups together having the right to two-thirds of the seats on joint boards.[68]

Pater in May argued strongly against their demands, urging the Ministry to be firm because the hospital service had to be organized on the basis of local authority direction. Thus, in opposition to the voluntary hospital's demand for a board on the national level like the one offered to the doctors, he argued 'If there is a case here for a Central Hospitals Board, it is for a board representing local authorities only.'[69]

Maude shared these sympathies,[70] but he had earlier led Goodenough of the Nuffield Trust to believe that some of these demands would be met[71] and found it difficult to change tack later. In May he agreed to establish a Central Hospitals Council but on an advisory, not executive, basis and it would not pass judgement on local schemes. He assured voluntary hospitals of representation on joint boards and saw no difficulty in giving them an unofficial advisory committee of their own. But he refused their request for a joint statutory advisory committee because that would pit municipal against voluntary hospital representatives.[72]

On finance he was equally anxious to preserve local authority influence. The voluntary hospitals had cried 'Don't put us on the rates — that would end all hope of voluntary subscriptions.'[73] They wanted all or nearly all their public money to come from the Exchequer. What was uppermost in their mind was the fear of municipal control if finance remained in local authority hands.

Maude rejected their proposal outright. It would, he warned, lead to a similar demand from local authorities 'and logically to a national and not a local government service'.[74] Some money had to come from local authorities to ensure co-ordination and regulate voluntary hospital development[75] However, Maude did provide public funds from the centre. 'Beveridge' money — part of social insurance contributions — would be pooled and distributed to voluntary hospitals on the advice of a central body composed of their representatives alone.

A different method was to apply to the distribution of the 'unit grant', amounting to £1 per week per bed. This was to be paid by the local health authority with an additional allowance subject to negotiation. Now, in place of the latter, the Ministry proposed a standard 50 per cent grant, thus removing discretion from municipal hands.[76]

Local authorities still had charge of planning and inspection, but they were not happy with the way their financial influence had been undermined. Most disliked even more the joint board concept, despite the 60 per cent majority local authorities were to enjoy on all committees to be formed. Municipal interests did not always coincide and joint board rule, particularly with its precepting power, threatened to deprive many authorities of autonomy. This applied particularly to the smaller district councils who had been given a minor role in the Ministry's scheme, being assigned a place only on district committees that were to be formed under joint boards.

In June, the Urban District Councils Association protested strongly against the joint board concept, and demanded direct representation if the proposal went ahead. Even more, district councils were unhappy with the loss of powers with which they were threatened — not only over infectious disease hospitals but maternity and child welfare clinics, school medical inspections, and supervision of midwives. Their interests, they recognized, coincided with the voluntary hospitals and, to the horror of many in the municipal world, the Association upheld the value of the voluntary sector as a supplement to local authority work.[77]

Throughout May resistance to the joint board concept rose and led to a demand for the reform of local government so that each of the larger authorities would be big enough to form a health authority on its own.[78] The proposal was supported by the Nuffield Trust because it feared the creation of joint boards would force a split in the service, with the boards responsible for hospital care, while individual local authorities were left in charge of domiciliary services.[79] In April the Labour Party had contributed to the movement by calling for new directly elected regional bodies to administer the health service.[80]

Maude had been strongly attracted to this idea, recognizing that it offered the best chance of salvaging his plan. On 19 April he put forward the proposal in Cabinet quarters, suggesting that a new authority might be possible if other duties (police, fire, education, highways, planning) were added to health.[81]

Wrigley registered a strong dissent. The department, he argued, could not wait for local government reform because of the need to have the health service ready before doctors discharged from the armed forces settled back in practice. If the service were not ready by the end of the war, then 'the most favourable opportunity of establishing a public medical service will have been lost'. But that was not his only concern; more important was the effect he feared on housing, and he was in charge of the housing section of the department. Housing did not need wider areas of government — indeed, that might make the task more difficult — and the public had a greater stake in preserving local authorities as they were: 'The interest of the general public in housing has during the past 25 years been much greater than that in health services, and housing has played a more important part in local elections.'[82]

Maude later left the department to take up the challenge of local government reform, but meanwhile the main force of Wrigley's argument prevailed; whatever the effect on housing, the health service could not wait for a second tier. Joint boards were the only alternative, and this led to a municipal demand for the split in service which the Nuffield Trust feared.[83]

Maude tried to stem the movement, but that only led to further wrangling over the composition of joint boards. Local authorities were determined to reduce medical and voluntary hospital influence, going so far in Scotland as to oppose representation without the vote. Johnston strongly upheld this demand. He was an ardent defender of local government, and opposed all thought of reform,[84] but he was more pragmatic than Maude and more in control of his department than Brown. As far as he was concerned, there was only one way out; give the doctors what they wanted and run the GP service from the centre.[85] The split in the service which Maude so feared had thus become a pressing danger; in England and Wales at least, he hoped to preserve unified direction.

The doctors' response was to extricate themselves from further involvement with local authorities. In their view, the concessions made by Maude were not enough; municipal influence in health centres would still be too strong, and a complete salaried service seemed to be the direction in which the department was heading. In the hopes of saving the situation, Maude was ready to offer the doctors representation with voting power, but that was not acceptable to the Scottish Department, and it was doubtful if it would have been tolerated by local authorities in England and Wales.[86]

To the doctors there seemed only one alternative; extend the panel system so that it covered 'dependants and specialists', moving gradually towards wider provision. In the process they hoped to squeeze the approved societies out — which was probably the main reason why Hill stressed the importance of removing the economic barrier between doctor and patient.[87] In an Exchequer-financed service covering 100 per cent of the population, there would be no room for approved societies dependent for their existence on the contributory principle. A new type 'insurance' committee' could be formed without the 60 per cent majority the approved societies enjoyed. In short, what the doctors wanted was insurance administration without insurance finance — unless the latter could be realized without agencies like the approved societies.

Was the salary scale offered too low?

The first round of discussions thus ended in August with Maude's plan in shreds. At least one BMA negotiator had regrets; this was Dr A. Talbot Rogers, a member of the SMA's executive committee and a fervent advocate of a salaried service.[88] Throughout the course of discussions he did his best to support Maude's plan, and years later he claimed that it failed only because the salaries offered were too low.[89] This was doubtful. The amounts rantged from £400 to £1,600 with £1,000 as the average. Though the earnings to be expected from the capitation system were raised substantially above this level before the NHS began — to an average of £1,777 (see page 101) — that was largely the result of the price inflation that followed the start of discussions in 1943. A year earlier the same scale had been proposed by Professor John Ryle, the leading academic proponent of a salaried service and closely associated with the SMA.[90] When the salary scale was made public in May 1943, one section of the Beaverbook press, the *Daily Express*, did its best to stir medical hostility by stressing the starting salary of £400 and failing to mention any figure above £650.[91] But another paper under Beaverbrook control, the *Evening Standard*, had to admit the scale was generous.[92]

It was no doubt galling to GPs to have their salaries compared with public health officers as the Ministry was prone to do. They preferred their pay to be linked with consultants who were to have salaries ranging from £1,000 to £3,000.[93] But that was not the main reason why the doctors rejected Maude's plan; the root cause lay in their aversion to municipal control. As one Scottish doctor told the Department: 'It was the glory of the profession that in the main they were masters in their own house.'[94] And a former assistant secretary of the Scottish Department agreed. This was J.W. Vallance, who was retained by the BMA to aid the profession in Scotland throughout the course of negotiations. In his view, a new *ad hoc* authority had to be formed to deal adequately with health and 20 per cent of its members should come from the medical and allied professions.[95]

Chapter six

Resistance to compromise

Despite the strong feelings displayed by the doctors, Maude had hopes of salvaging his plan. Those chosen to speak for the profession were mainly older men and Maude believed they did not reflect the sentiments of younger doctors, many of whom favoured a salaried service.[1] Medical men who returned from the armed forces would have to start afresh and nearly all, Maude thought, would welcome the security of health centres.[2] Moreover, he did not think the profession recognized the implications of its MPC report; it accepted group practice but rejected salary — yet the two in Maude's mind were indissolubly tied.[3] The doctors had acknowledged the need to cover nearly the whole population but, Maude pointed out, they did not see there would then be little difference between payment by salary or capitation.[4]

Maude was sure group practice in health centres would grow, but there was another link in his thought; it was vital that GPs be associated with their colleagues in the hospital world, and for that to happen all had to come under the same management. This, in Maude's eyes, meant local authority rule, for he could conceive of no other body being responsible for hospital provision.[5] He was therefore willing to make more concessions to persuade the profession to accept municipal direction.

Others felt too many concessions had already been made. The first sign of resistance came after the outline of the White Paper had been prepared by Hawton in July. Macgregor, who had been in charge of panel pay negotiations since February 1941,[6] objected to the way the section on health centres had been modified: 'What I am afraid of is that unless the centre business is tackled at the outset and not left as something to be worked for "over" a substantial period, a new vested form of hybrid practice will take root and we will never see the centre.'[7] From his experience with panel practitioners, he was sure they would welcome health centres as originally conceived and since they treated 90 per cent of the population (dependants of insured persons being covered on the private side), that meant the bulk of the profession would assent.

The next sign of resistance came from the Scottish Department, then under pressure from local authorities to resist any form of medical representation, even without the vote. On 19 July, Henderson conveyed this feeling to Maude: 'If we concede the principle of membership to the medical profession, we may not be able to stop there; similar claims will no doubt come from the organisations representing nurses, dentists, pharmacists and opticians.'[8] So strongly did the Scottish local authorities feel about the issue that they were ready to give up administration of the GP service, hopeful that this would relieve them of health centre costs as well.[9] Johnston found it easy to raise a demand for GP affairs to be handled from the centre, under the direct control of his department.

Debate at Cabinet level

Nevertheless, Maude held firmly to the need for municipal rule. Now that a White Paper was to be issued, he had the task of justifying it to the Cabinet ministers on the Reconstruction Priorities Committee. The surest way was to stress the need for a unified service, and to make that plausible Maude had to remove all doubt about where control of the GP service would lodge: was it to be under individual local authorities or joint boards? Maude came down firmly in favour of joint boards since they were to arrange hospital care.[10]

Morrison did not respond kindly. He held pride in the LCC hospital service which had developed under his direction, and believed strongly in the value of local government. Above all else, he wanted to keep municipal hospitals under local authority control and not have its influence diluted by joint boards. But he did not feel the same passion for the GP service and, like Johnston, was ready to let that sector pass under central direction. Since the local authorities that provided hospital care were not always the same as those that ran municipal clinics, Morrison was ready to see the service split three ways.[11]

Maude's reaction was to advise retaining the joint board until the White Paper was issued and then make concessions as needed. He feared that anything else would evoke a demand from the BMA to leave the panel system intact and merely extend provision to dependants. In defence of the joint board, Maude stressed that it would be dominated by the larger local authorities whose autonomy Morrison was anxious to protect. All these views were expressed by Brown or in Brown's name as he was the Minister responsible for department policy.[12]

On 18 August the Reconstruction Committee came down in favour of Maude's position, but in deference to Morrison gave larger local authorities the option of running their own hospitals.[13] Maude — strongly supported by Hawton[14] — was not pleased. If joint boards did not control hospitals, their existence would be meaningless: 'they would be little more than spectators of a hospital system for which they are themselves answerable but which would be carried out by other bodies acting under other medical advice'. The GP service would have to move under central direction because the doctors would never accept direct local authority control.[15]

This argument proved persuasive. On 8 September the Reconstruction Committee dropped the local authority option and upheld joint board control of hospitals.[16] No doubt the stand taken by Scottish local authorities influenced the decision. On 30 August they accepted joint board control because the vast majority were too small to support a hospital service, thirty-two out of fifty-five local authorities there having a population under 50,000.[17]

But the fate of the GP service was still undecided. Maude attacked Johnston's proposal and upheld the need for the unification in the strongest terms he could present:

A single panel doctor service could no doubt be administered centrally and nationally, as long as it was regarded as a separate and self-contained service. But it can no longer be so regarded. The essence of reform is to bring together and correlate all stages of medical care as parts of a single process of health treatment. That is just what has been lacking in the past, and it is one of the main reasons for the changes in prospect.[18]

To lose the GP service, Maude warned, would be a greater blow to local government than the creation of joint boards. Earlier, he had sought joint board control of health centres to unify the service, but now he found it prudent to compensate Morrison for municipal loss of hospital management. He suggested that health centres be put under direct local authority rule since they fell in the rightful sphere of local government.[19] In this way the centres would be linked with the most widely-used municipal clinics — those dealing with maternity and child welfare — but not with the hospital service. Since it was hoped that GPs would eventually take over child welfare work, that part of the department's plan remained intact.

This proposal brought Maude back into conflict with the Scottish Department. On 14 September Johnston maintained that medical resistance to municipal control 'is real and unrelenting'.[20] He suggested a different way of unifying the service than through joint boards. In Scotland, seven EMS hospitals had developed under department direction, and its regional medical officers, acting through a Supplementary Medical Service under the Clyde Basin Experiment, had been able to establish a link between hospitals and GPs. This point had been brought forcefully to Johnston's attention by a member of the profession's representative committee.[21]

It was clear that Johnston did not attach the same priority to unification as Maude. He was more pragmatic and preferred 'to sacrifice some degree of apparent unity to get our reforms introduced in an atmosphere of goodwill'.[22] The Highlands and Islands medical service showed what could be done. It had evolved under department direction and the doctors employed in it had found a salaried method of payment acceptable. As one of them put it, 'He knew that the Highland and Island doctor would prefer to be left under State administration than have to come under local authorities.'[23]

These arguments impressed the Reconstruction Committee and, like Maude,[24] its members recognized that they could not let the Scottish pattern diverge too greatly from the English.[25] Where pay and general conditions of service were concerned, agreement was reached; they would be decided centrally since joint boards could not deal with such questions while they contained medical representatives employed under them. But in England and Wales joint boards would still be responsible for routine aspects of the GPs' service on the insurance committee pattern; only in Scotland would they be confined to hospital administration.[26]

Furthermore, to secure something like the unified direction Maude desired, joint boards in England and Wales would be given the task of integrating the service. Hospitals would be under joint boards, GPs mainly under central oversight, and the most widely used municipal clinics under individual local authorities — but joint boards would be responsible for co-ordinating the lot. Though Maude had not achieved full unification, he had managed to preserve an important role for joint boards. As he put it to Brown on 4 September, 'To secure larger areas and larger authorities for the hospital service would in itself be a big achievement and it may be worth while going all out for this at the expense of logic and consistency.'[27] Rucker, who shortly thereafter returned to the department as Deputy Secretary after a two-year spell on special duties, thoroughly agreed.[28]

Health centres

There still remained the question of group practice in health centres: would it develop or not? This had been the centrepiece of Maude's plan, the point around which all his hopes for GP reform revolved. Yet Johnston had moved Brown so far from Maude's goal that he almost seemed to abandon the concept. That was how it appeared to Attlee, who criticized Brown severely at the meeting of the Reconstruction Committee on 15 October, thereby possibly contributing to Brown's departure from the Ministry a few weeks later.[29]

Attlee wanted a full-time salaried service, he was opposed to private practice,[30] and like Maude he saw groups in health centres as the best way to reform GP care. Bevin, Morrison, and most labour MPs agreed, so much so that Johnston had to reverse himself to maintain his standing as a socialist. On 3 November he supported experiments with health centres so as not to rule out the prospect of a whole-time salaried service.[31]

During November a number of changes occurred which tended to push influence in a Conservative direction. A Tory, Mr (later Sir) Henry Willink, replaced Brown as Minister of Health, the two reconstruction committees (one dealing with 'priorities', the other with 'problems') were combined into one under the head of a non-party but Conservatively-minded businessman, Lord Woolton, and Rucker, who had been 'wholly uncritical' of Neville Chamberlain's appeasement policies while serving as Parliamentary Private Secretary to the Prime Minister in 1939,[32] was given the main task of preparing policy for the White Paper (while Hawton was left to do the job of drafting it).

But none of this stopped the health centre movement from gathering force. The four Labour members — Attlee, Bevin, Jowitt, and Morrison — still dominated the Reconstruction Committee and they managed to stir a surprising degree of radicalism among the others.[33] Not only did Woolton display it in opposition to a hotel charge for hospital patients (see page 163) but so did the non-party ex-civil servant Sir John Anderson (later Lord Waverley) who had become Chancellor of the Exchequer upon Wood's death in August 1943.

Anderson had a long experience of the panel system, having served with the English NHI Commission and the Ministry of Health between 1912 and 1919. During the debate on the Beveridge Report in February 1943 he had declared his faith in the free choice principle for family care, but saw nothing incompatible between that and group practice.[34] He made his support for health centres clear to the Reconstruction Committee on 11 January 1944, only a few weeks before the White Paper was published: 'The Government should go out boldly for the health centre scheme, and the Health Departments would find that they had the support of all the more progressive doctors because of the facilities the scheme would afford the medical profession.'[35]

In the face of this feeling, Johnston and Willink made no attempt to stop the health centre movement. Johnston merely insisted that in Scotland health centre development should come under department direction. Since Willink followed Maude's lead and adhered to local authority provision, the subject came in for diverse treatment in the White Paper. Throughout Britain as a whole the CMB was to act as the employer for GPs, but in England local authorities were expected to have some say over those who worked in health centres.[36]

Furthermore, within health centres everywhere something like the salaried model was to be followed. Maude's distaste for competition found its way into the White Paper: 'It seems fundamental that inside a Centre the grouped doctors should not be in financial competition for patients.' There was 'a strong case for basing future practice in a Health Centre on a salaried remuneration or on some similar alternative which will not involve mutual competition within the Centre'.[37]

Outside health centres doctors were to be paid by capitation, but even there provision was made for salaried remuneration (at Johnston's urging) if a practitioner desired it.[38] However, on the queston of private practice rights, the Reconstruction Committee departed greatly from Maude's preference. It will be recalled that he wanted to restrict the privilege to existing doctors, not allow it to new entrants.[39] So strongly did he object to any modification that he seemed ready to exclude higher income groups from the service.[40] In that way, he hoped, the emergence of a double standard of treatment might never arise.

However, the pragmatic Johnston took a different tack, one that was more likely to please the profession. He left private practice open to all doctors but suggested that a limit be imposed on list size on those who undertook it.[41] Maude had earlier considered such an arrangement, but had dropped it.[42] The Reconstruction Committee brought it back. In the White Paper, even doctors who worked in health centres would have the privilege, although they could not treat private patients within the centre itself.[43] Otherwise, a ban was to be imposed on new entrants only during their first few years of practice; if the CMB deemed it necessary, they would have to work whole-time in the public sector. This, it seems, was certain to apply during the apprenticeship period through which all young doctors would pass after leaving the hospital world.[44]

Maude also failed to realize his aim of abolishing the sale of practices. This was surprising because the profession had shown less concern about retaining that right than about preserving private practice. Where health centre practices were concerned, even the MPC had contemplated its abolition.[45] But all of this changed after the doctors came to regard Maude's plan as a threat to freedom. Then, the right to trade in practices became an essential part of the profession's preference for the panel system.[46]

Maude, however, insisted that the custom be totally abolished, and he maintained that position until the drafting of the White Paper began.[47] At that point Rucker took over and advised against complete abolition, stressing that its removal was not needed to implement the new form of general practice. Indeed, he argued, it would be disadvantageous to do so because the Ministry would have to set up machinery to fill each vacancy: 'This removes one of the remaining elements of freedom in medical practice and is a big step forward towards a full State service.'[48] Jameson agreed and urged Maude to move slowly on such a controversial issue.[49]

Rucker thought the custom should be barred only to doctors who worked in health centres and to those who practised in over-doctored areas. This view was accepted by the Reconstruction Committee, which was also intent on preventing any inflation in values due to patients added by the new service. A statement to that effect appeared in the White Paper, but even then the subject was left open for discussion with the profession.[50]

Medical representation in administration

Though Maude's plan had been greatly diluted, he could take pride in the fact that a commitment to health centres remained and that in England, at least, they would stay in municipal hands. But would this be acceptable to the profession? Maude knew there was little chance of that unless the doctors secured what they most ardently desired — the same right of representation in administration as they had under NHI.

On the national level, considerable effort had been made to please the profession. Not only was a CMB to act as the employer element in the GP service, but the doctors were to have a place on a CHSC that would advise on policy. In both instances, however, the medical members were not to be appointed in the way the doctors desired. The Minister, as the result of Rucker's intervention, reserved the right to make appointments after consultation with the profession[51] — and in the case of the CMB, some of those selected would become full-time bureaucrats who were more likely to be concerned with sound administration than with GP demands.[52] Willink, in deference to Maude, argued strongly for direct representation on the CHSC, but the Reconstruction Committee rejected it.[53]

Sir John Anderson, reflecting Treasury opposition, was concerned with its legitimacy from the standpoint of the Machinery of Government Committee which was then sitting.[54] The BMA had seen all of this before, because in 1919 it had failed to secure the same rights on Dawson's medical consultative council, thus setting the stage for the demise of that body.[55]

On the local level, the doctors found themselves in a worse position; they were denied any place on joint boards, local authorities, or their committees, even without the vote. Maude (through Brown and Willink) pushed hard for some concession but Johnston refused to budge and he was backed by Morrison, leader of the municipal forces on the Reconstruction Committee.[56] At first the question was left open, but when the White Paper appeared the government came down strongly against it: 'on balance', it declared, 'the risk of impairing the principle of public responsibility . . . outweighs any advantages likely to accrue'.[57]

What did all these changes add up to? From the time the first draft of the White paper appeared in November, nine alterations had been made and the main effect was to strengthen departmental and municipal control at the expense of the doctors.[58] Though the larger local authorities lost direct management of hospitals, they won primacy of place in local administration, particularly over health centres in England and Wales.[59] At one point even the title '*National* Health Service' was dropped, but was later restored because of its public appeal.[60]

Some concessions were made on private practice and no decision was taken on the sale of practices, but the Reconstruction Committee left little doubt that a salaried system in health centres was the ultimate goal. The doctors could take little comfort from the proposals presented in the White Paper.

Yet that was not how it appeared to the civil servant in charge of panel affairs, F.F. Marchbank. Under NHI, he noted, funds were regarded as the collective property of insured persons and they were administered by bodies which represented them, the approved societies:

> In the White Paper the situation is entirely different. The insured person has dropped into the background and you have almost a scheme to provide benefits for the medical profession to be administered by the medical profession. 'Government of the people by the people for the people' is replaced by 'Government of the people by doctors for the doctors' and I am afraid that when parliament gets down to details this line of attack will be taken by the approved societies and may well wreck the whole scheme, compelling the Government to start again with a fresh scheme in which the doctors will be kept severely in the background.[61]

Marchbank was an old hand in the department. He had entered the LGB in 1914 and moved into the Ministry of Health when it was created in 1919. His whole career, like that of Maude's, had been spent in a period when conflicts in medical administration were rampant. For some thirty years the approved societies had presented a countervailing force to the doctors, though their influence had waned in the 1930s. But they were soon to disappear and no one seemed to be aware of the revolution this would produce in the Ministry's relations with the profession.

Chapter seven

Doctors reject White Paper

In 1929, when the department was searching for some way to unify maternity services under municipal control, it encountered an insuperable obstacle:

> Administration by the local authorities of the medical part of the service would mean disciplining of the doctors by the public health committee advised by the Medical Officer of Health which the doctors would never stand without the power to appeal in every case to the Minister, which the local authorities would not stand.[1]

Maude worked hard to find a way out of this dilemma and he thought the White Paper had supplied it. Local authorities would be involved only in health centres, and even there their role would be limited. Conditions of employment would be set nationally after agreement with the profession, and no doctor could be removed from the service without the intervention of a CMB containing a medical majority. The result, Maude and his colleagues believed, is that 'the profession is likely to feel that it is getting a very favourable deal'.[2] If anyone had grounds for complaint, it would be local authorities, not the doctors.

The scheme did contain a number of provisions that, in the Ministry's view, were likely to annoy the profession: it denied the right of direct representation; it attempted to establish a salaried practice in health centres; and it introduced restrictions over the location of practices. But these and other proposals were not seen as insuperable obstacles: they were merely negotiating points. As someone in the department (probably Hawton) put it, the doctors would not 'feel so hotly as to try to smash the whole scheme'.[3]

Medical reaction

The doctors did not take long to respond. On 18 February 1944, shortly after the White Paper was issued, the BMA held a meeting to consider it. Dawson, who as president chaired the gathering, described the White Paper as a 'genuine and statesmanlike endeavour to meet an extremely difficult situation'.[4] In private, he told the Ministry observer, Mr Harding, that the Paper was 'a remarkable piece of work — well written and lucid'. (For this, Hawton could take credit since he had prepared the document.) However, in his public address, Dawson did criticize the proposals for their failure to give adequate recognition to voluntary hospitals. Also, he warned that any scheme would take years to implement because of the shortage of doctors in the hospital world.

BMA leaders were similarly circumspect where general practice was concerned. They regretted the absence of direct representation rights but implied a willingness to accept it if wider areas of local government were formed. On the issue of universal coverage, they expressed the fullest sympathy', indicating that the profession 'will play its full part in achieving this object'.[5] In private, Hill was even more encouraging; he told the Ministry observer that 'even if they were whole-heartedly in favour of the service — as some of them were — it would not be politic to say so at this juncture with a flourish of trumpets'.[6] In his public address, Hill went as far as he dared to calm medical fears. According to a senior medical officer of the LCC who was present, Dr Letitia Fairfield, Hill implied that 'the health centres would not be used as the thin edge of the wedge for introducing a full-time medical service'.[7] Where the sale of practices was concerned, he was insistent 'that whatever happened the present system of buying and selling practices was undesirable and would probably have to go'.

The Scottish Department was so encouraged by this response that it expected a bill to pass through Parliament by Whitsun 1945.[8] No one seemed concerned with the consultant reaction because they were so few in number and so little had been said about them in the White Paper.[9] Indeed, detailed planning of the consultant service did not begin until later in 1944, when it was undertaken by a semi-official body set up by the royal colleges under the direction of Lord Moran (see page 123).

This euphoria was short-lived; BMA followers failed to view the White Paper as sympathetically as the Ministry expected or medical leaders desired. According to Fairfield, Hill's stricture on the sale of practices was 'coldly received' and she believed he had misled his colleagues on the purpose of health centres. In her view they were intended to be the precursor of a salaried service:

> It seems to me that B.M.A. must face up to the fact that, whether they like it or not, this will be the inevitable result of the experiment. It is, in fact, the method whereby the Government are conciliating the State Service supporters, and we might as well acknowledge this from the start.[10]

Within the ranks of the profession that fear had been growing for months, fed by a new force in the medical world that was opposed to state control in any form. This was the Medical Policy Association (MPA) which had been formed by a group of doctors who reflected in their first bulletin an addiction to the paranoid anti-semitic theories of the social credit leader, Major Clifford Douglas.[11] In 1943 they had issued a questionnaire to mobilize medical opinion and of the 10,000 doctors who responded, 77 per cent opposed the principle of central control — an objection which MPA leaders interpreted to mean that the profession did not want any state service at all. Though there was reason to doubt the accuracy and objectivity of the survey, it was clear that MPA views, as expressed in the many bulletins it distributed to the 7,000 doctors on its mailing list, made a disturbing impact on medical thought. Policy groups sprung up around the country — the most important being in Guildford — and a number of BMA divisions adopted resolutions on MPA lines.[12]

This challenge unnerved BMA leaders and their plight was not made easier by the activities of the SMA, the only medical–political group which had been given a place on the MPC. Throughout 1943 SMA leaders sought in vain to stem the rising tide of medical opinion against a salaried service, and when the White Paper appeared, one of them — Dr David Stark Murray — reasserted the need for such a service in the *Sunday Express*, declaring his position as a member of the MPC.

This led some doctors to question the SMA's role in BMA affairs. As one of them put it:

> That a doctor should write this article is bad enough. That it should be printed in a Sunday newspaper over the name of a doctor who announces himself as a member of the B.M.A. Medical Planning Commission is one of the gravest matters that has confronted the Association.[13]

The profession's fears were fed further by Souttar's contention that 'the White Paper was very largely based on the work of the Association through the Medical Planning Commission'[14] — which he chaired. By this he mainly had in mind the fact that the concept of a comprehensive health service covering the nation as a whole conformed closely to the doctors' own plan since they had excluded only 10 per cent of the population. But that was not how it was viewed by many medical men. As a *BMJ* leader observed in May:

> Apparently many voices have uttered the fantastic suggestion that the Representative Committee was responsible for the White Paper. If the Representative Committee can be said to have had any influence at all it was in preventing the Government from drafting a document plainly advocating a whole-time salaried service, and leaving little or no room for further discussion on this point. Of the emotional cross-currents in the life of the profession to-day, the strongest is suspicion.[15]

A critical mood emerges

Because of this suspicion Souttar lost his seat as chairman of the BMA's council and head of the representative committee that dealt with the Ministry. His place was taken by Dain, a popular negotiator whose method of appeasing militants was to put forward proposals which he expected the department to reject.[16] This made him appear aggressive in the eyes of some civil servants, but the main force in BMA circles was Charles Hill who became secretary after Anderson suffered a heart attack in October 1943, and died in January. Even as deputy, Hill had taken the lead since Anderson lacked the ability to make decisions.[17] According to Dr Frank Gray, a member of the BMA's representative committee, Anderson helped Maude with his salaried plan because he wanted a knighthood.[18] He certainly did not openly oppose it, as it was Hill who launched the attack in May 1943 (see page 57). That warmed the hearts of medical militants and made Hill the darling of the rank and file. He did not want to lose that affection in 1944 and had to tread carefully.

The first sign of Hill's caution came in March when, in two addresses to medical audiences, he said that he had detected an authoritarian touch in the White Paper, stemming mainly from the power given to the CMB to order young doctors to work on salary in health centres:

> A Minister, by means of these directions, would be able to change the whole character of the general practitioner service by a series of actions which he need not report to Parliament, making the service increasingly a whole-time one under local authorities.[19]

A similar change in attitude appeared in the analysis the BMA issued in March to accompany the questionnaire on the White Paper that had been prepared by the British Institute of Public Opinion.[20] The statement cast doubt on the Ministry's intentions: health centres were not to be limited to experiments, as the doctors desired; young doctors had to work whole-time during their first years in the service; and compensation for loss of the right to sell practices was to be given only to doctors who worked in health centres. Taken together, these proposals seemed to suggest that the department still had as its ultimate aim the creation of a salaried service.

Even more vigorous criticisms were directed at the administrative structure, since it did not allow direct representation. The CMB, it was pointed out, was not a representative, but a quasi-corporate, body with a civil service structure like that of the Board of Control. And on the local level doctors were not given representation on local authorities, joint boards, or their committees. This fell short of what was provided in the recently-passed Education Act (which required local authorities to establish education committees and co-opt experts), and also of the present position of the larger local authorities. Though the power was rarely exercised, some authorities did make room for outsiders on health committees.

The same critical mood appeared in the contributions made by medical spokesmen to the parliamentary debate on the White Paper in March. In the Commons the lead was taken by an ardent defender of the voluntary hospitals, Sir Ernest Graham-Little, a dermatologist who only a few days earlier had addressed a meeting organized by MPA supporters in Guildford.[21] The Ministry, however, paid more attention to the debate in the House of Lords, where criticisms were made by three leading consultants — Dawson, Horder, and Moran.[22] Though Dawson still welcomed the White Paper, he now saw its health centre provisions as an insidious attempt to introduce a salaried service. Horder was more concerned about the threat posed to private practice and the voluntary hospitals, but it was Moran — president of the Royal College of Physicians since 1941 and the most forceful personality in consultant circles — who most alarmed the Ministry.

Moran directed his remarks mainly at the weakness of medical representation in the administrative structure, pointing to its absence on the local level and the inability of the advisory body on the national level (CHSC) to publish its own work without the permission of the Minister. To this the department in an internal document responded as follows:

> The Government has given concrete proof in the White Paper of their desire and of their intention to give the expert the fullest possible part in planning and guiding the operation of the health services. At the same time the full responsibility for the provision of the services must rest squarely on the shoulders of a body or bodies responsible to the people for whom the services are provided, and nothing must be done to weaken or divide that responsibility.[23]

Discussions begin

This was the atmosphere when Hill and Dain met privately with Willink and his officials in April. Significantly, Maude was not there; he deeply resented the way Hill had attacked his salaried plan and it was no doubt politic if the two met as infrequently as possible. From this point on, Rucker and Jameson assumed the burden of negotiating with the profession: Maude only occasionally appeared.

Before these talks began, the doctors' representative committee sent a list of forty-four questions to the Minister covering many aspects of the White Paper, in addition to those raised above. Hill and Dain took these up, reporting through the *BMJ* in May the replies made by the department.[24] But the meeting also gave Hill a chance to express opinions, based on his reading of the medical mood. From this it was clear that he personally supported the health service idea, for he opposed pay beds or payment for other amenities not only on the grounds that they would reduce the scope for private consulting practice but also because such preferential treatment might tend to depress the quality of the public service.[25]

The main point raised by Hill was the need to grant the profession the right of direct representation throughout the administrative structure. Where the CHSC was concerned, the doctors did not think it sufficient merely to suggest names to the Minister. As for the CMB, the profession feared it was in danger of becoming a 'caucus', out of touch with practice problems because of its bureaucratic nature. So concerned were the doctors that Hill thought they might prefer joint board control if some form of medical representation were allowed, even without the vote. But he soon had second thoughts, out of fear that the profession might want to avoid any tie with local government. He therefore came down for a continuation of the structure that had existed under the panel system.

At this meeting Hill pressed the Ministry to make a clean sweep of the custom of selling practices. Since doctors entering health centres would not need to purchase them, that could have an adverse effect on the value of practices outside. When asked if the profession preferred total abolition of the custom, Hill (and Dain) indicated that there was no strong feeling on the subject.

On the crucial question of health centres, the department was urged to make only controlled experiments and to allow the doctors who worked in them to be paid by capitation.

Many other points were discussed — the talks proceeded smoothly over three days — and the two BMA leaders hoped to continue the practice in the future, giving the department the benefit of their advice. But they indicated that they faced difficulties, and this became apparent in May when the BMA Council issued a report severely criticizing the Ministry's plan.[26] Though the profession, the *BMJ* proclaimed in its review of the report, had long accepted the 'excellent principles' laid down in the White Paper, it found them contradicted by the proposals it contained. For GPs, the key point was the establishment of health centres by local authorities, with the government favouring payment by salary: 'If in fact such a proposal is accepted and acted on, then it is difficult to see any other fate for the future general practitioner than that of a whole-time salaried servant of the State.' The real issue, then, was not whether money for health services should be collected or distributed in a certain way 'but whether the medical profession is to be socialised'. And on that threat, the *BMJ* left no doubt where the bulk of the profession stood:

> Except for a vocal minority of doctors grouped round a party political flag [i.e. the SMA], by far the greater part of the profession is rigidly opposed to a whole-time State salaried medical service, and it is upon this one issue that opposition must be unshakably offered in the coming months.

To press the point home, the BMA Council voted to end all discussions with the Ministry.[27] Future action had to await not only the results of the poll of medical opinion (which was not published until August) but, more crucially, the decisions taken by the Representative Body. And because of transport restrictions arising from the war, that body had to postpone its annual meeting from July to December.[28] This meant that, except for one exchange in August, the doctors did not hold talks with the Ministry until January 1945, when negotiations formally began. In the interim, a fierce battle was fought within the medical world for the control of BMA policy.

Ministry reaction

The department reacted angrily to the BMA report, stung by the criticisms made of the White Paper. No one in the department (except possibly Jameson, and he left few papers behind) seemed to be aware of the forces in the medical world exerting pressure on BMA leaders. Maude had done his best to satisfy medical demands but the doctors did not appreciate his efforts. Maude's sensitivity to criticism became apparent in a speech the department prepared for Willink to deliver at his Croydon constituency in May. In it, the suspicions and accusations of the profession were dismissed, while BMA leaders were chastized for doubting the Ministry's good intentions.[29]

It could not be denied, however, that the White Paper had failed to deliver the direct representation rights the doctors demanded, and in the months that followed the Ministry did its best to repair the omission. By April the department was ready to acknowledge that it had to make concessions to the doctors and voluntary hospitals, but its only method was to give them a place on joint boards without the vote.[30] It did not dare to go further on the national level because the Reconstruction Committee had firmly opposed direct representation on the CHSC.

Weak as this concession was, it failed to win sympathy in municipal quarters. The LCC had always set its face against a medical presence, and now it was joined by the CCA. In the spring of 1944 the CCA adopted a resolution condemning direct representation as a 'dangerous impairment of the principle of public responsibility'.[31] And in June it joined hands with the LCC to oppose the right without the vote. All they would tolerate was a measure of co-option, together with the right of a local advisory body (Local Health Services Council) to present its views.[32]

Nor were local authorities the only bodies to set their face against the medical demand; opposition arose from PEP,[33] as well as from an influential Conservative Party health committee headed by Henry Brooke.[34] The latter must have taken the department by surprise because the committee contained two doctors who were playing a prominent part in negotiations: Professor Henry (later Lord) Cohen, a leading figure in the BMA and the Royal College of Physicians; and Dr Edward Gregg, an influential spokesman for panel practitioners within the BMA in his capacity as chairman of the Insurance Acts Committee.

In August, Dawson led a small group of medical representatives to the Ministry in an attempt to retrieve the position. Previously Dawson had been satisfied with an advisory role alone (see page 55), but now he urged medical representation on joint boards, preferably with the vote.[35]

At this point, Willink made his influence felt on Ministry policy. He knew there was no hope of placating the profession without a radical change in the government's plan. Within the department, Maude and his colleagues held fast to joint board rule, believing there was no other way to unify the service. And since joint boards were to cover the health service as a whole, the concept offered a convenient excuse to resist medical and voluntary hospital demands for representation. Only on groups or committees confined to community or hospital matters might some place be found for outsiders, but they would still be subject to the overriding control of joint boards.

However, resistance to this concept was growing; it came not only from the doctors and voluntary hospitals but from local authorities. The latter wanted to manage their own hospitals and this applied particularly to the county boroughs in which most of the larger municipal hospitals were located.[36] They were willing to accept joint boards for planning purposes only, and the same stand was taken by the voluntary hospitals[37] as well as by the Conservative committee headed by Brooke which was so concerned about their welfare.[38]

The doctors held similar views. They had long favoured local government reform to produce the wider areas needed for hospital organization, but it appeared they would be denied representation within that structure as well. So they put forward a proposal for regional councils without executive powers, leaving them only with planning and advisory duties. In that way the profession thought it might secure representation rights, while administrative control would pass to the centre as the doctors always wanted.[39] Some elements of this proposal had already been put forward by others; the Hetherington Committee (concerned with hospital organization in Scotland) proposed regional advisory councils;[40] while the Conservative Party report advocated something similar, with joint boards or regional councils confined to planning.[41]

Hawton, backed by Maude and Rucker, tried to resist the movement, contending that the power to plan would be useless if it could not be implemented.[42] Local authorities would never take orders from a body they did not dominate, while joint boards had to have administrative duties to be effective. A paper prepared in June spelled out the department's thinking on the subject:

> This 'planning only' doctrine is one of the most formidable things we have to face, because it will command the agreement of everybody who does not really want to change the present situation. . . .
>
> The plain fact is that the joint board needs to take over and own and be responsible for running all the publicly provided hospital services over the planned area because that is the only way of ensuring that all those hospital services are run entirely as one, without dissenting interests and conflicts of view; the only way of ensuring their full relationship to each other, interchange of staff, pooling of resources, and so on; the only way of operating the plan throughout them, without the joint board having constantly to call on the Minister to intervene.[43]

Willink's two-tier plan

Willink refused to accept this advice; he was intent on devising a structure that would open the way to 'outside' representation, no matter what the price. If joint boards were transformed into planning bodies, and local authorities were left in command of their own hospitals, that might make the municipal world less resistant to medical and voluntary hospital spokesmen. He had his staff prepare a new structure to present to the Reconstruction Committee in October.[44]

The department duly complied, but made every effort to preserve a large degree of municipal control. The result was a two-tier structure for planning on regional and area level, with hospital management normally left in local authority or voluntary hospital hands. Only in exceptional cases might local authorities be compelled to form joint boards if they were not able to support a hospital service on their own. The doctors and voluntary hospitals would have representation on both levels but despite the demands raised by the voluntary hospitals (who also wanted a Central Hospitals Board to match the doctors' CMB),[45] it was not to be an equal share; Willink's staff reserved a majority place for local authorities. Only on advisory groups subject to the overriding control of the municipal majority might the doctors and voluntary hospitals expect equal representation.

As for consultants, their position was not clearly defined. The regional bodies might have a hand in their appointment to hospital posts, but otherwise they would be left to the direct rule of municipal and voluntary hospital management committees.

GPs would have a separate structure under the CMB, and Willink tried to ease their concern over the development of a salaried service in health centres. He wanted to drop the whole-time requirement for young doctors, modify the directive powers of the Board, lessen local authority involvement in health centres by confining it to a landlord role, and secure a co-opted place for doctors on municipal health committees similar to the one arranged for teachers under the 1944 Education Act.

This structure represented a compromise between conflicting interests. It offered the doctors and voluntary hospitals some place in administration, while retaining control in municipal and Ministry hands. Aside from their majority place on planning bodies, local authorities would manage their own hospitals, and be a funnel through which some funds would be channelled to GPs (in health centres) and voluntary hospitals. When the latter, in October, tried to avoid all payment from the rates, a department document made the municipal role clear: 'this service is — rightly or wrongly — primarily a local government service. The *duty* of ensuring an adequate service, in accordance with the settled plan, is a local government duty.'[46] Already, the paper complained, municipal control over the voluntary sector had been reduced to 'a token' and the Ministry refused to go further.

Willink's bias, however, lay in the voluntary hospital direction, and so did that of his party's Health Committee. Tories as a whole rated voluntary hospitals above their municipal counterparts because (among other reasons) they gave the doctors more freedom.[47] Though Willink left the management of municipal hospitals with local authorities, he did not neglect to note that they 'hitherto have scarcely shown evidence that they could rise to a fully effective hospital service'.[48] And he was similarly impressed by the opposition to whole-time service in the BMA poll of medical opinion. Had Willink enjoyed a free hand, he would have excluded local authorities from health centre operation, but he was dealing with civil servants and Cabinet ministers who were intent on municipal development.

Unfortunately for Willink, Johnston did not fully support his plan. In Scotland, joint board rule was confined to the hospital sector and Johnston refused to go beyond it when a planning structure was substituted. Though he was willing to make some concessions to the voluntary hospitals, he refused to grant more to the doctors. Health centres in Scotland had been put under direct departmental control in deference to their wishes, but that was as far as Johnston would go. He rejected their demand for a place in administration without voting power, and he was supported by his civil servants and Scottish local authorities.[49]

All of this reinforced the Reconstruction Committee's long-standing objection to the representation principle. Though the Committee did make room for 'outsiders' on the area level, it rejected the demand of the doctors and the voluntary hospitals for an equal place because they might be able to force the expenditure of public money. And they ruled out any seat for a person employed in the health services covered by the planning body.

On the national level, the Committee was even more resistant, rejecting the plea of both health Ministers for the doctors to have direct representation and publication rights on the CHSC. (Only a few *ex officio* appointments were allowed, and Council reports would still be subject to departmental veto.) And though the Committee was willing to drop the whole-time requirements for young doctors and alter the location powers of the CMB as Willink desired, it refused to confine local authorities to a landlord role in health centres; 'The health centre experiment had great potentialities and it was important that nothing should be done to weaken this part of the scheme.[50]

The doctors reacted predictably. Though they welcomed the new planning structure, they objected to the denial of direct representation rights, going so far as to call for the scrapping of the CMB concept, leaving the old Ministry–insurance committee pattern in its place.[51] Nor was that all; forces were at work in the medical world trying to turn the profession wholly against state provision, leaving the nation with at most a modest extension of the panel system.

BMA leaders under pressure

This pressure derived mainly from the MPA. Its influence gathered strength in August when the results of the BMA poll appeared.[52] This showed over half the doctors (53 per cent) to be unfavourable to the White Paper, and 80 per cent thought it had infringed their objection to municipal control. Though critical aspects of the scheme were approved — coverage of the whole population (60 per cent), the principle of health centres (68 per cent), abolition of the sale of practices (52 per cent) — the overwhelming majority (80 per cent) wanted direct representation on joint boards and 53 per cent thought local authorities should not be party to health centre contracts. Incredibly, the poll failed to contain a direct question on the profession's attitude toward municipal administration of personal health services, but it did come close enough with other queries to make medical feeling clear: the doctors wanted nothing to do with local authorities.

These results were close to the stand taken by the BMA's Council, so it could be said that medical leaders did reflect medical opinion.[53] Nevertheless, suspicions mounted throughout the summer, stimulated by MPA propaganda. In

November Hill even found himself forced to defend the right of the Guildford Division (the MPA's stronghold) to publish an intemperate pamphlet attacking the proposed health service from the patient's point of view. Guildford claimed to have the approval of the BMA's public relations adviser — which was not true — and Hill set that straight when the Stratford Division protested. But he had to defend the right of publication because of the BMA's constitution; it was (and is) composed largely of autonomous units which were free to express whatever views they saw fit.[54] In anticipation of the long-awaited representative meeting in December, many divisions put forward motions similar to those proposed by the MPA.

BMA leaders tried to counteract the movement by dissociating themselves not only from the SMA but from another organization that had become the target of MPA abuse — PEP.[55] Hill (and Webb-Johnson) wrote letters to the public press criticizing the White Paper, while Dawson used the correspondence columns of *The Times* to express BMA concern with the political activities of the SMA.[56] All of this provoked a retort from the SMA's leading proponent in BMA circles, Talbot Rogers. In September he wrote a long letter to the *BMJ* dismissing the accusations levelled at medical leaders by the MPA.[57]

Still, nothing seemed to stem the rising tide of rank-and-file suspicion. The postponement of the BMA's representative meeting meant that no decisions could be made until December and that, as someone in the Ministry observed, left the way open for a 'sniping policy by the opposition doctors'.[58] The writer urged the department to organize a counter-attack using medical men known to be sympathetic to the White Paper, like the left-wing professor of social medicine, John Ryle.

Lord Cherwell, the Paymaster-General and trusted adviser of the Prime Minister, called for a similar campaign in the public press,[59] but it was the Director of Home Intelligence at the Ministry of Information who devised the most effective strategy. This was Stephen Taylor, who had caused a stir in 1939 with his call for a takeover of the voluntary hospitals (see page 19). At the end of 1941 he had joined the Ministry of Information, but remained in close touch with medical affairs as the leader of a young group of doctors, some 200 in number, all under the age of 45, calling themselves Medical Planning Research. In November 1942, just before the Beveridge Report appeared, they had published a report in *The Lancet* that was even more sympathetic to the concept of a national health service than the one issued earlier by the MPC.[60] This tended to confirm the view, strongly held by Maude and his colleagues, that the younger members of the profession — most of them without ties to existing practices — would welcome a salaried service.[61]

Though Taylor came from an old Liberal family, he had been a socialist from his schooldays and served on the Council of the SMA (with which he retained close ties until 1956) as well as on the Public Health Advisory Committee of the Labour Party before becoming a Labour MP in 1945.[62] He lost his seat in 1950, but was made a peer in 1958 and aided the Labour cause in the House of Lords until he left the Party in 1981 out of concern for what he called its Marxist tendencies.[63]

Taylor in 1944 was thus deeply involved in socialist politics but in his attempt to contain the MPA he did not reveal his Labour sympathies or even his own name, since as a civil servant he was not allowed to do so. Most doctors leaned to the right of the political spectrum and Taylor used both a pseudonym (Gordon Malet) and a conservative journal (*The Spectator*) to propagate his views.[64] From May 1944 onwards his articles appeared regularly, and on 29 September he added to the Talbot Rogers letter in the *BMJ* a strong attack on the MPA, revealing the unsavoury tactics it had used to influence BMA policy.[65]

This led to a long debate, conducted in the *BMJ* as well as *The Spectator*, which lasted until the representative meeting in December. During it, the attempt to discredit BMA leaders by linking them with Malet, the Ministry, the SMA, PEP, and other organizations clearly appeared in a letter written by one of the MPA's strongest supporters, Dr E.U. MacWilliam: 'It can truly be said that of these that though they march separately they fight together.'[66]

Alarmed by the threat of central control, those doctors who followed the MPA's lead proposed the New Zealand refund scheme as a way to avoid it. Under that system, the patient paid the bill and secured reimbursement, leaving the medical man in the middle free from contact with the state.[67] The proposal attracted the support of several BMA divisions who put it forward for the representative meeting in December,[68] but the panel doctors who met at their annual conference in October devised a different method; they rejected the concept of a service covering everyone and called for a cautious extension of the system they knew best — NHI.[69] By then it was clear that the approved societies would go no matter what happened on the medical side, so the profession had lost all fear of insurance finance. And as a member of the BMA Council observed in November, that method of funding offered a better chance of securing the representation rights the doctors desired than Exchequer or rate finance:

> One of their ideas in preserving the insurance relation had been that it was through that machinery that the medical profession got representation on central and local bodies which they had never got in relation to other medical and public health services.[70]

Yet another method was proposed by two doctors from Scotland, A.F. Wilkie Millar and F. Martin Brodie. They wanted to sever all ties with social insurance and have the medical service considered afresh.[71] In that way the percentage of population covered could be left open. By linking insurance contributions with health provision, Beveridge had forced the 100 per cent principle on Ministry policy, and that posed a threat to private practice. Who would want to pay extra for medical care when he had deductions made from his pay packet each week for the public service? The fact that only 10 per cent of health costs would come from this source would not be understood; the public would think their contributions covered everything.

The only way to avoid confusion was to have all funds from taxation, but Hill warned of the threat of municipal control if the insurance principle were abandoned.[72] Perhaps as one BMA division suggested, that danger could be averted if insurance contributions were confined to the hospital service, leaving the government free to set an income limit for GP care.[73] But this ran counter to what Maude and Beveridge intended for, by associating insurance payments with GP care, they hoped to leave scope for hospital contributory schemes (see pages 37 and 39). Within the doctors' negotiating committee, Webb-Johnson strongly backed this view. He and his fellow surgeons hoped to protect voluntary hospitals and private specialist practice by confining the insurance principle to the GP sector.[74]

The December meeting

Such was the medical mood when the representative body met in December. At the start the MPA made a show of strength, some eighty out of 270 representatives supporting its point of view. But by the time the meeting ended on the 8 December its followers had dwindled to twenty-seven.[75] The overwhelming majority of representatives held fast to the BMA lead, though they did register wider disapproval of the White Paper than the 53 per cent proportion in the poll suggested. It was the 100 per cent issue that aroused most concern. The doctors made it clear that they would not man a comprehensive service until they were satisfied with the administrative structure, and that meant they had to have direct representation. As a leader in the *BMJ* stressed, 'From the point of view of the profession, the essence of administration is that doctors should have an effective voice at all levels of organization, and that this effective voice should be secured by electing medical men on to the various responsible bodies.[76]

Since that position had been secured under NHI, this was the method by which the profession wished to advance, moving cautiously towards a comprehensive service. First would come hospital and specialist treatment, thereby forcing wider areas of administration and averting the danger of local authority control. Only when that had been accomplished would it be safe to widen the GP service by adding dependants and others of like economic status.[77] In making this decision, the doctors hoped to preserve a place for private practice but they unwittingly reversed a priority which the BMA leader, Sir Henry Brackenbury, had taken twenty years to construct. He wanted dependants to come first to strengthen the family and social orientation of general practice (see page 8).

Medical policy had thus moved a long way from the position expected by the Ministry when it published its White Paper. It was true that the worst had not happened; the MPA failed to persuade the BMA to break off negotiations. A new negotiating body was appointed (now clearly labelled as a negotiating committee) so that the process of altering the White Paper could begin. But the mood of the profession was ugly, so much so that two BMA leaders — Talbot Rogers and J.A.L. Vaughan Jones — feared that all hope of a new health service might be lost. Through Joan Clarke, Fabian secretary of the Social Security League set up to promote the Beveridge Report, they appealed to Beveridge to save the day, but the social insurance expert pleaded lack of time, fearing that the subject was too difficult and delicate to handle in a hasty way.[78] Willink and his civil servants thus did not find a receptive audience when negotiations began in January 1945.

Chapter eight

Retreat to the panel system

Negotiations with the doctors began in January 1945, and it was clear that direct representation rights would be their main concern. Before the BMA meeting in December, Rucker warned Willink that there was no hope of securing medical approval of the new two-tier plan without this concession being granted.[1] A statement was prepared for the Reconstruction Committee, but Willink, meeting privately with the Scottish Secretary on 20 December, found Johnston rigidly opposed, citing strong feeling in the municipal world. Local authorities, Johnston declared, 'would not for a moment contemplate that medical representatives should be co-opted to local authorities or their committees'.[2]

Only in England and Wales did the doctors have hope of a place on the planning bodies, but it was not to be in the direct representation manner they desired. Local authorities, furthermore, held fast to their 60 per cent majority on the area level. Only on the regional tier and on the hospital group formed under the area body did the doctors, together with the voluntary hospitals, have expectations of a more equal share.[3]

Where the GP service was concerned, this issue had implications throughout the administrative structure. GPs in separate practice would remain in their own surgeries and have little contact with local authorities. They would be affected mainly by area plans and decisions to develop health centres. For them, protection would lie in the medical representation provided on the area and regional planning bodies. They also might be able to secure support from the CHSC if the profession could induce the Ministry to let that advisory body exert greater influence over the siting of health centres.[4]

GPs who entered health centres would be more exposed to municipal oversight. Though the exact nature of the relationship was not spelled out in the White Paper, MOHs expected GPs eventually to be treated like other local authority employees. This was the way the journal of their society saw the plan when it was issued in Febraury 1944:

> Whereas it may be assumed . . . that practitioners working singly or in voluntary groups will be paid by capitation fee, as soon as they join an official centre their remuneration will be by whole-time or part-time salary and they will

enter into a side-contract with the local authority. It appears to be contemplated, therefore, that general practice will sooner or later come under the management of county and country borough councils.[5]

The profession proposed to resist this development in two ways: by confining the municipal role in health centres to a landlord–tenant relationship; and by securing a place for doctors on local authority health committees.

Otherwise, GPs everywhere would be subject to oversight by a CMB which would establish local committees to handle complaints and deal with other duties. The Ministry itself had offered this protection to mitigate GP fears about municipal direction. But the doctors lost interest in the CMB because of its bureaucratic composition, preferring the NHI pattern it had come to trust. Under that structure, the Ministry would retain oversight of the GP service and all the doctors expected on the local level was a recast insurance committee deprived of its approved society majority. In future they wanted the professions involved in the family practitioner service (GPs, dentists, chemists, but not opticians) to have an equal place with laymen and, if feasible, they wanted none of those laymen to come from the local authority world. Despite the fact that municipal (and Ministry) appointees on insurance committees had been regarded as neutrals in the struggle with approved societies, the doctors no longer could trust them. If a place had to be found for local authorities, the profession wanted their share confined to one-third of the whole (or two-thirds of the laymen), with the Ministry appointing the rest.[6]

Medical demands

Because of the differences between the health departments on this issue, Johnston wanted to tackle the hospital service first, leaving the GP sector until later.[7] But Willink did not think this wise and so negotiations began with the profession's role in administration unresolved and the fear of municipal control underlying its main demands.

Thus the doctors wanted to separate the health service from social insurance and develop it slowly by extending NHI because they feared a co-ordinated approach might lead to coverage of the population as a whole and that might produce a salaried service under local authority rule with no room for private practice. In the profession's view, the pace was being rushed to ensure careful certification of cash benefits, and they wanted the health service to be considered in its own right, not as an appendage to the needs of a new Ministry of National Insurance.[8]

Similarly, the doctors reiterated their demand for a Ministry confined to health alone, not only as a means of giving the subject proper attention but also as a way of breaking the department's tie with local government through its housing role. To all it was clear that the most ardent advocates of municipal control in the Ministry were those who started their career in the old Local Government

Board or who were involved in housing administration. (For the names, see page 41.)

For similar reasons the doctors wanted to strengthen the role of the CHSC and increase their influence on it. The moving spirit here was Dr R.W. Cockshut of Hendon, a GP active in BMA affairs. He presented proposals similar to those which Dawson had put forward in 1919 in a fruitless attempt to buttress the Ministry's first medical consultative council.[9] To be effective, Cockshut stressed, the council had to be a small body which met weekly and which contained medical members who could give enough time to counter the influence of the civil service.[10]

When the doctors learned that the CHSC was to be split into separate medical and hospital groups as the voluntary hospitals demanded, they objected, fearful (among other considerations) that this would weaken their hold on policy.[11] (In the end it was decided to retain a single advisory body but form separate standing committees under it.) They also wanted more than the bare medical majority the Ministry proposed — nineteen to eighteen, as opposed to eighteen to fifteen in Scotland — with an increase in the number of *ex officio* appointments from four to six so as to compensate for the denial of direct representation. (With local authorities demanding an equal place, the Ministry found it impossible to expand the medical majority but two *ex officio* appointments were added.) Lastly, the doctors pressed hard for the CHSC's right to publish an annual report and they accepted only reluctantly the department's insistence on veto restrictions if the report was judged not to be in the public interest.[12]

Even greater medical concern was focused on the planning bodies because the area tier was to retain the 60 per cent municipal majority (eighteen out of thirty-two members) that had been proposed for joint boards. For the Ministry this was the critical point in the structure if any semblance of public responsibility was to remain. Only reluctantly did it agree to establish a separate hospital planning group with a medical and voluntary hospital majority (eight to four), but like the regional council (where a similar medical–voluntary hospital majority applied), this group would not have power to decide plans. That would stay firmly in the hands of the municipal majority on the area tier.[13]

The doctors' way of circumventing this barrier was to shift powers upwards to the regional council or the Ministry. Consultants had a particular interest in strengthening the regional tier since it was at that level that candidates would be short-listed for hospital appointments. Moran wanted to transform the regional councils into executive bodies with power to alter area plans and advise on the distribution of Exchequer grants.[14] GP efforts, meanwhile, were concentrated on methods of removing health centres from area control, thereby arousing suspicions among consultants that they might lose BMA backing for their demands at regional level. (For more on this, see page 134.)

Willink's concessions

Willink knew, when negotiations began, that he would have to resist most of these demands, but he softened the blow in the manner Charles Hill suggested — by presenting the service as a natural transition from NHI:

> Although we are going for a comprehensive service from the start, we are not proposing to uproot all medical practice and change its whole design by some revolutionary stroke. In the main, it will be the well-known foundation of insurance practice — capitation, a local 'i c' [insurance committee], panel lists, and so on — on which we build. The process is essentially one of evolution.[15]

This statement did not preclude all change. Group practice in health centres with doctors on salary still remained the ultimate goal, but bit by bit Willink was driven back to the point from which Maude started. Medical pressure forced him to retain the essential features of the panel system.

The first to go were the two concessions that had been accepted by the Reconstruction Committee: young doctors would no longer have to work whole-time; and the CMB would not have licensing powers over the location of practices. When the profession objected to 'negative' controls (i.e. the closure of areas judged to be over-doctored), Willink dropped these as well, retaining only the subsidies available under NHI to induce doctors to practise in remote communities.[16]

Once these duties disappeared, the doctors saw no point in the CMB and that went as well.[17] The Ministry still hoped to retain municipal involvement in health centres along with a salaried payment for doctors who worked there. At the start of negotiations Willink went so far as to propose a basic salary for all GPs so as to lessen competition,[18] but the medical negotiators rejected the idea, not wanting it to apply even in health centres. To them, competition was a force to be fostered, not suppressed:

> The profession did not accept the view that financial competition between practitioners in health centres was inadvisable: financial partnership might be desirable in some cases but co-operation in work (which was accepted as essential) did not necessarily depend on financial partnership.[19]

This reaction did not please the local authorities and they told Willink they would have nothing to do with health centres unless a salaried payment applied.[20] They were also disturbed by the addition of a regional tier. This, together with the other bodies containing non-municipal majorities, made them fearful of a weakening influence and they registered a strong protest in March.[21] Willink must have been further rattled by a report issued by his own Conservative Party in May which warned of 'forces in the Ministry' working for a full salaried service and the destruction of private practice.[22] He and Rucker found it essential to add 'outside' experts to municipal health committees and they stuck to this proposal despite objections from local authorities.[23]

Sale of practices

These issues were difficult enough, but the one that aroused the strongest feelings was Willink's decision to let the sale of practices continue until it could be seen how values were affected by the start of the Health Service and the introduction of health centres. In two or three years' time he proposed to establish a committee of inquiry and if abolition were decided, then compensation would go to all doctors and not just to those who practised in or near health centres. However, no amount would be allowed for any increase in value due to the new service.[24]

Johnston and the other Labour Ministers on the Reconstruction Committee objected to this concession but Woolton silenced them by claiming it to be essential for BMA approval of the new service.[25] There is reason to doubt the validity of this claim. Woolton was ready to drop the proposal — an inclination he hid from the Prime Minister[26] — and he may have exaggerated the profession's feeling to silence his Labour colleagues. Only a few weeks earlier Hawton had come to the conclusion that the doctors were willing to end the sale of practices as long as compensation was paid to everyone who entered the service with a practice value in hand.[27] Any delay, he feared, would make abolition more difficult and he opposed Johnston's call for an immediate enquiry (instead of the two or three year delay that Willink proposed). That, Hawton argued, would produce nothing new and it could create pressure to postpone the bill until the study was completed. Nor was Hawton deterred by the difficulty of abolishing the custom. He recognized that a ban might be evaded (as indeed it has been) by selling a house and surgery at inflated value,[28] but that did not stop him from favouring the restriction.

A review of medical opinion suggests that Hawton made the more accurate judgements. There is no doubt that the doctors were ambivalent. Though the MPC report called for abolition in health centre practice,[29] feelings changed after the profession saw how that might pave the way for a salaried service. Then the mood became uncertain: some doctors wished to press ahead with abolition to free themselves from debt; others wanted to do so out of fear of a fall in the value of practices if the new service began before the issue was settled. But on one point the profession agreed; if compensation were paid, it should apply universally or not at all. Health centres might spread too fast if payments were limited to those who entered them.[30]

This ambivalence gave Charles Hill room to manoeuvre and from the moment the White Paper appeared he pressed strongly for abolition (see page 73). But medical fear of a salaried service rose throughout 1944 and the BMA, at its representative meeting in December, voted to retain the sale of practices.[31] Thereafter the negotiating committee (with the exception of Talbot Rogers) objected to interference with the custom.[32] But the poll taken earlier by the BMA had shown a clear majority of GPs (53 per cent) in favour of abolition when compensation was to apply to all practices, and this no doubt influenced Hawton.[33]

However, Woolton's claim won over the Reconstruction Committee and Willink reported the concession to Parliament on 3 May 1945,[34] the day on which the BMA held a special representative meeting to consider all the concessions that had been made.[35] And what they learned did much to please the doctors present. As far as GPs were concerned, the new plan represented a retreat to the panel system. The sale of practices was to continue, and all bars on entry or attempts to regulate the profession were dropped, even those designed to secure a more equal distribution of doctors. Though the BMA representatives were given the option of a CMB they made clear their preference for the NHI pattern. Insurance committees, together with their local medical committee counterparts, won a new lease of life, and they would no longer have a 60 per cent approved society majority. The doctors, along with other family practitioners (dentists and chemists, but not opticians) were given half the places, while laymen — two-thirds selected by local authorities, one-third by the Ministry — made up the rest.

The only significant addition to the panel system was the provision for municipal involvement in the development of health centres and that, despite local authority objections, would be limited to a landlord–tenant relationship.[36] To make the profession feel more secure, local authorities would have to form health committees and co-opt medical experts. In return, all Willink sought was acceptance of the principle of universal coverage and that, at long last, was grudgingly agreed. The 100 per cent issue, the doctors acknowledged, was one for Parliament to decide.[37]

Labour reaction

Those who had their hearts set on a salaried service did not react approvingly. A loud protest arose in Labour circles, particularly from those who led the SMA and the local authority on which the SMA's president (Somerville Hastings) and other members served — the LCC. They now felt free to speak because of the change of government in May. With the war in Europe over and a general election imminent, Labour ended the coalition, leaving a Conservative caretaker government to carry on until July.

Before he departed from office, Bevin had expressed concern about the concessions made by Willink,[38] while Johnston had timidly tried to hold the line on abolition of the sale of practices.[39] But these efforts were nothing compared to the protests that arose after Willink's plan became known. Though the BMA meeting in May was held in secret, the report the Council prepared was sent to every doctor, and SMA leaders had no inhibitions about making the contents public. Latham in March had told the Ministry that he was disturbed by the 'successive surrenders' in policy: 'This was so marked that it could even be described as "not selling out but giving away".'[40] Now he and others said the same thing in public.[41] So strong was the reaction in Labour circles that it forced the TUC to harden its stand on the health service and suspend its alliance with the BMA.

Before 1945 the TUC had taken a soft line with the doctors drawing on their aid to promote an industrial medical service[42] and recognizing the need for the profession's goodwill if the new health service was to succeed. Not only did the TUC allow scope for private practice but it demanded full consultation with the doctors and ample remuneration because the provision of medical care was a 'sacred trust'.[43] The TUC at this point showed every inclination of leaving administrative control to the conscience of the individual practitioner.

It was therefore not surprising that the BMA welcomed the appointment of the TUC's social insurance director, J.L. Smyth, as the representative of consumer interests on the official committee (chaired by Sir William Spens) charged with the duty of working out a new pay deal for GPs.[44] And Smyth did not disappoint the profession because he pressed so hard for higher incomes that at one point he was labelled 'doctor' in the minutes of the committee's proceedings.[45]

In public the TUC could not be so helpful after Willink's concessions became known. Then it demanded that practitioners in health centres be given the option of salary and it wanted medical shortages met by requiring young doctors to work in specified places on a whole-time basis. It objected strongly to the medical majority on the CHSC as well as to the medical–voluntary hospital majority on the regional bodies. It also condemned the doctors' attempt to enlarge the scope of private practice by allowing patients to contract-out of the payment to be made to the health service from social insurance contributions. But it directed its anger at the concession Labour hated most — continuation of the right to sell practices.[46] Only the TUC's medical adviser, Dr Morgan, himself a member of the BMA's Council, made any attempt to defend the profession.[47]

Until May, Willink, had not made his plan known to Parliament and he was criticized for divulging it first to the profession. But all that was to be put right with a second White Paper showing the changes that had been made since February 1944. However, after much agonizing, the Cabinet decided against publication, mainly out of fear of an adverse reaction to the concessions made on the GP service. The public would applaud the government's intent to create a comprehensive system in the first session of the new Parliament, and that pledge was made in the Conservative Party's election manifesto. But, it was feared, that same public would condemn the fading prospect of health centres and the abandonment of attempts to even out the distribution of doctors.[48] Indeed, the results of the BMA's poll suggested that Willink had made more concessions than the profession expected.

Nor was the GP service the only point of concern. Hospital negotiations were deadlocked, with no way in sight of resolving the conflicting aims of local authorities and voluntary hospitals.[49] In May, power had been removed from the proposed regional bodies in response to local authority demands.[50] The effect was to leave the area tier with greater control over planning, inspection, and finance, and on this level the municipal majority remained. As a Ministry document put it, though the regional bodies would still be in a position to offer advice on area plans 'the public responsibility for the plans will rest firmly with the area body having a local government majority and with the Minister'.[51] In London this meant that the LCC would be in charge since it covered an area large enough to constitute a tier on its own. It did not take consultants and the voluntary hospitals long to protest at the loss of regional powers, and they demanded the division of London into sectors on EMS lines as a way of forestalling the emergence of a more powerful LCC.[52]

With the Ministry holding fast to the last remaining vestige of local government control, the Cabinet decided it would be wiser to wait. Though printed in proof form, the second White Paper never saw the light of day.[53]

Chapter nine

Bevan the pragmatist

Labour came to power in July 1945 with a surprising choice as Minister of Health — Aneurin Bevan, a fiery Welshman whose burning socialism had been fired by years spent as an unemployed youth coping with the harshness of the means test.[1] He blamed that on Conservative policy, and his hatred of the party burned so deeply that when the struggle of creating the NHS was over he had the audacity to call the Tories 'lower than vermin'.[2]

Such a man was not likely to appeal to a profession imbued with middle class sympathies. Nor were the doctors likely to look kindly on the close association Bevan once had with the medical aid society in his home town of Tredegar.[3] A.J. Cronin's *The Citadel* describes vividly the indignities the profession suffered at the hands of coal miner management committees in the medical clubs of South Wales.[4] From the nineteenth century, the BMA had tried to destroy such societies in a struggle that became known as 'the battle of the clubs', and nothing angered the doctors more than the way the medical aid societies had managed to secure a foothold in NHI.[5] Between the wars the BMA repeatedly sought to dislodge them, but nothing worked. With the creation of a new service, medical leaders had reason to hope that they would at last be rid of the medical club incubus — yet here was a Minister of Health who sprang from the same source. At the age of 47, he was the youngest member of the Cabinet and, like many of his colleagues, lacking in ministerial experience.[6]

Why, in the face of such medical feelings, did Attlee choose him? The reason is not clear, but several considerations were apparent. Bevan, from his trade union experience, had become a skilled negotiator and someone was needed to unravel the knot in which health planning had become tied.[7] Even more important was the determination and strength of character the Welshman had displayed. Once Bevan embraced a goal he pursued it relentlessly, and Attlee wanted someone who could reverse the concessions Willink had made. During a debate in Parliament in 1941 Bevan had declared his belief in a salaried GP service,[8] and the Labour Party itself had made that its goal, together with municipal control, in a report issued in 1943.[9] No doubt that was the reason why Bevin, despite a long-standing feud with the Welshman, claimed to be responsible for his appointment.[10] Like Attlee, Bevin wanted someone who could put across the health centre idea.

At first, Bevan seemed intent on pursuing that goal. In April and May 1945 he had been among the first to condemn the concessions Willink had made and, when the Minister refuted the charge, Bevan threatened to reveal all he knew about the department's discussions with the municipal world.[11] When the new House of Commons convened on 17 August, Greenwood declared Bevan's intent to 'go back to the White Paper because of the terrible muddle in which the health plan was left'.[12]

Yet no sooner did the new Minister start to unravel the knot of health planning than he dropped all thought of a salaried service and municipal direction; in the hospital world as in general practice, he adopted a flexible stance. Far from being a dogmatic socialist, Bevan proved to be a pragmatic reformer. His greatest success, as one Labour MP put it, 'was the way he applied the anaesthetic to supporters on his own side, making them believe in things they had opposed all their lives'.[13]

Bevan's tactics

The first and most important change came in hospital policy. Breaking completely with past direction, Bevan took all (or nearly all) hospitals under national control. No other way seemed possible to unravel the knot in which negotiations had been tied. How Bevan arrived at this decision will be discussed later (see page 172), but it is important to note that it was not anticipated by Labour policy. Before it came to power in 1945 the Party had been committed to municipal direction, its stand being largely dictated by Somerville Hastings and other SMA activists in its ranks.[14]

Having removed the hospitals from local authority control, Bevan felt the need to give MOHs and their staffs something more than clinic work.[15] Willink had left them with only a landlord role in health centres and he planned to sanction only a few experiments. Bevan had to do more to satisfy the health centre lobby in Labour ranks and he led them to believe he would develop the centres at a faster rate than he intended or building shortages would permit.[16] Years later, Bevan claimed his main interest was in group practice and that could be organized by the doctors themselves in their own surgeries.[17] But in 1946, he did not talk this way; then, he assured his Parliamentary colleagues that health centres would be 'encouraged in every possible way'.[18]

Whatever were his real intentions, medical resistance to municipal control made it certain that Bevan would have to move cautiously. He could not offer local authorities more than a landlord role in health centres and, to the dismay of his friends in Tredegar, he ruled out the medical aid societies that had plagued the profession for so long.[19] Furthermore, he felt bound to defend the capitation system so as to preserve the principle of free choice.[20] But when pressed on his reasons for rejecting a salaried service, Bevan replied 'I do not believe that the medical profession is ripe for it.' And later he gave a clearer hint: 'There is all the difference in the world between plucking the fruit when it is ripe and plucking it when it is green.'[21]

Still, some suggestion of a salaried system was built into his remuneration structure. Though GPs would be paid mainly by capitation, Bevan restored the basic salary element which Willink had dropped, and he applied it to all doctors, not just to those who worked in health centres. Furthermore, Bevan did not grant GPs in health centres the right to use those facilities for private practice; only in their own surgeries could they continue the custom.[22] Even more important, Bevan made clear his determination to end the sale of practices and this also would apply to all GPs who entered the service. Lastly, he indicated his intent to restore the 'negative' control over the location of practices which Willink had dropped. GPs in practice would be allowed to stay where they were, but new ones would not be able to enter 'over-doctored' areas without the permission of a Medical Practices Committee which would carry out the task of classification.[23]

These measures were a pale shadow of what Brown and Maude had envisaged, nor did they even carry the GP service back to the modified conditions proposed in the White Paper. But there was enough to satisfy the more militant proponents of the health centre idea. SMA leaders were impressed most of all by Bevan's decision to abolish the sale of practices, since that, they believed, would inevitably lead to a salaried service. And to a Christian socialist like Somerville Hastings, the decision had moral significance. He hated commercialism in medicine and this custom represented business practice in its worst form. To him, the sale of practices was an evil thing which had to be uprooted, even if it were not needed to even out the distribution of doctors, the purpose with which it had long been associated. Hastings was overjoyed when Bevan agreed with him,[24] and after the decision was taken he was prepared to accept any concession the Minister might make, a disposition he publicly acknowledged in 1950.[25]

Bevan's concessions

The Minister's concessions were quick to come. Bevan had no hope of securing even modest reforms without giving the profession something in return, and he had no doubt of the place to start. What the doctors demanded above all was a place in the administrative structure — which meant that they preferred to elect those who would represent them, not leave the selection to others. Willink had offered precisely that with a recast insurance committee, and Bevan slavishly followed him. In place of the 10 per cent proportion which the doctors had enjoyed under NHI, they and the other family practitioners (dentists and chemists, but not opticians) were to have half the seats, with only a chairman to break deadlocks, and doctors along with other family practitioners were not excluded from holding the post.[26]

Henceforth among the lay members, approved society representatives would no longer be found; only the municipal and Ministry appointees who had always been considered 'neutrals' in the struggle for control of medical benefit under NHI. Other than this and in the provision of health centres, local authorities would have no role in GP administration. Bevan sternly rejected the demand raised by Latham and the local authorities for half the places on the hospital bodies and the new executive councils that would administer the family practitioner service.[27] The doctors would remain independent entrepreneurs, and executive councils, like insurance committees before them, would have local medical and other professional committees to guide them. The terms of service would be set as under NHI – by direct negotiation between the Ministry and the profession. Central control of wages and working conditions was what the doctors had wanted from the moment the panel system began and central control was what Bevan gave them.[28]

Nor was that the limit of the Minister's concessions. He felt he ought to do more to protect the profession within a service that would cover everyone. Under NHI, a doctor could be expelled from the panel for delinquent behaviour and still have a large cushion of private practice to fall back on. No such retreat seemed possible in future. Bevan therefore added an independent tribunal to the cumbersome complaint procedure that had evolved under NHI. Henceforth, before a doctor could be dismissed from the service, the decision would have to be made by three bodies — executive council, tribunal, Minister — rather than two.[29]

To his Labour colleagues, Bevan justified these changes by invoking the principle of worker's control; if it were right for coal miners, he cried, how could it be wrong for doctors?[30] Still, he took care not to extend its application too far; direct representation rights were granted only to GPs and consultants in teaching hospitals, not to other hospital doctors or the rest of the NHS world.

Medical reaction

It soon became clear that GPs would not respond in the way Bevan expected. With Labour and a left-wing Minister of Health in charge, their fear of a salaried service returned, and it was further aroused by the basic salary Bevan added. Something like the mood of 1943 revived, only this time it was not tied to a dread of municipal control. Local authorities had only a limited role to play in health centres and the profession was more concerned with the way the Minister's powers had grown as a result of his decision to nationalize the hospital service.

The doctors were also alarmed by the influence of the civil service. It had been evident from the moment discussions began in March 1943 that Maude and his colleagues were the driving force behind the Ministry's plan for a salaried service. During 1945 the profession's hopes of countering departmental advice had failed to materialize; the proposed CHSC did not receive the powers the doctors desired. Under NHI the profession had been content to deal directly with the department on the major conditions of panel practice, leaving insurance committees with routine duties. But this new service would cover everyone and Bevan's offer of a tribunal was not enough; the Minister would still have the final say as to whether a doctor should be expelled for delinquent behaviour.

In defence, the profession sought the right of appeal to a court of law. Such a demand had been pursued in the 1920s (with the MPU taking the lead), but it had died as a result of the representation rights the profession won under the disciplinary procedure.[31] Now neither these nor the tribunal Bevan offered were considered sufficient. To the doctors, the spectre of an all-powerful Minister arose, causing them to forget the preference they had shown for central control.

The MPA saw the opportunity. From the time it was formed in 1943, its bulletins had harped on the danger of central control, but as long as local authority fears predominated, that theme had limited effect.[32] However, once Bevan announced his intent to nationalize the hospital service, the focus of medical concern shifted, and MPA propaganda found a more receptive audience.

BMA leaders rose quickly to the challenge. At the critical representative meeting in December 1944 they had managed to stave off the MPA attempt to reject negotiations,[33] but now their position was again under threat. The only way to meet it was to steal the MPA's thunder and Dr Alfred Cox, the BMA's wise former secretary, showed the way. No sooner was the Bill published in March 1946 than one MPA acolyte (A.C. de B. Helme of Guildford, the main centre of MPA influence) denounced it in these terms:

> It was extraordinary what powers the Minister took to himself under the Bill. He was made an autocrat, almost a dictator. If this Bill comes into operation in anything like its present form it will represent something very much like that regime that is now coming to its sorry end in Nuremberg.[34]

The same tactic was used by anti-vivisectionist doctors within the MPU, then probably working in tandem with MPA leaders. Though the MPU group had flirted with fascism in the 1930s, they now found it expedient to disassociate themselves from the Hitler regime and they did this by linking the target of their attacks with the excesses of Nazism. Thus in 1947 Dr Maurice Beddow Bayly launched an assault against vivisection in the MPU's journal by equating it with the horrors of concentration camps: 'every vivisection laboratory throughout the world is a Belsen'.[35] Similarly Dr James Burnet, Bayly's main ally in the MPU, linked doctors who performed animal experiments with 'sadists, like the arch-criminals of the Belsen camp'.[36]

Cox, who only three years before had cast doubt on the need for the free choice principle (see page 49) swiftly sounded the same theme in the *British Medical Journal*:

> I have examined the Bill and it looks to me uncommonly like the first step, and a big one, towards National Socialism as practised in Germany. The medical service there was early put under the dictatorship of a 'medical Fuehrer'. This Bill will establish the Minister of Health in that capacity.[37]

He and BMA leaders were now forced to resurrect a demand they were anxious to drop — the right to sell practices. To the profession at large, the preservation of property rights seemed the surest way to secure protection against a salaried service. On the eve of Labour's election victory, the BMA's representative body had voted overwhelmingly to retain the custom.[38] MPA leaders did not lose sight of the opportunity. They made the demand their own, despite the fact that its debt implications conflicted with their devotion to social credit ideals. They, above all others, were intent on freeing the profession from the burden imposed by money-lenders, yet their call for the preservation of property rights promised only to prolong the bond.[39]Nor did the MPA abandon the demand after the NHS began. In 1952, its honorary secretary called for restoration of the custom, condemning the ban on the sale of practices 'as an infringement of the ordinary rights of property and as constituting discriminatory legislation'.[40]

BMA leaders could not call attention to the contradiction without acknowledging the challenge posed by the MPA. At first they tried to ignore the issue; nothing about it (or the need for an appeal to the courts) appeared in the seven principles of professional freedom published in December 1945, before talks with Bevan began.[41] But in the face of the rising storm over Minister's powers, they found it necessary to restore the demand, with Cox again leading the way.[42] But Charles Hill, in a private meeting with the new Permanent Secretary of the Ministry, Sir William Douglas, made his true feelings known about the proposal to abolish the sale of practices. On 10 May 1946, before the final round of negotiations began, he told Douglas that he 'wants to isolate this as the only big outstanding point, and then advise the profession to swallow it.'[43]

Would the doctors acquiesce without an assurance on salary? In view of the fears that had been aroused by Maude's original plan, that seemed unlikely. Hill himself had no delusions. When the profession was asked to pass judgement on the package of proposals which Bevan presented at the end of 1947, Hill made the point painfully clear: 'There is one criterion by which as a profession we can measure these matters. . . . It is whether these proposals do or do not bring us closer to a whole time salaried service of the State.'[44]

Bevan did not heed the warning until it was almost too late. Following the example set by Lloyd George in 1911, he left the method of payment to GPs out of the NHS Bill so as to secure the flexibility needed to press the basic salary proposal.[45] But the House of Lords refused to follow his lead. In October, the peers added a capitation clause and the move was supported not only by Horder but by Moran. The RCP president wanted the basic salary element dropped, insisting that capitation was needed to give GPs an incentive to do good work.[46] Bevan duly rejected the amendment when the Bill returned to the Commons, and the Act emerged with his original intention intact.[47] But the damage had been done; even Moran had chosen to defy the Minister. This gave the militants in medical ranks the opening they needed to stir discontent. Every time Bevan conceded one demand they raised another and the only way of thwarting their tactics was to delay the critical concession until just before the NHS began.[48]

By then it was evident that nothing short of an amending Act barring salary would suffice, but Bevan was reluctant to make the move until he was sure his Labour colleagues would acquiesce. A precedent had been established early in 1948 by the Unionist government in Northern Ireland; the NHS Act it formulated did specify a capitation payment for GPs.[49] The critical moment came in March and Bevan let Moran force his hand. Though two out of three doctors still opposed the Act in the final plebiscite in May, the concession broke the back of GP resistance; too few doctors dissented to warrant a boycott. With Cox again showing the way,[50] BMA leaders advised acceptance and GPs flocked into the service, propelled by fear of a disastrous drop in income if they stayed out. Not only would they have lost all their panel pay — since, as Bevan repeatedly warned, NHI terminated with the start of NHS and National Insurance in July — but much of private practice.

Even more vital was the need to qualify for compensation for loss of the right to sell practices before the government's time limit expired — which, despite the profession's protests, had been set as the date when the NHS began, 5 July 1948. On this issue, Bevan refused to bargain because he considered the custom 'an intrinsic evil'.[51] Even if it had not been needed to smooth out the distribution of doctors, he would have insisted on its abolition. Nor did he leave the profession in doubt about his intentions; unlike the method of payment, the abolition of the sale of practices and the terms of compensation had been written into the Act.[52]

In January 1948 a warning about the danger this posed to medical solidarity had been sounded at a representative meeting of the BMA:

> As the Act now stands it seems clear that a doctor must, on the appointed day, engage in the new service or lose any compensation for the goodwill of his practice, and it does not matter whether the doctor is single handed or in a partnership. Doctors of all ages are affected, the older because they cannot afford to stay out of the service and so lose their compensation for goodwill; the younger, who may have a debt on their practice, are virtually offered a liquidation of this debt if they go into the service. This in effect places a pistol at the head of the practitioner and may force him into the service against his better judgment, as otherwise he will be involved in very considerable financial loss.[53]

Sale of practices

In this way the detailed arrangements made to abolish the sale of practices assumed critical importance and we need to examine how they evolved. Despite the stand taken by the representative body in July 1945, opposing abolition, BMA leaders agreed to discuss the subject in December.[54] At that point the government based the cost of compensation on practice values in 1939, with no allowance for price increases during the war. This produced a figure of £40 million to £43 million.[55] When the doctors protested, the Ministry replied: 'It would be unjust to base compensation on current values because those were affected by the war and the publication of the White Paper.'[56] The government, it explained, was offering only a measure of compensation, not full value.

However, not long after, the department did relent and the actuaries who did the detailed work took account of price increases during the war. They settled on a figure of £66 million (covering practices in England, Wales, and Scotland, but not Northern Ireland) and that was accepted by the Treasury.[57] To this amount was added the cost of a new superannuation plan, with GPs bearing 6 per cent of contributions.

The £66 million figure was based on a formula traditionally used to set practice values — two times yearly gross income. Lower ratios — some below one-and-a-half times — had prevailed during the war due to dislocations in practice, the movement of patients, and uncertainties over the future. But after some hesitation the Ministry accepted the doctors' argument that the 'two times' ratio should apply.[58] In the process, the actuaries applied a slightly lower ratio — 1.9 times — based on a study made by the BMA's actuary in 1943.[59]

To determine average gross income, the government relied on a study conducted for the BMA by Professor Bradford Hill. He produced a figure of £1,572 for the years 1936–8 and to this was added a 16⅔ per cent betterment allowance to take account of price rises during the war.[60] That brought the amount available to £3,668, but the average amount paid was no doubt higher because only about seven out of ten doctors (or 14,000 out of 20,000 practices) qualified for compensation.[61] (The rest were newly registered or had no practices to return to after the war.) This became evident in 1950 when the BMA was urged to seek additional compensation because many more GPs joined the service than anticipated. (Some 20,000 entered as opposed to the 17,900 used in computation of the £66 million.) The doctors decided it would not be wise to request more because the number who applied for compensation 'was considerably below the figure of 17,900'. If the issue were raised, it was feared that the Ministry might demand a downward adjustment of the £66 million.[62]

The average amount paid may thus have been about £4,700 and this compares with a pre-war value of some £3,100, an increase of over 50 per cent. But there is reason to believe the percentage gain was greater because many doctors failed to respond to Bradford Hill's questionnaire and many who abstained were thought to be low earners who did not want to depress the average. Data obtained earlier from the Inland Revenue showed incomes at lower levels, with 61 per cent of a sample of 548 doctors in 1938 earning less than the £1,000 net income found by Bradford Hill.[63] If, as the Ministry assumed in 1943, average gross earnings were only £1,350,[64] that would have produced a selling price of £2,700 instead of £3,100, and the £4,700 paid in compensation would have meant a gain of 63 per cent.

The government's generosity was stimulated partly by the recommendations of the Spens Committee, which called for a substantial increase in GP pay from the low level that prevailed before the war. Bevan accepted the Spens recommendation, which had been stated in terms of 1939 prices, but did not translate it into 1948 values in the manner desired by the profession. Though prices had doubled by 1948, average GP income rose by only 60 per cent — from £1,111 to £1,777. The matter was put right by Justice Danckwerts in 1952 (to whom the issue was referred for adjudication) when he raised the amount to £2,222.[65]

Nevertheless, even with a 60 per cent increase, GP incomes were set at a more generous level than had prevailed before the war, and the same applied to compensation payments. The Treasury failed to grasp the implications of the Spens Report, but there is no doubt that Bevan did; he clearly saw it as a way to lure GPs into the new service.[66] Alternatively, the profession might have been allowed added years for past service under the superannuation plan that was to start with the Act; indeed, Maude preferred that method in 1942, with lump sum payments given only to doctors burdened with debt.[67] Had that route been chosen, then only £35 million or less would have been needed for compensation purposes.[68] But these added years could have been given only to doctors who had served under NHI, and the department wanted to offer an inducement to all doctors, including those who had previously shunned the panel. And more to the point, added years would not have held out the allure that a large lump-sum payment would present.

Furthermore, the Ministry took care to offer compensation in a way designed to produce the maximum effect; it was given only to GPs who joined the service when it began and only to those who undertook to treat a reasonable number of patients (at least 400). The doctors wanted the same three-year leeway that had been granted to midwives when a salaried service was created under the 1936 Midwives Act, but the Ministry, which had even considered a cut-off date before the Health Service began, ruled that out on 5 January 1946.[69]

Thereafter, no attempt was made to alter the ruling because of the stand taken by the BMA's representative body in 1945 and 1946; it refused to contemplate any loss of the right to sell practices.[70] Agreement had been reached on the global sum only because Rucker insisted on discussion before the Bill was presented to Parliament (since the amount was to be included in the statute).[71] During the prolonged period of negotiations in 1947, the issue was not raised. Not until the end of the year did the doctors realize the mistake they had made, and Hill made no attempt to correct it.[72] Nor did he have to; because of ambivalent feelings within the profession, medical leaders still felt reluctant to discuss the subject. As Dain put it at the time, 'The general practitioner is in this cleft stick, that if the Act starts and he has not come in, then he loses the right to compensation.'[73] There was also the danger that his debts might be called in, since practice loans were often made on condition that the doctor maintained contract work like that provided by NHI and the new NHS.[74] No greater security was prized by the lender.

In January 1948 BMA leaders did make a half-hearted attempt to save the custom by offering financial aid to young doctors for the purchase of practices. The idea was to make the selling price and interest charge low enough so that the debt could be discharged in ten years or less. But when Dr F.M. Rose proposed a plan to that effect — with practice values based on one or one-and-a-quarter years' gross income instead of two — his colleagues baulked.[75] Older doctors were anxious to promote medical solidarity but not if it meant they lost money in the process.

The department also took care to prevent departures from the service after the right to compensation was won; no payments were made until doctors died or retired, with exceptions allowed only in cases of hardship. Meanwhile, the amounts held in reserve accumulated at the going rate of interest, then only 2¾ per cent. It was left to the profession to decide how much each doctor should receive, the Ministry's role being limited to payment of the global sum. Only a few records are available to indicate how this was done; no overall summary was compiled showing the amounts paid to each doctor or the average compensation realized.

Because of inflationary conditions in the post-war period, many GPs treated the 'small' payments they received with contempt. But that was not how the profession saw the arrangement in 1948; then, the amounts appeared more generous and the Ministry made it clear that the full £66 million would not be paid unless 17,700 GPs joined the service.[76] Even before the appointed day, that condition was met. One doctor publicly declared his desire for compensation to free himself from debt[77] — while Cox, who had taken a strong stand against abolition of the right to sell practices, was forced to admit that few in the profession thought the issue worth fighting for.[78]

Health centres deferred

Such was the main thrust of the strategy that led to the start of the NHS in July 1948. The details were more complex, involving an array of issues that were gradually resolved over the three year period that began with Labour's accession to power in July 1945. To complete the story, we need to review them here.

Bevan's first concern was to break the deadlock in negotiations that had bedevilled hospital planning. He did it in the simplest manner possible — by bringing all, or nearly all, hospitals under national control, 3,105 in number (1,771 from local authorities and 1,334 from the voluntary sector).[79] This was debated and resolved within the department between August and October. The decision was then referred to the Cabinet where, over the heated opposition of Herbert Morrison, it was approved in principle on 18 October.[80]

Bevan's next concern was to reverse Willink's decision and end the sale of practices. This was decided within the department on 5 October and approved by the Cabinet without dissent on 3 December.[81] Discussions with the profession on the amount of compensation started immediately and £66 million was agreed in March 1946, just before the Bill was presented to Parliament.[82]

Before the issue was referred to the profession's negotiating committee, the Ministry sounded out the Treasury on a demand the doctors were expected to raise — the right to receive past service credits (equal to half the time spent in panel practice) in addition to a lump sum compensation payment. Mr (later Sir) Edward Hale and his civil service colleagues at the Treasury not only resisted the idea — they did not see how the sale of practices could be outlawed as long as doctors remained independent entrepreneurs. It was too easy to evade the ban through house sales at inflated prices (surgeries normally being sold along with residential accommodation) or partnership agreements which left the junior partner with more than his fair share of the workload or income.

Bevan tried to meet this objection by denying a doctor the right to select his successor. That still left house sales open to abuse, but Bevan expected that problem to be solved by the development of health centres together with the greater freedom of patients to choose and change doctors. Hale did not agree (as it turned out, with some justice), nor did he consider it necessary to consult his political chief, the Chancellor of the Exchequer, Hugh Dalton.[83] The Ministry did not press the issue despite the dissatisfaction it stirred in Scottish circles. If a choice had to be made, the Scottish Secretary, George Buchanan, preferred to offer past service credits, but the English department held fast to lump sum compensation.[84] Charles Hill later sought to obtain both, but neither he nor his colleagues pressed the demand when it was rejected.[85]

From this exchange an influence became evident which had long been known in civil service circles; the Treasury, like Maude, was intent on pushing the doctors in the direction of a salaried service. Sir John Anderson, during his tenure as Chancellor, had offered more than a hint of this by the strong support he had given to health centres (see page 68). Such feeling was understandable. Treasury officials were fearful of the costs of a health service that would cover everyone, and saw a salaried service as a way of restraining them. Not only would that method provide a cheaper and more predictable way of rewarding GPs but it might lessen the temptation to prescribe drugs or issue sickness certificates too freely. *Competition between doctors was seen as the enemy of an efficient health service.* In this respect they shared the view not only of colleagues in the Ministry of Health but of the socialists who made up the Labour Party. The demands of finance made strange bedfellows.

However, since there was no hope of persuading the profession to accept a salaried service, Bevan had to search for other ways to restrain competition, and this produced his basic salary proposal. The doctors had rejected the idea when Willink raised it in 1945 (see page 89) but it had been proposed by the BMA's own MPC[86] and medical negotiators put it forward in 1943.[87] Bevan justified its reintroduction because it had been endorsed by the Spens Committee on GP Remuneration,[88] while Charles Hill thought medical opposition might be overcome if it were called by a different name so as not to imply the start of a salaried service.[89] Jameson suggested the words 'guaranteed minimum salary'[90] but Bevan, who had left-wing critics to appease, stuck to the 'basic salary' designation. Not until 1966 was a more acceptable term devised — 'practice allowance'.

Early in 1946 the Cabinet made clear its desire for a high basic salary — 'say ⅔rds' of GP income — to minimize competition. The Ministry prepared a paper on the subject and included in it other devices to restrain rivalry: controls over the location of practices so as to even out distribution; higher pay for all GPs so as to lessen the need to compete; firm action against lax certification; and the promotion of group practice in health centres.[91]

The last was most important. Within the Ministry, health centre development was envisaged on a large scale, eventually embracing all GPs.[92] When that structure was complete, most doctors would be working in groups and that would weaken competitive pressures, even without a salaried service. Bevan may have thought this could be done simply by encouraging doctors to form groups of their own, but that was not how it was seen by the officials in his department. Even empiricists like the newly-elected Labour MP, Dr Stephen Taylor, stressed the need for health centre development: 'The health centre proposal is really the key to the general practitioner service as constituted in this Bill. The thing will stand or fall by the success of health centres.'[93]

Doctors resist municipal development of health centres

Resistance to the plan arose before Bevan presented the Bill to Parliament, and Bevan had partly himself to blame. Instead of freeing health centres from a municipal bond, he stuck to Willink's plan for local authority development. Though councillors and clerks would have only a landlord role, they would be responsible for provision. Indeed, in December 1945 Bevan stressed the need for local authority involvement.[94]

This stirred the old fears of the doctors. They not only reasserted their demand for slow development on an experimental basis, but doubted whether health centres were wanted at all. What GPs really needed, the *BMJ* contended, was access to the experts and diagnostic facilities of the hospital world: 'The general practitioner does not so much want consultation with another practitioner in a health centre as with the man who has expert knowledge he does not possess himself.'[95]

Medical fears rose to the point where the doctors sought to end all municipal involvement, shifting responsibility for health centres to the regional boards that were to oversee hospital development. This would not only bring the English pattern closer to the Scottish (where health centres remained under direct department control) but would help to bridge the gap between GPs and the hospital world.[96] The *BMJ* added to the clamour by attacking one MOH for restricting hospital admissions — a portent, it warned, of bureaucratic interference to come. This produced a protest from the president of the Society of MOHs to the Council of the BMA, but he received no support and it was dismissed. That may explain why the Society failed to register any complaint in 1943 when GP attacks on municipal control were at their height.[97]

These views were communicated to Bevan on 6 February 1946.[98] At that point they had to be kept confidential because the Bill had not been presented to Parliament. Before he became Minister, Bevan had criticized Willink and others for negotiating in advance.[99] Though he held three meetings with the doctors before the Bill was published on 20 March, he did little more than listen. Bargaining did not formally begin until after the Act was ratified in November.

However, on 26 February 1946 a leading local authority spokesman made it clear that his group no longer wished to be involved in health centre development.

This feeling had been growing in the municipal world since 1945, fed by Willink's retreat from a salaried service. Local authorities did not want to be responsible for health centres if the doctors were left in competition. They were also angered by Bevan's refusal to grant half the places they sought on executive councils. Now, in 1946, an added factor arose: the cost of the health centre to be built in Manchester was estimated at £5 million. Sir Miles Mitchell of the AMC wanted the duty transferred to the hospital service, leaving local authorities responsible only for rental payments for the municipal clinics that were to be held in health centres: 'His real objection to the local authorities taking over the health centres was the large capital cost involved.'[100]

The CCA spokesmen did not agree, but their interests lay more with hospitals than health centres. They were alarmed by the impending split between hospital and community care and were willing to abandon all involvement with health services to avoid it. They were ready to let the new regional hospital boards (RHBs) assume responsibility for everything.[101]

Only Latham of the LCC felt strongly about preserving a local authority role for health centres. He was afraid of losing control of municipal clinics if the LCC did not retain a place in health centres. For over a year the LCC had been locked in a battle with the metropolitan boroughs, the boroughs contending that the LCC covered too large an area for clinic administration. Willink, they claimed, had promised to put health centres under their control, but Bevan turned a deaf ear to borough demands. According to Willink, Bevan refused because he had made an agreement with Latham under which the LCC would accept the takeover of its hospitals providing it were given control of all, or nearly all, borough health services.[102]

Bevan's missed opportunity

The loss of municipal interest in health centres provided Bevan with a rare opportunity, one that had not been available to his predecessors; he could have given the doctors the health centre structure they wanted. If Bevan had let RHBs assume responsibility, the profession might have welcomed the development of health centres and then not only group practice but a salaried service might have evolved.

But Bevan did not seize the opportunity: he left health centres in municipal hands. The main reason was dictated by finance; the health centres Bevan envisaged were to be simple and small, consisting primarily of consulting rooms for GPs. As administrative bodies, he maintained, the RHBs were too remote and they had enough to do with hospital development[103]

Bevan was also anxious to placate MOHs: with their hospital empires gone, they needed something meaningful to do. For Jameson, municipal involvement was essential 'if there was to be the desired close link between general practitioner work and the Local Authority Health Services'.[104] But someone in the department did express concern about the split this would cause between hospital and domiciliary care. For him, 'the only real remedy is to entrust all personal health services to the Regional Boards', but that 'is not practical politics now'.[105] In England and Wales, health centres remained in local authority hands.

The doctors thus had no reason to change their view. For them, health centres remained a diagnostic facility and that was the role Bevan stressed when he presented the Bill to Parliament.[106] But this interest would remain only so long as GPs were denied direct access to pathology and radiology services in the hospital world. In a few places the right had been won, but staff shortages and fear of abuse made its widespread application a distant prospect.[107] Not until the 1960s did an 'open door' policy become prevalent. Then, however, the department had reason to be grateful, for 'direct access' proved to be far less costly than the health centre alternative.

With health centres remaining in municipal hands, the stage was set for the demise of the idea. During the negotiations that followed in 1947 the doctors showed no interest, and Bevan, in January 1948, announced that few were likely to be built because of building shortages.[108] As the head of a department charged with housing as well as health, he found it prudent to give priority to houses and hospitals. During the 1950s only a few experimental health centres were built and the most ambitious — Woodberry Down in London — proved too costly and too large to set a pattern for the future.

Basic salary abandoned

With the health centre prospect fading, Bevan held fast to the basic salary idea; that seemed the surest way to reduce competition among GPs. He hoped the amount of GP income to be paid in salaried form would rise as group practice spread. A financial incentive in the guise of a capitation payment, he told the Cabinet, would be needed only at the start of NHS; gradually, it would be replaced by the pressure for better clinical work coming from colleagues working in groups.[109] In an attempt to secure medical assent to a small basic salary, Bevan lowered the amount to £300 from the higher figure desired by the Cabinet, but that did not pacify the doctors.[110] Any suggestion of salary filled them with fear, and so large did the issue loom in February 1948 that Douglas saw it as the only real obstacle left to overcome.[111]

The profession made its feeling clear in the plebiscite taken in January 1948, but Bevan did not relent until Moran offered a diplomatic way out in March. The Minister then agreed not only to a legislative ban on a salaried service but, at Moran's suggestion, to a concession on the basic salary as well.[112] It was now to be confined to young doctors during their first three years of service. An added influence may have come from Northern Ireland; William Grant, the Unionist Minister of Health and Local Government there, restricted the basic salary to doctors working in rural districts. Though Northern Ireland had a Unionist government, its Parliament operated on the principle that its social services would conform with the pattern set in Britain. However, Grant went out of his way to appease the doctors, giving them rights which Bevan had rejected. On several issues

Bevan later followed suit, but he held firm to his denial of an appeal to the courts against dismissal from the NHS: that was allowed only in Northern Ireland, not Britain.[113] In the negotiations that followed his announcement in April, Bevan went further. Though he widened the instances in which a basic salary might be paid, he added the need for executive council approval.[114] In effect, that meant few doctors would receive it unless the local medical committee approved.

This marked the end of all attempts to start a salaried service; in the 1949 Amending Act, GPs even won the right to treat private patients in health centres.[115] That should have been sufficient to overcome medical resistance, but several issues remained. Much concern had been expressed about the effect of the Act on partnership agreements, particularly if one partner entered the NHS and the other did not.[116] That would make it difficult, if not impossible, for the other partners to sell their practices, thus forcing the break-up of partnerships before the appointed day. How ironic for a service that purported to promote the development of group practice — such was the taunt the doctors threw at the Ministry in 1947. In December Bevan agreed to examine the problem and introduce amending legislation if needed.[117] Though no satisfactory solution emerged and a large number of partnerships were dissolved, the Minister's gesture did defuse the issue.

Nor did the profession's objection to controls over the location of practices present a serious problem. Though the doctors wanted entry to NHS to be as free as it was under NHI and under the Northern Ireland NHS Act, they were ready to tolerate restrictions in areas judged to be over-doctored. Certainly those in practice in such places would present no objection. Bevan held fast to the restriction.

More feeling was expressed over the right of appeal to the courts against dismissal from the service. Many doctors did not think Bevan's tribunal offered sufficient protection and their fears were heightened by the clamour over Minister's powers. Under the Northern Ireland Act an appeal had been allowed and Norman Brook of the Cabinet office was ready to allow the same procedure in England and Wales.[118] But Bevan held firm; if the doctors received the privilege, he feared that miners and railwaymen (whose industries were also being nationalized) would make the same demand and that would lead to 'judicial sabotage of the socialised services'.[119]

Maternity services

Where maternity services were concerned, Bevan made a major concession; he agreed to pay all GPs who did the work, not just those who held the desired qualifications. In an attempt to restrict the duties to doctors who could meet conditions favoured by the obstetricians, the Ministry confined not only payment but even the right to practise midwifery in the NHS to GPs who had postgraduate education or the continuing experience needed to maintain competence (defined as a minimum of twenty cases per year).[120] Some reform like this had been tried by local authorities before the war, but had failed.[121] The start of the NHS offered the chance to make another attempt.

However, in Scotland and Northern Ireland too many GPs did the work to impose restrictions, and that made it difficult to apply them in England and Wales. Furthermore, the profession feared that once selection became the rule in mid-wifery, it would spread to other areas of general practice.[122] From the moment the proposal was raised, the doctors protested, and just before the NHS began Bevan gave in. He offered payment to all GPs for midwifery, the only difference being that those who possessed the necessary qualifications would receive two guineas more (seven as opposed to five) for the full array of services.[123]

Within the department, Jameson found it hard to accept the freer terms; from his long service in the public health world, he had come to see the need for selec-tion.[124] Nor could the arrangement be managed without protests from the Treasury. In January 1948 the department gave notice of intent to raise the fee for midwifery from three to seven guineas (with the work still being confined to selected GPs). Hale reacted angrily, giving the Treasury view that the doctors were 'already being generously treated'. But by then the Ministry had already made the offer since it thought Treasury consent had been given for a payment as large as ten guineas. That left Hale no option but to acquiesce. Still, he gave warning of the Treasury's intent to take legal action against the department under section 75 of the NHS Act if similar concessions were made in future.[125]

The Ministry gave the Treasury no cause for concern when the doctors made similar payment demands for minor surgery. Here, Bevan and his civil servants held firm. Fee charging for services beyond the range of panel care had been an unending source of abuse under NHI and the department was determined to stop it. In future, Ministry officials pointed out, such treatment would be available in the hospital service and there was no reason why GPs should be paid. If they wanted to remove such things as sebaceous cysts, they were free to do so but they would receive no additional fees. Only if this imposed too great a burden on the hospital service might the subject be reviewed.[126]

The decision was silently welcomed by many in the consultant world. They were concerned by the way GPs had exceeded their competence in cottage hospitals and done damage to patients. Though major operations were the main concern, they felt it safer to offer no financial incentive for those of a minor nature. GPs were more likely to accept this arrangement if payment for midwifery were left open, so in effect the Ministry 'traded midwifery for surgery'. In the long run, the department may have recognized that GP interest in midwifery would weaken. No doctor liked to spend endless hours waiting for mothers to deliver babies, so in time GP interest might be largely confined to the ante-natal sphere — and that, indeed, was what happened.

But in 1948, obstetricians did not react favourably. With a severe shortage of qualified specialists, they needed GP aid, but wanted it done on a selective basis. In their view, GPs without the necessary qualifications should not be allowed to practise midwifery, and at one point it looked like that revolutionary principle would be incorporated in the NHS. But by the time the service began, the work had been opened to all GPs and all were to be paid. With the trend toward hospital confinements, doctors who wanted to deliver babies would have to have access to beds. A 'battle of the beds' was about to begin in obstetrics and it would not take long for consultants to complain about the 'most unsatisfactory state' of the domiciliary midwifery service.[127]

Part 3
Moran's Consultant Service

when everyone is able to obtain the services of a consultant who
has had a proper training, it will be the greatest single step in advance
in my lifetime . . . . You may be surprised to hear that there are
great areas of England, towns with a population of 100,000 where
the major surgery and everything else is done by general practitioners . . . . All this must end; it is one of the greatest evils of
our time in the medical world.

*From Moran's maiden speech in the House of Lords, 1 June 1943,
volume 127, column 752*

Chapter ten

Moran organizes consultants

We have seen how the interests of GPs and consultants diverged during negotiations on the Health Service. Not only obstetricians but all specialists were involved. What they had in common was a desire to create a proper consultant service and remove GP-specialists from the hospital world. Doctors who combined specialism with general practice were pinned with the derogatory label 'consultoids', or sub-consultants. In this chapter, and the next two, we shall see how Moran, as RCP president, paved the way for their exclusion from the hospital world.

The division in British medicine

The separation of general practice from hospital work, which is more pronounced in Britain than in most countries, has a long history, stemming from social class divisions that split the profession from the middle ages. Physicians headed the pecking order, surgeons came next, and others such as GPs (when they arose) were at the bottom.

The advance of medical science from the middle of the nineteenth century reinforced the division by making specialization necessary across a broad front. More and more specialists joined the ranks of fully-qualified consultants, but their numbers did not grow fast enough to man the expanding number of hospitals that arose at the end of the century. In many places, GPs who practised part-time as specialists had to be used, so much so that by the 1930s they made up over half (57 per cent) of the staffs of voluntary hospitals. But most of the hospitals in which they worked were small, containing only 17 per cent of the total number of beds.[1] In the larger institutions, and particularly in Britain's prestigious teaching hospitals, no GPs were to be found.

The growth of a publicly-financed GP service from 1911 gave the profession the chance to make a fresh start by freeing it — at least in part — from the divisive forces inherent in private practice. But neither GPs nor consultants took advantage of the opportunity; instead of closing the gap, they let it widen further, and the medical world became alarmed by the damage done by GPs in the field of surgery. Many doctors in cottage hospitals performed operations beyond their competence — or so it was widely believed — and this cast a stigma over the whole corps of 'consultoids'.[2]

Nor was this the only difficulty caused by the GP presence. The growth of small hospitals without resident or fully-trained staff created financial problems for the voluntary sector: 'It is these hospitals which account for the anomaly that whilst the total income of Voluntary Hospitals is greater than their expenditure, practically all general and teaching hospitals are in debt.' Most of the paid work went to the cottage hospitals; patients seeking free care turned to the larger voluntary hospitals, which remained largely true to their charitable tradition. This complaint could not be lightly dismissed for it was made by a Liverpool physician influential in BMA as well as royal college circles — Henry Cohen.[3]

By the time the Second World War began, consultant leaders were determined to act; specialism had progressed too far to be left in untrained hands. They wanted nothing more to do with the 'consultoids' who had stolen their patients, lowered their incomes, and frustrated the development of proper clinical standards in the consultant world.[4] A partial reform was provided by the EMS since it extended consultant influence throughout the land. But its effect was limited: it was created mainly to serve those who had been injured by war, not the larger civilian population. Even more telling, the organization of the service left hospital management — and hence staff appointments — largely intact. Regional consultant advisers did much to raise clinical standards in outlying hospitals, but they could not carry out a complete reform.[5] As for the Ministry, all it did was arrange contracts for services from municipal and voluntary hospitals, restricting its attention to supplies and the material aspects of hospital operation. It did not interfere in clinical matters or the way hospitals made staff appointments.[6] In 1942 Jameson and another Ministry official 'made it clear that the Ministry never accepted any responsibility for clinical treatment of any branch of medicine nor instituted any supervision over the clinical treatment afforded by local authorities'.[7] If this were the case with municipal hospitals, it applied even more to the voluntary sector; regional consultant advisers had to make judgements on their own.

But even if the will were there, no way was open to carry through a complete reform; there were simply not enough qualified consultants at hand. 'Consultoids' had to be used, whether consultants wanted them or not. Nor was there hope of altering the situation without a substantial infusion of state aid. Not many young doctors could afford the long wait to consultant status and a secure place in private practice. Though the EMS offered payment for work in voluntary hospitals, it was doubtful if the custom would continue after the war. Just before NHS began in 1948, Lord Horder was startled to find that two-thirds of the voluntary hospitals in London still clung to the honorary tradition.[8] Teaching hospitals in particular had long been notorious for their parsimony, relying on the prestige attached to their posts to attract good men; teachers found compensation in the steady flow of private patients from the GPs they trained.[9] The whole hospital system — municipal as well as voluntary — needed a large injection of Exchequer aid to increase the consultant corps and place it adequately around the country.

BMA dominance in medical politics

From the moment EMS planning began in 1938, Moran had seen the opportunity, and it was his hand, with its pattern of sector organization, that avoided LCC rule of the London region.[10] But Moran was then only treasurer of the RCP; he had to wait until he became president in April 1941 before he could exert much influence on national policy. Though the college he headed was the most prestigious in the medical world, it had become an 'effete institution',[11] concerned mainly with academic and ceremonial affairs. The dominant place in medical politics was occupied by the BMA, which owed its rise to the 1911 Insurance Act. That statute brought the profession into direct relation with the state, but since it covered only primary care, only an organization that embraced GPs could negotiate.[12]

Some consultants did manage to influence medical policy between the wars. Dawson was the outstanding example and he served as RCP president from 1931 to 1938.[13] But, like other consultants in public life, he acted mainly in an individual capacity; the College as a corporate body carried little weight in Whitehall. Its main accomplishment was to win private practice rights for consultants in the EMS after the war began. Together with the BMA and the other royal colleges, it persuaded the Ministry to let consultants on whole-time duty undertake private practice while receiving £500 per year for standby emergency duties.[14] But that was apparently all the RCP president, Sir Robert Hutchison, wanted the College to do; thereafter, he suggested it be closed for the duration.[15] When, in April 1940, the president of the Royal College of Obstetricians and Gynaecologists (RCOG) — Dr (later Sir) William Fletcher Shaw — proposed that something be done about the future of the consultant service, Hutchison refused to act, leaving it to the BMA (which had been propelled into action by the MPU) to create the MPC five months later.[16]

Nothing angered Moran more than the humiliation he felt when discussions on the Health Service began in 1943. The Ministry asked the BMA to form a representative committee covering the whole profession, and at the first meeting in March the three college presidents were introduced to the Minister by the chairman of the BMA's council. 'Perhaps', Moran later declared, 'at no time in the history of the College had its influence over public affairs fallen so low.'[17]

Moran was determined to change that. Even before he became president, he tried to persuade the colleges to act independently. At a meeting of college leaders in October 1940 he implored his colleagues to reject the BMA's invitation to serve on the MPC: 'I do not see how 2 or 3 representatives are going to influence the opinions of the existing 45 members of the Commission.'[18] Though the BMA later conceded more places on the MPC's Teaching Hospital Committee, giving the colleges a two-thirds majority, it refused to do so on other committees dealing with hospital planning. As Anderson, the BMA secretary, put it in May 1941, 'The concern of special practice and matters connected with hospitals have a far wider application than the members of the College alone.'[19] Throughout this exchange Anderson defended his right to act because it was the BMA, not the colleges, that had earlier negotiated consultant salaries with the LCC.[20]

Neither Hutchison nor the presidents of the other colleges were pleased by this response, but they refused to go it alone. They preferred to leave economic and financial matters to the BMA. Only Fletcher Shaw felt differently, angered by the smaller place on the MPC given to his college as compared with the older colleges.[21] Dispute over the extent of college representation raged on for months, causing the MPC to delay the start of its deliberations until May 1941, but in the end Moran was forced to accept BMA dominance.

What bothered him most about this situation was the extent of GP influence in the larger organization: 'The truth is that the B.M.A. committees are ruled by the general practitioner and he calls the tune.'[22] This, he declared, meant that the BMA was obsessed with material demands:

> We shall go to the Ministry of Health to demand 2/6 extra pay, not to insist on proper standards. The interest of the Colleges, whatever their faults, is to preserve and maintain standards of consultants and resist men practising as consultants who have not been trained for the job.[23]

All of this made Moran suspicious of BMA leaders and of consultants who worked with them. With Anderson, whom he respected, he used flattery, making the BMA secretary an honorary fellow of the RCP.[24] Dain also won Moran's admiration for his honesty and 'guts';[25] only later did he become aware of weaknesses long recognized by the Ministry (see p. 74).[26] But with Charles Hill, Moran always felt uneasy, seeing him as his great rival in NHS negotiations and developing a paranoid suspicion of every move the BMA secretary made.[27]

Moran thought Hill was devious, yet that was the very charge GPs levelled at him with the nickname 'Corkscrew Charlie'. And in his capacity as personal physician to the Prime Minister, he did not endear himself to Churchill's aides. They found Moran vain, egotistic, indiscreet, over-critical, and imbued with an inflated sense of self-importance. Not only did he exert far less influence than he imagined, but he fashioned appointments for himself (Provost of Eton, Minister of Health) which the Prime Minister could not possibly award. Nor did he hesitate to make judgements on subjects beyond his competence. When, after Churchill died in 1965, Moran published diaries detailing records of the leader's illnesses, he shocked Churchill's family as well as the medical profession at large.[28]

Underlying Moran's behaviour was an unshakeable faith in his own judgements and an ardent desire to get things done. Once he embarked on a course of action, he would let nothing stand in his way. The RCP's oligarchic constitution (see below) gave him freedom to act like an autocrat and he could neither understand nor tolerate the BMA's democratic processes. Medical spokesmen, in his view, had a duty 'to lead instead of waiting like the B.M.A. for three months to find out what the rank and file really think'.[29]

Hill must have been aware of Moran's foibles for he went out of his way to placate the RCP president and satisfy the demands he made.[30] Moran, in turn, had to acknowledge the worth of Hill's work in drafting the MPC report[31] as well as the 'great gifts' Hill displayed in the discharge of his secretarial duties throughout the course of negotiations.[32] There was no one in college circles who could match the aid Hill and his staff brought to BMA affairs.

Nevertheless, there were good grounds for tension between the two because Hill and his colleagues did resist the attempts of Moran and the colleges to adopt an independent stance. What BMA leaders feared above all was a recurrence of the split that had damaged the profession in 1912. Dr Alfred Cox, the BMA's secretary at the time, was still alive to remind his successors of the danger.[33] With the large membership, funds, staff, and experience at their command, BMA leaders felt themselves better able to represent the profession in negotiations with government.[34]

Divisions among consultants

Yet to unite consultants was no easy task, for though few in number, specialists were more sharply divided than generalists. Those in teaching hospitals lorded it over their counterparts in the non-teaching sector, provincial consultants felt neglected by their colleagues in London (where the main teaching hospitals and all three colleges were located), whole-time municipal specialists comprised a lower class and, as salaried employees, had different interests than those on honorary service in the voluntary sector, and all who engaged in private practice found themselves in competition with neighbours, there being nothing to unite them the way GPs were by local medical committees and periodic negotiations over panel pay. With the colleges preoccupied with academic affairs, consultants had to fend for themselves, and the depression between the wars made the going rough. Outside the EMS, the voluntary hospitals still expected them to give their services free — or almost so. No organization had their economic interests at heart.

The BMA tried to fill the gap in the 1930s. It formed a variety of groups catering to individual specialties as well as one (divided only on geographical lines) that embraced consultants and specialists as a whole.[35] For those concerned with the profession's welfare, this was a welcome move. Consultants like Henry Souttar (a surgeon) and Peter Macdonald (an eye, ear, nose, and throat specialist) had long been active in BMA circles and they threw their weight behind the specialty groups.[36] Others turned to the groups because there was nothing better, and some — like Lawrence Abel and Arthur Dickson Wright (both surgeons) — stayed with the BMA throughout the 1940s because it was more democratic.[37] This feeling was shared by many London consultants who made the Marylebone Division their home,[38] and they elected the most prestigious specialists in their ranks — like Lord Horder — to press their demands at BMA meetings.

Still others like H.J. McCurrich from the Royal Sussex County Hospital felt they had no choice; they came from non-teaching hospitals in the provinces and, together with their municipal brethren, occupied the lower rungs of the consultant ladder. Many felt more confident with the 'consultoids' at their side than with their counterparts in the teaching sector. Since this group formed by far the largest proportion of hospital staffs, the BMA had much to gain by offering them a voice.[39]

Yet others from provincial teaching hospitals tried to straddle both worlds. This applied particularly to the most influential in their ranks, Henry Cohen. He found the atmosphere in the BMA more receptive to physicians from Liverpool, but his teaching hospital interests and keen sense of diplomacy led him to seek a place on college committees.[40] As a result, despite Moran's suspicions and criticism of his behaviour,[41] he did more to shape consultant policy than any except the college presidents.

Nevertheless, despite the wide range of consultants from which it could draw, the BMA never managed to attract more than a small number of specialists before the war. The organization was too involved in panel affairs and too much concerned with general practice. Most consultants preferred to work through their own committees rather than on those, such as the BMA formed, which included GPs and 'consultoids' likely to out-vote them.[42] One professor of obstetrics — E. Farquhar Murray — found it impossible to devise a satisfactory maternity policy in 1936 after eighteen months of infighting within his BMA division in Newcastle.[43] After the war began, few BMA groups met and those that did were poorly attended.[44] According to Moran, Anderson confessed before he died that 'his failure to get the confidence of the consultant world was the one great blot on his career'.[45]

Differences between the royal colleges

The colleges were no better equipped to rally support; indeed, their medieval, oligarchic structure made them less able to mobilize consultant opinion. They were governed by a body of fellows answerable to no one, the College of Physicians being even more elitist than the College of Surgeons.[46] As opposed to the 2,700 surgeons who were awarded fellow status, only 700 physicians secured the title.[47] Voting rights were reserved for fellows who together formed the Comitia and elected the officers and council. Few fellows bothered to attend the infrequent meetings of the Comitia so that, once elected, the president ran the college much as he pleased, with only limited help from the council.

Sufficient records are available from the RCP and RCOG to gain insight into their operation. This is not the case with the RCS and that makes judgements difficult. Webb-Johnson, who served as president throughout the course of negotiations on the NHS, made only occasional reports to his colleagues and, except for council minutes, we have no record of the internal debate that went on within the College committee concerned with the subject.

It is clear, though, that surgeons had a greater stake in private practice than other consultants and posed greater resistance to the concept of universal coverage.

With the large number of fellows in his ranks and the overwhelming majority from the non-teaching sector, Webb-Johnson could have found life difficult if he had followed Moran's lead and chosen to act in an independent capacity. As it was, we find him repeatedly preferring to leave negotiations and economic matters to the BMA.[48] In that way, he secured more room to manoeuvre; as the son of an MOH from Stoke-on-Trent, he may have harboured more sympathy for a national health service than his colleagues realized.[49]

But there was another, more compelling, reason for wanting to keep his College out of financial affairs; Webb-Johnson could then be sure of protecting its tax-free status as a charity. For the RCS, this was more important than for the other colleges because it was (and is) deeply involved in research and education. Moran's college, by contrast, did no routine teaching, established no special departments for research, and confined its role largely to that of an examining body for the MRCP (member of the RCP).[50]

Webb-Johnson's concern on this score became clear in June 1948, when the amount of consultant remuneration came under consideration. At that point he was reported as opposing college participation in negotiations because, for one reason, 'he did not wish to involve his College in any way which might affect the payment of Income Tax on certain funds'.[51]

Perhaps, also, the RCS lacked the means to go it alone. Only the RCP, it seems, had the resources to reject BMA aid; during discussions with the Ministry, it paid the expenses of all college members (from the RCS and RCOG as well as the RCP) involved in the process.[52]

The RCOG also faced financial difficulties; it was too new and too small to act independently. That was one of the main reasons why Fletcher Shaw feared Moran's attempts to have the colleges set up their own planning commission and negotiating committee.[53] The RCOG had only been formed in 1929, it could not add the word 'Royal' to its name until 1938, and because of legal wranglings over a large bequest left by its first president, William Blair Bell, it had to wait until 1947 before it received a charter from the Privy Council. This meant the College could not be given a seat on the GMC, or have its degrees added to the Medical Register, until it won corporation status. That process was only completed with the passage of a Medical Act in 1950.[54] Before then, obstetricians and gynaecologists generally had to be fellows of the RCS before they could secure appointments to the larger hospitals.[55]

With these handicaps, the College carried little weight in official circles and it was weakened further by the three-year limit it placed on the president's term of office. Whereas the two older colleges kept the same presidents (Moran and Webb-Johnson) throughout the course of negotiations, the RCOG had no less than three — Fletcher Shaw to 1943, Eardley Holland to 1946, and William Gilliatt thereafter. During the 1940s, the BMA gave the RCOG a smaller place on negotiating bodies than it offered the two older colleges.[56] Most telling of all, its president in 1945 (Holland) was not included among the select six chosen to meet Bevan informally at the Café Royal on 25 October. Hill, who arranged the meeting, asked only Moran and Webb-Johnson to join him and three other BMA leaders — Dain, Souttar, and J.B. Miller.[57]

Similar indignities were felt within consultant circles. The two older colleges had opposed the new one when it was created in 1929, and they did not ask it to join the standing committee they formed in 1933 to 'consider matters of common concern'.[58] Not until 1941 was the new college asked to participate. Moran extended the invitation because he needed a central agency to start the preparation of lists of *bona fide* consultants and provide a forum where college efforts could be coordinated free from the taint of 'consultoid' influence. Once again, it was the Nuffield Trust that prompted the move because it needed the names of proper consultants to provide services to the middle class members of a provident insurance scheme it was about to launch.[59]

However, it was not enough simply to add RCOG representatives to the college standing committee: Moran needed an agency that would cover the consultant world as a whole. Consultants from the north of England had felt so neglected by their colleagues in London that, in January 1942, they formed a Provincial Teaching Hospitals Staff Association. Also, aside from the BMA's specialty groups, there were numerous specialty associations that had emerged partly because the two older colleges were dominated by the interests of general physicians and general surgeons. Orthopaedists and radiologists were among those who created separate bodies.

Moran's attempts at unity

Moran started a movement to bring all these consultants together after Ministry discussions began in 1943. He used as a nucleus a planning committee he had formed at the RCP in 1941. It came to be called the 'Beveridge Committee' and its members were extended in 1943 until it covered all sections of the consultant world. By the time the White Paper on the NHS was issued in February 1944 the amalgamation process was nearly complete and its name was officially changed to the Consultant Service Committee (though it was still referred to as the 'Beveridge Committee').[60] It was only at this point that detailed planning of the consultant service began; a sub-committee of this body was given semi-official status to carry out the task, estimating the number and distribution of doctors by specialty. But despite Moran's wishes, his 'Beveridge Committee' did not become the negotiating body for the hospital service as a whole. That remained in BMA hands and Hill took care to forge close links with the largest organization in the voluntary hospital world, the BHA, serving himself on its negotiating committee.

From the moment the BMA's representative committee was formed in 1943, Moran tried to remove the hospital service from its remit,[61] but he destroyed the chance by a disastrous misjudgement. When Maude proposed his plan for municipal control, Moran was inclined to accept it and strive only for a stronger medical voice within the administrative structure. He knew nothing of local government and relied on an MOH to guide him — Dr (later Sir) John Charles, an RCP fellow and MOH for Newcastle since 1932.[62] With a father who, as a colliery surgeon, had long been active in BMA work,[63] Charles was highly regarded in Ministry circles, so much so that he was appointed deputy CMO in 1944, and succeeded Jameson in 1950. His friendship with Moran no doubt helped him win this high place since Jameson, being an ingenuous extrovert, needed Charles' aid to help overcome a fear of failure 'with some of the more Machiavellian characters in the medical world'.[64]

Moran had a high regard for Charles' intelligence and learning but did not realize how much the MOH world had been blinded by the prospect of municipal control. Charles, like everyone in public health circles, did not question the force of Maude's movement, and endorsed Moran's judgement:

> I share your conviction that the profession would in the long run be wiser to concentrate on the provision of safeguards rather than to waste itself in opposition to the Government plan. Proper and wisely devised safeguards will not only preserve the rights, dignities and status of the profession, but will give added stability and greater administrative efficiency to the comprehensive health service.[65]

No advice could have been more wrongly conceived or foolishly given. Moran was subjected to a barrage of criticism, not only from his own Comitia but from the consultant world as a whole. The strongest reaction came from Dr T.L. Hardy, a prominent physician in Birmingham. He warned Moran that consultants in his area would fight municipal control 'to the last ditch'.[66] With these words ringing in his ears, Moran swiftly changed front and assured Hardy that he would lead the fight against local authority direction: 'I think you are likely to find me as tenacious as the Dawsons of this world.'[67]

He was true to his word; from that point on, Moran became an ardent opponent of municipal control. But the damage had been done; even Fletcher Shaw warned him against attempts to form a separate negotiating body. Though the RCOG president acknowledged that most consultants would prefer the colleges to the BMA, he told Moran that he doubted 'if this feeling is as universal as you think'.[68] Moran heeded the warning and abandoned attempts to negotiate separately.

Still, his role as college leader was further undermined by his close tie with Churchill and the frequent trips he made with the Prime Minister during the war. Some consultants came to believe that Moran was responsible for the White Paper.[69] All of this no doubt added to Webb-Johnson's lack of enthusiasm for the 'Beveridge Committee' and made him want to see it disbanded before negotiations began in 1945.[70] Only the need for a separate stance on regional organization, it seems, quieted his fears. (See page 134 for differences with the BMA on this issue.)

Threat from McCurrich and non-teaching consultants

A more serious and sustained threat to Moran's leadership arose from McCurrich, leader of the non-teaching consultants. Though 'only' a provincial consultant, McCurrich was a formidable opponent, having won status as an RCS fellow in 1923. From there he rose to the post of medical superintendent of the Brighton Hospital in 1925, upgrading it dramatically before he moved, as assistant surgeon, to the Royal Sussex County Hospital in 1931, becoming gynaecologist in 1939 and full surgeon in 1946.[71]

Throughout this period, McCurrich displayed a deep interest in social and political affairs. In 1926 he won the Rogers prize from the University of London for an essay on the treatment of the sick poor and, from 1938, he moved upwards in BMA circles, first as chairman of the Brighton Division (1938–41), then as a representative at annual meetings, and finally as a member of Council (1943–44) and the negotiating committees that dealt with the Ministry (1943–8).

It was the BMA's Council decision to elect McCurrich to the representative committee in March 1943 that aroused Moran's fears,[72] for as leader of the non-teaching consultants, McCurrich could demand a substantial following. Over 3,500 in number, as opposed to some 800 in the teaching sector, they made up more than 80 per cent of the consultant corps.[73] Together with their counterparts in the provincial teaching sector, they comprised over half the fellows of the RCP and an even larger proportion of the RCS.[74] If enough of them chose to attend Comitia, they could exert considerable influence. It was only by holding meetings in London that Moran and Webb-Johnson could keep them at bay.

Moran's main link with the provincial world was through Dr J.H. Sheldon of Wolverhampton, an RCP fellow with appointments in teaching as well as non-teaching hospitals. As planning proceeded, Moran relied on Sheldon to hold McCurrich in check.[75] Both were appointed to the BMA's negotiating team, but Moran took care to exclude McCurrich from the 'Beveridge Committee' when it was first enlarged in 1943.[76] At that point, Moran made room for members from 'non-teaching areas' but since no peripheral organization existed, choices were made in a haphazard manner. Not only McCurrich but others loyal to the colleges condemned the arrangement; they wanted more control over those who spoke for them.[77]

Moran's way to provide it was to start a non-teacher organization of his own. In November 1943 he came very close to doing so.[78] But Webb-Johnson opposed the move and Moran reluctantly abandoned the idea. The RCS president preferred to work through the BMA and did not want to alienate its leaders.[79]

Moran then tried a different approach. He made room on the 'Beveridge Committee' for all twenty members of the BMA's Central Consultants and Specialists Committee. He also agreed to hold consultant meetings around the country so that non-teachers and others could say they had not been ignored. In future, BMA leaders had reason to hope, consultants everywhere would have the chance to voice opinion and elect those who represented them.[80]

Among the twenty BMA representatives appointed to the 'Beveridge Committee' was McCurrich but, again, Moran found a way to isolate him. The 'Beveridge Committee' was now so large that it could not do detailed planning; its operation was confined to general principles and quarterly meetings.[81] The real work was assigned to a smaller sub-committee whose members were hand-picked by Moran with the aid of the other college presidents and Dain.[82] With Charles of the Ministry as a member, the body assumed semi-official status and Jameson gave it his blessing.[83] But McCurrich found no place and Moran thought it wiser to exclude Sheldon as well. Instead, he appointed two others from the non-teaching world who had not been prominent before — Dr C.J. Fuller, a physician from Exeter, and Mr Gerald Alderson, a surgeon from Leamington who had been recommended by Sheldon.[84] Though Alderson was president of the Provincial Surgical Club, he and his organization attracted so little attention that he did not rate an obituary notice in the *BMJ* or *The Lancet* when he died in 1961.[85]

McCurrich forms a new association

But McCurrich was not done. He was furious at the way the sub-committee had been appointed and the difficulty he faced in finding out who had been chosen. Though the initial selections were made in February, McCurrich was not officially notified until July despite his presence on the 'Beveridge Committee'.[86] The stage, in his eyes, was being set for non-teaching hospital domination by teaching hospitals or local authorities. McCurrich did not want either; his long service in the municipal sector had made him more fearful than Moran of local authority rule. As he read the White Paper, only the teaching hospitals had hope of escape; their fate, at least as far as financial aid for teaching was concerned, would not be decided until the Goodenough Committee reported.[87]

In McCurrich's view, the time had come to form a new association. In March he sent a circular to seventy-seven provincial hospitals inviting staff support, and he followed this with progress reports in June and September.[88] In them, McCurrich condemned the way non-teachers on the 'Beveridge Committee' had been hand-picked, no attempt being made in some areas to hold elections. The same applied to the all-important sub-committee of the 'Beveridge Committee', as well as non-teacher appointments to the BMA's representative committee. On the sub-committee, one of those selected (Alderson) was not even a member of the 'Beveridge Committee', while McCurrich described himself was the only one on the representative committee committed solely to the non-teaching sector as Sheldon had teaching as well as non-teaching appointments.

Charles Hill added to the clamour by complaining about the failure of the colleges to hold meetings in the provinces. To correct that, the BMA wanted to act as joint convenors and make sure that non-teachers had the right to attend all consultant meetings, including those arranged for teachers. In Moran's eyes, Hill was using 'this stuff to make out that the Colleges neither have the business ability nor the energy to do consultant work which he would rather see done by the B.M.A.'.[89]

Moran rejected both demands, but that only added force to the growing chorus of complaints. Even Charles Kindersley of Bath, one of the colleges' own area representatives on the 'Beveridge Committee', condemned the way the sub-committee had been appointed.[90] As for the general run of consultants in places like Shrewsbury, they did not even know a 'Beveridge Committee' existed.[91]

All of this threw Moran into a panic and he accused McCurrich of trying to divide consultant forces.[92] In a desperate attempt to stop the new association, he doubled the number of non-teachers on the 'Beveridge Committee' from twelve to twenty-five, thereby enabling smaller areas to be formed so that consultants would find it easier to attend meetings.[93] He then wrote furiously to provincial colleagues, asking them to reject the new association.[94] 'McCurrich', he warned, 'is violently anti-College and is in addition a wild fellow.' The colleges in his view had been betrayed by the BMA; as a sign of goodwill, they had put the BMA's whole Central Consultant Committee on the 'Beveridge Committee' but now a member of the BMA's Council (McCurrich) was starting a rival organiza-tion. Moran expected Hill to check McCurrich's ardour, 'but it seems to me that Hill is waiting to see what success McCurrich has'.[95]

The new association held its inaugural meeting at the end of September and Moran thought only about thirty hospital staffs would join, but in the end, nearly a hundred did.[96] All opposition was swept aside by the example set in the teaching sector; if provincial teachers could form a separate association, why not one for non-teachers? There would be no attempt to obtain separate bargaining rights; that would be left to the 'Beveridge Committee', which would make all consultant appointments to the BMA's new negotiating committee.[97]

This did nothing to ease Moran's fears, for the same assurances had been given by provincial teachers. In 1943 he managed to persuade them to drop a demand for separate representation on the BMA's committee[98] but the chairman of their association, Professor T.H. Oliver of Manchester, raised it again in 1944.[99] This time he would not be dissuaded, and Moran was saved only because the BMA rejected it. Nevertheless, Hill made the most of the occasion, raising doubts about the ability of the colleges to represent consultant opinion.[100]

The challenge from non-teachers was harder to dismiss. Since they were so many in number, Moran thought the BMA might be prompted by McCurrich's association to propose new machinery in place of the 'Beveridge Committee'. His only hope of stopping it was to retain the loyalty of the rest of the consultant world. As he put it in August, 'If we can carry the Provincial teaching centres in spite of Oliver, and if Specialties [i.e. the specialty associations] agree with us, then provided Webb-Johnson does not rat, we must win.'[101]

By then Moran had already succeeded in dividing non-teachers in London from the provinces. At the end of July, he helped form a new association covering the staffs of 157 voluntary hospitals outside the teaching sector in London.[102] It was called the Volims Committee and, once its support was assured, Moran turned over to it the three places reserved for the London area on the 'Beveridge Committee'.[103] In November he also made room for the Association of Municipal Specialists, thereby bringing salaried consultants within his ranks.[104] McCurrich, meanwhile, found it impossible to persuade his colleagues to seek separate bargaining rights. They welcomed his association as a way to spur the 'Beveridge Committee' but they still wanted the colleges to represent them in negotiations with the Ministry.[105]

Fragile unity in the consultant world

None of this did much to raise Moran's spirits; he was depressed by his failure to stop McCurrich. As he told Alderson in July, 'We have missed the bus very badly, primarily owing to Webb-Johnson. I was dissuaded from organising the association of non-teaching hospitals.' But he warned Alderson to keep his concern confidential: 'In particular I don't want any views on B.M.A. and how far they are behind this association to be revealed. I've got to work with them.'[106]

As more and more hospital staffs joined the new association, his gloom deepened, so much so that by December he was ready to leave medical politics completely. Churchill, he hoped, would offer him a way out by making him Provost of Eton. Only a sharp rejection by the Prime Minister's Private Secretary dissuaded Moran from presenting a formal request for the appointment.[107]

All of Moran's fears were realized when negotiations began in January. The BMA's negotiating committee made no attempt to consult the 'Beveridge Committee' and the latter found it impossible to act because of the obstructive tactics adopted by the new members that came from the BMA's Consultant Committee. As Moran later described the impasse, 'It was impossible to control the meeting, because a certain section tried to sabotage it. They wanted to break up the Committee from the beginning.'[108]

Meanwhile, McCurrich's association gathered strength when Lawrence Abel, a candidate for the RCS Council and a prominent figure in BMA circles, took command in London. Moran tried to hold the non-teachers in check by sending college supporters to their meetings, but he rejected a request from the new association to be consulted, agreeing only to pass on the minutes of 'Beveridge Committee' meetings.[109] Hill, however, made sure non-teachers were no longer excluded from consultant gatherings. In March he told Moran that the time had come to seek consultant opinion and that the BMA would arrange joint meetings. Would Moran, he asked, be willing to address those held in London?[110]

None of this did anything to strengthen consultant influence on policy. By May negotiations were at an impasse, the doctors having done little to alter the Ministry's insistence on some form of municipal control (see page 135). The only way for consultants to protect themselves was through the planning work done by the semi-official 'Beveridge' sub-committee. This led the Volims Committee — which had earlier accepted Moran's reasons for exclusion[111] — to demand direct representation, and so urgent did it feel the need that it sent its request by telegram on 24 May.[112]

Bit by bit, then, control of consultant affairs was falling out of Moran's hands. By July, when Willink left office, the fragile unity Moran had so laboriously constructed was near collapse and influence was passing into the hands of those associated with the BMA. The RCP president now must have wondered whether he would ever be able to create a proper consultant service.

Chapter eleven

Who is a consultant?
Who should decide?

With the start of negotiations on the White Paper in January 1945 the time had come for Moran to pursue his aim of a consultant service free from 'consultoid' influence. GP aid in the hospital world, he told the Spens Committee on GP Remuneration in October, was needed only as an interim measure. Once the shortage of qualified men was overcome, GPs who practised as consultants were not wanted:

> I do not believe that you should aim ultimately when the lifetime of these men is over at having general practitioner consultants. *I think you must aim at a sharp division eventually.* I want to make it perfectly clear that he cannot practise as both.[1]

GMC blocks Moran's plan

From 1941 Moran led a movement in this direction, using the hospital survey as an excuse to compile a list of qualified consultants. In so far as possible, 'consultoids' would be excluded and the list would eventually serve as a register from which hospital appointments would be made under the new health service.

Moran feared the BMA would frustrate his plan. In 1931, when the Hospital Savings Association sought to obtain a 'closed' panel of true consultants for its low-cost specialist service, the BMA had baulked, and by offering a fee of only one guinea per consultation in place of the prevailing three guinea rate, it managed to open the panel to the 'consultoid' class.[2] Moran did not want the BMA involved in the preparation of consultant lists.

But he did not want the GMC to participate either. On the face of it, this was surprising, since the GMC had maintained a statutory register of a general nature since 1858, and if a specialist section were contemplated, it was the natural body to carry out the work. But in Moran's view it contained too many members who might be hostile to his plan. Of the thirty-nine on the GMC, only nine came from the colleges, while seven were directly elected by the profession, and they were usually GPs with BMA backing. Moran could not be sure that the remaining twenty-three members — eighteen from university faculties, five appointed by the King (including some laymen) — would always side with the colleges. From the nineteenth century, relations between the colleges and the universities (particularly in London) had been punctuated by disputes over who should hold examinations and award practice qualifications.[3] Nor were all the college appointees suitable in Moran's eyes; at one point in 1944 he expressed doubts about the 'three elderly English surgeons' on the GMC.[4]

For Moran, the safest way to conduct the study was for the colleges to do it alone, and because of the financial constraints under which the RCS and RCOG operated, he had the RCP bear all the costs itself, devoting £3,500 to the work.[5] But Moran soon realized that Ministry backing would be needed, not least because of the official stamp of authority this would convey. In February 1942 he managed to secure Jameson's blessing because the Ministry needed to know the number and distribution of hospital doctors to plan the new service.[6] It is possible that Jameson made this gesture without being aware of the larger implications of Moran's proposal.

Initially, the study was to be conducted by a triumvirate consisting of Moran, Mr (later Sir) Ernest Rock Carling (formerly dean of the Westminster Medical Schol but then a surgeon on the war-time staff of the Ministry and one who enjoyed the full confidence of the RCS), and Sir Francis Fraser, director-general of the EMS.[7] Having secured Ministry backing, Moran no doubt hoped the GMC could be ignored — but he was wrong. No sooner did its fiery registrar, Michael Heseltine, hear about the study than he sent a strong memorandum to the department, asserting the GMC's right to maintain anything that resembled a register of specialists.[8] Since Heseltine had once been a most able member of the Ministry's staff, his claim could not be lightly dismissed. Pater, in an internal memorandum, had to acknowledge the strength of the GMC case.[9] Jameson now faced an uphill task persuading his lay colleagues to let the study proceed.

Moran thought he knew the way. In March 1943 he added university professors to his directing group and changed its name to the Central Medical Academic Council (CMAC).[10] On the local level, where area committees had to be created to select appropriate names, university members were also included. This machinery was needed because in many places few doctors who practised as consultants had college or other qualifications. Some method of 'local recognition' had to be devised and Moran put vice-chancellors in charge of the committees that chose them. Jameson told his lay colleagues they should convey sufficient authority to let the study proceed.[11]

Maude was embarrassed and did not know how to respond. For weeks he did nothing, hoping the dispute would fade away. But Heseltine would not be deterred. In June, he sent another memorandum, setting forth the whole affair,[12] and this was followed by a letter from the vice-chancellors, expressing concern about the larger implications of Moran's study. On 28 June, in a letter which found its way into Ministry hands, Lord Percy of the University of Durham wrote angrily to Moran:

It seems to me that the whole scheme has changed in character since the Vice-Chancellors originally considered it. It is no longer simply a question of ascertaining the present distribution of consultants for the information of the Ministry of Health. It has become the first step in the preparation of a register, exclusion from which will exclude a medical man from consultant practice. If you allow me to say so, I think you have hardly appreciated how serious this change is.[13]

Percy also expressed concern about the legal status of the choices made. If they were not 'privileged', then doctors excluded from the list might resort to libel action. The Scottish members of the GMC had an additional cause of alarm; if the English colleges prepared the lists, they might exclude holders of Scottish qualifications from posts in England.[14]

Moran lost no time in writing to the Minister, rejecting the GMC's claim. He had taken legal advice, he told Brown, and found that the GMC had no right to prepare a statutory list of consultants; its authority was limited to the purpose for which it was created — the maintenance of a general register. As for the Scottish concern, there was no cause for alarm; the college study would cover only England, Wales, and Northern Ireland. Scotland would make its own arrangements and the English colleges would be glad to help them.[15]

Moran's arguments were to no avail. The next day, Sir Herbert Eason, the GMC's long-standing president, led a heated deputation to the department, declaring that nothing short of a statutory register would suffice. The colleges, the deputation warned, could not be left to prepare lists that would have a formal effect once the new health service was established; they, after all, were only professional and examining bodies, not teaching institutions like the universities that dominated the GMC.[16]

In the face of this pressure, Maude was forced to admit the Ministry's error: 'We had not realised originally quite how big a formal undertaking this would be — otherwise, the G.M.C. would have been consulted.'[17]

Moran's study was now in peril. The only way to save it was to drop all thought of a register for hospital appointments and concentrate on the survey needed by the Ministry. Brown asked Moran to proceed on these lines[18] but Eason and Heseltine were not satisfied and Maude had to assure them of Ministry backing when the time came to create a statutory register.[19] However, in view of the shortage of consultants, that moment was sure to be long deferred; as Moran later indicated, it would take ten to fifteen years to develop an adequate corps.[20] Meanwhile, 'consultoids' in one form or another would have to be used.

Moran seeks BMA aid

Moran had long recognized the need for 'consultoid' aid and that meant the BMA could not be ignored. In many areas, 'local recognition' was the only test that could be used for inclusion on the consultant list and the BMA's consultant groups contained those most likely to be familiar with the doctors who practised there.[21]

When the CMAC was formed in March 1943, Moran made room for the BMA's leading spokesmen — its secretary (then Anderson) and its chairman of council (then Souttar).[22] Flattery was used to win Anderson's support; shortly thereafter, he was made an honorary fellow of the RCP.[23]

But after Hill took over at the start of 1944 it was clear that flattery would not be enough to win BMA backing. Moran raised the number of BMA representatives on the CMAC from two to five, but took care to exclude McCurrich.[24] He also made room for spokesmen from the various specialty organizations.

Hill now found himself in a difficult position. As a disciple of the Brackenbury school of general practice, he had no special concern for 'consultoids' and no doubt was ready to see them excluded from the hospital world.[25] He wanted the colleges to go ahead with the preparation of consultant lists, and made this clear in a private interview in January 1944. He also placed the blame for the dispute with the GMC on Heseltine who, he claimed, had 'an unbalanced mind and looks for every opportunity of making trouble with the Ministry of Health'.[26]

But Hill dared not say this in public because of the BMA presence on the GMC, two of its leading Council members, Dain and J.W. Bone, being members. During a heated exchange at the CMAC on 8 February, Dain dismissed the college list exercise as a waste of time since the BMA's Central Medical War Committee had already compiled one.[27]

Even stronger opposition had been expressed by the TUC's medical adviser and Labour MP, Dr H.B.W. Morgan. In a wildly emotional letter to Brown in August, he gave vent to all his bitterness at the way his specialty, industrial medicine, had been ignored by the colleges and the GMC. Neither, he told the Minister, were fit to select consultants since all the bodies involved were undemocratic, with the exception of the BMA.[28]

When the consultant survey was formally announced in the medical press in January 1944, Heseltine found the time ripe to have an MP ask a question in Parliament, and this forced Willink to give assurance that the lists would not be used to make hospital appointments.[29] Percy, to this point, had refused to include names in the list he compiled, but after a plea from Jameson he complied.[30]

But Heseltine and his colleagues were not satisfied. No matter what assurances Willink gave, the lists still had the semblance of an unofficial register and the only body qualified to maintain that, they believed, was the GMC. Heseltine therefore put forth a demand for enabling legislation. In an attempt to stop it, Moran turned to Churchill for aid, supplying him with notes for an address he was to deliver at the RCP in March. But before the speech was prepared, the Ministry of Health was given the chance to comment and the civil servants there made sure the Prime Minister stayed out of the dispute. As Michael Reed, Willink's private secretary, put it in a letter to Churchill's office, 'Generally, my Minister feels that the notes prepared by Lord Moran are rather dangerous material as they stand.'[31]

Thereafter, no documents appear in the Ministry of Health's file. But the dispute did not die, and Moran was angry at Jameson for leaving the question unsettled, accusing him of saying one thing to the colleges and the opposite to the GMC.[33] Years later, when Moran recalled the events of the 1940s, it was evident that he harboured a deep distaste for the CMO.[33]

RCOG fears Moran's consultant lists

In January 1945 Moran was dealt another blow when the RCOG Council broke ranks; it suddenly reversed its policy, and came out for a register by a statutory body.[34] The Council was sharply divided on the issue but what tipped the scales was a fear of the secrecy surrounding the lists prepared by the two older colleges. Since RCOG qualifications were not yet registrable, some obstetricians and gynaecologists wondered whether their names might be excluded.

Beyond that, there was a fundamental difference between the manpower needs of the RCOG and the other two colleges, certainly where the RCP was concerned. The RCOG did not so much want to exclude the GP-specialist as make him more competent. The demands of midwifery and the severe shortage of obstetric consultants made it impossible for RCOG leaders to be exclusive. How could they bar GPs from midwifery when so many labours were conducted in homes? Some doctor had to be on call for minor emergencies. As one RCOG leader (James Wyatt) told the Spens Committee on GP Remuneration, 'there should be something between the specialists and the person who has no special knowledge at all'.[35]

Holland's way of ensuring this was to confine the work to doctors with six months of postgraduate experience. For years he had been trying to have his college adopt the principle, but had encountered much resistance.[36] Fletcher Shaw, his predecessor in the presidential office, thought the move would be 'suicidal',[37] since the older colleges were satisfied with four-month preregistration appointments and the Goodenough Committee had suggested the same for midwifery. But one of Holland's colleagues, Professor Andrew Claye, urged him to stand fast: 'We can be fairly sure that if we do not strive for this ideal, no one else will.'[38]

Aided by another colleague, Professor James Young, Holland had managed to have the principle adopted in 1944 and was determined to see it implemented in the new health service. If he could secure something like a statutory register for GP midwifery, he would be satisfied. He was therefore inclined to accept Moran's plea to abandon the demand for a larger register and persuaded his Council to reverse its stand again. But his colleagues added an important proviso; they would not recognize any existing list of consultants.[39] If Moran still had hopes of having his lists determine hospital appointments, he must have been badly shaken.[40]

Those hopes were dealt a final blow when the lists finally appeared. Most of the doctors on them did not have a college qualification or anything that would justify their ranking as a consultant. It was experience only that counted and as a result, the lists showed 'a considerable variation in standard'.[41] Moran now realized that it would be difficult to explain why one doctor had been put in and another left out except that the decision had been made by a committee sitting in a university town.[42]

Heseltine and his colleagues were still wary of Moran's lists, and in 1946 they had a bill prepared giving the GMC power to create a specialist register.[43] But nothing ever came of it. The decision as to who would rank as a consultant was left to the administrative bodies that would make hospital appointments. In this way the structure and control of the hospital service became the focal point of college concern. Moran now put all his efforts in that direction.

Chapter twelve

The struggle for regional control

Consultants, like GPs, had long opposed municipal control of health services, demanding wider areas of administration on regional lines. But unlike GPs, they had economics on their side because hospitals needed large populations to operate efficiently.

It had long been recognized that the areas covered by local authorities, aside from large cities like London, were too small for efficient hospital administration. Since the 1930s the BMA had been calling for the reorganization of local government.[1] The EMS, when it was created in 1938, lent force to the movement since it brought a regional perspective to hospital operation.[2] Even more influential was the Cancer Act of 1939, since the costly radium treatment it provided required a large patient intake to justify expenditure.[3]

The doctors thus had every reason to reiterate their stand when they published their MPC report in 1942 and, on this occasion, they called for all health services to be managed on a regional basis, not just the hospital sector.[4] But no one expected this to be done through the creation of regional bodies concerned with health alone. Not even a royal commission that favoured regional administration dared to make such a suggestion; in 1937, one on local government in Tyneside thought it could be done only if other services (education, police, fire brigade, highways) were linked with health.[5]

For most people, even that was not enough; somehow the concept had to be allied with all of local government, and this meant new boundaries had to be formed. But how could such a mammoth task be carried out in the midst of war? It would take years to reconcile conflicting interests, and that made the doctors ready to accept joint board administration as long as the 'outsiders' — doctors and voluntary hospitals — received one-third of the places.[6]

Moran clashes with the BMA

Such was the mood when discussion with the Ministry began in 1943 and that, combined with Maude's passion for local government, may explain why Dawson as well as Moran were resigned to municipal rule (see page 120). But there was another consideration where Moran was concerned; at that point the Ministry's plan dealt mainly with general practice, and he wanted to see GPs securely ensconced in health centres before hospital planning began. Only in that way could consultants be sure that GPs would confine their speciality interests to the narrow limits set by local authority clinics. Child care, in Moran's view, was safe for GPs to undertake; surgical operations and the more heroic forms of medical treatment were not. As he told the Spens Committee on GP Remuneration in 1945, 'My point is let your child welfare man specialise in things, but you must sharply differentiate what things can be specialised by picking up as one goes and what requires an original basic training.'[7] This, more than the concern he showed for team work in general practice, explains why Moran continued to promote health centres long after GPs lost interest.[8] If general practice *per se* could be made more attractive, then few GPs would feel the need to take on the role of consultant.

Once planning of the consultant service began in 1944, Moran's mood changed. Then he would tolerate no thought of municipal control, and insisted on regional administration. The royal colleges, he told Willink, consider this 'the most vital part of the White Paper' and wanted more power to the regional body under the two-tiered plan.[9] At that point, only the area authority with its 60 per cent municipal majority was to have planning powers, and it would receive funds directly from the Ministry. In Moran's view, this would place the voluntary hospitals and consultants at its mercy. The regional tier, he demanded, must have more influence; there, a two-thirds medical–voluntary hospital majority would rule and Moran wanted the regional body to have planning duties as well as advisory functions on finance. Even more important, he wanted consultant appointments made at regional level; under no conditions must they be dependent on municipal choice.

At the end of January 1945 Moran went to Yalta with Churchill and left his registrar, Dr Harold Boldero, in charge of RCP affairs. At a meeting with the Ministry on 6 February, Dain and Hill failed to give Boldero the support on regional powers which Moran expected, leaving that tier with no place in the funding process. When Boldero reported this to Moran, the RCP president was white with rage and suspected Hill of collusion with Rucker. As for Dain, Moran wrote 'he did not support you over finance and I have no doubt doesn't care a damn about Regions even if he doesn't really want them to have no power'.[10]

Moran suspected that the 6 February meeting had been delayed so that it would coincide with his absence and he wanted the next meeting postponed until he returned. If this were not done, he instructed Boldero, Willink should be told the College would withdraw from negotiations, but he did not think the BMA would follow suit: 'I am quite certain Hill is seeing Rucker (I wish we could establish this) and telling him that the B.M.A. will not pull out over Regions.' Hill, he told Boldero, should be handled 'roughly': 'Hill will only be influenced if he feels that any action of mine may do him harm with his constituency.'[11]

Underlying this exchange was a tension in the medical world that had not appeared before; Moran predicted it would emerge as soon as the colleges insisted on a proper training for consultants.[12] During 1943 the focus of attention had been on the GP sector and BMA leaders were more concerned about municipal control there than in the hospital sector. Moran and his college colleagues felt the opposite, and this created a situation in which one group of medical leaders may have been tempted to 'sell-out' the other. Thus, Moran would have been satisfied if only hospital services were administered on the regional level, whereas BMA leaders wanted all of health provision there.[13]

However, the test never came because the Ministry refused to bargain; it was too afraid of offending municipal feelings. The department left the decision to local authorities and, at a separate meeting with them on 27 April, the doctors discovered that neither the CCA nor the AMC would consider any erosion of area powers: 'The local authorities could not contemplate a position under which the regional body, with its less intimate knowledge of area conditions and requirements, would be empowered to submit to the Minister's plan in opposition to the proposals of the area body.'[14] All they would allow the regional council to do was make its disagreement known to the Minister.

In Moran's absence, the BMA leaders on the negotiating committee were inclined to compromise in May,[15] but the RCP president was in no mood to bargain. He rejected the two-tiered plan and condemned the department for its municipal stance. Looking back on events from the vantage point of 1946, he described the situation as follows:

> Some members of the Committee in the course of these negotiations received the impression that the Ministry was like a horse tethered to a peg, the Local Authorities; they could not wander far without being pulled up with a jolt, and the peg seemed driven so firmly into the ground that it did not give at all . . . on this central issue, whether the Region was or not to have power, the Ministry did not budge an inch.[16]

Willink thus left office in July with negotiations deadlocked. To someone with Moran's aspirations, national control of the hospital service must have seemed the only way out. The fragile unity he had fostered in the consultant world was on the point of collapse and, encouraged by Ministry backing, the GMC had refused to abandon its pursuit of a statutory register. Dawson, in 1944, had rejected the idea of national direction when the voluntary hospitals, led by the BHA, had demanded a Central Hospitals Board to protect themselves from municipal influence: 'The central control of hospitals would take the heart out of local government and lead to an inanimate uniformity.'[17] But he, too, was alarmed by the limited powers given to the profession in Willink's plan and, had he lived on, might have seen no alternative to central direction.

Ironically, the medical world was witnessing a repetition of the events of 1911 when BMA leaders had to seek central control of the panel system to free GPs from friendly society domination.[18] Moran now found himself forced to pursue a similar course for consultants.

A national solution

When Bevan took over in August, there was every reason to expect him to come down on the municipal side. Like the Labour Party in general, the new Minister had given no hint in the socialist paper he edited, *Tribune*, that he was committed to anything but local authority rule.[19] Yet no sooner did he enter the department than his thoughts turned in a national direction.

Perhaps, as has been claimed, one of his civil servants made the suggestion (see page 173). Or Bevan may have come to the idea with the help of medical friends. But Moran also had the chance to influence him during private meetings at Prunier's Restaurant,[20] and he certainly gave the Minister every support once the decision was known.

The same could not be said of his medical colleagues; many doctors found the nationalization idea hard to accept. Though they preferred central to municipal direction, they hated to see voluntary hospitals disappear. At first, this feeling was not evident; in January 1946 the consultants on the BMA's negotiating committee were ready to let the voluntary hospitals go to remove the municipal threat.[21] McCurrich was particularly averse to local authority rule and he carried his non-teaching colleagues with him. As for the college members, they could not but welcome the special status given to teaching hospitals.

Considerably more dissent was expressed when the 'Beveridge Committee' considered the proposal in March. Webb-Johnson led the opposition. Souttar as well as Hill tried to devise a face-saving formula that would leave the ownership of hospital assets, particularly trust funds, in hospital hands.[22] Thanks to a proposal from the King's Fund,[23] Bevan had made the concession to teaching hospitals and the doctors wanted to extend it more widely. As it turned out, the demand failed; the Minister insisted that trust funds outside the teaching sector be spread across a region as a whole (see page 139).

Moran had to employ all his oratorical skills to turn his colleagues around. You cannot, he told the 'Beveridge Committee', have public money without public control: 'It must be either the local authorities or the Minister.'[24] Only a Labour minister, he argued, could impose a national solution; even Latham had accepted the loss of the LCC's vaunted hospital service out of party loyalty. With McCurrich proposing the motion, Moran put the concept across, only one member (probably Webb-Johnson) still registering dissent.

RCP follows Moran's lead

Thereafter opposition mounted due to feeling stirred by the BHA. At an informal meeting in February, its chairman, Sir Bernard Docker, had failed to persuade the doctors to break the pledge of secrecy which surrounded Bevan's proposals,[25] but the BHA's secretary, J.P. Wetenhall, dropped all restraint after the White Paper was published in March. A few days before the RCP Comitia was due to consider the Bill, he sent a circular letter to fellows urging rejection.[26] Moran thought it prudent to defer a decision until May and, meanwhile, he mounted a meeting of RCP members to marshall support. With Dr (later Sir) Richard Doll speaking on behalf of young doctors in the armed forces, who saw the new health service as a way to secure consultant status, Moran managed to have a motion endorsing nationalization carried by a large majority.[27]

Still, power rested with the fellows in the Comitia and there the outcome was uncertain. As a result of Wetenhall's campaign, feeling among non-teaching consultants was turning against nationalization. In March the Council of McCurrich's Association had approved the proposal as long as RHB composition was satisfactory, but in May it reversed its stand as the result of opposition from area committees.[28] The surgeons who made up the majority of the Association were less sympathetic to nationalization than physicians and no longer willing to follow McCurrich's lead.[29]

Moran felt he could take no chances. Shortly before the Comitia met, he wrote to some fifty fellows urging them to endorse Bevan's hospital plan and let him negotiate.[30] To one such fellow, he gave a warning of the Tory reaction if the opposition won: 'I happen to know, though the information came to me privately, that if the profession does have a head on collision with Bevan and rejects the Bill that the Conservative Party will not back them in this attitude.'[31] That, among other factors, turned the tide, and the Comitia dutifully gave Moran power to negotiate.

But his ordeal was not over. The BMA, at a special representative meeting in May, registered a resounding vote (210–29) against Bevan's hospital plan.[32] This gave Horder reason to mount another challenge to Moran, and in 1948 he almost fulfilled his lifelong ambition of becoming RCP president. Once again, Moran had to write furiously to fellows to hold office,[33] but years later he did not hesitate to admit that the majority opposed the NHS with its nationalization concept.[34]

RCOG supports nationalization

Though obstetricians and gynaecologists had much to complain about, they did not resist Bevan's hospital proposal.[35] What worried them was the division of maternity services produced by NHS's tripartite structure. In the years between the wars, they had striven to develop a unified service, finding in the 1936 Midwives Act a way to narrow the gap between hospital and domiciliary care. Some means were still needed to bring in GPs, but Bevan's plan threatened to undo all their good work. Holland registered a strong protest when the negotiating committee met the Minister in January 1946.[36]

Still, Holland and his colleagues were as anxious as Moran to remove the hospitals from municipal control. Though some local authorities had done yeoman work in the maternity field, most had failed to use specialist advice in the manner desired by the RCOG. Too many MOHs had acted on their own or relied on GP-specialists for aid.

RCOG leaders hoped the EMS would give them the chance to put matters right.

With its provision for regional consultant advisers, obstetricians and gynaecologists would join physicians and surgeons in devising new arrangements. But to their bitter disappointment, maternity care was left out of the EMS and put in an emergency service under local authority control.[37] Few MOHs would have tolerated any other arrangement. Municipal services had developed furthest in the maternity sphere, and it was hard to classify the birth of babies as a war casualty.

Still, at one point in 1942, it looked like the organization of emergency maternity services would follow the EMS pattern. Obstetrical advisers had been appointed in Scotland and it was expected that similar posts would be created in England and Wales. The Ministry, indeed, accepted the principle — but then took fourteen months to work out the details. The delay meant Treasury approval could not be expected since it could argue that the emergency had passed.[38] Fletcher Shaw had foreseen the consequences before the war began:

> I am unhappy about these [emergency maternity] schemes. Unless we can so arrange matters that these women are put under the care of trained obstetricians, we shall find that after the war the whole maternity service is taken from the obstetricians and left entirely in the hands of local authorities.[39]

Holland thus had as much to gain as Moran from a hospital service under national control. Indeed, with Jameson's support, he went further and had a provision inserted in the Bill that promised to alter the pattern of GP care. In future, midwifery practice was to be confined to selected GPs.[40] In the face of BMA demands, he was forced to let experience count as much as an RCOG diploma,[41] but Holland thought his successor, Gilliatt, went too far by accepting pre-registration posts as well. 'Even as a result of expediency', Holland declared, 'he did not feel the principle should have been conceded.'[42]

Nevertheless, at that point in the negotiating process (1947), some measure of selection survived and it had been accepted by the BMA representatives involved.[43] But before the NHS began, all restrictions were dropped; any GP could do midwifery and all who did so were paid for the work (see pages 108–10). The only semblance of selection left was the establishment of an obstetric list, with higher payments made to GPs who qualified to have their names enrolled. But even that test failed to hold when the Ministry refused to give guidance to local committees charged with the duty of preparing lists.[44] In most areas, doctors found it easy to have their names added; by 1975, 75 per cent of GPs in England and Wales were included.[45]

RCOG leaders were furious, but their College was too weak to resist. All Gilliatt could do was write a tame letter of protest to the *The Times*.[46] In it he was careful to exclude any criticism of the department 'as it was felt that there was nothing to be gained by quarrelling with the Ministry officers at this stage'.[47]

Surgeons resist nationalization

Many surgeons resisted the NHS with its national hospital idea and deplored the loss of voluntary hospitals.[48] Webb-Johnson had greater difficulty than the other presidents in rallying college support and, according to one RCS fellow, Reginald Payne, he did so in an irregular manner. The main resistance to Bevan's plan came from surgeons; alone among college fellows, those in the RCS opposed entry to the Act when the final vote was taken in the April 1948 plebiscite. And it was Webb-Johnson's severest critic, Payne, who, in November helped Horder gather all the medical dissidents into a new organization called the Fellowship for Freedom in Medicine.[49]

The immediate cause of surgeon resistance lay in their expectations of private practice. More than other specialists, surgeons had hopes of supplementing NHS income from private sources and they did not want a national hospital service to deprive them of beds. It was Webb-Johnson, not Moran, who persuaded Bevan to leave nursing homes alone and permit pay beds in NHS hospitals.[50] And it was Webb-Johnson who forced the colleges to back the BHA demand for trust funds to remain under hospital control.[51] In that way, consultants could be sure that voluntary hospitals would have the means to maintain pay beds after national direction passed into Ministry hands. Bevan rejected this demand; only teaching hospitals were allowed to retain control of trust funds — with the hope, no doubt, that they would be used mainly for research and education. Otherwise, the funds were pooled into a Hospital Endowments Fund and the income assigned to RHBs to spend as they pleased.[52]

But there was a more fundamental reason for the distinctive stance taken by surgeons; unlike physicians (or obstetricians), they did not have the same need to exclude GPs from hospital practice because they were protected by the nature of their speciality. Where surgical operations were concerned, GPs had undermined their position by the damage they had done in cottage hospitals; their failings were not so obvious when it came to medical care.

As early as 1928,[53] Moran had called attention to this difference and he reiterated the point in 1946:

> You can see whether a man is cutting with an established technique. It is awfully difficult to say whether X or Y is not competent to give a first class opinion as many people are. There is no way of judging a physician as there is a surgeon.[54]

No matter how the hospital service was structured, surgeons could be reasonably certain that only qualified men would be used for major operations. Moran noted in 1945 that every report which appeared during the war was 'critical of people doing surgery without adequate training'.[55] Physicians had no such certainty where hospital appointments were concerned; as long as the decision remained in local hands, 'consultoids', might be used. Voluntary hospitals were no different in this respect. Indeed, their management committees were more likely to appoint

GP-specialists than municipal counterparts. They could also be more arbitrary than municipal counterparts. (They could also be more arbitrary than municipal counterparts. One physician had such bitter experience that he told Moran in 1943 that he preferred local authority management with safeguards to the unfettered rule of the voluntary hospital's lay committee. This surprising preference was expressed by an ardent opponent of bureaucratic control, a doctor who later emerged as a severe critic of the NHS – Dr Ffrangon Roberts.[56]) Moran needed national control and regional appointment boards to create a clear distinction between physicians and GPs.

In an attempt to rally support, Moran cited the views of Rock Carling, his partner in the preparation of consultant lists and a surgeon who enjoyed the confidence of the RCS.[57] Like Moran, Carling was disturbed by Willink's two-tiered plan with its dearth of powers at regional level. For Moran, this meant the need for a national solution, and Carling agreed — although he did not like the way the RCP president made public use of his views.[58]

Webb-Johnson had to act even more cautiously and that may account for the strong stand he took against Bevan's plan before the 'Beveridge Committee' in March 1946.[59] But once support was given, he went along with the decision[60] and followed Moran's lead. RCS fellows had few opportunities to protest, and those that did complained about the secrecy surrounding College decisions.[61] When they did finally have the chance to vote in April 1948, they made it clear that they wanted nothing to do with Bevan's plan.[62]

But with Webb-Johnson striving to keep the College out of economic affairs, the RCS offered no vehicle for opposition. If surgeons wanted to resist the Act, they had to do so through the BMA, and there they found consultants of all kinds from the non-teaching world ready to join them. As negotiations proceeded, provincial consultants grew ever more fearful of college domination, particularly after Moran, acting through official channels, managed to foster a system of distinction awards for the top third of consultants. This was the result of a recommendation made by the Spens Committee on Consultant Remuneration. Though Rucker tried to stop Moran's appointment to the Committee, he failed and the Chairman, Sir Will Spens, could not contain the RCP president. At one point, Spens complained about Moran's determination 'to share in writing the report' and wanted a new member (to replace one who had resigned) to act as 'a counterweight'. Spens suggested Maude or Sir Ernest Gowers but neither was available and Moran's influence predominated.[63] Non-teachers felt they had little chance of selection and through the BMA's Central Consultant Committee (with *BMJ* support), made their opposition known[64]

As a result, Moran again almost found his organizing work undone. Since the war, more and more consultants had joined the BMA; by 1947, over 80 per cent were in its ranks, a higher proportion than was the case with GPs.[65] This encouraged BMA leaders to form a new system of regional consultant committees to deal with RHBs. Thirty-five years earlier it had provided the same service for GPs in the form of local panel committees under the 1911 Insurance Act and that had led to BMA dominance in medical politics. At the centre, the local panel committees had a voice — the Insurance Acts Committee (after 1948, called the General Medical Services Committee) — which bore the brunt of negotiations with the Ministry, and the BMA formed a similar central committee for consultants.[66] If this action went unchallenged, the BMA would become the bargaining agent for consultants as well as GPs, and non-teachers would have a majority.

Webb-Johnson, as always, was content to let the BMA take the lead; he did not want his College involved in financial affairs.[67] Moran, on the other hand, wanted to displace the BMA and have the colleges act alone, but even the RCP lacked the funds and staff required; consultants, like GPs, needed the BMA's able secretariat.[68] The only way college control could be maintained was through a majority of places on a joint committee and that, with Hill's co-operation, was arranged. On the new body, the colleges were given eleven seats and the BMA only six; not until 1962, when many 'consultoids' had retired, was the BMA share raised to ten.[69] But non-teacher distaste for distinction awards remained, and in 1956 the BMA's representative body called for its abolition. It took all of Moran's oratorical powers to persuade the BMA to reverse its stand.[70]

Phasing out 'consultoids'

Once NHS began, there was no question but that hospital appointments would be made, and distinction awards decided, in the manner Moran desired. Because of the shortage of consultants, 'consultoids' had to be used, but they were employed in a sub-consultant grade, given the derogatory title 'SHMO', acronymn for senior hospital medical officer, and phased out as soon as the growth of consultant firms permitted.[71] Some 2,000 were admitted to the hospital service when NHS began,[72] but many did not apply out of fear of losing compensation for loss of the right to sell practices. Only doctors who entered NHS as GPs were eligible, not those who opted for the hospital service.[73]

Talbot Rogers, himself a GP-specialist, tried to preserve a place for 'consultoids' in health centres as well as hospitals, but failed because of opposition from GPs as much as consultants. Frank Gray and other BMA leaders did not want GPs to work in hospital; like Brackenbury, they thought general practice had a more important role to play in the community.[74]

Through a public service with hospitals under national control, Moran thus realized his dream of a consultant service free from 'consultoid' influence. The division in British medicine was finally complete. Underlying Moran's view was a belief in the hierarchical structure of the profession with specialists at the top and GPs at the bottom: 'general practice', he declared, 'was entered by those who failed on the specialist ladder'.[75] His judgement was not unique; a similar statement may be found in the war-time records of the Fabian Society.[76] But at least one socialist disagreed; in 1946, Dr Stephen Taylor told the Fabian Society, 'it is quite as difficult to be a good general practitioner as it is to be a good specialist'. Both, he argued, should receive the same pay under NHS. But Taylor could not ignore the failings of general practice. Citing the views of Canadian doctors who had been in Britain during the war, he noted that 'they were absolutely appalled at the average level of British working-class practice'.[77]

Later, a College of General Practice was formed to give substance to Taylor's claim, but it failed to impress Moran. He had set forth his 'ladder' thesis behind the closed doors of the Spens Committee in 1948, and repeated it a decade later before the Royal Commission on Doctors' and Dentists' Remuneration.[78] This time, since the hearings were held in public, Moran's remarks raised a storm of protest. (The writer was present at that historic meeting and witnessed the furore that followed.)

What we see here is a remarkable persistence of the pecking order in British medicine. In Moran's view, the advance of specialization had done nothing to alter the old social class divisions; instead, it reinforced them. Nevertheless, he felt uneasy about the separation he sought, fearing that it would take serious cases out of GP hands and make his role uninteresting: 'If that goes on there is a real danger the general practitioner's work will become less attractive and that will affect the men going into the profession.'[79] In 1945 his way of coping was to give GPs a stake in minor specialties like child welfare; only later did he see the need to bring some GPs — the better ones — into the hospital world.

Chapter thirteen

Bevan's concessions — more to consultants or GPs?

We have seen how the interests of GPs and consultants diverged during negotiations over the NHS. Bevan was aware of the differences and skilfully exploited them, doing all he could to satisfy consultants and then relying on their goodwill to force GP acquiesence. It has been suggested that this was the deciding factor in the struggle; if Bevan had not 'stuffed their [consultants'] mouths with gold',[1] he might not have created the NHS. In this chapter we shall examine the validity of that thesis.

Concessions to consultants

Bevan made the most important concession to consultants before negotiations began; he removed the threat of municipal control and brought all (or nearly all) hospitals under state ownership. Many consultants preferred to leave the voluntary hospitals intact, but in view of their parlous financial state that was not feasible. Nor was it possible to envisage a voluntary hospital takeover of the municipal sector. Even dissidents within the consultant world accepted the need for an integrated service[2] and the only way to secure it was through national or municipal means. Given that choice, nearly all consultants would have preferred the former.

Bevan also took care to protect consultants from the way the hospitals were administered. Though municipal members were given a place on RHBs and HMCs, they were kept in a minority and not appointed in a representative capacity. Moreover, the absence of a financial tie weakened their interest in administration; after 1948 it was found that they were not the most zealous attenders of NHS meetings.[3] Daley, in February 1946, predicted this would happen: he told Boldero not to worry about the municipal demand for a majority of places on RHBs because local authorities were divided and, since they did not have to put up the money, municipal members would be inclined to accept medical advice. Financial concern, he explained, had underlain their resistance to the regional tier in Willink's plan; if given more power, regional authorities might make rate demands.[4] For the same reason, municipal leaders had expressed concern about the precepting powers in Brown's joint board plan (see page 54). Now that

Bevan had swept financial considerations aside, the doctors could be sure of a dominant role in the hospital sector.

Where London was concerned, the Minister was even more considerate of consultant wishes; he put its twelve undergraduate teaching hospitals, along with teaching hospitals generally, each under a separately-administered board of governors and divided the rest of the city's hospitals into four sectors on the EMS pattern Moran had fashioned. When the LCC asked to be consulted on the way this was done, Rucker refused[5]; he wanted to avoid the suspicion that the LCC might be perpetuated as an administrative unit.[6]

Throughout the administrative structure generally, every effort was made to give the consultants the influence they desired. Not only were they allowed advisory as well administrative representation within the RHB–HMC structure, but those in teaching hospitals received the same direct representation rights on boards of governors as GPs had on executive councils. Of the first 364 appointments to hospital bodies, 120 went to doctors.[7]

Consultants also stood much to gain from the imminent expansion of the hospital medical corps. Though the country had some 7,000 doctors who called themselves specialists, only about half were properly qualified,[8] and it was recognized that twice that number would be needed.[9] But growth would not only come at the top: more juniors had to be trained and they were needed to cope with the expected mass of hospital work.

Consultants were thus to be leaders of teams of 'firms' or doctors that would have beds of their own and operate with almost complete autonomy.[10] Such freedom had long existed in voluntary hospitals, but payment was not normally provided; that was the price consultants had to pay to escape the rule of medical superintendents in the municipal sector and to keep GPs out of the larger hospitals. Now payment was to be combined with freedom; the voluntary hospital method of staffing was to extend over the hospital world as a whole.[11] Though no one recognized it at the time, this was the counterpart to consultants of the compensation given to GPs for loss of the right to sell practices.

Furthermore, the payment provided was as generous as Bevan led consultants to expect. When the Bill passed through Parliament, the Minister acknowledged the need to raise consultant earnings[12] and the Spens Committee on Consultant Remuneration concurred when its recommendations were published in June 1948. Initially, the Committee thought a salary of £800 would be sufficient for a junior doctor in training at age 30, but this was raised to £1,200 as a result of a plea by Moran.[13] With the salary scale based at an £800 level, he feared the loss of manpower to general practice.

For consultants the amounts were more generous, with startng salaries of £1,500 at age 32, rising to £2,500 after eight years, and to that were to be added distinction awards of £500, £1,000, or £2,000 for 34 per cent of the corps.[14] A consultant at the top of the scale thus had the prospect of a £4,500 income (plus whatever he could earn from private practice) instead of the £3,000 the Ministry had in mind in 1943.[15] As in the case of GPs, these amounts were far above those prevailing before the war, when the average consultant had a net income of some £2,000, and nearly one-third earned less than £1,500 at the peak of their income capacity.[16]

It had long been recognized that consultants would be easier to woo than GPs.[17] They needed hospital facilities and if the voluntary sector was to disappear, that would leave only beds in poorly-equipped nursing homes. Once the decision was taken to bring nearly all hospitals under state control, most consultants had no choice; in particular, those who wanted to retain posts in the country's prestigious teaching hospitals would have to enter the NHS. GPs might be engaged as independent contractors but not consultants; they had to accept a more direct form of employment on a sessional or salaried basis.

But like GPs, consultants wanted an escape route in case state service proved unsatisfactory. And in view of the shortage of hospital beds and expected long waits for operations in the new service, many consultants — particularly surgeons — had reason to hope that the private sector would survive. Bevan had no wish to outlaw the custom, but he did not want to see it grow. His aim was 'to provide so good a service that nobody would want to buy anybody else'.[18] His civil servants shared this concern because of their experience with the panel system; they did not want to perpetuate the double standard of care that had plagued its operation.

But there was a harsh fact that no planner could ignore; Britain had only 3,500 consultants to treat a population of 47 million and it was essential to make full use of their time. Just to lure the majority of consultants into the NHS, Bevan had to offer the option of part-time contracts on a sessional basis, but he did not want those who chose it to race back and forth between public hospitals and private nursing homes. The way to avoid that was to give part-timers the right to treat private patients in public pay beds, in some cases without any limit on the fees they could charge.[19]

GPs were initially not given the same privilege in health centres; there, no fee payments were to be allowed. But few GPs appeared to resent the ban; not many health centres would be built and little demand was anticipated for private GP care. Furthermore, from their experience with the panel system, many doctors had developed a preference for the less demanding patients in the state sector. As long as they could treat private patients in their own surgeries, GPs felt secure. Later, when Bevan extended private practice rights to health centres, few GPs seemed to care; they preferred to practise on their own rather than in premises provided by local authorities.

Medical attack on Minister's powers

When Bevan first presented his proposals to the profession's negotiating committee in January 1946, he found a favourable response.[20] Even the militant Dr Roland Cockshut was pleased:

We assembled at that first meeting expecting that our beautiful profession was to be hung, drawn and quartered. Instead, we were reprieved. It was the most dramatic moment I can ever remember. On one point after another — control by local authorities, the free choice of patient and doctor, clinical freedom — the Minister had accepted what we were demanding before we had the opportunity of asking for it. We were jubilant and stunned.[21]

The euphoria did not last long. BMA leaders feared they would be accused of betrayal if they accepted the plan. After all, Bevan had insisted on abolition of the sale of practices, and the basic salary proposal might portend worse to come. In the legal opinion provided for the BMA, Cecil Havers, KC, had pointed out the dangers,[22] and MPA leaders were ready to exploit any weakness in the BMA stance. Charles Hill could not afford to take chances. Over the heated protests of Moran, he and the BMA Council prepared a critical report for the special representative meeting in March. It was at this point that Dr Alfred Cox found it expedient to brand Bevan as a 'Medical Fuehrer' (see page 98).

Bevan did not respond to the attack. He was surprised by its ferocity but encouraged by the support he had received from consultants. Not only Moran but Webb-Johnson and Souttar welcomed the Bill he presented to Parliament at the end of April. Nevertheless, considerable dissent was to be found among consultants, emanating from the group around Horder. Earlier, Horder had lent support to the concept of a wider state service,[23] but at the start of 1945 he changed tack and delivered a blistering attack on 'nationalized medicine', which he equated with a whole-time salaried service.[24] Later, after Bevan's proposals had been made public, he broadened the target to include the takeover of voluntary hospitals and the extension of Ministerial powers.[25] This led him into fierce fights with Moran for the presidential office of the RCP. Though Moran successfully resisted the challenge, Horder did not lack a following; he emerged as the leader of disgruntled surgeons and the group of 'lesser' consultants — those employed mainly in non-teaching hospitals — who made the BMA their home. Over the consultant world as a whole, specialists opposed the new service as much as GPs.

GPs made their opposition clear at two representative body meetings held in May and July. With only a handful of doctors dissenting, the BMA rejected the key features of Bevan's plan — state ownership of hospitals, controls over the location of practices, the basic salary proposal, and, most heatedly of all, abolition of the sale of practices. Only by the narrowest vote did the doctors decide not to reject the Bill in its entirety.

This forced BMA leaders to change tack. They had intended to concentrate on a few amendments; now they had to combine the profession's grievances into an overall attack on the Minister's powers. Whether anyone realized it or not, MPA policy had become BMA policy. Bevan made minor concessions, but on the principle of Ministerial control he would not and could not budge. This put BMA leaders in the position where they had to sound out medical feeling before proceeding with negotiations. A plebiscite was conducted in November 1946, after the Bill passed through parliament, and it resulted in a 54 per cent majority against, with rejection among GPs alone rising to 64 per cent.[26] Fearful of attacks from militants in their ranks, BMA leaders had done their best to secure this adverse vote, but it was evident that feeling against the Act was running stronger in GP than in consultant quarters.

This gave college leaders room to manoeuvre and in a letter to Bevan on 2 January 1947 the three presidents tried to break the deadlock. They asked the Minister to let negotiations continue, on the understanding that the profession would retain the right to reject the Act once talks had been completed. Bevan complied and indicated a willingness to reconsider the basic salary proposal. Furthermore, he not only extended the private practice privileges of consultants by giving them access to pay beds after they had reached the NHS retirement age, but offered GPs the increase in NHI's capitation rate which they had long been seeking.[27]

This put BMA leaders in an awkward position, but they found a way out by insisting on the possibility of further legislation if the talks, which were to be comprehensive in scope, produced the need. It was on this basis that negotiations began in February 1947. However it was evident that the first open division in medical ranks had appeared because many GPs were angry at the initiative taken by consultant leaders to break the deadlock. Negotiations, they cried, should be left to the BMA, not arrogated by academic bodies like the royal colleges.

Negotiations begin

Thereafter a misleading calm fell over the profession. Negotiations — conducted through six separate committees — were long and arduous, with the understanding that nothing would be disclosed until they were completed. Where general practice was concerned, one obstacle was overcome when agreement was reached on the question of collective responsibility. Under NHI, the profession had assumed obligation for the treatment of all insured persons, whether registered with a doctor or not, but the negotiating committee did not want to do this in a universal service out of fear that it might rule out private practice.[28] In the end, the doctors decided to accept it because they wanted to be paid for patients they might be liable to treat. Only patients not likely to use the NHS were excluded and the Ministry estimated their number at 5 per cent of the population, roughly the same percentage as of insured persons that had failed to use NHI. A central fund was to be established, similar to the one under NHI, which would ensure payment to the profession as a whole at the prevailing capitation rate for 95 per cent of the patients at risk.[29]

In the midst of this process, the rank and file did show signs of restiveness at the BMA's representative meeting in July. A critical resolution, introduced by Dr Harold Goodman of Newcastle, expressed fear of 'subversive elements on the Negotiating Committee'.[30] But he and others were silenced by the militant

Cockshut who, as a member of the committee, assured his colleagues that 'nothing had been given away'. Similar support was supplied by Lawrence Abel who, with Arthur Dickson Wright, represented surgeons and other consultants who preferred to work through the BMA. All the personalities involved in this exchange were BMA loyalists and their intervention had the effect, no doubt intended, of forestalling any challenge from the MPA.

The calm in relations was shattered in December when negotiations ended and the negotiating committee produced a report dismissing the Act as 'unacceptable'.[31] To Bevan and his civil servants, it seemed as if the long months spent hammering out details had been fruitless: nothing would satisfy the profession. The Minister feared the reaction from Morrison and others in his Party who were waiting for the chance to upset his plans and restore control to local government.

Bevan exploits division in profession

In Bevan's view the time had come to exploit the division in the profession, and when he met the doctors in December he was 'rude, blustering and threatening' to GPs, but 'smooth and amiable' to consultants.[32] It was at this point that he offered consultants the right to some pay beds without a ceiling on the fees they could charge. But he warned GPs he would cut their capitation fee if their resistance caused fewer than 95 per cent of patients to sign on in the new service. Needless to say, he offered no concessions on the issues that mattered most to GPs — a legislative ban on a salaried service, the basic salary proposal, abolition of the right to sell practices, controls over the location of practices, and the right of an appeal to the courts against dismissal from the NHS.

The doctors were also dismayed to hear Bevan disclaim any intent to introduce an amending Bill before the Act had been given a chance to demonstrate its worth. Some changes, he proclaimed, might be made later, but under no conditions would the general structure of the service be altered. In his eyes, the erosion of Minister's powers had gone far enough; deceived by the calm that had settled over the profession the previous year, he refused to make more concessions. The negotiating committee went away empty handed.

For BMA leaders, this was a call to arms and Hill delivered a blistering attack in January, which Bevan dismissed as 'politics' since the BMA secretary had become the Liberal and Conservative parliamentary candidate for Luton.[33] But Hill and his colleagues did not rely on words alone: they conducted another plebiscite to show the strength of medical feeling. This time, all ballots had to be signed with the doctor's name and address, not left in the anonymous state in which voting had been conducted before. The change was an innocent one, designed to forestall criticism from the MPA and similar quarters; in 1944 Graham-Little had condemned the anonymous procedure used then, in an attempt to discredit the BMA poll on the White Paper.[34] But Bevan did not see it that way and he castigated the BMA in Parliament for arranging what seemed to be a method of voting that was 'a long way from the secret ballot and the workings of democracy as we know it in this country'.[35] Because the Minister was protected by Parliamentary privilege, the BMA could issue no challenge but it did win libel action against Dr Morgan, Somerville Hastings, and two other SMA leaders, when they made a similar charge in the press.[36]

Nor was that the only change in the voting procedure; this time, a special rider was added. Because GPs far outnumbered consultants and no boycott could be effective without their support,[37] it was decided to require opposition from at least 13,000 GPs out of the total of 20,500.[38] Bevan had made it clear that NHI would end when NHS began and many doctors would face financial ruin if they lost their panel income.[39] Consultants needed beds as badly as GPs needed panel patients, but BMA leaders were prepared to arrange a boycott only if a decisive majority of GPs (63 per cent) refused service. We thus see where the critical group in medial ranks lay.

Bevan at this point lost patience. He issued a public statement attacking the doctors and staged a special debate in Parliament to justify his position.[40] If he thought this would alter medical opinion, he was mistaken, for even the *Lancet*, which had been sympathetic, criticized him. The result of the plebiscite was overwhelming. On an 84 per cent poll, nine out of ten doctors rejected the Act, and this included not only 17,037 GPs but all but 269 consultants.[41]

Thus, despite Bevan's attempts to divide the profession, it remained united. Only Moran and his influential coterie felt differently, but Horder tried to undermine their position at the special representative meeting the BMA held in March:

> I am sometimes accused of being too much a 'B.M.A. man', but I do not lose any equanimity over that. I am more and more a 'B.M.A. man' because I realise that if we stick together we must have a focus point for our power, and that focus point is the B.M.A. There are certain other distinguished bodies within the ambit of medicine, but, whether from their constitution or some other reason, the immediate fight lies not with them.[42]

Medical feeling now rose to new heights, so much so that the doctors refused to contemplate service even if a salaried payment were barred by an amending Act. In private session, they set on foot an independence fund to prepare themselves for a boycott. Though the fund failed to attract much support, it did receive £400,000 from a trust created earlier for a similar purpose under NHI.[43] Before the meeting, BMA leaders hinted at a readiness to compromise, but not afterwards. Once again, negotiations were deadlocked.

And once again it took Moran to break it. He not only urged Bevan to introduce an amending Act that would bar a salaried service but suggested that the basic salary proposal be restricted to new entrants during their first three years of service. He also thought the issuance of regulations should be subject to a special procedure because of the profession's fear of Ministerial power.[44] Bevan was swift to respond and announced his intent to include the requested ban on a salaried service in legislation that had been contemplated for 1949.[45]

This exchange had the hallmarks of a carefully planned manoeuvre; indeed, it has been suggested that Moran's intervention was 'partly contrived in the Ministry',[46] though there is nothing in the Public Record Office to document it. For Bevan, the move offered an immense advantage since it swept aside all issues except the salaried payment, leaving him free to hold fast to the reform that mattered most — abolition of the sale of practices. Events, as it turned out, had moved exactly in the way Hill desired when he met Douglas in May 1946 (see page 99). Dr Hugh Clegg, editor of the *BMJ*, had 'always feared a last ditch struggle over buying and selling', but he was confident that not more than 15 or 20 per cent of GPs would stay out because of it.[47]

BMA in disarray

Hill, however, did not have freedom to act. At the BMA's representative meeting in March, the doctors had made it clear that a ban on salary would not be enough. Besides the right to sell practices and other concessions, they wanted power to appeal to the courts against dismissal from the NHS, and they were not deterred by the fact that Rab Butler for the Tories had meekly supported their demands during the Parliamentary debate in February.[48] Nor were they concerned by the way public opinion had swung against them. GPs were angry at Moran's intervention, and militants in their ranks were doing all they could do to whip up opposition.

It needed strong leadership to deal with such a situation but the BMA had as Council chairman the vacillating Dain. The only way to resolve the issue was to hold another plebiscite but Dain feared this would be seen as a sign of weakness, and could not make up his mind; first he was for the plebiscite, then against. It took Hill to put the proposal across at the fateful Council meeting on 15 April. But those who opposed Bevan's offer made sure the memorandum sent with the voting form contained these words: 'Bearing in mind that what we have secured falls short of what we sought, the Council's view is that, while progress has been made to that end, the freedoms of the profession are not sufficiently safeguarded.'[49]

Dain went further: in a fighting speech at Shrewsbury on 18 April, he urged the profession to reject the offer. He was supported not only by twenty-six members of the BMA's Council and Representative Body but by Horder and his group of London consultants. At an angry meeting on 22 April, Horder's followers voted 196 to 1 against the Act.[50] Four days later, a 'rebel' group of fellows, led by Reginald Payne, tried to turn Webb-Johnson and the RCS against the Act. This was only the second meeting at which fellows had been given the chance to express their views since the Bill was introduced, and some 250 attended. Despite the president's attempt to prolong debate and silence opposition, a resolution opposing service was forced through by the narrow majority of sixty-seven to fifty-eight.[51] But by declaring the proceedings secret, Webb-Johnson managed to shorten the report in the medical press, only a brief editorial appearing in the *BMJ*, nothing in *The Lancet*.[52] He also merely forwarded the resolution to the

Minister and negotiating committee without comment, thereby failing to convey the strength of feeling expressed within the College.[53] The president's way of dealing with awkward motions was to leave individuals to fend for themselves, regardless of the stand taken by the RCS Council. If any fellow wanted to boycott the Act, he was free to do so but the College itself could not organize resistance.[54]

Bevan had done his best to woo consultants, but it was evident that many still opposed the Act. What concerned them most were the conditions of service: the Spens report on consultant remuneration did not become available until 19 May and the terms had to be negotiated after that. With dissatisfaction still rife among GPs, the outcome was uncertain. No one could be sure the NHS would begin as scheduled on 5 July.

Dain, however had gone too far for some of his colleagues in BMA House; Clegg was particularly alarmed. He had pushed hard for concessions, but Clegg made it clear to Moran where his own sympathies lay: the *BMJ* had to give space to medical dissent but he personally welcomed the RCP president's intervention (see Appendix, page 219). As for Hill, he did not want to repeat the mistake made in December 1912, when the BMA Council voted to boycott the NHI Act while GPs flocked onto the panel. Cox reminded the profession of the danger in a letter to the *BMJ*.[55] Clegg decided not to report Dain's speech at Shrewsbury and the Council chairman was forced to retreat, issuing a statement which left each doctor voting in the plebiscite 'to make up his own mind on the facts'.[56]

The results appeared early in May. A majority still opposed the Act (25,842 to 14,620) but the number included only 9,588 GPs, far short of the 13,000 the BMA had set as necessary for resistance.[57] Though the Council agonized over the final decision, it had no choice: it advised doctors to join the service, provided Bevan delivered the promised amending Act. Bevan not only duly gave assurance but added other concessions, including payment for maternity work to all GPs.[58]

That marked the end of medical resistance. By the closing days of May, 26 per cent of GPs had enrolled in the new service and the proportion was even higher in Scotland (36 per cent) and Wales (37 per cent). Nearly all the rest followed, so that by the time the NHS began on 5 July only some 10 per cent remained outside. Nor were patients more reluctant. By the appointed day, 75 per cent had put their names on GP lists and the proportion reached 97 per cent a few months later. There, give or take a few percentage points, it has remained ever since.

Resistance from consultants

Only among consultants did significant resistance remain. Those who followed Moran welcomed the Act — as did a group of orthopaedic radicals led by Sir Reginald Watson-Jones.[59] But Horder and his London followers were unrepentant. Together with MPA dissidents and diehard GPs, they condemned BMA leaders and tried to reverse their action at the representative meeting in May.

One motion called for the resignation of the BMA's council while another demanded the dismissal of Clegg, but neither managed to attract more than a few votes.[60] In contrast to the 1913 fiasco, BMA leaders came through with flying colours.

Horder could not reconcile himself to the collapse of medical resistance and formed a new organization called the Fellowship for Freedom in Medicine to act as a ginger group within the BMA.[61] Though the body failed to attract much support, and has remained impotent ever since, Horder performed a great service for the professon since his action hastened the departure of the MPA. By the time the NHS began, MPA influence was ebbing; its leading advocate in Guildford — Dr Arthur C. de B. Helme, whose father, Dr. T. Arthur Helme of Manchester, had been one of the leading opponents of NHI in 1911 — could not attract enough votes to win a seat on the BMA's Council.[62] (The irony goes even deeper; Helme's main opponent in Guildford was Dr Donald Whitaker, son of Sir James Whitaker, the BMA secretary in 1911 who moulded the Bill in the profession's favour before he was accused of betrayal for taking a post with the NHI Commission.[63]) Perhaps this effect is what Horder intended, since his abrupt change of attitude toward state intervention in 1945 has never been explained. Hill was also puzzled by Horder's ambivalence on the proposal to abolish the sale of practices; in private he accepted it, but before the House of Lords he condemned it as a gross infringement of personal liberty.[64]

Among diehard opponents of the Act, GPs were more numerous than consultants, but this was only because they came from a much larger corps. When proportions are taken into account, the standing in the final plebiscite is reversed; consultants formed a higher percentage — 60 per cent as opposed to 53 per cent for GPs.[65] Within Horder's group, GPs were also more numerous, but consultants made their presence felt, particularly from the ranks of surgeons. Horder drew his strongest support from Payne and others like the young Reginald Murley who could not make their views felt within the RCS.

How, in view of Bevan's efforts to woo consultants, can this paradox be explained? The uncertainty surrounding hospital appointments was the critical factor, more important than the uncertainty surrounding remuneration. Consultants could not enter the NHS as freely as GPs, and among Horder's group were many who feared rejection. The BMA tended to attract consultants from the periphery of the hospital world; some held minor hospital posts and spent most of their time in nursing homes or practice premises. They had much to fear from a service that would cover everyone; without a hospital appointment and access to the pay beds Bevan offered, they might have few private patients to fall back on.[66]

The consultants at the head of the royal colleges, on the other hand, drew their strength from the teaching hospitals, and it was there Bevan directed his favours. Moran and his colleagues had reason to believe the NHS would be good for them. Bevan not only exploited the division between consultants and GPs — he played off one group of consultants against the other.

Furthermore, though he delayed the ban on salary until the psychological moment, he did not neglect the demands of GPs. He could not offer them as much as consultants because Willink had conceded nearly all they asked for before he arrived. This forced Bevan to restore reforms (like abolition of the sale of practices) which he considered essential and that made him appear less generous to GPs. But he did go beyond Willink in some respects and added the prospect of higher capitation fees. Only where practice reform was concerned did Bevan (and Willink) falter, but there GPs had only themselves to blame because they failed to give the Minister the support he needed to secure Treasury funds for new methods of working.

It was true that Bevan had greater reason to satisfy consultants. For the most part, those in private practice had not experienced state payment before the EMS began, whereas GPs had gone through thirty-five years of NHI and learned to like it. Since Bevan made only minor changes in the panel system, he had reason to expect GP acquiescence.

In any case, there were so many GPs that even if some held back there would have been a sufficient number to start the service. Consultants, on the other hand, were in short supply and Bevan needed all he could get to launch the hospital service. This was partly why some 3,000 medical refugees who fled to Britain from Nazi oppression were given permanent status on the Medical Register in 1947. Those with specialist qualifications were badly wanted in the hospital world.[67] Indeed, in 1949 the Ministry of Health told the Home Office that it normally favoured the admission of an alien doctor to Britain 'only if he proposed to practise within the NHS scheme'.[68]

Consultants thus became the recipients of special favours, but Bevan could not ignore GPs: he had to satisfy both to make the NHS work. In May 1948 one of Horder's followers went so far as to declare that the Minister had adopted 'a more conciliatory attitude towards general practitioners than towards consultants'.[69] So satisfied were GPs with the conditions they found that in 1966 they agreed to adopt the basic salary proposal (under the new name of 'practice allowance') which they so strenuously resisted in 1948. Even more striking was the attitude adopted by the profession as a whole in 1988; with the NHS itself under attack, the strongest support for Bevan's plan came from consultants as well as GPs.

Part 4
National Hospital Service

It is the aim of the Government to enable the voluntary hospitals to take their important part in the service without loss of identity or autonomy. But it is essential to this conception that the hospitals should still look substantially to their own financial resources, to personal benefactions and the continuing support of those who believe in the voluntary hospital movement. So long, and so long only, can they retain their individuality. If once the situation were to arise in which the whole cost of the voluntary hospitals' part in the public service (a service designed for the whole population) was repaid from public money, or indeed in which it was recognised that public funds were to be used to guarantee these hospitals' financial security, the end of the voluntary movement would be near at hand.

From the White Paper on an NHS issued by the Ministry of Health and Department of Health for Scotland, February 1944, London, HMSO, Cmd. 6503, page 23

Chapter fourteen

No charge for hospital care

We have seen how the medical services evolved and how hospital issues affected their development. But hospital reform had a life of its own and to follow it we need to return to October 1941, when the Ministry issued its statement of intent on post-war hospital policy (see page 28).

Post-war hospital policy

It will be recalled that this statement was forced by the action of the Nuffield Trust and did not go far beyond what was planned before. Local government was to be the centre of hospital development and though voluntary hospitals would have a place, they were expected to co-operate with local authorities and look to them for financial aid. That, rather than the EMS pattern of Ministry funding, was implicit in the 1941 statement; Maude opposed giving voluntary hospitals a direct Exchequer grant.[1] Though they would have the same right of appeal to the Ministry against local authority plans as had been allowed under the Cancer Act, voluntary hospitals were expected to take their lead from the municipal sector.[2] Only teaching hospitals were exempt; their funds — at least those devoted to medical education — would come from the UGC. Yet in the long run Maude also expected teaching hospitals to establish links with the municipal sector.[3]

This plan did not satisfy everyone. Some in the municipal world wanted to force voluntary hospital co-operation, even without financial aid. That, indeed, had been the position taken by the Cathcart Committee in 1936; it wanted to stop voluntary hospitals from adding beds without consulting local authorities.[4] Menzies, in August 1941, reminded the Ministry of the failure of voluntary hospitals to co-operate in the development of LCC clinics between the wars. When asked to make space in their own buildings, the hospitals refused, making it clear that they would have 'no truck with the Municipal Authorities'.[5] Yet the LCC, like local authorities generally, depended on them for aid in the treatment of cancer, TB, and VD cases.

Though the Scottish Department may have leaned in the compulsory direction, that was never the English Ministry's intention. In March 1943 Maude told the voluntary hospitals that he had taken care to restrict municipal powers so as to safeguard their development.[6] Nevertheless, Ministry officials did not think voluntary hospitals could survive in the long run,[7] and many in the municipal world agreed. In 1940 one-fifth of the larger voluntary hospitals (over 125 beds) were in deficit — 32 out of 154 — and ten were teaching hospitals.[8] Thereafter the EMS, with its £32½ million of Exchequer aid, saved them, but that would disappear as soon as the war ended.

Daley, the LCC's MOH, expected the voluntary sector to face difficulties because of the way they had refused admission to private patients to make room for war casualties.[9] As a result, many private patients had turned to LCC hospitals and become accustomed to municipal service. Added to this was a sharp fall in income from contributory schemes, which hit provincial hospitals hard. Brock, who had once been the department's expert on voluntary hospital finance, was sure the schemes did not provide enough income to ensure survival. Even the most successful — the one in Merseyside — had failed to cover capital costs.[10]

Searching for ways to save voluntary hospitals

Treasury officials were not at all pleased with this prospect. If the voluntary sector could not survive, that would place a heavy burden on the Exchequer. In June 1939, Sir Frank Tribe, the Treasury's Principal Assistant Secretary, did not want EMS doctors paid a salary because that might hasten the end of voluntary hospitals.[11] This was another reason why Brock was pessimistic about the future of voluntary hospitals. Once their doctors became used to payment, they would not want to return to the old days of honorary labour.[12]

However much Maude may have desired the end of voluntary hospitals, he could not ignore Treasury feeling. Nor did he face meaningful pressure from local authorities. Indeed, the fear of Daley and others lay in the opposite direction as a result of the Nuffield initiative and voluntary hospital dominance of the EMS scheme. They preferred to have voluntary hospitals form their own regional organization separate from local authority development.[13]

In the 1941 statement, therefore, Maude took care to protect voluntary hospitals. Though the post-war hospital service would be open to everyone, those who could pay were expected to do so. During the spring of 1942 Ministry officials set forth various possibilities.[14] At first, they considered a system employing means tests and the recovery of charges, but that was ruled out because the amounts produced in the past had been so meagre. Then it thought about adding a hospital benefit to NHI, as Beveridge had in mind, but that was rejected on several grounds. In the first place, it would have raised contributions beyond the reach of many insured persons because of the heavy costs involved. Secondly, it was apparent that the approved societies had no desire for development in this direction. They were content to rely on the charity of voluntary hospitals and focus their attention on other extensions, like coverage for dependants of insured persons. But the most important factor inhibiting the Ministry was the fear that such a plan would destroy contributory schemes and imperil the whole voluntary hospital structure.

In the department's view some way had to be found to make use of contributory schemes, but enrolment could not be compulsory because that would confine coverage to employed persons and leave out the large number of non-insured who needed hospital treatment. On the other hand, if no one were required to join, many people might evade charges and that would undermine the system.

Despite the risks involved, the Ministry came down on the side of contributory schemes operating in their traditional voluntary manner. No other method promised to raise so much from private means and impose such a small burden on the Exchequer. At first the department proposed to do this through something like an approved society system, giving 'official approval' and financial aid only to hospitals that raised sufficient funds through private means. But Maude had reservations; because of the difficulties encountered with the approved society system, he thought it better to leave the schemes free to operate without minimum rates of contributions and benefits. The only point at which the Ministry might intervene was to ensure that no scheme was tied to one hospital, but spread its favours fairly over the municipal sector. Contributory schemes were notorious for the way they made larger payments to voluntary hospitals.

Beveridge suggests a charge for 'hotel expenses'

This was the point Ministry planning reached when the Beveridge Report appeared in November 1942. In it, Beveridge assumed the creation of a comprehensive health service available to everyone 'without contribution conditions in any case'.[15] However, he did leave open the question of whether part of the cost of treatment should be included in the compulsory contribution which all employed and self-employed persons had to make to be eligible for cash benefits. If so, that would not entitle them to special treatment under the health service but it would make them less likely to seek private care or make donations to voluntary hospitals. Who would want to incur extra charges when they had already made direct payments to the state?

Though Beveridge did not state it openly, he was ready to see the end of private general medical practice and made no effort to protect it. But he was concerned about the future of voluntary hospitals. They could be shielded if payment from compulsory contributions were kept low, pegged at a level to cover only GP care as under NHI. That would leave scope for voluntary payments for hospital treatment at the time of use or through contributory schemes. And since Beveridge wanted to promote the schemes, he stressed the need for the contributory principle to overcome reluctance on the part of patients to seek hospital treatment.[16] If patients had to pay contributions, they would be more likely to enter hospital when service was required.

All of this was carefully worded and hedged with arguments on both sides so as not to prejudice the outcome of negotiations on the health service. Maude had implored Beveridge to show this caution.[17] But along with defenders of voluntary hospitals, the Permanent Secretary was anxious to do more to protect contributory schemes, and Beveridge made some effort to accommodate him. Those in receipt of disability benefit, Beveridge suggested, might be required to make payment toward the cost of their board as 'hotel expenses' whenever they entered hospital as in-patients:

> With the small benefits provided by national health insurance hitherto, this question could hardly be raised. But, if the social insurance scheme is to provide benefits in future designed to cover the food and fuel requirements of the insured person and his dependants, it may appear reasonable that, while the person is getting his food and fuel in a hospital and not in his home, the money provided for that purpose should be directed to the hospital.[18]

However, Beveridge had only a small charge in mind — 10s. a week from a benefit normally of 40s. — and he recognized that it was 'not perhaps of great importance to the finance of institutional treatment'.

The pressures on Maude

Two of Maude's colleagues thought it would take more than this to make contributory schemes viable. Soon after the Beveridge Report appeared, Pater and McNicholl prepared a paper which foresaw no place for them because the schemes did not fit in with Ministry policy, based as it was on local government. In their eyes the schemes were out of favour because of the way they were tied to the voluntary sector. Perhaps, Pater and McNicholl suggested, the time had come to make provision for hospital insurance in the general social insurance contribution, thereby raising subscriptions above the level Beveridge thought desirable.[19] Here as elsewhere Ministry officials betrayed a distaste for the voluntary sector. One civil servant went so far as to claim that no voluntary hospital administrator had 'a tithe of the experience in administering a hospital service' as the medical department of the LCC or the EMS staff of the Ministry.[20]

Maude did not dare to go this far. If he were to satisfy the Treasury, he had to hold the line on Exchequer finance and that would only be possible if voluntary hospitals could raise sufficient funds on their own. This, indeed, was one of the main assumptions on which the Ministry based its estimate of £130 million as the cost of the new service (see page 197). Even if private funding held up, the voluntary hospitals would still have a deficit of £6 million, but that amount would be reduced by £1 million with the modest hotel charge Beveridge proposed, and Maude had a larger payment in mind.[21]

Nothing, then, must be done to upset the fragile structure of private finance if voluntary hospitals were to survive. That message was delivered to the department by the leading figures in the hospital world — Goodenough and Hyde of the Nuffield Trust, Docker of the BHA, and Sir Ernest Pooley of the King's Fund.[22]

The provincial hospitals were particularly vulnerable because a large share of their income came from contributory schemes. But money, the hospital spokesmen stressed, was not the only benefit the schemes offered; they also injected a democratic element into administration. Without the representatives to which the schemes were entitled, hospital boards of management would consist of little more than self-appointed persons.[23]

Maude had also the municipal world to consider, and their spokesmen did not react favourably to the payment proposed in the Beveridge Report.[24] Local authorities had been forced to levy charges under section 16 of the 1929 Local Government Act as the result of pressure applied by voluntary hospitals.[25] Previously, payments had only been required in municipal maternity homes but neither there nor more generally after 1929 did local authorities make much effort to collect them. Means tests were anathema to the working class and municipal officials found the process distasteful. So little money was accumulated that the effort seemed pointless. As the depression deepened, public pressure mounted and in the 1936 Public Health Act (sections 181 and 184) outpatient treatment was exempted.[26] Meanwhile in Scotland, the whole power remained permissive until 1937, when the Maternity Act brought GPs into the network of municipal care.[27]

Scottish voluntary hospitals oppose hotel charge

The demand for patient payments was thus associated more with the voluntary than the municipal sector. But when the Reconstruction Committee came to consider the question in October 1943, the call for rejection came from voluntary hospitals, and it was from Scotland that the cry originated.[28] There, many voluntary hospitals were barred by charter from imposing charges and few relied on contributory schemes. In 1938, patient payments to Scottish voluntary hospitals amounted to 27 per cent of income, as opposed to 46 per cent in England and Wales.[29] The money Scottish hospitals received was more in the nature of a 'thank offering' than payment for services rendered.[30] That, among other factors, made them receptive to state control. Scotland thus had the anomalous situation where hospital treatment tended to be freer in the voluntary than the municipal sector.

Maude was fully aware of the Scottish situation. Not only did the voluntary hospitals there display different characteristics, but many areas had been short of beds because of inadequate muncipal provision. No fewer than thirty-two out of fifty-five local authorities had populations of less than 50,000 and were in no position to support a hospital service.[31] The task was left to the Scottish Department, and during the war it put seven EMS hospitals in operation. What was to be done with them when the war ended?

To sort this and other problems out, a Committee on Post-War Hospital Problems, under the chairmanship of Sir Hector Hetherington, was appointed at the end of 1941. Its main task was to propose a partnership between municipal and voluntary hospitals. When it reported in August 1943 it rejected charges for hospital services, whether they involved maintenance or treatment. Why, the committee asked, should the payment Beveridge proposed be restricted to holders of disability benefit? But if it were extended to others, a means test would be required and that the committee utterly repudiated.[32]

This view, as Johnston later pointed out, reflected 'the great weight of public opinion in Scotland' and was 'fully shared by voluntary hospitals and local authorities'.[33] Instead of charges, the committee proposed compulsory insurance and it wanted a contributory system for hospital treatment to be created separate from the one to be established for cash benefits in the Beveridge Report.

Maude had been fearful of the Hetherington Committee from the moment it was formed. Early in 1942 he warned the Scottish Department of the need to uphold charges so as to protect contributory schemes in England and Wales: 'Rightly or wrongly, I think probably rightly, the leading people in the voluntary hospital world regard these Savings Funds as the sheet-anchor of the whole hospital movement.'[34] To soften the impact of charges, he raised the possibility of exempting chronic cases and those suffering from infectious disease. He also proposed to keep the amount low and apply it uniformly throughout the country. Since Beveridge expected the Social Security Fund to contribute £15 to £20 million (later raised to £40 million) to the cost of medical treatment, that was an additional reason for holding the charge down.

These arguments failed to impress the Scottish Department. When the Hetherington Report appeared, Maude was furious. He dismissed its call for compulsory hospital insurance as 'a quite impracticable suggestion' because it would necessitate a weekly contribution too high for the lower paid to support.[35] As much as 2d. would have to be added to the weekly contribution of 4/3 for men and 3/6 for women proposed in the Beveridge Report.

Pater and McNicoll did not share Maude's view. They themselves had raised the possibility of including hospital insurance in the Beveridge contribution, and before the Hetherington Report appeared they had opposed an hotel charge.[36] This failed to move Maude, but Beveridge, with his call for only 10s. to be deducted from disability benefit, had set a limit as to how far the Permanent Secretary could go to protect contributory schemes. In March 1943 the department had under consideration a charge of 15s. to 20s. a week except for those suffering from TB and infectious disease.[37] In July, just before the Hetherington Report appeared, Maude raised the amount to a firm £1.[38]

Hotel charge dropped

The issue came before the Reconstruction Committee in October 1943. A £1 charge, the Ministry claimed, would not have a harmful psychological effect. Since few patients stayed in hospital beyond three weeks, the maximum most would pay would be £3. But unlike Beveridge, the Ministry wanted this charge to apply to everyone, not just to those who received disability benefit. Otherwise, it reasoned, contributory schemes would not have room to operate and that would mean the end of voluntary hospitals.[39]

Brown argued for the charge, Johnston against, and he was supported by Bevin who had been pressing hard for hospital coverage in the social insurance scheme since 1941. Bevin did not like contributory schemes because they created 'a great deal of work and some friction'.[40] Not until the meeting on 1 November was a possible compromise found. Then at the suggestion of the Chancellor of the Exchequer, Sir John Anderson, the committee decided to favour the Beveridge method and confine the charge to those in receipt of disability benefit and possibly family allowance. The charge was set at or below the level Beveridge proposed — 7s. for married men, 10s. for single men.[41]

Now it was the turn of the English voluntary hospitals to object, and they forced the new Minister, Willink, to renew the call for a £1 charge at the committee meeting in January.[42] When Johnston again rejected the proposal, it was left to the new chairman, Woolton, to settle the issue. Surprisingly, he came down on Johnston's side and called only for 'some' deduction from disability benefit along the lines proposed in November. The voluntary hospitals, he told Willink, had adopted the wrong approach: 'Put quite bluntly, the hospitals are relying on the element of fear to stimulate charitable contributions from the public.'[43] They should raise their appeal to a higher plane, he advised, and the government could help by stating in both Houses of Parliament how dependent it was on the voluntary hospitals for the creation of a national health service.

When the White Paper appeared in February, no mention was made of contributory schemes and the only reference to a hotel charge was the possibility of a deduction from disability benefit.[44] That was to be decided later — when the government had completed its proposals for social insurance — and before they were announced the idea was dropped.[45] All of the new service, including long stays in hospital, was to be free to everyone. Not until 1955 was the idea of reducing sickness benefit (after eight weeks in hospital) resurrected and implemented.

No opposition from voluntary hospitals

Ministry officials were surprised by this turn of events because Hawton had expected violent opposition if the hotel charge were dropped.[46] Instead, the voluntary hospitals let it go without a whimper. Indeed, their journal, *The Hospital*, came out against a charge after the Hetherington Report appeared.[47] Later, Docker found himself reeling from Woolton's strictures, forcing him to declare that all the hospitals wanted was the public to realize their plight; they needed more than state aid if their costs were to be met.[48] By February, when the White Paper appeared, his BHA was even claiming to be responsible for the 100 per cent principle which made the service available to everyone: 'In fact, some six months before the Beveridge Report, they had themselves adopted this as one of several major points in their post-war policy.'[49]

163

Finally, in March, a spokesman for voluntary hospitals in Scotland declared his preference for the public health form of finance — from rates and taxes rather than from compulsory insurance. This was J.W. Vallance, a former civil servant who was acting as an adviser to the BMA (see page 63). The tax method, Vallance proclaimed, would be less likely to deter the public from making the charitable contributions upon which the voluntary hospitals would now depend: 'The imposition of a weekly contribution on the individual will operate as a psychological bar in a way that payment from taxes and rates will not.'[50]

Nor were the voluntary hospitals the only ones to change direction; equally surprising was the altered stance of the Treasury. One of its leading civil servants, Sir Bernard Gilbert, might express discomfort at the wide-ranging nature of the service offered in the White Paper (see page 200) but it was his political chief, Sir John Anderson, who undermined Maude's attempt to impose a hotel charge. That act, as Pater noted at the time, dealt a 'death-blow' to contributory schemes.[51] Nor did the White Paper make provision for capital allowances. Somehow the voluntary hospitals had to raise substantial funds on their own or seek full compensation from the state. But this, as Moran warned, put them 'in a cleft stick':

> If we don't get margin made up we will be in financial difficulty. If we demand full payment in a few years time municipal hospitals will see this is not an economic bargain. It would not pay the voluntary hospitals to have full payment made.[52]

Chapter fifteen

Deadlock in negotiations

Maude wanted to preserve voluntary hospitals in the interests of Treasury finance, but from the moment planning began their future was in doubt. How could the voluntary sector hope to attract sufficient funds when the whole population would be covered by a public service? Everyone — or nearly everyone — would be paying rates, taxes, or insurance contributions, and if free care could be obtained at a municipal hospital, who would want treatment elsewhere? Only if the service were better (or quicker) in the voluntary sector would a significant demand arise, but one of the Ministry's main aims was to remove the stigma that had plagued municipal service. If hospital treatment had been confined to insured persons the way GP care had been since 1911, then half the population would remain outside and that would leave scope for voluntary endeavour. But once the war began the long-standing movement to add dependants to NHI gathered force, and from there to the 100 per cent principle was but a short step.[1] The Beveridge Report with its call for comprehensive coverage made inclusion of the whole population virtually certain.

Maude saw this pressure growing from the moment the Beveridge Committee started work in 1941. How could he hold a place for voluntary hospitals? They drew their funds from three main sources — contributory schemes, patient payments, and charitable donations. After the White Paper only the last offered hope, and it was doubtful if it would prove fruitful. But planning proceeded on the assumption that, if it did not, the state would make up the difference.[2]

The problem confronting the voluntary hospitals was how to prevent this financial dependence from being translated into municipal control. The Ministry was intent on making local authorities the centre of hospital development, and if all funds were chanelled through them that would bring on the prospect voluntary hospitals were most anxious to avoid. Throughout 1944 they concentrated their efforts on forging different avenues of finance. Ideally, they wanted all state aid to come from social insurance contributions, since that, as the White Paper acknowledged, represented payments which might otherwise have gone to the voluntary sector.[3] But despite the concern Beveridge had shown for their welfare, his report did not help them. Though he called for £40 million for the health service from insurance contributions, this was intended more for GP care than hospital treatment (see page 194). The hotel charge was Beveridge's main way of helping the voluntary hospitals, and that was subsequently discarded.

It was the Hetherington Report that recommended a system of compulsory insurance for the hospital service, but this, as Maude noted, was impracticable. How many workers — or, indeed, employers — could have borne the heavy contributions involved? Both found their interests better served by having hospital costs met by the state. The voluntary hospitals, however, did not want aid to come from the rates. That would have strengthened the case for municipal control and it might also have dimmed the prospect for charitable donations since money paid through local government was more likely to be a deterrent.[4]

On every count the voluntary hospitals preferred their funds to come from the Exchequer, but that was in conflict with the Ministry's aim of basing hospital development on local authorities. In Maude's scheme of things some money had to emanate from the municipal world, or at least be channelled through it.[5] And local authorities had to have a majority on administrative bodies if there was to be co-ordinated planning.

The Treasury also favoured a municipal focus to shift costs to the rates. Local authorities as well as voluntary hospitals offered the prospect of Exchequer relief. Of the £80 million allowed for hospital expenditure in the White Paper, £36 million was to come from the rates and voluntary hospitals were expected to raise an additional amount on their own.[6] Between the two, the Treasury would have been relieved of over half the cost of the hospital service. Willink found it difficult to depart from the administrative pattern in the White Paper, and that forced him to produce a plan of unworkable complexity in an attempt to satisfy the conflicting interests involved.

Initial Ministry proposals

The process began with the proposals presented by the Ministry in 1943.[7] Then planning was concentrated on the GP service and only a few details were added for hospital development. Administration for both would be based on local government, with combinations of counties and county boroughs being required wherever wider areas were needed for hospital operation. The department had long been aware of the limitations of the joint board concept as applied to isolation and mental hospitals,[8] but it could see no alternative unless local government was reformed and that would take years to realize. Central control had been ruled out on various grounds but mainly out of a belief in local government. However the local health authority was to be constituted, the Ministry would make sure it was dominated by county and county borough appointees.

This was the framework in which voluntary hospitals were expected to fit. Though they would continue to be managed by their own governors, they had to adhere to plans made by the health authority, and with that body they would have only vaguely delineated rights. The intention was to follow the precedent set under section 17 of the 1939 Cancer Act and permit one-third of joint board members to be co-opted. But later it became clear that neither the doctors nor voluntary hospitals would be allowed more than a few nominees and they would be in a minority on all committees.[9] Just as the approved societies held a 60 per cent majority on insurance committees, so the new health authority would have a 60 per cent majority on any committees it created.[10]

Furthermore, specific measures were to apply to key aspects of hospital operation. Voluntary hospitals were expected to adopt national rates of pay for nurses as laid down by the Rushcliffe Committee in 1943, and they would no longer have complete freedom over medical appointments and patient admissions. The Ministry was determined to stamp out 'in-breeding' and the exclusion of the chronic sick.[11]

In return for accepting these conditions, public aid would be provided — a flat payment of £1 per week for each bed made available to the state plus the prospect of a discretionary grant from the local health authority. In addition, voluntary hospitals would be entitled to the proceeds of the hotel charge under consideration. Though this money might be raised through contributory schemes, all the proceeds would be disbursed by the health authority. Financial control was placed firmly in the hands of local government.

Reactions to Ministry proposals

For the most part these proposals were welcomed by the municipal world, though concern was expressed over the precepting power of the joint authority. Furthermore, only the AMC was ready to give 'outsiders' a voice in municipal affairs.

That did nothing to soothe the feelings of the voluntary hospitals, who were as angered by the department's proposals as were the doctors. Though three bodies spoke for them, the main voice came from the BHA. The influence of the King's Fund did not extend beyond London, while the Nuffield Trust had been formed to promote the interests of provincial hospitals. Only the BHA, it maintained, could speak for the hospital world as a whole.

The BHA's way of protecting voluntary hospitals was to seek a separate structure within the state service. With the support of the King's Fund, it proposed a central hospitals board to run the hospital service. On it, voluntary hospitals would have the same number of places as local authorities (six each), while the three seats reserved for the Ministry would be matched by three for the doctors. All payments to voluntary hospitals would be made through this body and the money would be for services rendered rather than in the form of a subvention or subsidy from public funds. In this way the discretionary element would be eliminated and finances would be put on a business basis without the implication of municipal control.[12]

On the local level, where the detailed plans would be drawn, protection would come from an advisory board that would have the right to challenge all health authority decisions, disputes in effect being settled by the central board. On the health authority, only one-third of the places would be given to voluntary

167

hospitals and doctors, but this relationship would be reversed on the advisory board. Nor was there to be interference in the appointment of medical staff or patient admissions; all hospitals were to make such decisions on their own.

These proposals were totally unacceptable to Maude, and his department slavishly followed him.[13] Nor, in view of municipal resistance, could the Ministry now hold out much hope of 'outside' representation on the joint board; only advisory bodies might be created.[14] As for funding, a certain amount of 'Beveridge' money (i.e. from social insurance contributions) might come from the centre, but the rest would have to be channelled through the local health authority. The only way in which the latter's influence might be moderated was to have the latter disbursed in the form of standard service payments along the lines suggested by the Nuffield Trust.[15]

White Paper proposals for a hospital service

That, essentially, was the pattern proposed in the White Paper. A CMB with executive functions was suggested for the doctors, but nothing comparable for voluntary hospitals; they were to have only a few places on the CHSC. Nor was their position on the local level any stronger. The Reconstruction Committee ruled out 'outsiders' on the joint authority, leaving only another advisory body, the Local Health Services Council, as a means of influencing policy.

For the most part the White Paper followed the structure originally proposed by the Ministry. A new joint authority was to administer the hospital service and, unlike the GP sector, it would apply to Scotland as well. Though several methods of forming such bodies were suggested, the White Paper came down on the side of the joint authority which would consist of representatives from the larger local authorities, the counties, and county boroughs, not the smaller district councils.[16] However, such combinations would not be needed in places like London where the local authority was large enough to act on its own.

Since voluntary hospitals were denied a place on the joint authority, their only hope of influencing policy was through the Local Health Services Council, but both the composition and functions of that body were left vague. Though this Council could lodge appeals with the Ministry, its main function was to provide 'the expert point of view on technical aspects'.[17]

If a voluntary hospital wished to retain complete freedom, it could stay out of the public service, but then it lost all hope of financial aid. To qualify for that, it not only had to implement area plans but undergo periodic audits and inspections. These would be wide-ranging and would cover both the number and kind of patients treated, as well as the way medical and other staff were paid. For the most part the inspections would be carried out on a national basis — by panels of doctors and other experts like the teams which conducted the hospital surveys. But the joint authorities could arrange to make inspections on their own if they thought it desirable and then they would rely on their chief medical officer.[18]

Despite the objections raised by voluntary hospitals, the financial arrangements also called for joint authority involvement. Though one grant based on the number of beds would come from 'Beveridge money', a second would spring from the rates and take account of the kind as well as the number of patients treated. Only the setting of standard service payments would limit the discretion in joint authority hands.[19]

In either case it was the Ministry's responsibility to see that the conditions of the grant were fulfilled. But elsewhere the White Paper stressed the importance of local government.[20] It was the responsibility of the new joint authority to provide a complete hospital service in each area. The Minister, sitting in far-off Whitehall, could not do that, not even with an able corps of civil servants. Local government was the basis on which the new hospital service would be formed; the Reconstruction Committee made sure that was added to the White Paper from the vaguely-worded draft Hawton had prepared (see page 70).

Nor was that the only change the committee made; it ruled out a hotel charge, leaving only a small deduction from disability benefit and that was subsquently discarded. What hope was there for contributory schemes? The White Paper left the voluntary hospitals in a more perilous position than they had been before. In May 1944 the BHA started a nation-wide campaign against the Ministry's proposals, and the Nuffield Trust as well as the King's Fund joined the attack.[21]

'Freedom with finance'

There now seemed no way for the hospitals to raise funds except through charitable donations, and Florence Horsbrugh, the department's Parliamentary Secretary, still clung to that possibility: 'I regard the work of the voluntary hospital as private enterprise without profit.'[22] But Sir George Aylwen, treasurer of St Bartholomew's Hospital, knew better: he did not see why the voluntary hospitals should have to raise any funds in a 'free' service. The state, he maintained, should foot the entire bill but not in a way that raised the danger of municipal control.[23] In essence, what he and his colleagues wanted was 'freedom with finance'.

Surprisingly, a possibility of securing it arose from the municipal world. For the most part the LCC was satisfied with the structure in the White Paper since it was large enough to constitute a health authority on its own. Though they had reservations, the county councils in the CCA were also willing to accept it in the hope of securing access to borough hospitals.[24] But this feeling was not shared by the AMC: it insisted that hospital management remain in local hands, leaving only a planning function for joint boards.[25]

That proposal would leave voluntary as well as municipal hospitals in command of their own resources but it did not satisfy the teaching hospitals or their prestigious consultants. They wanted to raise standards, not leave them in their pre-war state, and the best way to do that was to create regional bodies based on medical schools, thereby enabling the royal colleges to exert greater influence on policy.

To Willink this suggested the need for a second tier, since his civil servants could not contemplate the abolition of joint authorities. He had his staff devise a complicated planning structure on two levels — area and regional — with hospital management left in voluntary and municipal hands. Led by Hawton, Ministry officials objected to this concept, fearful that it would pose a barrier to change, but Willink forced it through to give the doctors and voluntary hospitals the representation they demanded (see page 79).

Though the BHA preferred its central hospital board and reiterated the demand in August 1944, it was worn out by the Ministry's repeated rejection and was ready to consider the two-tier plan at the end of the year.[26] What voluntary hospitals feared most was municipal domination of the main planning body at area level. Willink was sympathetic and took up their demand for equal represen-tation, but the Reconstructon Committee refused to consider it.[27]

The area council thus emerged with a municipal majority of eighteen as opposed to twelve for the rest. Only three seats were reserved for voluntary hospitals. In Scotland they did not even receive that because Johnston refused to grant representation to outside interests. He had gone as far as he could to placate GPs and refused to make further concessions.

However, in both countries voluntary hospitals would have representation on a hospital planning group under the area council on which they would have the same number of places as the local authorities and the doctors. Furthermore, any plans made by the area council would have to be submitted to the regional council and the Minister before they were approved, and on both levels voluntary hospitals would be able to exert influence.[28] On the regional council they would not only have the same number of seats as local authorities (four each) but they could usually count on enough support from the four medical and three university members (one of whom would be chairman) to override municipal objections. Similarly, though the Minister would make the final decision, he would be advised by a standing committee with a majority likely to support the voluntary hospital view. Nine members each would go to voluntary hospitals and local authorities, but six others would come from the medical profession.

The financial arrangements were also made more satisfactory to voluntary hospitals. Some funds would come from local authorities but payments would be made through an area 'clearing house' that would keep them at a distance from the municipal sector.[29] The BHA still had many reservations, but with the war in Europe over, it was anxious to obtain an alternative source of funds before the EMS ended.[30] Willink, who was under pressure from Churchill and Woolton to reach an agreement before the general election, managed to wring a reluctant acceptance from the BHA in April 1945.[31]

Deadlock in London

But a few weeks later the issue was again in doubt. In response to local authority pressure, Willink removed powers from the regional tier, leaving the municipal majority on the area body with greater control over planning, inspection, and finance. Moran and his colleagues shivered with fear. Woolton was mistaken when he reported to the Cabinet in June that agreement had been reached with all parties except the LCC.[32]

In London the parties were so far apart that no legislation was possible. We have seen how strongly Latham objected to the concessions made to the doctors, and he felt the same about those made to voluntary hospitals. Unlike local authorities generally, the LCC was to retain enormous power since it was large enough to act as an area planning body on its own. In the face of Willink's concessions, the Labour majority not only held fast to its stand against outside representation but, together with the CCA and AMC, demanded a 60 per cent municipal majority on the hospital planning group.[33] Consultants had reason to be concerned, because in January 1944 the medical superintendents who ran the LCC's hospitals had made clear their intent in the new service: 'in every Government hospital *every* clinician must be answerable to someone. The clinical autonomy enjoyed by the head of a medical or surgical firm in a voluntary hospital cannot persist in a Government hospital.'[34]

To avert the threat, Moran and his collegues demanded the division of London into sectors on the EMS model and they were supported not only by the King's Fund but by Horder and his group in the BMA.[35] However, the proposal was not entirely welcomed by local authorities or voluntary hospitals in the six home counties; they viewed sector rule with suspicion because of the way teaching hospital needs had dominated EMS administration.[36] In June Docker went so far as to consider an alliance with the LCC,[37] but after the Labour victory in July he threw BHA support behind the King's Fund.[38]

Far from agreement having been reached, negotiations were hopelessly deadlocked when Bevan became Minister in August. At the root of the stalemate was the department's insistence on some vestige of municipal control. As the secretary of the King's Fund, A.G.L. Ives, later lamented: 'The White Paper was coloured by the local government mentality which has dominated the Ministry of Health since the days when it was the Local Government Board.'[39]

Chapter sixteen

The hospitals are nationalized

Bevan's way out of the deadlock in negotiations was to nationalize the hospital service. No better solution was in sight. With 30 per cent or less of funds coming from their own resources, the voluntary hospitals would have found it difficult to maintain an independent existence, and no one in the municipal world, not even Latham, was anxious to foot the bill. That left the Exchequer as the main source of finance, and grants to local authorities that might run as high as 80 or 90 per cent would have alarmed the Treasury. The Ministry had to assume the task of organizing the hospital service.

Moran was pleased by the prospect and so (if he has been correctly identified) was Charles Hill; he felt the move 'would be so beneficial — if linked with independence for the teaching hospitals — as to outweigh almost all other considerations'.[1] Nor did any dissent arise from the medical experts who carried out the hospital surveys; Carling, Sir Henry Gray, and Professor George Gask all supported Bevan's decision and they were in the best position to judge.[2] The study they carried out revealed a state of chaos in the hospital world, uncovering divisions that only a system of central control could cure. As a summary of the surveys prepared by the Nuffield Trust put it:

> From all these criticisms it is clear not only that a damaging cleavage lies between the two separate systems, municipal and voluntary, but that the two are not in fact systems at all, since the members of each too often strive after an impossible self-sufficiency. The present position in most places may be unfortunately but not unfairly summarized thus: 'In no area is there a genuine pooling of facilities in an attempt to extract from the combined resources the maximum advantage to the population.'[3]

Who suggested nationalization?

If the solution was so obvious, why did Willink not consider it? He told Parliament in 1946 that no one in the department had made the suggestion during his twenty-one months in office.[4] Perhaps the Conservative faith in free enterprise acted as a deterrent. Who in the Ministry would have dared to raise the proposal when the Tory party's health committee had pleaded so strongly in 1944 for the preservation of voluntary hospitals?[5]

But that was not the only reason. More compelling was the department's belief in local government and its long-standing aim of putting all of health care under municipal control. Maude was devoted to the concept and not until he retired was another solution possible. The Ministry had considered a takeover of voluntary hospitals in 1939 and rejected the idea (see page 18). No one dared raise the subject again. In 1944, following the recommendation of the Hetherington Committee, Johnston had announced his department's intent to turn Scotland's seven EMS hospitals over to local authorities.[6] Similarly, Horsbrugh made clear the English Ministry's antipathy to central control of the hospital service; it would, she told Parliament, produce 'an appalling uniformity and lack of local interest'.[7]

After Maude retired, inhibitions remained because of Rucker's concern for voluntary hospitals. Maude let him take the lead from the moment Willink arrived in November 1943, probably because of Rucker's close tie with Neville Chamberlain (whom he served as Principal Private Secretary in 1939) and the respect he commanded in Conservative circles. Douglas leapt over Rucker's head in 1945, but he was new to the task and lacked authority. As Deputy Secretary, Rucker was most able to influence policy.

However, it was doubtful if Bevan let him. The new Minister found Hawton more compatible and relied increasingly on his advice.[8] When Rucker retired in July 1947, Hawton became Deputy Secretary, winning the admiration of his colleagues for the devotion he displayed to the concept of a national health service. Before the 1945 election he was said to have prepared alternative plans likely to fit the policies of the victorious party.[9] Labour at that time had no intent to nationalize the hospitals; under the influence of Hastings and the SMA, it was committed to municipal control. (The Medical Service Group of the Fabian Society felt differently, but its severe critique of municipal administration was never published).[10] Yet Hawton's closest colleague, John Pater, has claimed that Hawton was responsible for Bevan's decision.[11]

Pater may be right. Before Bevan arrived, Hawton was caught between Maude's passion for local government and Rucker's concern for voluntary hospitals. Only after Maude retired did Hawton have freedom to suggest an alternative, but he had to move cautiously because of Rucker's seniority. Still, there is nothing in the Public Record Office to support Pater's contention. At no point did Hawton submit a paper on the subject. Those he did prepare show him to be a synthesizer rather than an original thinker. Pater did not witness any exchange on nationalization between Bevan and Hawton; his claim is based solely on what Hawton told him.[12] But like many in the civil service it is possible that Hawton found it hard to accept the thought that politicians were capable of original suggestions. Civil servants from the old school tend to see themselves as the fount of all wisdom, and Pater himself is said to belong to that school.[13]

If Hawton did plant the idea in Bevan's head, he did so privately or else the written record has been lost. Charles Hill, for one, is certain the proposal did not come from the civil service [14] — while Godber inclines to the view that Bevan, in a flash of insight, conceived the thought himself.[15]

It is possible that Bevan was influenced by someone outside the civil service, and the person with the strongest motivation was Moran. By the time Labour came to power, his plans were in ruins (see page 135). Some way had to be found to break the deadlock in negotiations and create the conditions needed to establish a proper consultant service. Moran could have led Bevan to the nationalization idea during private meetings at Prunier's. Moran himself made this suggestion to Michael Foot for his biography of Bevan. Foot faithfully reproduced the conversation,[16] but now believes 'the full impetus for nationalising the hospitals came from Anuerin Bevan himself'. Foot notes that Bevan 'sometimes used the skilful device of making one with whom he had the conversation think he was making the proposal'.[17]

Once the decision was made, there was no doubt that Moran as well as Hawton gave it full support. As Moran told the House of Lords when Bevan's proposals were first put before it in April 1946:

Every discussion among consultants and specialists . . . has been dominated the last few years by one fact, by one fear, that the hospitals would come under the control of local authorities. It is because the White Paper appears to lift that menace from the profession that so many consultants and specialists are reconciled to the passing of the voluntary system. It is that dread which on the whole makes them prefer the proposals of the present Minister of Health to those of his predecessor, which handed us over, bound hand and foot, to local authorities.[18]

Hawton died in 1982, a year after Pater's book appeared, without affirming or denying the claim made by his colleague. We shall probably never be able to resolve the issue; it is possible, as Sir Alan Marre has wisely suggested, the idea arose from many directions at once.[19] What is clear is that Bevan put the department to work on the subject as soon as he became Minister, seeking detailed data on the state of voluntary hospital finance.[20] When he learned that 70 to 90 per cent of funds would come from public sources, he was not content to leave management alone; in future, he proposed, the state should take control by appointing more than half a hospital's governing board.

Rucker resists nationalization

Rucker reacted immediately. He opposed taking control even if 100 per cent of hospital maintenance costs had to come from public funds, since the state would still benefit. The voluntary hospitals, he argued, had substantial capital assets and expertise that would be at public disposal: 'What we, in fact, propose to do is buy their services — at a cheap rate because we propose seldom, if ever, to pay the full cost.'[21] All the Ministry had to do was make sure it received value for money and it could do that by appointing a few representatives to hospital boards, adding only the safeguard of inspection and sanctions. If the state went further and took control of management, it would destroy the voluntary system. The teaching hospitals, he warned, should not be subject even to this minimal control because they offered 'a tested kind of public service with which it is not necessary, in the public interest, to interfere'.[22]

Bevan was not impressed. Could he rely on subsidized service from the voluntary sector? Would consultants accept little or no pay if the hospitals they worked in made their services available to the state? The answer to both questions was 'no'. A warning had been given the year before by a prestigious spokesman for the Nuffield Trust — Sir Farquhar Buzzard, Regius Professor of Medicine at Oxford. He declared the voluntary hospital system dead because many doctors had become used to EMS salaries and costs were escalating.[23]

Rucker made another attempt to dissuade the Minister and this time he stressed the threat to local government. He submitted a paper which purported to present a balanced view, setting forth the arguments for and against nationalization, but by the time one reached the end it was clear that the author was on the side of the two-tier plan Willink had left. Nationalization, Rucker warned, 'would undeniably cause the biggest reduction yet made in the power of local authorities', a loss that surpassed even the transfer of means-tested benefits to the Assistance Board: 'It would be particularly unfortunate if there had to be a major clash between local authorities and the Ministry of Health — whom they have always regarded as their principal protector.'[24]

But his strongest argument came at the end. It would, he noted, take time to work out a new scheme — yet 'We cannot afford to wait much longer for a general plan if we are to hold the improvements gained from the E.M.S.' Even more serious was the threat this posed to the certification of sickness benefits:

> There cannot be national insurance without a national health service. From this point of view, it may be a pity to discard a plan [i.e. the one left by Willink] which gives us much, if not all, of what we want, which is practically ready, and which would have a very large measure of agreement in its passage.

If, Rucker concluded, the Minister insisted on nationalization, the department must work to a 'tight schedule' and be ruthless in negotiations with local authorities and voluntary hospitals. The aim was to have a bill ready by March 1946.

The debate in the Cabinet

Rucker's arguments failed to move Bevan, and he had his staff prepare a nationalization paper for the Cabinet. In it Bevan laid stress on the extent to which voluntary hospitals would be dependent on public funds, amounting in some cases to 80 or 90 per cent of income. Under such circumstances, he could not justify leaving them in private hands, but he ruled out a municipal takeover because most local authorities could not support a hospital service. Not only were the geographical areas they covered too small but their financial resources were too meagre. That was why their record had not been good. A Poor Law atmosphere pervaded nearly half their ordinary hospitals, while their general hospital service was 'of questionable efficiency'. The only way to secure uniform provision was by a national organization operating through regional boards. If local government were reformed, the situation might be different but there was no prospect of that in the immediate future.[25]

Bevan at first exempted the teaching hospitals because of their special role in education and research, but he changed tack after his Scottish colleagues protested. More than a quarter of voluntary hospital beds in Scotland were in teaching hospitals and the Scottish Department could not exclude them without undermining its service.[26] Bevan proposed to take them over — twenty-two over the country as a whole, with twelve in London.[27] But before he did so he gave them a special status that exceeded the demands they had raised the year before. Not only was London divided into sectors for hospital adminstration, but teaching hospitals everywhere except in Scotland were given an independent board of governors. Consultants who taught in them, furthermore, were allowed direct representation, in contrast with colleagues generally.[28] On the regional boards, the profession had the right only to suggest names; it was the Minister who made the final selection.

Not all the members of the Cabinet were happy with Bevan's plan; formidable opposition arose from Herbert Morrison, Lord President of Council. For him, nationalization was anathema because it threatened to destroy the hospital service he had spent a decade in building — the vast network of the LCC which covered ninety-eight hospitals and 72,000 beds, one-fifth of the total in the municipal sector.[29] In his rebuttal to the Cabinet, he stressed the devastating effect nationalization would have on local government, warning that the hospital service might be only the first of their health duties to go. In time, he implied, local authorities could lose child welfare, district nursing, and health centre provision as well. Nor was there a mandate for the proposal: nothing in *Let us Face the Future* (Labour's manifesto for the 1945 election) had hinted at nationalization. Though, Morrison admitted, joint boards had their failings — and he had been their severest critic in 1943 (see page 65) — he now saw them as the only feasible solution.[30]

In preparing this argument, Morrison was aided by a civil servant with the initials, 'J.M.'. This was certainly John Maude, still active in government circles as Deputy Commissioner of the Boundary Commission, a body charged with the duty of redrawing municipal areas. Here was the start of a process which Maude hoped would one day enable local authorities to assume the task of hospital administration, thereby paving the way for the unified control of the NHS that had eluded his grasp. He made this clear a decade later while serving as a member of the Guillebaud Committee, created by a Conservative government to examine the cost of the NHS.[31]

Morrison's arguments did not impress Bevan. The Minister stood fast, confident that his proposals offered the most efficient solution. The Lord President, he pointed out in a second memorandum to the Cabinet, had not seriously disputed this contention.[32] Nor was it practicable to return to joint boards; that would split municipal services in half and leave voluntary hospitals separate. The only alternative to nationalization was Willink's two-tiered plan, and that had satisfied no one. As for the fear that state control would concentrate too much power in ministerial hands, Bevan stated his intent to delegate duties to regional boards and district committees.

The main weakness of municipal control, the Minister warned, lay with finance; local authorities could not bear the heavy cost of hospital administration. (That, he might have added, was the main reason why, as late as 1942, only twenty-five of sixty-six county councils had exercised power under the 1929 Local Government Act to remove hospitals from the Poor Law).[33] Under Willink's plan, local government was to assume only 31 per cent of NHS costs — yet, as Bevan pointed out, 'It was the common practice of local authorities to resist strenuously any denunciation of their powers and at the same time to complain of the burden on the rates and to demand ever increasing subsidies from the Exchequer.'

There was no need to fear the political consequences, Bevan added. Nationalization was the most sensible solution and that would be seen by most of the parties involved. The only danger lay in delay, but if the Cabinet settled the issue there was no need for a new round of negotiations. The Minister ended with a rousing plea for support. A chance like this, he warned, came only once in a generation: 'If it is not done now, it will not be done in our time.'

This exchange was in writing and when the protagonists came face to face in October, Morrison had only one argument left: let the decline of voluntary hospitals run its natural course and allow them to fall gradually under municipal control instead of raising a storm that would harm local government. To this Bevan issued a warning that his civil servants had not sounded before: there was nothing inevitable about the disappearance of voluntary hospitals: 'On the contrary Exchequer subsidies which it would be necessary to give to them would consolidate their position.'[34]

Bevan clearly had the better of the debate, but the Cabinet was not entirely convinced. Aside from Morrison, the strongest opposition came from the Home Secretary (James Chuter Ede), and reservations were expressed by the Lord Chancellor (Jowitt) and the First Lord of the Admiralty (A.V. Alexander). On his side Bevan had a founder of the panel system and Britain's first Minister of Health, Lord Addison, then Secretary of State for the Dominions and Leader of the Lords. Strong support also came from the Minister of Education (Ellen Wilkinson), despite her close personal ties (in all probability, his mistress) with Morrison.[35]

Had the financial implications been fully explored by the Treasury, the issue might have been settled there and then. But though Dalton supported the principle of nationalization, he needed time to consider costs, and Attlee deferred the decision so that the Cabinet's Social Service Committee could explore the proposal further. However, there is no reason to doubt the Prime Minister's own sympathy for the plan. Any reservations would have been overcome by the colleague whose judgement on health matters he most trusted, Addison; as neighbours in Buckinghamshire, they had personal ties.[36] The only member of the Cabinet who might have dissuaded Attlee was the Foreign Secretary, Bevin, and though he was not present at the October meeting, it is likely that he supported Bevan. As early as July 1943 he had favoured centralized control of the health service as a whole.[37]

The subject came before the Cabinet again in December. By this time, Bevan was able to present proposals covering the entire NHS, and the hospital question was not the only issue. But the huge costs of hospital operation were the main concern and it took Dalton to quiet the Cabinet's fears. The Chancellor wanted it made clear to local authorities that they could not expect rate relief once their hospitals were transferred to the state. He also insisted on close control of regional boards to satisfy the Treasury, concerned as always about spending powers being given to a body that did not have to raise the money.[38] Not until 8 January could Bevan offer assurances, so the drafting of the Bill did not begin until then.[39]

Still, the battle was not over. Morrison refused to accept defeat and found a surprising ally in Arthur Greenwood, who had returned to government as Lord Privy Seal. Greenwood had fought hard for health service development from the time the Ministry of Health was created in 1919 and in the 1929 Labour government had served as Minister himself. But by 1945 his interests seemed to lie more with cash benefits and the extinction of the approved society system.[40] Nothing, in his view, should threaten the passage of national insurance and from his experience with maternity proposals in 1930 he knew how difficult health negotiations could be. He supported Morrison's efforts to delay Bevan's measure. As late as 6 March they submitted a memorandum to the Cabinet, expressing fear that the NHS Bill would prove so controversial that it would crowd out other legislation.[41] Though they did not state it, perhaps they lacked confidence in Bevan's ability to deal diplomatically with the doctors.

In other circumstances their tactics might have succeeded, since they controlled the Parliamentary calendar — Morrison as Leader of the Commons, Greenwood as chairman of the Legislative Committee. Greenwood carried added weight as chairman of the Social Services Committee that examined Bevan's plan. Nevertheless, thanks to Addison — who as Leader of the Lords had a say in timing of legislation — the Bill went ahead unhampered.[42] It was clear that the payment of cash benefits could not begin until certification arrangements were in place. Bevan must have been disappointed by Greenwood's action and astounded at his blunder. The Lord Privy Seal's fondness for alcohol provided only a partial explanation, but it contributed to his removal from office and departure from government in 1947.[43]

Yet Morrison could not reconcile himself to defeat. Bevan had criticized him in 1943 for negotiating a Workmen's Compensation Bill with outside bodies before presenting it to Parliament,[44] and there was much bad feeling between the two. No sooner was the NHS Bill published in March than Morrison found another point to challenge — the term 'regional' to describe hospital boards. This was improper, he contended, because NHS regions did not coincide with those used by other departments.

This pin-pricking continued for some weeks, with Morrison suggesting the term 'divisional' instead,[45] but Bevan heeded advice (originating from Pater) to 'stick to our guns'.[46] Finally Morrison gave in, but three years later he had another chance to attack Bevan — this time over NHS costs, which vastly exceeded estimates.[47] From this it can be seen that Morrison could never bring himself to accept Bevan's nationalization plan, beneficent though it was; as late as 1958 he was harping on the need to return hospitals to municipal control.[48] Perhaps Attlee was right when he said 'Herbert cannot distinguish between big things and little things.'[49]

Local authorities submit

The LCC might have been expected to follow Morrison's lead, and, indeed, its former MOH did. Just before the NHS began in July 1948, Menzies started an 'imposing correspondence' in *The Times* to delay the service because of bed and other shortages.[50] Latham did not share the sympathies of his former leader: he hated the voluntary hospitals more than he loved the municipal sector. Nor, no doubt, did he relish the thought of having to repair the £20–30 million in bombing damage that had devastated London's hospitals.[51] Except for one sanatorium, all the LCC's ninety-eight hospitals were hit, with a loss of 4,456 beds, over 10 per cent of the total.[52] As long as the haughty teaching hospitals were taken into public ownership, Latham was satisfied.[53]

What did concern him was the way London was carved into four sectors (with the teaching hospitals separate) on EMS lines, but on this issue Rucker had his way.[54] Bevan held fast so that voluntary hospitals and consultants would be pacified. The Minister did much to appease Latham by consolidating the public health service in county and county borough hands.[55] Despite pressure from Willink, the metropolitan boroughs were forced to bring their maternity and child welfare services under the overriding control of the LCC.[56] Health centre development was also left with the major local authorities and the LCC took pride in constructing the first newly built one at Woodberry Down — at a cost, however, of nearly £200,000, and that excluded the amount for land.[57]

With the LCC so ready to give up its hospital empire, other local authorities saw little reason to resist. CCA leaders registered a feeble protest, restrained by relief at having a heavy financial burden removed. What bothered them most about Bevan's plan was the separation it produced between the hospital and domiciliary sectors. To avoid that, they wanted to leave both under municipal control, with only a joint planning body to give the breadth needed for hospital development. Failing that, they preferred to let the regional boards take over the domiciliary services left in municipal hands.

If the latter applied, then the CCA wanted half the places on the RHBs and hospital management committees (HMCs) that were to be created under them. With this proportion the LCC and AMC agreed and they wanted the same ratio to extend to the executive councils that were to administer the family practitioner service. Bevan summarily rejected these demands.[58]

Voluntary hospitals protest

Louder protests arose from the voluntary hospitals, but their resistance was undermined by medical behaviour. After decades of fruitless demands, the BMA decided that the time had come to end the tradition of honorary service; in November 1945 it sought payment of five guineas a session before the NHS began.[59] If the hospitals could not find the funds, then the BMA wanted them to seek aid from the Ministry of Health. This decision was taken by the BMA's Council without prior consultation with the voluntary hospitals and it drove the BHA to fury, but it stirred deep fears among hospital treasurers.

The first to react was Sir George Aylwen of St Bartholomew's: for him, there was now no alternative to state intervention and he urged his colleagues to accept national control.[60] Lord Donoughmore of the King's Fund agreed,[61] and so did Goodenough of the Nuffield Trust. Though Goodenough registered a mild dissent from Bevan's plan, he acknowledged the need for radical change.[62]

Instead of waging a fruitless campaign against nationalization, Aylwen urged his colleagues to concentrate on endowment funds: they, he argued, should remain under individual hospital control and not be spread across the NHS as a whole. In that way, something of a voluntary spirit would remain and encourage others to make gifts, even after 'their' hospital passed into the state sector. On this issue, Webb-Johnson offered strong support and he managed to carry Moran with him.[63] Pay bed provision, college leaders recognized, could be made more secure if hospitals retained control of trust funds.

The only real protest came from BHA quarters. Docker and Wetenhall were horrified by Bevan's plan, fearful that it would lead to closure of the smaller voluntary hospitals, many of the cottage type, that made up a large part of their organization. Only seventy-five out of 1,000 voluntary hospitals had more than 200 beds.[64] (However not until the 1980s were these fears realized, and it took intense financial pressure to ovecome the local feeling that successfully resisted closure during the 1960s and 1970s.)

In place of nationalization, the BHA again put forward its demand for a central hospital board, but Bevan deflected it with the point that his proposals 'were based largely on ideas provided by the voluntary hospitals themselves arising out of their study of the functional needs of a fully co-ordinated hospital service'.[65] From this exchange it was clear that BHA pressure no longer created anxiety in Ministry circles. Though the BHA was the oldest of the hospital organizations, having been formed in 1884, it had never been able to rally much support from a voluntary sector riven by competition for charitable funds. The BHA's weaknesses were so apparent that the Nuffield Trust had to be established in

1939 to give effect to the Sankey Commission call for hospital co-operation along regional lines.[66] Like the King's Fund, the Nuffield Trust had a financial weapon in hand; voluntary hospitals in need of funds were likely to heed its call for regional organization. The BHA, by contrast, could only rely on moral suasion.[67]

Nevertheless, before 1945 the BHA seemed best equipped to speak for the voluntary hospital world as a whole. Until then, its views were not at variance with those of the powerful London teaching hospitals (twelve undergraduate, fourteen postgraduate) that were allied with the King's Fund. But Bevan's plan produced a split in hospital forces and, encouraged by the Minister's efforts to satisfy their needs, the teaching hospitals joined the royal colleges in support of nationalization.[68] This left the BHA isolated and forced its leaders to turn elsewhere for aid.

Opposition from disgruntled specialists

They found new allies among disgruntled specialists. Some like Graham-Little were flatly opposed to state intervention, and sought to limit its scope no matter how the NHS was constructed.[69] Others like Horder were alarmed by Bevan's Act and wanted to preserve a place for private practice. Still others like Dickson Wright and Lawrence Abel were concerned by Bevan's efforts to divide the profession, and strove to rally specialist support behind GPs.

They were joined by a corps of doctors who feared displacement from the hospital world. This applied particularly to 'consultoids' — GPs who practised part-time as specialists. Under Bevan's plan, they might lose access to beds and thus destroy their hope for private practice. Hence their demand for all doctors, even those without appointments to NHS hospitals, to be able to treat patients in pay beds.[70] In this way their concern converged with the general concern among consultants, particularly surgeons, that a place had to be preserved for private practice.

With Horder in the lead, this collection of disgruntled specialists gave their allegiance to the BMA, but because of their small number (in relation to the profession as a whole) they needed GP support. When Bevan first met the BMA's negotiating team in January 1946 it looked as if that aid might not be forthcoming. No one then objected to hospital nationalization, concern being expressed only about the composition of regional and area bodies. Under no circumstances would the doctors tolerate a municipal majority, but in that respect BMA leaders were not unique: Moran and his college collegues shared the feeling.[71] Bevan duly assigned a minority of places to local authority nominees, while handing doctors more than their fair share: on the fourteen RHBs, 120 of 364 places went to the profession — sixty to consultants, forty to university teachers, and twenty to GPs.[72]

This did nothing to calm the Horder group since Bevan repeatedly refused to open pay beds to 'outsiders'. Access was confined to those with NHS appointments and the selections were to be made at regional level where royal college influence would be strong. Horder's followers shivered with fear.

Their solution was to seek the same freedom of entry to NHS as GPs had enjoyed under NHI and which all doctors in Northern Ireland were allowed.[73] To promote this and other demands, they had formed a specialist association to work in tandem with the BMA, and the movement gathered force in the spring of 1946 with the attack on Minister's powers (see page 136). The *BMJ* came out against a voluntary hospital takeover in April and the BMA followed suit at its special representative meeting in May.[74] From this point on, BMA policy diverged increasingly from that of the colleges.

The Tories, led by Richard Law and Willink, took up the protest in Parliament so that the BHA had the Conservative Party as well as the BMA on its side.[75] But with Bevan holding fast, the only chance of diluting the move was to shift powers downwards to the 377 HMCs in the hope that they, rather than RHBs, would make consultant appointments. Under that arrangement, it was thought, 'consultoids' would have a better chance. This movement gathered force in October when the Lords amended the Bill so as to give HMCs legal status and duties of their own.[76]

GPs still harboured many grievances, but at this point all that seemed to concern consultants was whether they would be allowed to treat private patients in NHS hospitals. Bevan gave assurances, and this made it possible for Moran to push the BMA into negotiations in February 1947.

By the time the talks finished in December only two major issues remained for the hospital service: how consultants were to be appointed; and whether chairmen would be selected by the Minister or by RHBs and HMCs. Consultants, in addition, wanted to make sure pay beds were available in all areas and they wished to charge private patients freely without the ceilings that were to be imposed by hospital authorities. Bevan could not guarantee the former, but he did concede some 'no ceiling' pay beds. On the key question of consultant appointments, however, he held fast: the power would remain in the hands of RHBs acting on the advice of special committees on which medical influence would be strong. Only junior hospital doctors would be appointed by HMCs.[77]

This left the Horder group writhing with uncertainty, but their spirits were raised by the anger that arose from GP ranks. In January the *BMJ* criticized consultants for accepting state-owned hospitals as a lesser evil than municipal ones, and warned of Bevan's attempts to divide the profession.[78] Horder allied his group behind the BMA and condemned the College of Physicians for its conciliatory posture.[79] In March he made another attempt to displace Moran and almost succeeded, but with the presidential office remaining in friendly hands, Bevan was able to break the deadlock and the NHS began, as scheduled, in July.

Horder and his followers remained recalcitrant, voting solidly against the Act in the final plebiscite taken in April (see page 152). What bothered them was the uncertainty of their appointments and the terms to be offered. Not until the Spens Report on consultant remuneration appeared in May did they realize how generous the salaries would be, but in any event they had no choice: without access to beds, they could not practise. Unlike GPs, consultants had to enter the

NHS, and despite the specialist shortage that prevailed, some did find it difficult to secure appointments.[80] Those in the 'consultoid' class who failed had no alternative but to practise as GPs.

End of the voluntary hospital

From 1946 the voluntary hospitals had little influence on their own: their fate depended on the outcome of the struggle with the doctors. Graham-Little might rant and rave, but the day of the voluntary hospital was over, and only by offering a doubtful array of supplementary benefits (like stays in convalescent homes) could contributory schemes hope to survive in the NHS.[81] The BHA did not even manage to let individual hospitals retain control of trust funds; Bevan allowed the privilege only to those in the teaching sector (see page 139).

Was Bevan's decision to nationalize the hospitals the right one? Even Willink came to think it was. During the 1946 debate in Parliament, he found it expedient to oppose the proposal, but when he came to write his memoirs in 1968 he felt differently

> I do not think the Conserative party would have agreed to this big change, but the financing of the voluntary hospitals in the years after the War would have been impossible, and it would, I think, have been impossible to organize a national plan for the hospitals of the country as a whole.[82]

Part 5
Free and Complete Care for All

The trouble with the national health insurance scheme is that it was never national. . . . [It provided a] limited insurance population with insufficient means to maintain themselves in sickness, and furnished a medical service which stopped short of the absolutely necessary specialised treatment and cut down the [cash] benefit when it was most needed.

Fifteenth Earl of Huntingdon in the House of Lords, 1 June 1943, volume 126, column 759

Chapter seventeen

Financial constraints

Before 1948 health care in Britain was governed by the insurance principle. Only persons who paid weekly contributions could count on free care from the state, and all they could be sure of was what a GP and chemist could offer. Some did manage to secure a wider array of services from approved societies wealthy enough to provide additional benefits. Others among the population as a whole could obtain hospital and specialist treatment from municipal or voluntary sources, but for the most part they had to have private insurance or pass a means test. Local authorities, like English voluntary hospitals, were expected to recover costs from all who could pay.

The start of the NHS produced a break with this pattern. After 1948 everyone was entitled to free care and they could hope to secure all that medical science had to offer. The insurance principle was dead. Though some money still came from the National Insurance Fund, no one had to pay contributions to use the NHS; nearly all its resources came from taxes levied by the Exchequer.

How did Britain come to abandon the insurance principle? In this chapter and the next two we shall trace the process as it developed within the Ministry of Health.

Expansion by way of insurance

When planning began in 1936, the Ministry assumed development would come by way of insurance, and not even the Fabian Society could propose an alternative: in March 1939 its health experts prepared a statement that ruled out the prospect of an expanded health service financed mainly from taxation.[1]

Of the £61 million spent on public health care in 1939, only £3 million came from the Exchequer; the rest arose from NHI contributions (£13 million) and the rates (£45 million).[2] Local authorities recouped some of their health costs from the £5 million added to the block grant in 1929, but no special Exchequer aid had been offered to upgrade Poor Law hospitals; whatever progressive authorities like the LCC did, they did on their own.[3] That no doubt was one of the main reasons why power had been given in permissive form. Had it been imposed as a duty, the Treasury would have had to help.

Nor did the voluntary hospitals fare any better. When the Sankey Commission called for regional organization in 1937, it hoped the government would finance the move, but the only money came from Lord Nuffield. Had the voluntary hospitals been willing to accept municipal direction, as the Cathcart Committee desired, the outcome might have been different but, since they did not, no public funds were forthcoming. Throughout the inter-war period, the Treasury took refuge in the belief that state aid would stifle the voluntary sector.[4] It left local authorities to decide how to use voluntary hospitals under section 13 of the 1929 Act and section 182 of the 1936 Public Health Act.[5] If beds and services were made available, payment would have to come from the rates.[6] The only money the Treasury offered was for medical education, and that was channelled to teaching hospitals through the UGC. Only 7 per cent of voluntary hospital income came from public sources in 1938.[7]

The initial plans made by the Ministry did not involve the hospital sector; they called only for the extension of NHI to 'dependants and specialists' (see page 13). Some Exchequer aid might be needed to foster development, but most of the money would come from NHI sources. Throughout the inter-war period, the Ministry assumed that the panel system could not be enlarged without higher contributions from employers and employees. Not until 1937 was the belief challenged, and the criticism came from a politician (R.S. Hudson, Parliamentary Secretary), not a civil servant.[8]

However, planning within the department was restrained by more than finance. No one (particularly Maude) was happy with the way panel practitioners performed and civil servants shared the trade union concern about the unequal benefits generated by approved society surpluses. It was far better, everyone agreed, to have health care under local authorities. Then the unemployed and others could be covered, not just wives and children of insured persons, and specialists could be linked with the hospital world. Indeed, in the opinion of the chief medical officer, MacNalty, it was no good offering specialist aid without a hospital tie.[9]

But this transfer could not easily be made. The doctors opposed municipal control and the approved societies clung to NHI funds, fearful that any loss would imperil their life. Was it safe, in any case, to give local authorities control over money they did not raise? This ran counter to the Treasury maxim of no administrative power without financial responsibility. Perhaps it was better to let services develop under NHI direction, since that method had medical approval. The doctors had favoured the addition of specialist services since the panel system began, and from 1929 they had called for the inclusion of dependants (see page 8).

For three years, from 1936 to 1939, the debate over these issues raged, but the department could not resolve them. Matters came to a head in April 1938, when the NHI world came close to an agreement on a plan to add specialist services. This proposal, Neville wrote, 'is likely to cause us some embarrassment'.[10] He and his colleagues preferred municipal development but there was no prospect of an Exchequer grant to start the process going. MacNalty was ready to forsake insurance money rather than have the service proceed under NHI direction.[11]

In the end, a policy of do nothing prevailed. Local authorities had long been developing their own special services, particularly for mothers and children, and the Ministry was content to let that process run. Only radium treatment for cancer received Exchequer aid. When this development was under consideration in 1938, the department (under the leadership of Kingsley Wood) did give some thought to adding the whole range of specialist care.[12] But the idea died as soon as the cost implications became apparent. The Treasury did not like the 80 per cent grant needed for the Cancer Act and was certain to resist further aid.[13] To the public, the extension of GP care to the dependants of insured persons held a higher priority but the huge costs involved (estimated at £10–12 million as opposed to £1½ million for specialist care)[14] ruled that out. Ministry officials, in any case, did not want to do anything to inflate the value of panel practices. In 1936 they had to offer midwives compensation before local authorities could establish a salaried service, and more generous amounts would be needed for GPs. 'Demo' took comfort in the thought that dependants were partly covered by the maternity, child welfare, and school medical services already established under municipal direction.[15]

Changes wrought by the war

The Ministry was roused from this lethargy by the impact of war. First came the need to care for air raid casualties and that led to departmental direction of hospital services; the EMS was run from Whitehall, not town hall. In the process, the call for a survey of hospital resources arose and that, as a result of Nuffield involvement, produced the post-war hospital policy statement of October 1941 (see page 26). The day of permissive powers was over; local authorities now had a duty to create the service envisaged in the 1929 Local Government Act. And from that arrangement the Treasury could not withdraw; in future, it would have to provide half the funds needed for hospital development. Indeed, it was the prospect of that aid that led Nuffield spokesmen to accept municipal direction. Goodenough and Hyde did not repeat the mistake made by voluntary hospitals and the Sankey Commission in 1937.[16]

Next came the need to expand the number of persons entitled to NHI care. For decades dependants had been waiting for admission, and the onset of war at last opened the door. A new sense of community pervaded the nation, stimulated by an evacuation programme that brought working class children into middle class homes and revealed the plight of the poor.[17] Coupled with this was a fear of infectious disease stirred by the destruction of homes and over-crowding in bomb shelters. Those who were healthy wanted protection from those who were ill, and this generated an irresistible demand for wider health coverage. The first clear sign came in 1941 when a million persons were added to NHI with an increase in the income limit from £250 to £420. If dependants had been included, 84 per cent of the nation would have been covered for GP care.[18]

These twin movements made a powerful impact on Ministry thought, enlarging its vision and making civil servants realize that it might be possible to move quickly: dependants and specialists, indeed hospital care as a whole, might be added at once. And then, it was hoped, the array of services would be so wide as to warrant the salaried service the department desired. In the process, insurance committees would go, and all of public health care could be put where everyone in the Ministry thought it belonged — under local authorities.

Financial dilemma

Still, the same old problem remained: how could the service be financed? The costs would be huge and local authorities would be no more willing than the Treasury to foot the bill. NHI offered a more promising source. The surpluses earned by approved societies were substantial and the weekly contributions paid by employers and insured persons produced a never-ending source of funds. The Treasury made it clear that it preferred the insurance method to the fruitless attempt of local authorities to recover charges after the event.[19]

By 1942 there was hope of a more receptive reaction from NHI quarters. In the wake of the community feeling generated by the war, the approved societies seemed more willing to let their funds go. The friendly societies, together with the assurance offices, had long resisted attempts to pool their surpluses, but in October 1941 they finally accepted the need to cover the cost of 'dependants and specialists'.[20] A few months later, in March 1942, the assurance offices went further; they told the Beveridge Committee they were ready for a comprehensive service open to everyone.[21] To those who knew anything about the NHI world, this was an astonishing change of attitudes.

But there were still difficult questions to resolve. If the approved societies put up the money, would they be willing to let administration go? And if some people had to pay contributions, would they be content to let the service be open to those who did not? Insurance tests and insurance administration might again be the dominating force in the enlarged system.

In any case, the funds required were too large to raise from NHI sources alone; few working men — or, indeed, employers — could have paid the contributions involved.[22] One way of alleviating the problem was to reduce the scope of the services, and Maude excluded dental and optical care, along with treatment in mental hospitals, from the department's initial plan.[23] He also set his sight on a salaried GP service in the hope of curbing prescription and certification costs as well as producing better care for the nation. And his preference for municipal control would shift much of the burden to the rates. Once the panel system went, the portion of costs borne by the Exchequer would fall from 64 per cent to 43 per cent.[24]

But Maude's main hope of financial relief lay with the voluntary hospitals. They had long provided a free service to the nation — so much so that the approved societies did not consider them suitable objects of aid; despite repeated exhortations, they had made only token donations to hospital funds.[25] The Treasury, if not the Ministry of Health, would insist on preserving the voluntary sector. Yet the charitable donations and subsidized services they attracted were no longer enough; no one — at least in English voluntary circles — thought their hospitals could survive without the aid of contributory schemes.

So no matter how the new service was structured, charges and patient payments would have to prevail in the hospital sector. This was the point policy making reached when Beveridge intervened.

Chapter eighteen

Beveridge pressure

During 1942 the Ministry stepped up its planning pace because of pressure from the Beveridge Committee. Yet Beveridge was the first to acknowledge that his inquiry would never have started but for 'the driving force of the Trades Union Congress'.[1] From the moment NHI began the unions had objected to the presence of industrial assurance offices, and their distaste widened as a result of methods employed by casualty companies in workmen's compensation. By the 1930s not even the assurance agents affiliated with the TUC could stop that body from a policy aimed at removing the industry from public provision; indeed, some agents welcomed it as a way of realizing nationalization objectives. They preferred to work for a public utility run by the state. And from 1937 the unions were aided by the doctors who had reasons of their own (stemming mainly from assurance agent exploitation of maternity benefit) for wanting the industry out of the welfare state.[2]

By 1941 Beveridge had come to the same conclusion. Though he had fostered unemployment insurance in 1911 and strove to protect it between the wars,[3] he did not feel the same sympathy for the approved society system. That system may have been necessary to start NHI in 1911, but it generated too much inequality for a nation needing to establish a national minimum. He not only called for its abolition but — prodded by the TUC[4] — assumed the creation of a comprehensive health service for everyone. In so doing, Beveridge went far beyond his remit, since his committee was supposed to consider only the financial relations between social insurance and health provision.[5]

Undermining the approved society system

Why did Beveridge become concerned with health care? In the first place, he saw it as necessary for its own sake: a wide-ranging service would promote public health and reduce the cost of the higher sick benefits he was proposing. But the subject also had a strategic purpose — it would put the finishing touch on the approved society system. As D.N. (later Sir Norman) Chester, secretary to the Beveridge Committee, revealed in 1943, 'It was the proposal to make medical provision comprehensive in scope . . . that provided the main argument against the Approved Society system.'[6] This may also have been a factor behind the Beveridge decision to include dental and optical care; they were enjoyed by too many insured persons (as additional benefits under NHI) to be ignored. By 1943 76 per cent of those covered by the Act were entitled to dental care, and 65 per cent to optical care.[7]

How should such a service be financed? If it were to cover everyone, there was in Beveridge's view only one way — 'on communist lines out of taxation'.[8] Any attempt to employ insurance tests would be out of place, since that would exclude those who could not pay contributions and it might provide an excuse to retain the approved society system. But Beveridge still had too much faith in the insurance principle to reject it completely. It would certainly apply to the provision of cash benefit; only those who could pay contributions to the new Ministry of Social Security (which would replace the approved societies) would receive the sickness and other benefits proposed. Yet he felt a need to apply it to health care as well: 'If importance attaches to preserving the contributory principle for cash benefit, it attaches also to contribution for medical treatment.'[9]

Beveridge's way of resolving this conflict was to have insured persons as a whole make contributions to the health service; on their behalf, the Ministry of Social Security would transfer £15 million a year from its Insurance Fund for domiciliary care.[10] This would give insured persons a sense that they had the right to use the health service and lessen reluctance to seek treatment, thus promoting recovery before illness became disabling:

> From this point of view, previous contribution is the ideal, better even than free service supported by the tax-payer. People will take what they have already paid for without delay when they need it, and they pay for it more directly as contributors than as tax-payers.[11]

Maude's dilemma

These views created problems for Maude as soon as he became aware of them. The first concerned the doctors: though they flirted with the idea of universal coverage for a fleeting moment in 1942, they preferred to exclude the well-to-do. Before the war the BMA had set 90 per cent as its population limit, and that stand was endorsed by the MPC in June 1942.[12]

Beveridge's response was ingenious. No such restriction could be imposed as long as the Insurance Fund contributed to the health service because that Fund covered every employed person, rich and poor alike. How could an income limit be set for health care when none applied to cash benefits? And Beveridge did not see how it could protect private practice, because those who had contributed to the national service would not want to pay again:

> If, therefore, it is desired to preserve a substantial scope for private practice and restrict the right to service without a charge on treatment to persons below

193

a certain income limit, medical service cannot be contributory. It must be provided out of general taxation as a free service, like elementary education.[13]

These words appeared in the first draft of the Beveridge Report and they must have taken Maude by surprise when he read them in July 1942. For Beveridge had now reversed himself: a tax-based service had become a way of excluding people rather than covering everyone, and the insurance principle was used to justify the inclusion of the well-to-do.

The final report did not appear in this form. Beveridge excluded the second sentence and changed the first to define 'contributory' more closely, ruling out only an *en bloc* contribution from the Insurance Fund if it were desired to exclude the well-to-do; they could be left out if contributions were levied on an individual basis.[14] But something of a contradiction remained which confused those who thought insurance principles were meant to restrict coverage rather than extend them.

The other difficulty involved the hospital service. Beveridge expected it as well as GP care to be free to everyone. As he put it in February 1942:

If there is any prospect whatever of a charge, the patient may delay applying. If the line is taken that health of the individual is a national and not an individual interest, medical service should be provided as freely as the services of a policeman or a soldier.[15]

But the Ministry, in its 1941 statement on post-war hospital policy, had called for patient payments through contributory schemes or otherwise. If GP care were divorced from NHI and made part of the public health service, it seemed logical to impose charges there as well. The department did not want to do that for reasons similar to those of Beveridge, so somehow it had to create a distinction between the two. Where GP care was concerned, it maintained, there was no tradition of payment. Some club practice remained, but it was not comparable to the £6 million raised by the hospital savings movement: 'It may, therefore, be predicted with fair certainty that an attempt to foster large scale voluntary savings movements in connection with domiciliary treatment would fail.' In any case, free access was needed for GP care to promote 'timely medical advice' and ensure certification of sickness benefits. Hospital access could stand on its own — 'the need for treatment is so often so urgent as to override any scruples on the score of expense'.[16]

Nevertheless, the scope for imposing charges was limited by the Beveridge view. The only way it could be defended was by confining it to hotel costs, since they represented a partial saving to the patient. Medical costs would be covered by the contribution from the Insurance Fund, but the Ministry wanted this to apply over the health service as a whole — to care provided by hospital doctors as well as GPs. Apparently in response to this demand, Beveridge raised the amount from £15 to £40 million, but he did not present a convincing case for a hotel charge and called only for a small deduction from disability benefit.[17] In the end, the

Reconstruction Committee decided the amount was not worth collecting, and so by the time Maude left the department in July 1945 the Ministry plan had evolved to the point where it offered free care to everyone.

By then the service was also far more comprehensive than Maude had intended. Mental hospital treatment was added due to demands from the doctors and the Scottish Department[18] — while dental care was included at the urging of the official Teviot Committee, despite the shortage of dentists.[19] With optical care incorporated as well, the plan assumed the wide-ranging dimensions that Beveridge envisaged.

Ministry adopts Beveridge view

In the process, the Ministry followed the lead of the Scottish Department in embracing the concept of universal coverage. When the Beveridge Report appeared, here was the way the civil servants from both departments justified the inclusion of everyone:

1 If a substantial percentage of the Social Security Fund is paid toward the cost of the health service as Beveridge suggests, then the service cannot exclude anyone who pays contributions.
2 Even if no such payment were made to the health service, every rate and tax payer should be entitled to use it since (as was then contemplated) it will be under municipal control: 'It would be contrary to the practice and tradition of local government to fix an income limit.'
3 An income limit would be welcomed only by the doctors, who want to protect private practice; it would be resented by the public and in particular by the middle class.
4 In any case, everyone needs to be covered to promote public health.[20]

Bevan, when he assumed office in August 1945, did not hesitate to adopt this creed. During the 1920s he had experienced hardship from the unemployment insurance system and that, combined with a distaste for means tests, led him to favour benefits of right.[21] Nor did he, with his roots in the south Wales coal industry, feel affection for the insurance industry; he knew all too well how employers and casualty companies had exploited workmen's compensation. By the time the Beveridge Report appeared, Bevan was a firm believer in the non-contributory principle and he applied it to the NHS, despite arguments raised by American friends.[22]

There was no question in his mind but that the service should cover everyone. Income limits, he feared, would perpetuate the double standard of treatment that had plagued the panel — and it would hit the middle classes hard; Bevan had no intention of excluding them from the benefits of the welfare state. Britain, as a result, did not repeat the mistake made by German socialists in the Weimar Republic.[23]

No one in the department dissented. Indeed, Maude was ready to include the upper as well as the middle classes as early as February 1942.[24] And Ministry officials were in no mood to adopt the contracting-out rights which had been permitted under NHI, an arrangement which enabled insured persons to seek attention from private or unorthodox practitioners instead of those on the panel. When the doctors raised the demand for a grant-in-aid of private practice in April 1945, Rucker rejected it: there was no case, he argued, for an exemption from Insurance contributions in a service financed mainly from rates and taxes.[25]

Unorthodox practitioners fared no better. Indeed, when Christian Scientists raised a similar demand, the department revealed a more important consideration behind its rejection: 'The real reason, of course, why we do not want Christian Scientists to contract out is that we do not think unorthodox forms of treatment will produce such good results as the National Health Service.'[26]

Chapter nineteen

NHS costs

With its plans in a preliminary state, the Ministry made no attempt to estimate costs until Beveridge pressed the point in March 1942, seeking data on existing services, public and private. Maude cited a figure of £185 million, taken no doubt from the estimate made by PEP before the war for Britain as a whole, but he thought it should be cut to £130 million because the department proposed to exclude mental hospital care. A further reduction, he added, should be made for cash benefits since they had been included in the amounts allowed for NHI, workmen's compensation, and other systems. No attempt had been made to confine the data to health care.[1]

At that point, only the GP service had been closely calculated and the amount specified — £35 million — included a figure of nearly £5 million for the 4,100 health centres Maude proposed to introduce. On average, each centre would contain five GPs caring for 10,000 patients and would cost some £1,200 with only £50 allowed for equipment — or £10 per doctor.[2] Epps was shocked when he saw these figures, and urged Maude to raise the figure for equipment to £200 per doctor. As the son of a well-known homoeopathic practitioner, Dr George Epps, the Government Actuary was in a position to know something about the problems of medical care, but Maude ignored the point and cited only the Ministry's hope of realizing savings elsewhere — on drug costs through a salaried service, and on GP efficiency by increasing list size to 2,500 in urban districts as opposed to 2,000 in rural areas.[3] Though the cost per health centre was later raised to £2,000 or £3,000, the total estimate for the GP service remained at £35 million when negotiations began in 1943, and that was condemned as too low by Latham and his municipal colleagues.[4]

Estimate for Beveridge Report

In July 1942 Beveridge pressed the point again, seeking a fuller estimate of costs based on the array of service he proposed to include in his report. This time, Maude drew on data supplied by his finance officer, H.H. George, and that showed a total of £100 to £120 million made up as follows:

Local authority hospital and health services	£30 million
Voluntary hospitals	15 million
GP for everyone	35 million
Dental care for everyone	20 million
	£100 million

To this had to be added spending on optical, Poor Law, and nursing services, thereby putting the gross amount between £100 and £120 million. But the net cost would be lower since the Ministry contemplated making a 50 per cent charge for dental, optical, and similar services, as well as a hotel charge for hospital stays.[5]

Only the total was given to Beveridge, but the details were supplied to Epps who judged the £100–120 million to be 'a conservative estimate'.[6] These figures covered only England and Wales and made no allowance for inflation. When £20 million was added for Scotland and the whole increased by 25 per cent to take account of price rises, the total came to nearly £170 million, and that was the figure cited by Beveridge in his report.[7] Aside from Epps, others thought this to be a reasonable estimate: both PEP and an Oxford statistician produced similar amounts.[8]

However, Beveridge added an assumption of his own: he made no allowance for an increase in expenditure between 1945 (when he expected the health service to begin) and 1965, £170 million being cited for both years. To justify that, Beveridge thought 'there will actually be some development of the service, and as a consequence of this development a reduction in the number of cases requiring it'.[9] In other words, he expected the health of the nation to improve as a result of the health service and that would offset any increase in costs.

Epps estimated a somewhat higher figure for 1965 — £180 million[10] — but the difference was not enough to deter him from accepting the Beveridge figure in the Actuary's appendage to the Report. The only point Epps added was a warning against an increase in the claims rate for cash benefits. Doctors, he suggested, might require longer periods off work to ensure recovery and patients might have a weaker incentive to return due to the higher level of benefits.[11]

Costs exceed estimates

After the Beveridge Report appeared in November 1942, George periodically altered the estimates to take account of changed provisions — like the removal of the hotel charge. But these changes did not significantly affect the total. In December 1945 the Ministry produced an estimate of £145 million for England and Wales, and that was the figure cited when the Bill was published in March 1946.[12] But costs rose sharply after the NHS began and when the Minister had to ask Parliament for a supplementary estimate in February 1949, he defended his earlier figure on the grounds that he did not want to prejudice pay negotiations: if the doctors had thought the costs would be higher, they might have wanted more for themselves.[13]

The estimated burden on the Exchequer for England and Wales rose from £110 million in 1946 to £179 million at the end of 1947 and reached a net annual rate of £242 million for the first year of the service — 1948-9.[14] This compares with the Beveridge estimate of £110 million after making allowance for the £40 million contribution from the Insurance Fund and £20 million for Scotland.[15] And the costs went on rising year by year, so that by 1965 they exceeded £1,200 million.[16] But as Brian Abel-Smith and Richard Titmuss (two academic experts employed by an official committee to analyse spending on the NHS) pointed out in 1956, the costs were reasonable when compared with the country's resources.[17] During the 1950s the proportion spent on the service actually fell, and thereafter it did not increase as rapidly as the rate in most of the developed world. By 1983, Britain spent only 6.3 per cent of gross national product on health care, compared with the 8 per cent to 9 per cent rate prevalent in the European Economic Community, while the American figure was as high as 10.8 per cent.[18]

Nevertheless, there is no doubt the Ministry grossly under-estimated the cost of the NHS. Why did the Government Actuary as well as others think the figure reasonable? Where they all went wrong was in the hospital service, and it was the additions to staff and pay that produced the largest increase.[19] No one took account of the way costs would rise in the voluntary hospitals once they passed into public ownership. Rucker, as late as August 1945, hoped to secure a subsidized service particularly from consultants, but all hope of that disappeared in 1948. Bevan's decision to nationalize the hospital service meant that everyone who worked in the old voluntary sector would receive the same pay as those who had been formerly employed in the municipal world.

Revenue costs rose sharply in the hospital service, but the same could not be said of capital expenditure. Indeed, it fell dramatically: by 1952-3 it was at a level less than one-third the amount (expressed in 1952-3 prices) spent in 1938-9.[20] Yet as the hospital surveys revealed, 'the state of hospital buildings in July, 1948 was far from satisfactory'.[21] An ambitious building programme was badly needed, but it did not begin until the 1960s and then it had to be cut in the 1970s when a world recession, triggered by a rise in oil prices, crippled the British economy.

Since then the hospital programme has failed to keep pace with needs, and Britain faces the same problem it had when the NHS began — revenue demands always take precedence over capital expenditure. In 1979 the department's policy planning unit issued a report on health capital which stressed the need 'to make the best use of the inherited stock'.[22] This was a prescription to 'mend and make do' rather than build new. Yet by then, according to the works officers who manage NHS buildings, as much as $4 billion was required to bring 2,300 hospitals and 4,000 other buildings up to modern standards.[23]

Treasury and Tory acquiescence

No one could have foreseen these problems when the NHS began — nor was any attempt made to relate costs to gross national product before Abel-Smith and Titmuss set the fashion in 1956. What concerned the Treasury was the cost to the Exchequer, and that is the main consideration today. Yet from the moment Maude produced his first estimate, successive Chancellors displayed an amazing acquiesence.

This was true even when the Conservative Kingsley Wood was in charge. He had been a proponent of assurance interests from the start of NHI, and his law firm — Wood, Williams, and Murphy — continued to act for the offices after Wood entered Parliament. But that did not prevent the Methodist solicitor from becoming an ardent advocate of health service development, displaying the same concern for wider provision as he had shown when the Ministry of Health was formed in 1919. At that point Wood was elected MP and held two junior appointments at the department before becoming a most able Minister of Health himself in 1935.[24]

It was then that the planning of the health service began, and Wood did not lose interest after he became Chancellor of the Exchequer in 1940. In that capacity he felt bound to speak out against the financial implications of the Beveridge Report, but his comments on the health side were subdued. Indeed, when Churchill sought his views in November 1942, Wood showed no enthusiasm for the insurance principle: not only did it rule out the prospect of universal coverage but, he warned, it would impose a heavy burden on British industry.[25] Far better to let the state bear the costs of health care in an economy so dependent on exports; that, indeed, was the advice given by a Keynes disciple in the economic offices of the cabinet, James Meade.[26]

But Wood did fear the American reaction because it might be felt that Britain was dividing the spoils before the war was won, a concern that was shared by one of Churchill's most trusted advisers, Lord Cherwell, himself an advocate of health sevice development.[27] That perhaps may partly account for Churchill's reluctance to make legislative commitments in February 1943, but he did endorse the basic principles of the Beveridge Report, including its call for a comprehensive health service.[28]

The civil servants at the Treasury were more cautious. They were alarmed by the £900 million estimate for cash benefits that Beveridge made and in August 1942 Sir Alan Barlow told Maude there would be little money for health care.[29] However, a Treasury committee headed by Sir Bernard Gilbert let the Ministry estimate of £170 million go forward for the world to see in the Beveridge Report. Perhaps Gilbert, like the doctors, thought a royal commission would study the problem before action was taken, but Beveridge had found a skilful way to stifle debate: by incorporating the health service as 'Assumption B', he made it appear as if the need were self-evident. Not until the White Paper was nearing completion did Gilbert show concern. Then, on 14 January 1944, he objected to the to the prospect of ' a comprehensive service for all'; this, he warned Maude, is 'no where qualified'.[30]

The Reconstruction Committee refused to be deterred and on 3 February it went ahead with a White Paper that promised to create a health service for everyone. Thanks to Woolton, not even a hotel charge survived: the Tory members of the Committee were as committed to the universal ideal as their Labour colleagues (see pages 162–3).

Where the parties did differ was on the question of a salaried service, and Woolton managed to persuade the Labour members to accept the compromise in the White Paper. But he and his Conservative colleagues had to offer something in return — the removal of the hotel charge and acceptance of universal coverage. They felt free to do so because of the Chancellor's attitude: Sir John Anderson deferred to Woolton on the hotel charge and raised no objection to the costs involved.[31] This led Cherwell to believe the Chancellor thought the additional expenditure 'will be worth it'.[32]

That was no surprise to those (like the doctors)[33] who were aware of Anderson's long-standing commitment to public health. He had not only helped to form the panel system but called for its reform as a member of the Royal Commission on NHI. When that body issued its report in 1926, Anderson and his colleagues made clear the direction in which the nation was heading:

> we feel sure that the wider the scope of these [health] services the more difficult it will be to retain the insurance principle. The ultimate solution will lie in the direction of divorcing the medical service entirely from the insurance system and reorganizing it along with all the other public health activities to be supported from public funds.[34]

Churchill's caution

The Prime Minister, however, had reservations. Churchill had not attended the critical Reconstruction Committee meeting and was surprised at Anderson's acquiesence: 'The Chancellor of the Exchequer seems very easy about great additions to the annual Budget.' With all his energies needed for the conduct of war, Churchill had no time to read White Papers 'let alone pass such a vast scheme of social change through my mind, under present conditions'. He feared the Cabinet had agreed too swiftly to the White Paper and, before it was published, he asked his Foreign Secretary (Anthony Eden) to give further consideration, consulting the Tories' shrewdest political advisers, Lord Beaverbrook and Brendan Bracken.[35]

Eden had already discussed the subject with Willink, who claimed he had 'the doctors squared'.[36] But the final decision was not taken until the Cabinet met on 15 February. Then it was felt the new service would pose no threat to private practice or voluntary hospitals; both would survive. This, together with the Chancellor's acceptance of the financial implications, was enough to convince

. the Cabinet and with other Ministers present (including Beaverbrook and Bracken), it approved publication of the White Paper.[37]

The imminence of D-day was an important factor behind Churchill's acquiesence. He did not want to do anything that might break up the coalition before the long-awaited invasion of the continent. But a year later the situation was different. The coalition broke up after the war in Europe ended and, with a general election pending, Churchill was anxious to protect his party's chances. Earlier he and Bracken had approved the concessions Willink and Woolton had made, but by June 1945 Churchill feared the process may have gone too far. He warned Willink that the changes offered doctors would be denounced by Labour 'as a betrayal of all that was promised to the nation by the Coalition Govt'. Before proceeding with the publication of the second White Paper, he advised Willink to consult Beaverbrook: 'I would expect he would be strongly in favour of your proposals. The only question is how will they strike the electors at this juncture?'[38] Beaverbrook apparently disapproved because the proposals were not published — but only Cherwell, it seems, protested: 'it would be a pity if the fruits of these prolonged discussions were jeopardized'.[39]

Treasury reaction to Bevan's plan

Churchill lost the election and Bevan proceeded to create a health service somewhat different from the one Willink proposed. Treasury officials may have been concerned about the Minister's decision to nationalize the hospitals, but they did not show it; Gilbert was worried only about the objection from municipal and voluntary hospital quarters.[40] One MP claimed that Treasury officials preferred central to local control because it enabled them to keep a tighter rein on spending.[41]

The other major change made by Bevan was abolition of the sale of practices, and the £66 million compensation he offered produced no reaction from the Treasury. The only point it challenged was the way the Ministry raised its offer to GPs for maternity work without prior approval (see page 109).

On one point at least, there was no dissent: Willink gave the support of every MP for the 100 per cent principle during the debate on the Bill in May 1946.[42] With that, Beveridge's own Liberal Party concurred. Indeed, four years earlier it had issued the sharpest denunciation made yet of the insurance principle:

> The idea of insurance is a limitation of benefit to known premiums and known risks; the idea of an adequate Health Service is the unlimited care of an incalculable number of persons during an incalculable period, and the provision of benefits limited only by the requirements of the individual case in accordance with the changing standards of modern medical practice. To call any scheme capable of meeting the actual needs of the Health Service to-day by the name of insurance is simply a misnomer, unless the word is used in its general and not its technical financial sense.[43]

Could the country afford it? To *The Lancet* — the enlightened voice of British medicine — there was no doubt: despite the nation's shaky finances, the NHS made sense. It would save work days and lengthen work life. Though gains in life expectancy could not be expected at the same pace as in the past, progress could still be made: 'As long as essentially preventable diseases like diphtheria exist, as long as there are big social gradients in mortality, whatever the cause, there is scope for fresh endeavour in the field of medical care.' In any case, the NHS could not be valued in terms of economics alone, for as Ruskin had said, in the long run 'there is no wealth but life'.[44]

Chapter twenty

Medical movement towards universal coverage

The NHS is unique: no country in the world makes a wider array of services available to all its citizens. For many years even foreign visitors could secure them without charge. Though optical services have now all but disappeared and substantial payments must be made for prescriptions and dental attention, the range of treatment is remarkable. Not even the Soviet Union can match it because there severe restrictions are placed on drugs and other forms of care.

How did such a service arise in a Parliamentary democracy noted for its conservative tendencies? Only twice in this century have politicians found the climate ripe to carry through wide-ranging reform — yet that was enough to create the most comprehensive health service in the world. Two Welshmen — Lloyd George in 1911, Aneurin Bevan in 1946 — devised the tactics needed to put the legislation across, but they could not have succeeded without the co-operation of doctors. Only qualified medical men can make the clinical decisions that health care requires. As a perceptive former civil servant at the Ministry of Health (R.W. Harris) put it in 1936: 'it is of the very essence of reform and progress in regard to the medical care of the nation that you should carry with you the medical profession itself every step along the road'.[1]

British doctors are no less conservative than their counterparts elsewhere, and yet despite the resistance they displayed during negotiations on the NHS, they proved willing to work it. Why did they acquiesce? That is the key question that needs to be asked to understand the emergence of a comprehensive service based on the 100 per cent principle, and the main answer lies in the panel system under the 1911 Insurance Act. That exposed the doctors to state payment and drained their fear of it. By the 1930s nearly all practitioners had joined the panel, leaving only a few thousand GPs, consultants, and specialists outside. Doctors who dreaded being turned into civil servants in 1943 were dismissed with these words: 'The fact is . . . that any of us engaged in panel practice are half Civil Servants already and not noticeably the worse for it.'[2]

Conditioned by this experience, the doctors were ready for a state-financed service covering 80 per cent of the population as early as 1929 and that policy was reaffirmed in 1938 and 1942. From there to 100 per cent coverage was a short step, but the profession feared to take it because the proposal became linked with the Ministry's plan for a whole-time salaried service under municipal control. That, the doctors feared, might subject them to managerial direction which would imperil clinical freedom. And the 100 per cent principle threatened to rule out private practice, an escape route they wanted to keep open in case state service proved unsatisfactory.

On this issue the surgeons were most concerned, since they had the largest scope for private practice, and the emergence of long waiting lists after 1948 made it a continuing object of their attention. GP leaders, by contrast, were ready to accept 100 per cent coverage provided they could secure changes elsewhere, but it took a series of concessions from Willink before their followers would acquiesce. Thereafter, Bevan threw the whole issue in doubt by restoring measures which Willink had dropped, but he eventually secured medical participation by placing a statutory ban on a salaried service.

From this brief review, it is clear that the 1911 Insurance Act was crucial: without the medical attitudes it engendered, no NHS would have emerged. So we need to push our query back further and ask a more fundamental question: how did the doctors come to accept the panel system? That, rather than in issues of hospital development, is where the movement for a health service began.

Freedom from friendly society control

The main reason for medical acceptance of the panel system lay in the nature of club practice that preceded it, and that was an offspring of friendly society development. During the nineteenth century, friendly societies began to employ doctors to provide rudimentary care and certify the cash sickness benefits they offered, but the pay and conditions of work were far from satisfactory. By 1895 the situation had become intolerable, and for the next fifteen years the profession fought a fruitless 'battle of the clubs' to free itself from friendly society control. The effort failed mainly because of a surplus of doctors; the friendly societies had no trouble replacing medical men who boycotted them.

In the end the doctors needed the help of the state to make medical life tolerable. They resisted the conditions offered by Lloyd George — mainly because he had been forced to concede too much influence to the friendly societies in the form of approved societies — but they flocked to the panel as soon as it began. The terms of service were not ideal but they were better than anything experienced in club practice.[3]

This, then, is what started the movement towards an NHS in Britain — the doctors needed state aid to free themselves from friendly society control. One Conservative MP (Sir Henry Craik), speaking for the BMA, made this clear during the debate on a critical amendment to the Insurance Bill in 1911:

> If you do not now place the administration of the medical relief under some public body . . . you will place the profession of medicine in perpetuity under the heel of private societies. . . . The doctors desire . . . to be brought into immediate contact with the State, whose servants they are.[4]

Dain, in 1959, believed the doctors would still be subject to club rule if it had not been for NHI.[5]

Lloyd George was sympathetic to the medical cause and gave all the help he could, but the friendly societies were too firmly entrenched for the process to be completed in 1911. The panel system emerged, with the approved societies able to exert considerable influence over the administration of medical benefit. A series of conflicts ensued which led to a critical clash in 1923 from which the doctors arose victorious. In the midst of this battle, the BMA's secretary (Dr Alfred Cox) again made the profession's preference clear:

> I would rather see the State provide the money. Our Civil Service is incorruptible. I would rather see the Government standing between the insured persons and the medical profession than the approved societies, some of which want the Government to stand aside.[6]

Thereafter, the story is one of increasing medical influence over administration. The main decisions were made at Ministry level and it was there that the profession exerted a growing force. By the 1930s the friendly societies were no longer a threat to British medicine.

However, a new protagonist had emerged in the form of the assurance offices; their opposition made itself felt during the controversy over maternity policy that raged throughout the 1930s (see page 6). And just when the doctors thought the danger of approved society interference in panel pay had disappeared, it arose again during a dispute with the Ministry in 1937.[7] GPs were divided on many issues, but where the approved societies were concerned they shared one aim — curb the growing influence of the insurance industry. Together with the unions, the doctors started a movement which led to the Beveridge Report and the end of approved society involvement in medical affairs.

Resisting municipal encroachment

Health services were part of this movement because the wider they became, the more difficult it was to retain the insurance principle. The doctors threw their weight behind an extended service partly to undermine the approved society system.

But there was a more important consideration — the threat posed by the growth of local authority services between the wars. Some BMA leaders welcomed the movement as a way of undermining the approved societies and stimulating GP interest in a community direction; they thought it might be possible to find a place for GPs in municipal work and form a satisfactory relationship with MOHs. But most doctors recoiled from the prospect; they feared any tie with local authorities and saw the development of municipal services as a threat to income. To counteract them, they favoured the extension of the panel so that it would cover persons and services being drawn into the municipal net.

This was the main reason for the publication of the BMA's 'General medical service for the nation' scheme in 1929; with the Local Government Act holding out the danger of a rapid expansion of municipal services, the doctors wanted the panel to cover 'dependants and specialists'. The BMA's secretary, Alfred Cox, sent a copy of the scheme to the Permanent Secretary of the Ministry, Sir Arthur Robinson, with this explanation: 'It is an attempt on our part to show how we think the medical service of the country ought to be developed during the next 10 or 15 years.'[8]

Neither Robinson nor his colleagues were impressed, and that included the CMO, Sir George Newman. From the moment he entered the new Ministry of Health in 1919 Newman seemed intent on expanding the public health service, but now he found the BMA scheme not only too expensive but 'too "socialistic" for the bulk of the profession'.[9]

BMA leaders refused to be deterred. They pressed their plan again in 1933 when 200,000 insured persons were threatened with the loss of medical benefit (due to unemployment) as the result of an Act passed in 1932.[10] The Ministry again refused to act. This time the Minister of Health, E. Hilton Young (later Lord Kennet), warned the Prime Minister, Ramsay Macdonald, against holding a conference to consider the possibility: 'I think it is quite likely that it would be stampeded into a recommendation in favour of the scheme and then if the conference had been initiated, or even formally recognised by the Government, we should be in a very difficult position.'[11]

The controller in charge of NHI, Sir Walter Kinnear, agreed. He was not only alarmed by the cost of the BMA scheme but fearful of where it might lead: 'Indeed it would be impossible to stop at the British Medical Association's scheme, which would cover only 80 per cent of the population. A proposal to provide this would at once raise the question of the provision of a State medical service' — and by that he meant one that would be extended to 'all sections of the population'.[12]

The department did not have long to wait for such a proposal to emerge. In October 1934 the MPU produced a plan calling for 100 per cent coverage, but unlike the BMA's scheme, it did not include specialist services; only GP care was to be provided to everyone. Public pressure, the MPU thought, would be sufficient to push the service beyond GP range: 'There is no turning back for the State in this matter of medical service, nor any standing still. The pressure of public opinion will undoubtedly compel greater and greater adherence in the direction of a full service.'[13] Nor was the MPU content to leave the movement to chance. Two months later it affiliated with the TUC and helped to lead that influential body in the direction of a service for everyone.

Yet another medical organization threw its weight behind the movement for wider care — the newly-formed SMA. Though its numbers were small, its influence was enlarged by its affiliation with the Labour Party, and in 1934 it won support for a motion calling for the creation of a state medical service open to all.[14] With Labour out of power, action was possible only at the local level, but led by Somerville Hastings, SMA leaders did much to make the LCC's municipal system the most comprehensive in the land.

The doctors who made up the SMA were moved by communal concern, but it was economic interest that drove most doctors on, making them favour reform in a narrow sense, and they recoiled as soon as that interest was imperilled. A wider public service was fine as long as it enhanced income and left working conditions alone; it was a danger when it threatened to turn doctors into salaried servants. The profession did not want to substitute MOH for friendly or approved society rule. Only the SMA favoured local authority direction, not the BMA or MPU. The MPU was a thorn in the BMA's side and challenged many policies, but on the issue of local authority control it registered no dissent. On the contrary, it was more strongly opposed to a municipal tie than some leaders of the BMA. Thus, when the BMA and TUC published their joint maternity policy in 1938, the MPU made clear precisely why most doctors objected to municipal direction:

> there is great annoyance now felt by medical men in many areas owing to the manner in which Medical Officers of Health are instructing midwives to call to their assistance only selected doctors. The doctors selected are usually women and persons with short experience, while older practitioners with long experience find that they are regarded by the M.O.H. as inefficient although he can have no knowledge of the real factors. It is this type of *uncontrolled personal administration* which makes members of the profession increasingly unwilling to allow maternity or other medical work to pass any further under the control of Local Authorities and their officers.[15]

Ministry inaction

Ministry officials ignored these warnings and failed to exploit the opening provided by the profession. If expansion came, they wanted it done under municipal direction. Robinson was anxious to abolish insurance committees, 'the cost of which is a sheer waste of money badly needed elsewhere'.[16] The BMA seemed willing to accept that, but Robinson doubted if local authorities would grant the co-opted place on public health committees the doctors desired.[17] They would also oppose the BMA's demand for extension of the free choice principle across the public sector — to means-tested patients (under public assistance committees) as well as to insured persons under NHI.[18] But it was the financial implications that alarmed Robinson: unless they were realized, holding a conference 'may in fact, not further, but set back the eventual synthesis in public health organisation to which I at all events was looking forward in working for the Local Govt Act, 1929'.[19]

Only the doctors refused to be deterred by finance; indeed, they declined to estimate costs when the department requested it. As Robinson complained in 1934, 'Their answer is that they cannot, and that they assumed that we should do this part of the business for them!'[20] Newman wanted to turn the BMA scheme down flat, but the government did not feel that to be politic.[21] So the Ministry gave consideration to the creation of a royal commission or departmental committee on the lines of the Cathcart Committee in Scotland.[22] Neither was appointed. The doctors were left to work out a plan for specialist services with the approved societies, and those talks collapsed in 1938.[23] This left only the Cathcart Committee as an engine of reform, and it finally forced the Ministry into action. But as the Committee's secretary, Neville, pointed out, the scheme recommended in Scotland was 'practically the BMA's plan'.[24] So throughout the 1930s it was the doctors who set the pace.

Medical pressure for extension

Though Ministry planning began in 1936, little was done until the war began, and efforts were concentrated on the hospital sector. The doctors were not content with that: they were tired of waiting for a wider panel system. The MPU was the first to act: in 1940 it pressed the TUC to demand the enlargement of the GP service to the nation as a whole. This, together with the impetus generated by the EMS, induced the BMA to create an MPC embracing all sections of the profession.[25] Five months before the Beveridge Report appeared, the MPC endorsed the extension proposals made by the BMA in 1929 and 1938: it wanted dependants added to state provision and since the income limit under NHI had just been raised to £420, this meant the doctors now favoured inclusion of 90 per cent of the population.

At that point — June 1942 — it looked like the profession would slip easily into a service covering everyone; indeed, at its representative meeting held shortly thereafter, the BMA approved the concept by a small majority (see page 44). Nor should it be forgotten that it was the BMA, backed by the Scottish Department, that forced the inclusion of mental hospitals before the lunacy law was reformed (see page 195). Only after negotiations began in March 1943 did the doctors reverse their stand, and that was because Maude pushed blindly ahead with his scheme for a salaried service. Thereafter, the doctors repeatedly raised objections to local authority control and the 100 per cent principle. (The MPU accepted the latter but not the former; only the SMA welcomed both.) Had the Ministry chosen to drop all thought of municipal involvement, agreement might have been reached in 1944, but the White Paper in February gave the doctors reason to believe that the department was still heading in a local authority direction. Not until that spectre was removed and the escape route of private practice protected did the profession accept the universal concept.

What the profession gained

Though the doctors resisted the creation of the NHS between 1946 and 1948, it enabled them to realize the two objectives they had pursued between the wars — freedom from approved society interference and local authority encroachment. But that was not the only benefit: universal coverage extended protection against the competition of unqualified practitioners. Unlike NHI, no contracting out was allowed from the NHS: if a patient wanted free care from the state, he had to consult a registered medical man, not one whose only qualification came from a school of fringe medicine.

State intervention thus proved beneficial to the profession; the movement for an NHS succeeded because it coincided with the interests of British doctors. Consultants still have much to gain from private practice but the same cannot be said of GPs; most are content to treat patients paid by the state. It was general practice, not the hospital world, that made universal coverage possible and the NHS will survive only so long as its needs harmonize with those of GPs.

Part 6
Assessment

Sir John Maude's insistence on the doctrine that local government provides the only possible framework for the new health service is essentially a relic of the past.

From the first draft of a paper by the King's Fund, GLC Record Office A/KE/355, 'Notes on doctrine of local government responsibility for the health service', 6 November 1944

Chapter twenty-one

Civil servants and doctors: their influence compared

The British civil service is inspired by high ideals and nowhere was this more evident than in the planning of the NHS. During the 1930s the depression cast a gloom over Ministry activity, inducing a resistance to reform even from its CMO, the revered Sir George Newman. But once restraints were broken by war conditions and pressure from the Beveridge Committee, Ministry officials worked hard to create a service worthy of the nation. The mountain of documents in the Public Record Office offers testimony to the strength of their concern.

But health care cannot be provided by civil servants alone: it requires the co-operation of doctors, and Ministry officials almost lost that aid by their obsessive desire for municipal control. For this, Maude and his colleagues were not solely responsible: the expectation had been part of government since the panel system was born. To politicians as well as experts, local authority direction made sense; even the doctors seemed ready to accept it in 1929 to stop municipal encroachment on private practice. The general medical service scheme published by the BMA in that year left open the question of insurance committee abolition.

But the disputes that followed changed all of that. Relations deteriorated to the point where GPs could not stand the sight of MOHs, particularly after a heated exchange at Croydon in 1937. When the BMA reissued its general medical service scheme the following year, the chairman of the committee that drafted it, Dr J.B. Miller, made the profession's attitude clear: 'In 1929 there was a feeling that the administration of National Health Insurance should be taken away from insurance committees and placed in the hands of local authorities. He thought that feeling had disappeared.'[1]

From that point on it was apparent that the doctors would pose the strongest resistance to municipal control, yet Maude pushed blindly in that direction and no one in the department dissented. To rational Oxbridge-educated civil servants, logic demanded local authority rule. Not only would it make for managerial tidiness but it was more in keeping with the dignity of a noble profession. Commercial competition had turned doctors into businessmen and degraded their ethical behaviour. Maude wanted to raise the quality of panel care and transform GPs into gentlemen. It was this, together with the desire for efficient organization, that made him so insistent on a salaried service. In the process he proved to be less pragmatic than the ardent socialist who became Minister of Health in 1945.

Importance of medical politics

What Maude failed to understand was the significance of medical politics. He needed someone at hand who could gauge the medical mood and tell him what the doctors would tolerate. Sir Weldon Dalrymple-Champneys, the Ministry's observer on the MPC, was not the man for the task. He was a dilettante, known as a 'playboy' within the department, who had no experience of clinical practice or panel negotiations. The son of Sir Francis Champneys, the venerable obstetrician who championed the cause of midwives, his progress within the Ministry probably owed more to his father's reputation than his own abilities. He was more interested in animal than human disease and was passed over twice for CMO, first to Jameson in 1940 and then to Charles in 1950. According to Godber, who shared an office with him, he never received an assignment that stretched his abilities.[2] Yet this was the man Maude relied on to tell him what the doctors would accept.

As for Maude's own perception, his insights did not extend far beyond the disciplinary procedure with which he, as a legal officer, had long been associated. For wider guidance he turned to another layman, de Montmorency, who found it difficult to offer independent advice; whatever the Permanent Secretary wanted was good enough for him. Jameson, as CMO, was better able to gauge the profession's mood and he had a medical advisory committee, composed partly of doctors from the BMA's negotiating team, to help him. But its members either accepted the department's view or failed to change it, their remit being confined to more technical subjects. Jameson himself was reluctant to challenge Ministry policy; with his municipal background, he could not resist the temptation to accept local authority direction. All the doctors needed for protection, in his view, was a CMB to deal with hiring and firing.

The medical leader who could have helped Maude most did not enjoy the Permanent Secretary's confidence. This was Charles Hill, the lively secretary of the BMA, who incurred Maude's wrath by the fiery way he opposed the salaried plan. As a Brackenbury disciple, Hill worked hard during the 1930s to forge an accommodation with local authorities and he did his best to push the MPC in that direction. The closest he came was the call for health centres to be provided by statutory means.

But the report the MPC issued was only an interim one in draft form. It did not present the profession's fixed position, nor could it have done so since the medical mood changed from month to month. Furthermore the report contained clear warnings against local authorities as constituted. It urged the formation of new bodies confined to health duties and — most important of all — containing many medical representatives. That could not be arranged in the time scale contemplated, nor were Maude and his colleagues inclined to work in that direction. They thought a little tampering with municipal health committees, combined with a CMB, would be sufficient to satisfy the profession; when ample salaries and improved working conditions were added, GPs would pose no objection to whole-time service.

How wrong these judgements were became apparent when discussions began in March 1943. In the face of medical feeling, Hill could not maintain the accommodating stance he had adopted the year before. Had he done so, the BMA might have lost the confidence of the profession and given scope to unsavoury forces lurking in rival organizations. Yet no one in the Ministry seemed to understand this, except possibly Jameson. When discussions began, Brown went so far as to demand that everything be held in confidence; no written documents were to be disseminated among the rank and file.[3] This was an impossible rule for the BMA to follow. When Hill broke it with Jameson's consent, Maude developed an undying hatred for the BMA official, which made it difficult for the two to meet. Not until Maude withdrew in 1945 did Hill find it easy to offer advice, but from that point on he did his best to steer the department in an acceptable direction. Moran himself bears testimony to this, and he was no admirer of Hill. When the RCP president was searching for a way out of the impasse in negotiations in December 1947, it was Hill who suggested the concessions needed:

> He did not seem to me to ask for a lot in the hope that he could get something but made an honest attempt to get a minimum that would alter atmosphere of GPs and displayed some ingenuity in making it as little provocative as possible.[4]

Medical influence on policy

Once negotiations began, the main policy-making force came from outside the civil service. Medical fear of Ministry and municipal control rose as Maude held to his salaried plan. The doctors tried to counteract it with a corporate body, and when that failed they proposed a strong advisory council under their direction. But their expectation of influence through that means was as unrealistic as the one held by Dawson in 1919.[5] The doctors could not hope to match the daily involvement of civil servants with policy and politicians. The only way to protect themselves was by insisting on negotiation with outside bodies before changes were introduced. The BMA's Insurance Acts Committee under NHI had shown the way; the same technique had to be applied to the new health service.

It did not take long for the BMA's Representative Committee to demonstrate its worth. Through that medium and that medium alone the doctors forced Brown and Maude to reverse their stand for a salaried service. One BMA leader (Dr Frank Gray) who participated in the process took pride in the result when he wrote his memoir in 1981: 'we had shown the civil servants no measure that embodies both their aims and the policy of the party in power can be imposed against the will of a united profession'.[6]

To harness that will required astute leadership, and Charles Hill supplied it. To do so required a *volte face* on his part. Before 1943 he (together with Anderson and Souttar) had shown every inclination to accept municipal rule; indeed, it has been claimed that Hill fought Dain on the issue.[7] But Hill was too wise an official to flout the will of the profession; once medical opposition appeared, he had to go along. Only in that way could he hope to mould negotiating policy and alter the views of the civil service. From 1911, BMA leaders had been thrown into the political arena and their association with NHI affairs had given them the skills needed to deal with Ministry mandarins.

Moran and his college colleagues had no similar experience. They were new to political processes and the autocratic manner in which they operated made it difficult for them to understand their BMA counterparts. Moran was no democrat and disliked democratic procedures; he wanted to lead the profession, not wait for the rank and file to speak. Even when Hill made an heroic attempt to support him in 1944, Moran thought he had taken the opposite stance.[8]

But the very nature of Moran's oligarchic rule had its advantages: it gave him freedom to take initiatives which were denied to Hill. Hill was more sensitive to the medical mood, but he was also imprisoned by it. He could not stray far from the stand taken by his followers without undermining his own position. Moran suffered no similar restraint, and the freedom he enjoyed fitted his temperament. Egotistic to the extreme, the RCP president displayed a boldness that not even Dawson would have dared to emulate. He was determined to create a proper consultant service and would let nothing stand in his way. What he failed to realize was that his arch-opponent in the consultant world, H. J. McCurrich, shared many of his aims and had McCurrich been given a proper place in college circles, the two might have worked together. As Godber has observed, all the bitterness about the role of the GP-specialist could have been so easily avoided.[9] Since it was not, Moran entered NHS negotiations in 1946 with divided ranks and Horder almost displaced him. Had that happened, the outcome might have been very different. It was only by the narrowest of margins that Moran was able to give the aid the Minister needed in the crisis of 1948.

In view of Moran's close tie with Churchill, it was remarkable that he was able to exercise so much influence with Bevan. Hill, in Moran's view, lost all weight with the Labour Minister because of his decision to stand as a parliamentary candidate for the Conservative and Liberal parties.[10] Yet Moran did not let his own relationship with the former Tory Prime Minister stop him from having private talks with Bevan at Pruniers. It was the very insensitivity of the man that enabled him to act so boldly.

Bevan's role

But one cannot ignore the character of the Minister himself. The civil service role changed radically after Bevan took over. Before 1945 Maude and his colleagues dominated policy-making, producing endless proposals for Ministers to consider. Elliot, Macdonald, and Brown all slavishly followed their lead. Brown counted so little in Maude's concern that he was not even shown the Ministry's salaried plan until Beveridge, Epps, Anderson of the BMA and others had been given the chance to comment.

Willink tried to depart from this procedure but ended by making so many concessions that he produced a plan of unworkable complexity. As he admitted in his memoirs:

> I was constitutionally unable to resist the temptation . . . to master too much detail. Another way to put it is, perhaps, that I was more a civil servant than a politician. I do not think very much went wrong: I do not believe any great opportunities were missed: but my tenure of the office was ordinary, not distinguished.[11]

All of this changed after Bevan took over; even Willink thought the new Minister was right to nationalize the hospital service. Bevan did not act like a civil servant, nor let the civil service dictate to him. Maude was removed before he arrived and Rucker went a few years later. The Welshman's method was to hold conferences and solicit views; if civil servants wanted to influence him, they had to do so openly.[12] This explains why so few position papers are in the Public Record Office for the period after July 1945.

More often than not Bevan made decisions by himself during the cut and thrust of negotiations. He was, as Godber has pointed out, capable of flashing insights. Yet few Ministers have shown the flexibility he displayed in dealing with the medical profession. He did not let his ardent belief in socialist principles stand in the way of necessary compromise.[13] The nationalization of the hospital service was his most brilliant stroke. Whether he conceived the idea himself or took advice from others was not so important as his willingness to implement it. Overnight he broke the deadlock in negotiations and made possible integration of the hospital sector. Had he stuck to Labour insistence on municipal rule, the division in the hospital world might have persisted to this day.

Whether the NHS itself owes everything to Bevan and the Labour government is more questionable. The onset of war probably made some kind of health service inevitable. Even before 1939, the gaps in provision and the failings of NHI had made the Ministry alive to change. The Beveridge Report and the community spirit generated by the war made that reform more comprehensive than anyone had dreamed before. Bevan had the good fortune to spearhead a movement that already had force. Lloyd George, by contrast, had no such advantage and that is why the task he assumed in 1911 was much more difficult than the one Bevan faced in 1945.

Civil service influence

The NHS was thus the result of a complex of forces, but in its development the civil service played no small part. Maude, Rucker, Jameson, and Hawton — all in that order exerted influence: Maude in attempting to impose a municipal structure; Rucker in finding ways to satisfy the doctors and voluntary hospitals; Jameson as a conciliator between medical negotiators and lay civil servants; Hawton as the synthesizer and idealist intent on seeing the NHS realized in its purest form. Douglas arrived too late to do much more than carry through policies initiated by others.

Of the first four, Maude was too much inclined to impose his view on others — while Rucker, who was known within the department as the 'great appeaser',[14] erred in the opposite direction. It was due to his influence that Willink made so many concessions as to leave negotiations in hopeless array. However, Rucker at least showed a willingness to adapt; his flexibility was matched neither by Maude nor Hawton.[15] Both took too rigid a stand. Only Jameson struck the right note in his efforts at conciliation.

In the end no one within the civil service could match the influence of those outside. The doctors — led by Hill and Moran — all but imposed their will on the department. It took a strong Minister like Bevan to hold the line and prevent the structure from being whittled away. But he too recognized the need to satisfy the profession, and it was this lesson above all that provided the guide for the future: without the doctors there would have been no NHS, and without their support there is no chance of its surviving.

It did not take long for the cost estimates of the new service to be shown to be too low. No doubt many in the Ministry expected this to happen,[16] but they clung to the modest amounts they projected in the hope of satisfying the Treasury. Only later was it shown how the growth in expenditure remained modest by international standards. Almost without realizing what they had done, the planners of the NHS created a system that was the most cost effective in the world.

But it did more than give value for money: far more vital, the NHS offered everyone the promise of care. Though shortages and waiting lists did much to undermine expectations, the basic principle remained intact: no one in Britain had to demonstrate ability to pay before he could secure the right to treatment. For Bevan, this was the realization of a socialist dream, but others saw it simply as the application of Christian principles. In a civilized society, they felt, health care was essential for the well-being of the nation. And it was a Conservative leader, not a socialist, who set the country on this course. As early as 1872, one of the great Prime Ministers of British history, Benjamin Disraeli, made the following declaration:

> the first consideration of a Minister should be the health of the people. A land may be covered with historical trophies, with museums of science and galleries of art, with universities and libraries; the people may be civilized and ingenious; the country may even be famous in the annals and action of the world, but, gentlemen, if the population every ten years decreases, and the stature of the race every ten years diminishes, the history of that country will soon be the history of the past.[17]

Appendix
The crisis in NHS negotiations,
April 1948

NHS negotiations reached a critical point in April 1948: something had to be done to ease the doctors' fear of a salaried service, and Moran persuaded Bevan to take the necessary action. Though GPs at large were furious at the RCP president's intervention, this did not apply to some of their spokesmen. Dr Hugh Clegg, editor of the *British Medical Journal*, strongly but secretly supported Moran's initiative. Following is a revealing exchange of letters that took place between them at the height of the controversy. Clegg's letters were written in his own hand.

British Medical Journal

B.M.A. House
Tavistock Square
London, W.C.1
13 April 1948

Dear Lord Moran,

Just after I spoke to you on the phone I went to Paris to take the chair at a conference on medical abstracting held by 'Unesco' — a dry enough subject but full of unexpected opportunities for controversy! So I wasnt here when your letter arrived with the news that the College resolutions were to be published on the Monday. It was magnanimous of you to urge the Minister again to re-consider the question of basic salary. And it worked! There is no doubt at all that his concession on this, coupled with the acceptance of the first of the Comitia's resolutions, has broken the deadlock and brought to an end a fight which, if continued to the end, would have been disastrous. I gather that yesterday he made further and important concessions. What I have always feared was a last ditch struggle over buying and selling. There will of course be a hullabaloo over this in our correspondence columns, but in the end I dont think that more than 15–20% of G.P.s will stand out of the Service on that account.

We are of course now receiving the usual letters about the wicked Presidents! I shall try to put the matter in perspective in a leader this week, and hope that this will discourage letter writers. But some of them will have to be allowed to blow off steam — the correspondence columns provide a useful safety valve.

May I end on a 'personal' note by saying that I think you have done a very great service to the medical profession, and that when the shouting has died down medical men will recognize this.

Yours sincerely,
Hugh Clegg

16th April, 1948.

Mr dear Clegg,

Many thanks for your letter and for what you say about my part in helping towards peace.

I am not so much worried about the numbers who will go into the service on July 5th as about the willingness with which they begin work under the new conditions. I would like to have seen the B.M.A. respond to the Minister by a gesture which I think would have greatly strengthened them. But perhaps I am expecting too much of human nature. As time passes it is, I think, easier to see things in perspective. Anyway one is increasingly interested in why people do things, or don't do them. What, for example, would have been the effect if four people had voted differently in the Presidential Election? Would there have been any forces then making for peace? and if not, what would have happened? Did many of those who voted give a thought to this? And, speaking more generally, what is so much needed in medicine is men who have the time and ability to think out things that are not part of their daily work. It was, I suppose, to provide such people that the Regius Professors of Medicine were created, but the posts do not seem to attract the kind of person who was Regius Professor in the days of Allbutt.

We seem to need a good deal of hard thinking and less emotion if we are to play our part as a profession in difficult times.

Yours sincerely,
(no signature but clearly by Moran)

Dr. H.A. Clegg, F.R.C.P.,
B.M.A. House,
Tavistock Square,
W.C.1.

Personal   British Medical Journal

B.M.A. House
Tabistock Square
London, W.C.1.
21 April 1948

Dear Lord Moran

Thank you for your letter. As I see it the Minister's concessions represent a great 'victory' for the Plebiscite. It was a great pity that the BMA did not make the first move: I suggested that this should be done, but all the Red (or Blue) Queens said 'off with his head'. I thought the RCP should have made a statement at the previous Comitia, but I freely admit now that I was wrong.

There is much in what you said about doctors coming in willingly, because I still believe that there will be something approaching chaos in the months after July 5: if medical men go in grudgingly then the disorder of the Service will be laid at their door.

Nobody knew Dain was going to make the speech at Shrewsbury! Fortunately I got my leader off to press before the meeting of our Council last Wednesday, and fortunately, too, Dain has written a letter for this week's B.M.J. which considerably tones down what he said last Sunday.

The trouble with so many people is that they find it easier to repeat certain verbal patterns than to think things out afresh at each stage of a situation which is continuously changing. My forecast is that 65% ± 5% of GPs will vote yes in the Plebiscite in spite of Shrewsbury.

Yours sincerely,
Hugh Clegg

These letters are on file in the library of the Royal College of Physicians, NHS papers, Box 1, Item 81.

Notes

Most references are to files in the Public Record Office at Kew. the following abbreviations are used:

ACT   Actuary's Department
CAB   Cabinet
HO   Home Office
LAB   Ministry of Labour
MH   Ministry of Health
PIN   Ministry of Pensions and National Insurance
PREM   Prime Minister's office
T   Treasury

Other abbreviations are as follows:

AMC   Association of Municipal Corporations
BEV   William Beveridge papers, British Library of Political and Economic Science, LSE
BHA   British Hospitals Association papers, British Library of Political and Economic Science, LSE
BMA   British Medical Association Registry, BMA Library, London
BMJ   *British Medical Journal*
CCA   County Councils Association
FAB   Fabian Society papers, Nuffield College, Oxford
GLC   Greater London Council Record Office, London
HAS   Somerville Hastings papers, Brynmor Jones Library, University of Hull
HC Debs   House of Commons Debates
HL Debs   House of Lords Debates
KF   King Edward's Hospital Fund for London papers, GLC
LCC   London County Council papers, GLC
LP   Labour Party papers, London
PEP   Political and Economic Planning papers, British Library of Political and Economic Science, LSE
RC   Reconstruction Committee of the War Cabinet papers, October 1943 to May 1945
RCOG   Royal College of Obstetricians and Gynaecologists papers, RCOG Library, London
RCP   Royal College of Physicians papers on the National Health Service, RCP Library, London
RCS   Royal College of Surgeons, Minutes of Council, RCS Library, London

RPC   Reconstruction Priorities Committee of the War Cabinet papers, March 1942 to October 1943

SJC   Standing Joint Committee of Royal Colleges papers, RCOG and RCP collections, London

SMA   Socialist Medical Association papers, Brynmor Jones Library, University of Hull

TUC   Trades Union Congress papers, London

WILL   Henry Willink papers, Churchill College, University of Cambridge

Chapter 1 Failure of reform

1 For development of medical services under the Poor Law, see Hodgkinson (1967).
2 For a summary of the medical provisions under the 1911 Insurance Act and the forces that led to their creation, see Honigsbaum (1979) pp. 9–21.
3 T 172/62, p. 10.
4 Ministry of Health, Consultative Council on Medical and Allied Services (1920). For an analysis of the report, see Honigsbaum (1979) pp. 64–72.
5 Honigsbaum (1979) pp. 73–8.
6 PIN 4/117.
7 MH 62/85 and 62/89.
8 Royal Commission on National Health Insurance (issued 1926, published 1928), pp. 114–35.
9 For a full account of this episode, see Honigsbaum (1983) pp. 515–24.
10 *Nursing Notes*, Dec. 1934, p. 174 (from a report in *Daily Telegraph*, 6 Nov. 1934). Baldwin (1955) pp. 66–7. Middlemas and Barnes (1969) p. 9.
11 Feiling (1946) pp. 2–3. Dilks (1984) p. 13.
12 PIN 5/11 and 5/29, minutes 10 Nov. 1927. See also MH 79/284.
13 *The Times*, 1929: 19 April, p. 19; 23 April, p. 18; 30 May, p. 9. *National Insurance Gazette*, 1929: 27 April, pp. 193–4; 1 June, p. 259.
14 MH 79/286. For details of the larger salaried scheme Greenwood had in mind, see the unpublished manuscript by the Research Department of the Labour Party, 'Suggested health service', no date (but certainly 1929), in HAS.
15 *BMJ*, 29 June 1929, Supp. pp. 258–62.
16 PIN 5/31, minutes 17 July 1929. MH 55/261.
17 For similar attacks on GP competence by spokesmen for these other interests, see *Medical Officer*, 16 April 1927, 1, pp. 177–80. *Maternity and Child Welfare*, Oct. and Dec. 1928, pp. 247, 319–20. National Conference of Labour Women, *Annual Reports*: 1929, pp. 39–40; 1930, pp. 85–6.
18 MH 79/285.
19 PIN 5/33, minutes 10 July 1931, and memos from Neill and Rockliff, 18 and 28 July 1931. See also PIN 5/49.
20 For the second reading debate, see HC Debs (265) 1,927–2,040, 11 May 1932.
21 *Maternity and Child Welfare*, Sept. 1933, p. 230. *BMJ*, 20 Oct. 1934, pp. 737–8.
22 Newman (1939) pp. 302–9.
23 RCOG (1944) pp. 28–30.
24 Abel-Smith (1964) pp. 368–83.
25 Honigsbaum (1979) p. 45.
26 MH 79/287, Maude to Minister, 9 April 1936.
27 PEP (1937) pp. 154–5.
28 Abel-Smith (1964) p. 374.
29 For the second reading debate of the Bill which became the Midwives Act, see HC Debs (311) 1,117–225, 30 April 1936. For the medical reaction, see *BMJ*, 3 Aug. and 30 Nov. 1935, Supp. pp. 62–4, 234–6; 2 Aug. 1936, Supp. pp. 82–4.

30 *BMJ*, 26 April 1930, Supp. pp. 165–82. See also the purpose of the plan as seen by the BMA's secretary in BMA 1,820/1, memo by Cox, 29 Oct. 1929.
31 Honigsbaum (1979) p. 157. For the detailed record of these discussions, see BMA 1,913.
32 Honigsbaum (1979) pp. 146–8, 325–6.
33 Royal Commission on NHI (1928) pp. 65–6, 161–5.
34 Honigsbaum (1979) pp. 190–4.
35 *BMJ*, 5 and 26 June 1937, Supp. pp. 355, 416–17 (Beauchamp).
36 Honigsbaum (1979) p. 219.
37 Honigsbaum (1979) pp. 217–26.
38 Honigsbaum (1979) pp. 227–38.
39 Honigsbaum (1979) pp. 219–20, 239–41. For the detailed record of this committee, see BMA 1,666, 1,709, 1,720; and TUC 840.1, 840.3, 840.11.
40 MH 55/442. PEP (1937) pp. 154–5. BMA, 1,709/Jt Com 1/3 (1937–8).
41 This criticism was made by David Bertram, a leader of the Ancient Order of Foresters in Scotland, but it was not shared by many in the approved society world. For the heated exchange prompted by his remarks, see *National Insurance Gazette*, 20 Sept. and 4 Oct. 1934, pp. 453 (Bertram), 475, 495, 499.
42 HC Debs (279) 961–2 (Skelton), 22 June 1933. See also (302) 2,122–4 (Lindsay), 6 June 1935.
43 McNicholl had close links with the PEP health group whose meetings he attended as an observer. PEP, WG 15/2, report of meeting 16 Dec. 1936.
44 Department of Health for Scotland (1936). For a comparison of the Committee's recommendations with BMA policy, see BMA 1,660/10 and 29.
45 HC Debs (319) 1,099–1,107, 28 June 1937.
46 Department of Health for Scotland (1936) pp. 356–7.
47 *BMJ*, 16 April 1938, Supp. p. 203. *Proceedings of Royal Society of Medicine*, 1935, volume 35, p. 649.
48 *Medical Officer*, 1938, 2, p. 154.
49 *BMJ*, 25 Dec. 1937, Supp. pp. 382–3.
50 *BMJ*, 1 Sept. 1945, pp. 294–6.
51 *BMJ*, 18 Feb. 1950, pp. 392–6.
52 *BMJ*, 4 Nov. 1944, Supp. p. 100.
53 Joint Committee of RCOG and the Population Investigation Committee (1948) p. 90.
54 RCOG and Population Investigation Committee (1948) pp. 67–8.
55 For the rejection by MOHs, see *National Health*, Jan. 1941, pp. 207–8, and *Public Health*, Sept. 1942, pp. 197–8. For the rejection by local authority clinic doctors and supervisors, see *BMJ*, 8 Aug. 1942, p. 166, and *Public Health*, Dec. 1943, pp. 30–1. For the rejection by health visitors, midwives, and inspectors of midwives, see *National Health*, March 1943, pp. 235–9 (Bayes, Parsons), and *BMJ*, 11 Dec. 1943, Supp. p. 97 (McIlroy). For the rejection by voluntary societies, see *BMJ*, 25 Dec. 1943, p. 824.
56 *BMJ*, 5 Aug. 1939, Supp. pp. 111–13 (Walker). See also the support for a salaried service from the Glasgow and Kensington divisions of the BMA, *BMJ*, 30 July 1938, Supp. pp. 99–100.

Chapter 2 Ministry rejects takeover of voluntary hospitals

1 MH 79/409, Neville to Secretary, 7 Nov. 1936; minutes of first office policy conference, 7 Feb. 1938.
2 Cooke (1972) p. 1083.
3 *BMJ*, 26 March 1938, Supp. p. 159 (Cook).

4   *Imperial Calendar*, 1914, p. 412b.
5   MH 79/409, Neville to Secretary, 7 Nov. 1936.
6   Honigsbaum (1979) p. 27.
7   For a review of his life, see the obituary notice in *The Times*, 4 Feb. 1957, p. 12.
8   For Chrystal's personnel file, see MH 107/37.
9   MH 79/409, Hudson to Secretary and Minister, 27 Jan. 1937.
10 MH 79/409, memo by CMO on provision of specialist services, 15 March 1937.
11 PEP (1937).
12 MH 79/409, minutes of first office policy conference, 7 Feb. 1938, and document circulated for conference, 'Development of the health services'.
13 For the section that deals with this in the PEP report, see PEP (1937) pp. 108–10.
14 MH 79/409, document prepared following first office policy conference, 'Outline of scheme for medical benefit for dependants of insured persons', 14 March 1938.
15 MH 79/409, minutes of second office policy conference, 6 April 1938, p. 1 (Chrystal).
16 MH 79/409, minutes of second office policy conference, 6 April 1938, p. 4.
17 For biographical details see his obituary notice in *The Times*, 15 Oct. 1959, p. 16, and *Who Was Who 1951–1960*, London, Adam & Charles Black.
18 MH 79/409, minutes of third and fourth office policy conferences, 31 May and 27 June 1938.
19 For the circumstances surrounding Addison's departure from the Ministry, see Morgan and Morgan (1980) pp. 120–48.
20 *Hospital*, Aug. 1934, pp. 213–15 (address by Somerville Hastings).
21 MH 80/24, draft by Wrigley, 'Hospital services', no date but precedes final draft, 18 Dec. 1940.
22 MH 80/34, memo by Minister of Health to Lord President's Committee on Post-War Hospital Policy, 14 Oct. 1941.
23 MH 80/24, 'The proposals for subvention of the London voluntary hospitals', 13 pp. typescript, no author, no date, but in file after minutes of second office policy conference, 6 April 1938. See also Rivett (1986) pp. 221–5.
24 MH 80/24, report of conference on financial aid to voluntary hospitals, 27 Jan. 1939. Another report will be found in GLC, LCC, Hospital and Medical Services Committee, presented papers, 13/DS10, 23 Feb. 1939.
25 MH 80/24, note on 27 Jan. 1939 conference by Dr T. S. McIntosh.
26 MH 80/24, report of conference, 27 Jan. 1939, pp. 5–6.
27 MH 80/24, 'The proposals for subvention of the London voluntary hospitals'.
28 For the development of the EMS, see Titmuss (1950) pp. 54–86; Dunn (1952) and Abel-Smith (1964) pp. 426–39.
29 HC Debs (344) 1,501–17, 2 March 1939.
30 HC Debs (344) 1,501–17, 2 March 1939. See also Rivett (1986) pp. 238–42.
31 Titmuss (1950) p. 75.
32 GLC, LCC, PH/GEN/1/41, conference of MOHs of London and home counties to discuss the EMS, 13 Aug. 1940. MH 77/22, Daley to Rucker, 4 March 1941, with memo by Daley, 28 Feb. 1941. See also Titmuss (1950) pp. 200–1.
33 GLC, LCC, PH/GEN/1/41, conference of MOHs to discuss the EMS, 13 Aug. 1940.
34 For Elliot's role here, see Chrystal's remarks in MH 80/24, Ministry of Health conference on casualty service and voluntary hospitals, 27 Sept. 1939. It should be noted, however, that in 1946 Elliot opposed Bevan's decision to nationalize the hospital service: HC Debs (431) 1,039–41, 10 Dec. 1946.
35 HC Debs (336) 2,130–1, 1 June 1938. In 1938 Haden Guest supported BMA as opposed to SMA policy and thereby won financial aid in the North Islington by-election: *BMJ*, 23 April 1938, Supp. p. 245, para. 180 of Council report.
36 MH 80/24, Forber to Chrystal, 17 Sept. 1939.

37 MH/80/24, MacNalty to Secretary on 'Proposed national hospital service', 21 Sept. 1939.
38 MH 80/24, MacNalty to Secretary, 22 Sept. 1939.
39 CAB 102/716, A.W.N. [Neville] to Secretary, 22 Sept. 1939. Rudolph Klein wrongly attributes this paper to Rucker: see Klein (1983) pp. 8–9.
40 For the report of the Sankey Commission, see Abel-Smith (1964) p. 412. For the proceedings, see BHA.
41 MH 80/24, Maude to Forber, 26 Oct. 1939.
42 *Lancet*, 28 Oct. 1939, pp. 945–51.
43 MH 80/24, Forber on 'A plan for British hospitals', 3 Nov. 1939.
44 MH 80/24, memo by Forber, 'Regional organisation of hospital services', 23 Nov. 1939.
45 MH 80/24, MacNalty on Forber memo, 8 Jan. 1940. A fuller version of MacNalty's memo appears later in the file with the notation 'Secretary's comments on Sir Edward Forber's Memorandum on regional organisation of hospital services', 18 Dec. 1939 (with 1939 crossed out and 1940 written in). This is not correct: MacNalty is clearly the author because the arguments are the same as those in his 8 Jan. 1940 memo. The quotation in the text is taken from the fuller version, with the underlining as it appeared in the original.
46 MH 80/24, Forber to Chrystal, 'Note on post-war hospital policy', 8 May 1940.
47 Department of Health for Scotland (1943) paras 116, 124–5. A copy of the report will be found in MH 80/26.
48 FAB, K10/3, memo by Health Services Sub-Committee of Social Services Committee, 'National health insurance', 14 March 1939.

Chapter 3 Ministry intent to create hospital service

1 HC Debs (365) 851–915, 17 Oct. 1940 (see cols 879–80 for Morgan's comment).
2 MH 80/24, comments by Maude at conference on post-war hospital policy, 7 Dec. 1940.
3 Cited by Florence Horsbrugh, Parliamentary Secretary to the Ministry of Health from 1939 to 1945, in HC Debs (398) 541–2, 17 March 1944.
4 Goodman (1970) pp. 80–2.
5 CAB 21/1583, Wood to Attlee, 15 Nov. 1940. For the establishment of the secretariat to the Reconstruction Committee, see CAB 21/1584. For Chrystal's personnel file, see MH 107/37.
6 Maude's personnel file is not yet available but for his obituary notice see *The Times*, 7 Feb. 1963, p. 14.
7 MH 80/24, Macgregor to Maude, 14 Nov. 1940.
8 MH 80/24, Pater's note on Macgregor's note, 14 Nov. 1940.
9 MH 80/24, Pater, 'Notes on hospital policy', 18 Dec. 1940.
10 MH 80/24, Pater, 'Notes on hospital policy', 18 Dec. 1940.
11 MH 80/24, Wrigley, 'Hospital policy and regionalisation', 18 Dec. 1940.
12 MH 80/24, memo by Maude on post-war hospital policy, 9 Jan. 1941.
13 MH 80/24, office conference on post-war hospital policy, 10 Jan. 1941.
14 MH 80/24, memo by Maude on post-war hospital policy, 9 Jan. 1941.
15 MH 80/24, office conference on post-war hospital policy, 10 Jan. 1941.
16 MH 80/24, note by Rucker, 6 Feb. 1941.
17 MH 80/24, Maude to 'Demo', 18 Jan. 1941.
18 MH 58/235 or 80/24, report of meeting with deputation from Nuffield Trust, 6 Feb. 1941.
19 MH 80/24, note by Rucker, 6 Feb. 1941.

20 MH 80/24, Forber to Maude, 9 Feb. 1941.
21 CAB 117/211, correspondence between Chrystal and Maude, 23 June to 15 Aug. 1941. Note in particular Chrystal's comments about 'Demo' in his letter to Maude, 1 July 1941. 'Demo's' personnel file is not available, but for his initial appointment to NHI administration, see *Imperial Calendar*, 1914, p. 412.
22 MH 58/204–7. See also Abel-Smith (1964) pp. 307–10.
23 MH 80/24,, Maude to 'Demo', 18 Jan. 1941.
24 MH 80/24,, notes by 'Demo' on Secretary's memo of 9 Jan, 11 Feb. 1941.
25 MH 80/24, Brock's comments are cited in note from 'Demo' to Maude, 12 Feb. 1941.
26 MH 80/24, Maude to Forber, 25 Feb. 1941.
27 MH 80/24, J.C.W. [Wrigley] to Hawton, 23 Jan. 1941. For the growing separation between GPs and the hospital world during the inter-war period, see Honigsbaum (1979).
28 MH 80/24, E.D.M. [Macgregor] to Maude, 20 Jan. 1941.
29 MH 80/24, E.D.M. [Macgregor] to Maude, 20 Jan. 1941.
30 For the pressure of work within the department, see MH 77/25, Maude to Brock, 25 Aug. 1941.
31 Nuffield Trust (1941) pp. 3, 9, 28–31; Nuffield Trust (1949) p. 10.
32 MH 58/316, Neville to CMO and Secretary, 21 Oct. 1937.
33 MH 58/235, Macdonald to Goodenough, 6 Jan. 1941.
34 Titmuss (1950) p. 275.
35 MH 80/24, 'Notes on certain special points in relation to hospital policy', no author, no date but follows document headed, 'Notes on hospital policy', 18 Dec. 1940, with Pater indicated as the author.
36 Latham's article appears in two files: CAB 117/211 and MH 77/25.
37 MH 58/235, Platts to Maude, 22 Aug. 1941, and documents which follow.
38 MH 77/25, Johnson to Maude, 23 and 25 Sept. 1941.
39 MH 58/235, Brown to Goodenough, 21 March 1941.
40 MH 80/34, War Cabinet — Lord President's Committee, memo by Minister of Health on post-war hospital policy, 14 Oct. 1941.
41 CAB 117/211, Chrystal to Maude, 23 June 1941, and correspondence which follows to 4 Oct. 1941.
42 MH 80/24, Secretary's memo, 'Suggestions for a post-war hospital policy', Aug. 1941, but no specific date indicated. It is likely that this memo was prepared by 'Demo'.
43 MH 80/24, Forber to Maude, 9 Feb. 1941.
44 MH 77/25, Brock to Maude with minute from 'Demo' to Brock, 29 Aug. and 4 Sept. 1941. See also MH 80/24, 'Demo' to Maude, 12 Feb. 1941, mimeographed copy with prefatory note from 'Demo' modifying views.
45 MH 77/25, Maude to Fraser, 20 Dec. 1941.
46 CAB 117/211, Maude to Chrystal, 4 Oct. 1941.
47 HC Debs (374) 1,116–20, 9 Oct. 1941.
48 MH 58/235, Maude note for file on meeting with Goodenough and Hyde, 13 March 1941.
49 CAB 117/211, Maude to Chrystal, 4 Oct. 1941. MH 80/34, War Cabinet — Lord President's Committee, memo by Minister of Health on post-war hospital policy, 14 Oct. 1941.
50 MH 77/22, Daley to Rucker, 4 March 1941, with memo by Daley, 'Hospital policy', 28 Feb. 1941.
51 MH 77/25, Menzies, 'Memorandum on hospital policy in London', Aug. 1941. See also note of conversation with Latham and Salmon of LCC, 29 Aug. 1941.
52 MH 77/25, Maude to Fraser, 18 Sept. 1941. See also Rivett (1986) pp. 244–6.
53 MH 77/24, Jameson to Buchan, 8 Feb. 1943.

54 MH 77/19. See also Nuffield Trust (1949) pp. 15–16.
55 MH 77/24, Jameson to Buchan, 8 Feb. 1941.

Chapter 4 A salaried service under municipal control

1   CAB 117/211, Neville to Chrystal, 14 Oct. 1941.
2   MH 77/26, Maude, 'Draft of a paper by Maude on a proposed GP service', Nov. 1942, p. 1, para. 2. For another copy of this paper, dated 5 Dec. 1942, see MH 80/24.
3   HC Debs (378) 2,132–3, 26 March 1942. For the records of the Goodenough Committee, see MH 71/59–76.
4   CAB 87/1, War Cabinet — Reconstruction Problems Committee, minutes 6 March 1941, p. 4.
5   HC Debs (374) 1,116–20 (Haden Guest and Brown), 1,660 (Messer), 9 and 21 Oct. 1941.
6   For the developments described here, see Honigsbaum (1979) pp. 239–47.
7   CAB 87/16, memo from TUC to Beveridge Committee, 2 Jan. 1942, containing report of TUC deputation to Minister of Health and Secretary for Scotland, 6 Feb. 1941. For another copy of this report, see TUC, Social Insurance Committee minutes SIC 4/1, 12 Feb. 1941.
8   CAB 87/1, War Cabinet — Reconstruction Problems Committee, minutes 6 March 1942, p. 2.
9   PIN 8/85, Greenwood to Brown, 10 April 1941.
10 For Bannatyne's own account of the origins of the Beveridge Committee, see his handwritten note, 16 June 1941, on the cover of PIN 12/94.
11 PIN 12/94, reports of meetings of civil servants which led to the creation of the Beveridge Committee, 16, 19, and 29 May 1941. These are full reports; an incomplete report will be found in PIN 8/85.
12 PIN 12/94, note on cover by Bannatyne, 16 June 1941.
13 Harris (1977) p. 376.
14 Beveridge (1942).
15 Beveridge (1953) pp. 296, 300–1, 306, 317.
16 CAB 87/77, TUC evidence to Beveridge Committee, 6 May 1942, Q. 2,290–308.
17 TUC, 150.5 II, verbatim report of Beveridge meeting with General Council, 16 Dec. 1941.
18 PIN 8/85, Brown to Citrine, 26 May 1941.
19 PIN 12/94, report of meeting of civil servants to establish Beveridge Committee, 19 May 1941, statement by Mr Tribe of Ministry of Labour.
20 PIN 12/94, note by Bannatyne on cover.
21 PIN 8/85, Chrystal to Maude, 2 July 1941.
22 BEV IXa/37 (part), document headed, 'Winston and William in parallel columns 1942 and 1943', p. 2.
23 PIN 21/65, Greenwood to Beveridge, 30 Jan. 1942; Bannatyne to Maxwell, 2 Feb. 1942.
24 CAB 87/79, note by Beveridge on future procedure, 4 Feb. 1942. HC Debs (377) 559–60, 27 Jan. 1942. For a query by an assurance industry spokesman as to whether there was any connection between these two events, see HC Debs (386) 357–8 (Mellor), 26 Jan. 1943.
25 *TUC Annual Conference Report*, 1943, p. 237 (Rowlandson).
26 CAB 87/76, Beveridge Committee, minutes 8 July 1941.
27 Beveridge (1942) p. 159, para. 428. For a clear indication that Beveridge favoured a salaried service, see MH 80/31 or BEV VIII/31/4, 'Some problems of medical treatment', with letter from Beveridge to Maude, 2 Feb. 1942.

28 Beveridge (1942) pp. 11 (point xi), 158–63.
29 For the creation of the MPC and the motives behind it, see Honigsbaum (1979) pp. 175, 184, 266. Confirmation of this interpretation was given by Sir Ewen Maclean, a consultant active in BMA affairs, at a joint meeting of royal college representatives to decide whether they should accept the BMA's invitation to join the MPC: RCP 22/1/1, shorthand notes of meeting 25 Oct. 1940, p. 2.
30 *BMJ*, 20 June 1942, pp. 743–53.
31 For the 1929 version see *BMJ*, 26 April 1930, Supp. pp. 165–82. For the 1938 version see *BMJ*, 30 April 1938, Supp. pp. 253–66.
32 For the progress of MPC proceedings as recorded by the Ministry, see MH 80/31, documents which list conclusions of GP and Hospitals Committees of MPC, 2 pp. typescript, no author, no date; Dalyrymple-Champneys to Secretary, note on draft report, 1 July 1942.
33 BEV VIII/31, Hill to Chester, 17 Dec. 1941.
34 ACT 1/684, Beveridge to Epps, 2 Dec. 1941, with first draft of memo, 'Heads of a scheme for social security', 2 Dec. 1941, p. 16. See also the second draft, 9 Dec. 1941, p. 18. Another copy of the second draft will be found in BEV VIII/27.
35 MH 80/31, Beveridge to Maude, 2 Feb. 1942, with document, 'Some problems of medical treatment'.
36 Beveridge (1942) pp. 57–9, paras 129–32. See also PIN 8/101, Min. of Health and Scot. Dept. of Health, 'Disability benefits: safeguards against abuse', 23 Feb. 1943.
37 MH 80/31, Maude to 'Demo', 20 Jan. 1942.
38 MJ 80/31, 'Demo' to Maude, 6 Feb. 1942.
39 MH 80/31, Maude to 'Demo', 9 Feb. 1942.
40 MH 80/24, Secretary's memo, 'Suggestions for a post-war hospital policy', Aug. 1941, para. 2.
41 MH 77/26, Maude, 'Draft by Maude on a proposed GP service', Nov. 1942, pp. 1–2. See also MH 80/31, Hickinbotham, 'General medical and hospital service — transitional stages', 1 April 1943.
42 MH 80/31, Maude, 'Post-war medical policy — GP service', Feb. 1942.
43 CAB 87/13, RPC, memo by Minister of Health and Scottish Secretary, 2 Feb. 1943.
44 MH 77/22, Brock to Maude, 4 Sept. 1941.
45 Jones (1972) pp. 89–90.
46 For the LCC efforts at integration, note reference in MH 77/22, memo from 'Demo', 29 Aug. 1941. For the doctors' concern, emanating mainly from psychiatrists, and Maude's response, citing the need to reform the mental health law first, see MH 77/26, Masefield to Ministry, 22 Oct. 1942; Maude to Anderson, 4 May 1943 (latter also included in MH 80/31).
47 MH 80/31, Maude, 'Post-war medical policy — GP service', Feb. 1942.
48 MH 80/31, Maude to 'Demo', 9 Feb. 1942.
49 MH 80/31, Maude to 'Demo', 9 Feb. 1942.
50 MH 80/31, Maude to 'Demo', 9 Feb. 1942.
51 MH 80/31, 'Demo' to Maude, 23 Feb. 1942.
52 MH 80/31, Maude to 'Demo', 20 Jan. 1942, underlining in original.
53 CAB 87/13 or MH 80/25, RPC, memo by Minister of Health and Scottish Secretary, 2 Feb. 1943, para. 4.
54 MH 80/31, report of meeting between Beveridge, Maude, Jameson and others, 17 Feb. 1942.
55 MH 80/31, note by Maude on meeting with Beveridge, 17 Feb. 1942.
56 MH 80/31, Maude to 'Demo', 4 March 1942, with copy of enlarged paper on GP service. For another copy of this paper, see MH 77/26.
57 Honigsbaum (1979) p. 208.

58 Honigsbaum (1979) p. 79.

59 MH 80/31, 'Demo' to Maude, 23 Feb. 1942.

60 MH 80/31, Maude to 'Demo', 4 March 1942.

61 MH 80/31, J.M.K.H. [Hawton], 'National medical service — w-t vs. p-t service', 12 March 1943.

62 MH 80/31, Maude to Beveridge, 4 March 1942.

63 MH 80/31, Maude to Hogan, 5 March 1942.

64 MH 80/31, Epps to Maude, 23 March 1942.

65 MH 80/24, 'Post-war medical policy. GP service', Sept. 1942, no author. This is an eight-page document comparing the MPC proposals with those of the Ministry.

66 *BMJ*, 26 Sept. 1942, Supp. p. 33.

67 Honigsbaum (1979) pp. 110–21, 147–8, 185.

68 MH 80/31, Maude to Minister, 20 May 1942.

69 *BMJ*, 31 Oct. 1942, p. 516.

70 MH 80/24, Maude to CMO, 26 Sept. 1942.

71 MH 80/24, Wilson to CMO, 2 Oct. 1942.

72 MH 80/24, paper comparing MPC proposals with Ministry's, Sept. 1942, pp. 4–5. See also MH 80/31, E.J.M. [Maude], 'Note on salaried service and payment by capitation fees for GPs', 12 March 1943.

73 MH 80/24, paper comparing MPC proposals with Ministry's, Sept. 1942, pp. 5–6. See also Maude to CMO, 5 Oct. 1942.

74 MH 80/42, paper comparing MPC proposals with Ministry's, 24 Sept. 1942, p. 2.

75 BMA 2075/GP 11 (1940–41).

76 Honigsbaum (1979) p. 186.

77 MH 80/24, paper comparing MPC proposals with Ministry's Sept. 1942, p. 4, para. 5.

78 MH 80/24, correspondence between Maude and Barlow, 17 and 18 Nov. 1942.

79 MH 77/26, Maude 'Draft by Maude on a proposed GP service', Nov. 1942, pp. 4–5, para. 10 (4).

80 MH 80/31, McNicholl, 'General medical service — some argumentative points', 26 Feb. 1943, underlining added.

81 MH 80/31, E.J.M. [Maude], 'Note on salaried service and payment by capitation fees for GPs', 12 March 1943, para 6.

82 MH 80/31, J.M.K.H. [Hawton], 'National medical service — w-t vs p-t service', 12 March 1943.

83 MH 80/31, Hawton, 'National medical service — w-t vs p-t service', 12 March 1942, p. 3. (1).

84 For the SMA's dogmatic belief in health centres, see Honigsbaum (1979) pp. 255–8.

85 MH 80/31, or BEV VIII/31/4, 'Some problems of medical treatment', with letter from Beveridge to Maude, 2 Feb. 1942.

86 MH 80/31, Dalrymple-Champneys to Secretary, 'BMA Medical Planning Commission — note on draft report', 1 July 1942.

87 MH 80/25, Cox to Harris, 18 and 22 Jan. 1943.

88 MH 80/25, Maude to Minister, 29 Jan. 1943.

Chapter 5 Doctors reject municipal control

1 MH 80/26, comments by Maude on BHA papers, 25 May 1943.

2 MH 80/25, Maude to Bridges, 19 Jan. 1943.

3 MH 80/24, Pater, 'Medical staffing of hospitals', 24 Sept. 1942.

4 MH 80/31, 'Specialists and consultants', no author but with papers dated April 1943.

5 MH 80/24, Pater, 'Salaried medical service', no date but with papers dated Jan. 1942. For another copy, see MH 77/26.

6 MH 80/24, Maude to Minister, 'Post-war medical service', 22 Dec. 1942.
7 ACT 1/708, Maude to Epps, 11 Aug 1942.
8 MH 80/31, Hickinbotham, 'General medical and hospital services — transitional stages', 1 April 1943. MH 80/31, report of Ministry meeting with medical representatives, 24 May 1943 (note word 'German' is typed in to designate the meaning of 'end of war'). MH 80/26, Maude, 'Discussions with the medical profession', 19 or 23 June 1943.
9 MH 77/26, Maude to Anderson, 10 March 1943. MH 80/31, notes for Minister's opening remarks to medical representative committee, 14 June 1943.
10 MH 80/26, Maude, 'Discussions with the medical profession', 19 or 23 June 1943.
11 MH 80/25, Maude to Henderson, 20 Feb. 1943.
12 MH 80/31, report of Ministry meeting with medical representatives, 9 March 1943.
13 MH 80/25, report of Ministry meeting with medical representatives, 15 April 1943. MH 80/26, Anderson to Maude, 21 May 1943, with BMA report of 17 May meeting.
14 For those first appointed, see MH 71/97, minute 4 March 1943.
15 MH 71/101, Maude to Minister, 23 June 1942. MH 80/26, A.N.R. [Rucker] to Secretary and Minister, 23 Dec. 1943, with historical note on advisory committee, 24 Dec. 1943.
16 For the papers of this sub-committee, see MH 71/103.
17 *BMJ*, 10 April 1943, Supp. p. 46 (A.V. Russell).
18 MH 71/101, quarterly report on medical advisory committee to Macgregor, 1 June 1944. MH 71/102, minutes 24 March 1944.
19 MH 71/103, papers and minutes, 24 March and 4 May 1944.
20 MH 71/102, papers and minutes, 4 and 10 May 1944.
21 MH 71/103, Hawton to Prescott, 22 July 1946.
22 Honigsbaum (1979) pp. 62–3.
23 MH 80/25, report of Ministry meeting with local authority representatives, 10 March 1943.
24 MH 80/26, memo by local authority associations and LCC on proposed financial basis of health service, 21 July 1943; report of Ministry meeting with local authority representatives, 27 July 1943.
25 MH 80/25, Maude, 'Note on administrative structure for local authority representatives', 12 March 1943.
26 CAB 87/13 or MH 80/26, RPC, memo by Minister of Health, 3 Sept. 1943, para. 14.
27 MH 80/26, report of Ministry meeting with local authority representatives, 27 July 1943.
28 CAB 87/13 or MH 80/26, RPC, memo by Minister of Health, 28 July 1943, para. 10.
29 MH 80/25 or 80/31, report of Ministry meeting with medical representatives, 25 March 1943.
30 MH 80/25, report of Scottish Department meeting with medical representatives, 20 April 1943, statement by Drs Lambie and McFeat.
31 MH 80/31, McNicholl, 'General medical service — some argumentative points', 26 Feb. 1943.
32 MH 80/26, Scottish Department, 'Note on local administrative machinery', 23 June 1943.
33 MH 80/26, report of Scottish Department meeting with medical representatives, 15 June 1943.
34 MH 80/26, report of Scottish Department meeting with BMA, 13 Sept. 1943, statement by Prof. G. McNeill.
35 MH 80/25, report of Ministry meeting with medical representatives, 25 March 1943. MH 80/26, report of Ministry meeting with medical representatives, 28 June 1943.
36 MH 80/25, report of Ministry meeting with medical representatives, 25 March 1943.

37 MH 80/25 or 80/31, E.J.M. [Maude], 'Composition of health authorities', 5 April 1943.
38 MH 80/25 or 80/31, report of Ministry meeting with local authority representatives, 29 March 1943.
39 MH 80/25 or 80/31, report of Ministry meeting with medical representatives, 25 March 1943.
40 MH 80/25 or 80/31, report of Ministry meeting with local authority representatives, 29 March and 16 April 1943.
41 MH 80/25 or 80/31, BHA commentary, 26 March 1943, and report of Ministry meeting with voluntary hospital representatives, 30 March 1943. See also BHA, executive committee minutes, March and April 1943.
42 *BMJ*, 20 Feb. 1943, pp. 227-8.
43 MH 80/25, correspondence between Pooley and Maude, 24 and 26 March 1943.
44 MH 80/25, Maude to Minister, 12 April 1943.
45 MH 80/25, report of Scottish Department meeting with medical representatives, 27 March 1943.
46 MH 80/25, E.J.M. [Maude], 'Composition of health authority', 5 April 1943.
47 MH 80/25, Maude to Minister, 12 April 1943.
48 MH 80/25 or 80/31, report of Ministry meeting with medical representatives, 15 April 1943.
49 MH 80/25 or 80/31, report of Ministry meeting with Anderson and Hill, 3 May 1943, with paper by Hawton attached.
50 Maude requested and no doubt secured the approval of the Minister for this procedure in MH 80/35 or 80/31, Maude to Minister, 3 May 1943.
51 MH 80/26 or 80/31, Anderson to Maude, 12 May 1943.
52 MH 80/26, Maude note for file on BMA letter, 14 May 1943.
53 *Daily Express*, 11 May 1943, p. 3. Brown was disturbed by this report: MH 80/26, report of Minister's meeting with medical representatives, 17 May 1943.
54 *BMJ*, 22 May 1943, Supp. pp. 61-2.
55 Goodman (1970) pp. 116-17.
56 MH 80/26, Maude to Bovenschen, 1 Sept. 1943.
57 MH 80/26, report of Minister's meeting with medical representatives, 17 May 1943.
58 MH 80/26, Anderson to Maude with note of phone conversation, 17 and 18 May 1943.
59 MH 80/26 or 80/31, report of Ministry meeting with medical representatives, 24 May 1943.
60 MH 80/26 or 80/31, report of Ministry meeting with medical representatives, 17 and 24 May 1943.
61 MH 80/26, Maude, 'Discussions with the medical profession', 19 or 23 June 1943.
62 MH 80/26 or 80/31, report of Ministry meeting with medical representatives, 3 June 1943.
63 MH 80/26, Maude, 'Possible combination of panel system with health centre system', 4 June 1943.
64 MH 80/26 or 80/31, Maude, 'GP service', 7 June 1943.
65 MH 80/31, 'Incentive within a salary scale', 3 pp. typescript, no author but with papers dated June 1943.
66 CAB 87/13 or MH 80/26, RPC, memo by Minister of Health, 28 July 1943, paras 30-3.
67 MH 80/26 or 80/31, Maude, 'GP service', 7 June 1943.
68 MH 80/26, BHA and King's Fund plan for national health service, 14 May 1943.
69 MH 80/26, Pater on BHA and King's Fund plan, 18 May 1943.
70 MH 80/26, Maude comments on BHA papers, 25 May 1943.
71 MH 80/25, Maude to Goodenough, 7 May 1943.

72 MH 80/26 or 80/31, report of Ministry meeting with voluntary hospital representatives, 26 May 1943.
73 MH 80/26 or 80/31, BHA and King's Fund plan for national health service, 14 May 1943.
74 MH 80/26 or 80/31, report of Ministry meeting with voluntary hospital representatives, 26 May 1943.
75 MH 80/25, Maude to Goodenough, 7 May 1943.
76 CAB 87/13 or MH 80/26, RPC, memo by Minister of Health, 28 July 1944, para. 44.
77 MH 80/26, memo from Urban District Council Association, 7 June 1943.
78 MH 80/25, paper by Dr Maples of CCA, 12 May 1943. MH 80/26, motion passed
at CCA Conference, 12 May 1943; Pritchard to Maude, 28 May 1943.
79 MH 80/26, Hyde to Maude, 29 May 1943.
80 MH 80/25, R.W.C. [?] to Maude, 22 April 1943.
81 MH 80/25, Maude to Maxwell, 19 April 1943.
82 MH 80/25 or 80/31, Wrigley, 'Health service', 21 April 1943.
83 MH 80/26, report of Ministry meeting with local authority representatives, 23 June
1943.
84 For a clear indication of Johnston's ardour for existing areas of local government,
see MH 80/26, report of Scottish Secretary meeting with BMA, 13 Sept. 1943.
85 MH 80/26, report of Scottish Department meeting with local authority representatives
and note on meeting, 12 July 1943.
86 MH 80/26, Henderson to Scottish Secretary, 28 June 1943.
87 MH 80/27 or 80/31, report of Ministry meeting with medical representatives, 28 June
1943.
88 Rogers joined the Executive Committee of the SMA in August, 1942 and remained
a member throughout negotiations on the health service. For his initial appointment,
see SMA DSM 1/6, Executive Committee minutes, 13 August 1942.
89 Rogers (1972) p. 112.
90 BMA 2075/GP 31 and *BMJ*, 21 Feb. 1942, Supp. pp. 33–5.
91 *Daily Express*, 11 May 1943, p. 3.
92 *Evening Standard*, 12 May 1943, p. 2.
93 MH 80/31, 'Specialists and consultants', no author but with papers dated April 1943.
94 MH 80/26, report of Scottish Secretary meeting with medical representatives, 26 July
1943, statement by Dr Cameron.
95 BMA 1448/C 13 (1942–3) para. 12; BMA 2343/C 9 para. 17, and C 12.

Chapter 6 Resistance to compromise

1 MH 80/26, Maude, 'Discussions with the medical profession', 19 or 23 June 1943,
pp. 11–12.
2 MH 77/26 or 80/24, paper comparing MPC proposals with Ministry's, Sept. 1942,
pp. 4–5.
3 MH 77/26 or 80/24, Maude, 'Draft of paper by Maude on GP service', 5 Dec. 1942,
p. 2, para. 6.
4 MH 80/26, Maude to Henderson, 30 Oct. 1943.
5 MH 80/24, Maude to Barlow, 18 Nov. 1942.
6 MH 62/243, E.D.M. [Macgregor] to Secretary, 24 Feb. 1941; Macgregor to Ritson,
11 April 1941.
7 MH 80/26, E.D.M. [Macgregor] to Maude, 16 July 1943.
8 MH 80/26, Henderson to Maude with draft of paper for RPC, Reconstruction Priorities
Committee, 19 July 1943, para. 4.
9 MH 80/26, report of Scottish Secretary meeting with local authority representatives,
30 Aug. 1943.

10 CAB 87/13 or MH 80/26, RPC, memo by Minister of Health, 28 July 1943, para. 5.
11 CAB 87/12 or MH 80/26, RPC, minutes 30 July 1943.
12 CAB 87/13 or MH 80/26, RPC, memo by Minister of Health, 13 Aug. 1943.
13 CAB 87/12 or MH 80/26, RPC, minutes 18 Aug, 1943.
14 MH 80/26, note by Hawton, 20 Aug. 1943.
15 CAB 87/13 or MH 80/26, RPC, memo by Minister of Health, 3 Sept. 1943, para. 10.
16 CAB 87/12 or MH 80/26, RPC, minutes 8 Sept. 1943.
17 MH 80/26, report of Scottish Secretary meeting with local authority representatives, 30 Aug. 1943. CAB 87/13 or MH 80/26, RPC, memo by Scottish Secretary 4 Sept. 1943. CAB 87/9 or MH 80/27, RC, memo by Scottish Secretary, 27 Sept. 1944, para, 6.
18 CAB 87/13 or MH 80/26, RPC, memo by Minister of Health, 10 Sept. 1943, para. 5. See also MH 80/26, draft of memo from Maude to Minister, 1 Sept. 1943.
19 MH 80/26, Maude to Minister, 4 Sept. 1943.
20 MH 80/26, memo by Scottish Secretary, 14 Sept. 1943.
21 MH 80/26, report of Scottish Secretary meeting with BMA, 13 Sept. 1943. See also HC Debs (390) 573–4, 8 June 1943 (Johnston).
22 MH 80/26, memo by Scottish Secretary, 14 Sept. 1943, para. 5.
23 MH 80/26, report of Scottish Secretary meeting with BMA, 13 Sept. 1943, statement by Dr Craig.
24 MH 80/26, draft of memo from Maude to Minister, 1 Sept. 1943.
25 CAB 87/12 or MH 80/26, RPC, minutes 16 Sept. 1943.
26 CAB 87/12 or MH 80/26, RPC, minutes 16 Sept. 1943.
27 MH 80/26, Maude to Minister, 4 Sept. 1943.
28 MH 80/26, Rucker to CMO, Secretary, and Minister, 'The White Paper', 6 Dec. 1943, para. 9.
29 CAB 87/12 or MH 80/26, RPC, minutes 15 Oct. 1943
30 For a clear indication of this, see CAB 87/5 or MH 80/27, RC, minutes 11 Jan. 1944.
31 MH 80/26, Henderson to Maude, 3 Nov. 1943.
32 Colville (1985 and 1986) p. 571 of 1986 edition.
33 Addison (1975) p. 236.
34 HC Debs (386) 1,655–65, 16 Feb. 1943.
35 CAB 87/5 or MH 80/27, RC, minutes 11 Jan. 1944.
36 CAB 87/7 or MH 80/27, RC, memo by Minister of Health and Scottish Secretary, 3 Jan. 1944, pp. 5–6. For the more evasive wording used in the White Paper itself, see Ministry of Health and Department of Health for Scotland (1944a) pp. 19, 31, 45.
37 Ministry of Health and Department of Health for Scotland (1944a) pp. 31–2.
38 MH 80/26, Henderson to Maude, 29 Nov. 1943.
39 For Hawton's advocacy of this restriction, see MH 80/31, 'Control of private work of part-time men', 5 April 1943.
40 MH 80/26, Maude, 'Private treatment by doctors in public service', 2 Sept. 1943. See also page 43.
41 MH80/26, Henderson to Maude, 1 Oct. 1943.
42 MH 80/26, Maude, 'GP service', 7 June 1943.
43 Ministry of Health and Department of Health for Scotland (1944a) p. 31.
44 Ministry of Heatlh and Department of Health for Scotland (1944a) pp. 34–5.
45 BMJ, 20 June 1942, p. 749 under 'Model health centre', section dealing with 'Conditions of service of medical staff'.
46 MH 80/26 or 80/31, report of Ministry meeting with medical representative committee, 28 June 1943.
47 MH 80/26, Maude to Henderson, 29 Sept. 1943; Maude to Gilbert, 12 Nov. 1943.
48 MH 80/26, A.N.R. [Rucker] to Maude, 10 Nov. 1943.

49 MH 80/26, J.E.P. [Pater] to Secretary, 12 Nov. 1943.
50 CAB 87/5 or MH 80/27, RC, minutes 11 Jan. and 4 Feb. 1944. See also Ministry of Health and Department of Health for Scotland (1944a) pp. 35–6.
51 Mh 80/26, A.N.R. [Rucker] to Secretary and Minister, 23 Dec. 1943. For the opposite stand taken earlier by Maude, see MH 80/26, Maude, 'Discussions with the medical profession', 19 or 23 June 1943, p. 3.
52 Dr Solomon Wand was the first to express concern about this possibility. MH 80/26, report of Ministry meeting with medical representative committee, 28 June 1943.
53 CAB 87/5 or MH 80/27, RC, minutes 10 Jan. 1944.
54 MH 80/26, note by A.N.R. [Rucker], 6 Jan. 1944. See also CAB/244, Fraser to Brook, 6 Jan. 1944; Brook to Minister (Woolton), 7 Jan. 1944.
55 Honigsbaum (1979) pp. 58–63.
56 CAB 87/5 or MH 80/27, RC, minutes 10 Jan, 1944. For Morrison's opposition, see CAB 87/13 or MH 80/25, RPC, memo by Minister of Home Security, 17 Aug. 1943.
57 Ministry of Health and Department of Health for Scotland (1944a) p. 20.
58 CAB 87/7 or PREM 4/36/3, note by Woolton, 'National Health Service: White Paper', 31 Jan. 1944.
59 CAB 87/5 or MH 80/26, RC, minutes, 10 Jan. 1944. Ministry of Health and Department of Health for Scotland (1944a) pp. 14–15.
60 MH 80/27, J.F.C. (?) to Wilkinson, 4 Jan. 1944.
61 MH 77/119, Marchbank to Hickinbottom, 24 March 1944. For an indication of general agreement with this view, see MH 80/26, 'After the White Paper', Jan. 1944, no author but probably by Hawton.

Chapter 7 Doctors reject White Paper

1 MH 55/285, memo setting forth arguments for and against local authority administration of maternity services, 29 April 1929, no author, 8 pp. typescript, quote on p. 8, item (b).
2 MH 80/27, 'After the White Paper', para. 6, no author but probably by Hawton, Jan. 1944.
3 MH 80/27, 'After the White Paper', para. 8. See also, 'The White Paper scheme,' para. 8 and 11, no author but probably by Hawton, 10 Feb. 1944.
4 MH 80/27, Harding, 'BMA conference on White Paper', 18 Feb. 1944.
5 MH 80/27, BMA statement on White Paper, Feb. 1944.
6 Mh 80/27, Harding, 'BMA conference on White Paper', 18 Feb. 1944.
7 GLC, LCC PH/GEN/1/13, Fairfield to Daley, 'Address by Dr Charles Hill on the White Paper', no date but probably 18 Feb. 1944.
8 MH 80/27, Henderson to Maude, 25 Feb. 1944.
9 Ministry of Health and Department of Health for Scotland (1844a) pp. 24–6.
10 GLC, LCC PH/GEN/1/13, Fairfield to Daley, 'Address by Dr Charles Hill on the White Paper'. See also BMA 1401/PR 18, Hill note on White Paper, 17 Feb. 1944.
11 Honigsbaum (1979) pp. 274–83.
12 For an early sign of MPA influence, see BMJ, 1 May 1943, Supp. p. 55 (MacWilliam). See also the leaderette, 'The opponents of the medical profession', in BMJ, 30 Oct. 1943, p. 552 and correspondence which followed.
13 BMJ, 19 Feb. 1944, Supp. p. 30 (Atkinson). For another exchange on this issue between Stark Murray and the Forfar Local Medical Committee, see RCP 25, agenda for MPC meeting, 16 March 1944.
14 BMJ, 18 March 1944, Supp. pp. 53–5.
15 BMJ, 13 May 1944, p. 663.
16 This was noticed within the Ministry as early as 1927 when Dain replaced a stronger

BMA leader, Henry Brackenbury, as chairman of the Insurance Acts Committee. MH 62/106, Brock to Secretary, 17 June 1927.

17 Hill (1964) pp. 52–3.
18 *Pulse*, 14 Nov. 1981, p. 13.
19 *BMJ*, 11 and 25 March 1944, Supp. pp. 40–3, 59–60.
20 MH 80/27, BMA, 'The White Paper — an analysis', March 1944.
21 HC Debs (398) 427–518, 16 March 1944. For Graham-Little's address at Guildford and his collaboration with the MPA, see *Surrey Times*, 31 March 1944, p. 4; and *Truth*, 14 and 28 April 1944, pp. 306, 338–9. See also Honigsbaum (1979) p. 284.
22 HL Debs (131) 70–116, 16 March 1944.
23 MH 80/27, 'Debate on NHS — Lord Moran's speech on his amendment', no author, March 1944.
24 *BMJ*, 13 May 1944, pp. 648–52.
25 MH 80/27, reports of meetings with Hill and Dain, 4, 11, and 12 April 1944.
26 For the report and leading article on it, see *BMJ*, 13 May 1944, pp. 643–8, 663–4.
27 *BMJ*, 20 May 1944, Supp. p. 113
28 *BMJ*, 27 May and 17 June 1944, pp. 727, 817. MH 80/27, correspondence between Maude and Hill, 1 and 6 Sept. 1944.
29 MH 80/29, draft notes for Croydon speech, no author, 17 May 1944.
30 MH 80/27, note on proposed local administrative structure, no date but with papers dated April 1944, p. 6.
31 MH 80/27, CCA, draft resolution rejecting direct representation rights for doctors, no date but with papers dated March 1944.
32 MH 80/27, report of meeting with CCA and LCC, 14 June 1944, p. 3, para. 14.
33 MH 80/27, PEP, 'The White Paper on a National Health Service', draft report and later section on 'Structure', 17 May and 12 June 1944.
34 MH 80/27, Conservative Party Health Services Committee, report on NHS proposals, 25 May 1944.
35 MH 80/27, report of Ministry meeting with medical representatives, 4 Aug. 1944.
36 MH 80/33, report of Ministry meeting with AMC representatives, 20 June 1944.
37 MH 80/27, BMA memo on White Paper, July 1944.
38 MH 80/27, Conservative Party report on NHS proposals, 25 May 1944.
39 MH 80/27, report of Ministry meeting with medical representatives, 4 Aug. 1944. See also *BMJ*, 13 May, 1944, para. 42–8 of Council Report.
40 Department of Health for Scotland (1943) para. 28–50.
41 MH 80/27, Conservative Party report on NHS proposals, 25 May 1944.
42 MH 80/27, Hawton, 'Report of Conservative Party Committee on health services', no date but with papers dated June 1944. See also 'The joint authority and the hospital services', no author but probably by Hawton, July or Aug. 1944.
43 MH 80/33, note on proposed local administrative structure, no author but probably by Hawton, June 1944.
44 MH 80/27, draft for RC, 'NHS', no date but with papers dated Aug. 1944.
45 MH 80/27 or 80/34, BHA memo on White Paper, July 1944; report of Ministry meeting with BHA, 3 Aug. 1944.
46 MH 80/34, 'Voluntary hospitals and payments from rates', no author but with papers dated Oct. 1944, underlining in original. Maude made the same point at a meeting with voluntary hospital representatives. MH 80/27, reports of Ministry meetings with BHA and King's Fund representatives, 5 and 17 Oct. 1944.
47 MH 80/27, Conservative Party report on NHS proposals, 25 May 1944.
48 MH 80/27, draft for RC, 'National Health Service', no author but with papers dated Aug. 1944, para. 18.
49 MH 80/27, revised draft of paper to RC from Scottish Secretary, 'Points arising on

the Scottish position', 20 Sept. 1944; Haddow to Hawton, 26 Sept. 1944.

50 CAB 87/6 or MH 80/27, RC, minutes 2 Oct. 1944.
51 MH 80/27, report of Ministry meeting with medical representatives, 10 Oct. 1944.
52 *BMJ*, 5 Aug. 1944, Supp. pp. 25–9.
53 *BMJ*, 16 Sept. 1944, Supp. pp. 57–9.
54 BMA 2342/C 10, agenda for Council meeting, 2 May 1945; 1459/PR 1, 2, 4, 7 (1945).
55 *BMJ*, 8 July 1944, pp. 47–9.
56 *The Times*, 16 Sept. 1944, p. 5. See also the leaders in *BMJ*, 23 Sept and 14 Oct. 1944, pp. 409, 506–7.
57 *BMJ*, 2 Sept. 1944, Supp. pp. 49–50.
58 MH 80/27, T.F.C. [?] to ? [possibly Hawton] 'National Health Service,' no date but with papers dated July and Aug. 1944.
59 MH 80/27, Rucker to Cherwell, 1 and 16 Aug. 1944.
60 *Lancet*, 21 Nov. 1942, pp 599–622.
61 MH 77/26 or 80/25, Maude, 'Draft of paper by Maude on GP service,' Nov. or Dec. 1942, p. 2, para. 6. See also in same files, 'Post-war medical policy. GP service', no author, March 1942, p. 12, para. 28. See also MH 80/26, Maude, 'Discussions with the medical profession', 19 or 23 June 1943, pp. 11–12.
62 See the profile of Taylor when he was adopted as a Labour candidate for Parliament at Barnet in 1945. *Barnet Press*, 28 April 1945.
63 For Taylor's resignation from the Labour Party, see *Pulse*, 18 July 1981, p. 9, and *World Medicine*, 25 July 1981, pp. 17–18.
64 For Taylor's admission that he was Gordon Malet, see *Update*, 1 Feb. 1979, p. 360.
65 *Spectator*, 29 Sept. 1944, p. 285.
66 *Spectator*, 10 Nov. 1944, p. 433.
67 MH 80/34, letter from Counties Practitioners' Group, Guildford, Nov. 1944. See also *BMJ*, 11 and 25 Nov., 9 Dec. 1944, pp. 115–17, 126–7 (Gough), 143.
68 *BMJ*, 7 and 28 Oct. 1944, Supp. pp. 77, 94.
69 *BMJ*, 28 Oct. and 4 Nov. 1944, Supp. pp. 95–8, 103–10.
70 *BMJ*, 11 Nov. 1944, Supp. p. 115 (Picken).
71 *BMJ*, 25 Nov. 1944, Supp. pp. 123–4. See also the debate on the proposal by the BMA's Council in *BMJ*, 11 Nov. 1944, Supp. p. 115.
72 BMA 1489/NC 12, minutes of negotiating committee, 12 Jan. 1945.
73 BMA 1399/27, motion and memo from City of Edinburgh Division, 22 June 1943.
74 BMA 1489/NC 12, minutes of negotiating committee, 12 Jan. 1945.
75 The number in opposition at the BMA meeting was cited by Dr Stark Murray of the SMA at a Labour party conference and reported in *BMJ*, 6 Jan. 1945, Supp. p. 3. For a view of the meeting from the MPA side, see the article in *Truth*, 15 Dec. 1944, p. 473; and by Dr E.U. MacWilliam in *Patriot*, 14 Dec. 1944, pp. 549–50.
76 *BMJ*, 16 Dec. 1944, pp. 794–5.
77 Honigsbaum (1979) pp. 122–30, 146–7, 156–7, 286–7.
78 BEV VIII/52, correspondence between Clarke and Beveridge, 1, 7, and 13 Dec. 1944.

Chapter 8 Retreat to the panel system

1 MH 80/27, Rucker to Minister, draft of paper for RC, 4 Dec. 1944, para. 17.
2 MH 80/27, report of meeting between Minister of Health and Scottish Secretary, 20 Dec. 1944, para. 5.
3 MH 80/28, Appendix to NHS (45) 8, 23 Jan. and (second revise — 23 Feb.) 1945.
4 MH 80/28, report of Ministry meeting with medical representatives, 20 Feb. and 13 March 1945.
5 *Public Health*, March 1944, pp. 61–2.

6 MH 80/28, report of Ministry meeting with medical representatives, 30 Jan. 1945; 'Note for further meeting with doctors', no author, Feb. 1945.

7 MH 80/28, report of meeting between Minister of Health and Scottish Secretary, 20 Dec. 1944, para. 7.

8 MH 80/28, report of Ministry meeting with medical representatives, 20 Jan. 1945.

9 Honigsbaum (1979) pp. 62–3.

10 BMA 1,400/NC (1945–6). MH 80/28, report of Ministry meeting with medical representatives, 16 Jan. 1945.

11 MH 80/27, report of Ministry meeting with medical representatives, 10 Oct. 1944. See also RCP 2/1/18, Moran to Boldero, 8 Feb. 1945.

12 MH 80/28, Appendix to NHS (45) 8, 23 Jan. and (second revise — 23 Feb.) 1945; 'Notes for further meeting with the doctors', no author, Feb. 1945; report of Ministry meeting with medical representatives, 16 Jan. and 13 March 1945; 'Central organisation — outstanding points', no author but with papers dated Jan. 1945.

13 MN 80/28, report of Ministry meeting with medical respresentatives, 23 and 30 Jan. 1945; Appendix to NHS (45) 8, 23 Jan. and (second revise — 23 Feb) 1945; 'Regional and area planning bodies', no author but with papers dated Jan. and Feb. 1945; report of Ministry meeting with AMC, 6 and 23 March 1945. MH 80/32, 'Dr Hill's list of points', no author but with papers dated March 1945, paras 25–6; 'Answers to Dr Hill's list of points', paras 23, 25–6.

14 MH 80/28, report of Ministry meeting with medical representatives, 13 March 1945.

15 MH 80/28, brief for Ministry meeting with medical representatives, no author, 12 Jan. 1945, addendum.

16 MH 80/28, report of Ministry meeting with medical representatives, 16 and 23 Jan. 1945.

17 MH 80/28, report of Ministry meeting with medical representatives, 13 Feb. 1945.

18 MH 80/28, report of Ministry meeting with medical representatives, 30 Jan. 1945.

19 MH 80/28 or 80/32, report of Ministry meeting with GP sub-committee, 24 April 1945.

20 MH 80/28 or 80/33, report of Ministry meeting with local authority representatives, 8 May 1945.

21 MH 80/28, report of Ministry meeting with various local authority representatives: AMC on 6 March, LCC on 9 March, CCA and LCC on 12 March 1945.

22 MH 80/28, Ministry notes on Conservative Party committee report, May 1945.

23 MH 80/28, report of Ministry meeting with local authority representatives, 6, 9, and 12 March 1945.

24 CAB 87/10, RC, memos by Minister of Health and Scottish Secretary on sale of practices, 5 and 6 March 1945.

25 CAB 87/10, RC, minutes 12 and 20 March 1945; memo by Ministers for Reconstruction and Health, and Scottish Secretary, 17 March 1945. CAB 124/245 or MH 80/32, Woolton to Prime Minister, 26 or 28 March 1945.

26 CAB 124/245, draft of minute from Woolton to Prime Minister, 24 March 1945. Compare this with the letter actually sent, 26 March 1945. For Churchill's approval, see PREM 4/36/3, Churchill to Peck, 30 April 1945.

27 MH 80/30, 'Compensation', no author but by Hawton, 8 March 1945.

28 For Ministry recognition of this danger, see MH 80/29, 'NHS — outline of the present proposals', no author, 4 Aug. 1945, p. 13, para. 32.

29 *BMJ*, 20 June 1942, Supp. pp. 746 (para. 35), 749 (para. 69).

30 *BMJ*, 13 May 1944, p. 647, paras 54–6 of Council report; 28 Oct. and 16 Dec. 1944, Supp. pp. 93–4 (Hill), 160–1. See also Honigsbaum (1979) p. 213.

31 *BMJ*, 16 Dec. 1944. Supp. p. 160

32 MH 80/28 or 80/32, report of Ministry meeting with medical representatives, 20 Feb. 1945.

33 *BMJ*, 5 Aug. 1944, Supp. pp. 28–9, Q. 33–4.
34 HC Debs (410) 1,602, 3 May 1945.
35 For the report presented to this meeting (a copy of which is in the writer's possession), see Honigsbaum (1979) p. 213.
36 MH 80/28, 'Further notes on local authorities and health centres', no author but with papers dated April and May 1945.
37 However, at a later date a leading article in the *BMJ* added a qualification: 12 May 1945, pp. 668–9.
38 MH 80/32, draft of letter from Willink to Bevin, no author but with papers dated April 1945.
39 CAB 87/10, RC, memo from Scottish Secretary on sale of practices, 6 March 1945.
40 GLC, LCC PH/GEN/1/16, report of LCC meeting with Ministry of Health, 9 March 1945. For the Ministry's minutes, see MH 80/28.
41 HC Debs (411) 1,533–4 (Griffiths), 12 June 1945.
42 LAB 14/315, Industry Health Advisory Committee, minutes 5 April 1943 to 9 March 1944.
43 TUC, *Annual Conference Report*, 1944, pp. 8–13, Supp. to General Council report, Section D, paras 80–1, 91–2. See also MH 77/73, Citrine to Brown, 29 Oct. 1943.
44 MH 80/32, note of appointments to Spens Committee, 20 Sept. 1944.
45 MH 77/173, Spens Committee, report of proceedings, 28 Nov. 1945, pp. 18–20; 11 Jan. 1946.
46 MH 80/29, TUC, 'National Health Service', 15 May 1945. See also TUC 847.3, Jt. SIC & WCFC 11/1.
47 HC Debs (411) 1,555–61, 12 June 1945.
48 MH 77/29, report of Cabinet meeting on health service, 6 June 1945. See also CAB 65/33, Cabinet minutes 15 June 1945, p. 60.
49 MH 80/29, 'NHS — outline of present proposals', no author but probably Hawton, 4 Aug. 1945, p. 7, para. 14.
50 MH 80/32, report of Ministry meeting with medical representatives, 24 May 1945.
51 MH 80/29, memo appended to draft paper to Cabinet from Minister of Health, 'NHS', June 1945.
52 MH 80/29, report of Ministry meeting with medical representatives, 6 and 20 Feb., 13 March 1945; report of Ministry meeting with King's Fund, 16 March 1945; Wetenhall to Rucker, 14 May 1945. See also GLC, LCC PH/GEN/1/16, Daley to Salmon, report on meeting of RCP, 21 April 1945.
53 CAB 21/2019, Cabinet minutes 6 June 1945. For the proof of the paper, see MH 80/28, 'Progress with the proposals for a National Health Service', June 1945. For the political considerations at Cabinet level, see CAB 21/2032, Woolton to Prime Minister, 1 June 1945; Paymaster General (Cherwell) to Woolton, 7 June 1945; Willink to Law, 20 June 1945. PREM 4/36/3, Churchill to Willink, 18 June 1945. See also CAB 65/53, Cabinet minutes 15 June 1945, p 60.

Chapter 9 Bevan the pragmatist

1 Foot (1962 and 1964) pp. 36–40 of 1964 edition.
2 Foot (1973 and 1975) pp. 17, 234 of 1975 edition.
3 Foot (1962 and 1964) pp. 63–4 of 1964 edition.
4 Cronin (1937).
5 Honigsbaum (1979) p. 13, 82, 125.
6 Foot (1973 and 1975) p. 16 of 1975 edition.
7 Foot (1962 and 1964) pp. 443–4 of 1964 edition; (1973 and 1975) p. 21 of 1975 edition.

8 HC Debs (373) 91–4, 8 July 1941. For possible wider political considerations behind Bevan's appointment, see Campbell (1987) pp. 150–1.
9 Labour Party (1943).
10 Campbell (1987) pp. 150–1.
11 HC Debs (410) 380–2, 2,635–7, 19 April and 17 May 1947.
12 HC Debs (413) 257–9, 17 Aug. 1945.
13 HC Debs (426) 426–32 (Messer), 26 July 1946.
14 Honigsbaum (1979) pp. 257–8.
15 HC Debs (Standing Committee C) 528, 6 June 1946.
16 Campbell (1987) p. 179.
17 Eckstein (1958) p. 252.
18 HC Debs (422) 57–8, 30 April 1946.
19 MH 80/30, 'Medical aid societies', no author but with papers dated Feb. 1946. It should be noted that a year earlier Bevan led a deputation to the Ministry pleading for medical aid societies to be given a place in the new health service because of the valuable experience they offered for the organization of group practice. A report of this deputation, which met Willink on 16 Feb. 1945, was issued by the Ministry of Health and a copy is in the writer's possession.
20 CAB 128/5, Cabinet minutes 8 March 1946, pp. 182–4.
21 HC Debs (422) 55, 392, 30 April and 2 May 1946. See also CAB 134/697, memo from Minister of Health to Social Services Committee, 17 Dec. 1945, paras 31–8; CAB 128/2, Cabinet minutes 20 Dec. 1945, pp. 338–40; MH 80/32, 'How to pay doctors in the GP service', no author but with papers dated Feb. 1946.
22 MH 80/30, report of Ministry meeting with TUC representatives, 8 Jan. 1946.
23 CAB 129/4, memo from Minister of Health on sale of practices, 23 Nov. 1945. HC Debs (422) 53, 30 April 1946.
24 HC Debs (Standing Committee C) 631, 19 June 1946.
25 HC Debs (472) 1,006–8, 14 March 1950. See also Honigsbaum (1979) pp. 292–3.
26 CAB 129/5, memo from Minister of Health, 13 Dec. 1945, p. 1, para. 4. See also Honigsbaum (1979) pp. 292–3.
27 MH 80/30 or 80/33, report of Ministry meeting with local authority representatives, 26 and 27 Feb. 1946.
28 Hongisbaum (1979) p. 17.
29 MH 80/32, 'BMA — notes on main points taken in BMA council's report on Bill', no author but with papers dated March and May, 1946.
30 BMJ, 15 Sept. 1945, Supp. p. 63.
31 Honigsbaum (1979) pp. 165–7.
32 Honigsbaum (1979) p. 280.
33 BMJ, 16 Dec. 1944, Supp. pp. 147–8.
34 BMJ, 30 March 1946, pp. 499–500.
35 Medical World, 7 Feb. 1947, pp. 827–8.
36 Animal's Defender, July 1951, pp. 12–13.
37 BMJ, 6 April 1946, p. 541.
38 BMJ, 4 Aug. 1945, Supp. p. 29.
39 See MPA Bulletin number 19, Jan. 1948, and MPA memo, 12 April 1948, in RCP 1/62 and 91. For the social credit origins of the MPA, see Honigsbaum (1979) pp. 274–8.
40 Daily Telegraph, 21 Oct. 1952, p. 6 (B. Steele).
41 BMJ, 15 Dec. 1945, p. 833.
42 BMJ, 9 Nov. 1946, p. 707.
43 MH 80/32, 'Dr Hill's points — interview with secretary', 10 May 1946, p. 2, point 4. For a clear indication of Hill's distaste for the abuses associated with the sale of

practices, see his interview with Dr Morgan, 3 Dec. 1935 in TUC 843.2.

44 *BMJ*, 10 Jan. 1948, pp. 61–4.
45 CAB 129/7 or MH 80/30, memo by Minister of Health on NHS Bill, 1 March 1946.
46 HL Debs (143) 510–22, 22 Oct. 1946.
47 HC Debs (428) 1,122–54, 4 Nov. 1946. BMA 1521/NC GP 2, 12 March 1947, p 2.
48 Foot (1973 and 1975) pp. 176, 197, 203 of 1975 edition.
49 For a summary of the Northern Ireland NHS Act, see *BMJ*, 3 April 1948, Supp. pp. 64–6.
50 *BMJ*, 15 May 1948, pp. 936–7, 149–50 (Cox).
51 HC Debs (Standing Committee C) 631–2, 19 June 1946.
52 NHS Act, 9 & 10 George 6, Chapter 81, sections 35–7.
53 BMA 1447/FH 5, Financial Hardship Committee, agenda 17 Feb. 1948, para. 4, minute 36 from report of Special Representative Meeting, 8 Jan. 1948.
54 MH 77/119, reports of Miistry meetings with medical representatives on compensation for abolition of sale of practices, 4 and 13 Dec. 1945.
55 CAB 134/696, Social Services Committee, minutes 29 Nov. 1945. CAB 21/3,028, A.G. [Arthur Greenwood] to Prime Minister, 1 Dec. 1945.
56 BMA 1,400/NC 59 (1945-6), report of Ministry meeting with medical representatives, 17 Jan. 1946.
57 MH 77/119 or 80/30, Harvey to Rucker, 15 Feb. 1946; Harvey to Douglas, 11 March 1946. BMA 1,400/NC 83 (1945-6). Of the £66 million, £7½ million went to Scotland and this may have been too large a proportion. In 1948, there were only about 2,000 doctors there but 2,290 was the figure used to calculate the proportion. MH 80/57, note on points arising out of meeting with BMA, 7 May 1948, para. II 4.
58 BMA 1,400/NC 49 and 68b (1945-6).
59 BMA 1,399/RC 43 (1943-4) and 1,400/NC 59 (1945-6).
60 The doctors wanted a higher increase of 25 per cent, but accepted the £66 million agreed by the actuaries. BMA 1,400/NC 78,83, 84 (1945-6) and letters from Hill to negotiating committee, 26 Feb. and 18 March 1946. See also MH 80/32, Hawton, 'Sale and purchase of practices — proposed compensation policy', no date but with papers dated Jan. 1946.
61 MH 77/26 or 80/24, Maude, 'Draft of paper by Maude on GP service', Nov. or Dec. 1943, pp. 1–2, para. 4. PIN 12/94, Official Committee on Beveridge Report, minutes 14 Jan. 1943, p. 14, para. 66.
62 BMA 1,514/Comp 1 (1949-50), Compensation Sub-committee, agenda 8 Feb. 1950, item 1. For earlier consideration of the same issue, see MH 80/57, various papers, May to Dec. 1948. By the end of 1948, some 17,000 doctors had applied for compensation, but many had practices of little capital value.
63 MH 80/26, samples of net earnings of doctors in 1938 from Inland Revenue, no date but with papers dated July 1943.
64 MH 77/26 or 80/31, Hawton, 'Remuneration of doctors', March 1943.
65 Ministry of Health and Department of Health for Scotland (1946); Stevens (1966) pp. 130–1.
66 Forsyth (1966) pp. 34–5.
67 MH 77/26 or 80/24, Maude, 'Draft of paper by Maude on GP service', Nov. or Dec. 1942, p. 12.
68 MH 77/119, George to Hale, 11 March 1946. MH 80/30, Harvey to George, 12 March 1946; George to Hawton, 16 March 1946.
69 MH 80/32, report of Ministry meeting with medical representatives on compensation for abolition of sale of practices, 13 Dec. 1945, 5 and 29 Jan. 1946. See also BMA 1,400/NC 49, 59, 68b (1945-6). For concern shown earlier in the Ministry about the likely damaging effects on recruitment if a three-year leeway on compensation

were allowed, see MH 80/31, McNicholl, 'General medical service', 26 Feb. 1943.

70   *BMJ*, 4 Aug. 1945, Supp. pp. 30–1; 11 May 1946, Supp. pp. 124–5; 3 Aug. 1946, Supp. p. 43 (Dain).

71   MH 80/32, report of Ministry meeting with medical representatives, 29 Jan. 1946.

72   *BMJ*, 8 Nov. 1947, Supp. pp. 106–7.

73   *BMJ*, 10 Jan. 1948, pp. 59–60.

74   BMA 1,447/FH 1 and 3 (1946–8).

75   *BMJ*, 24 Jan. 1948, Supp. p. 14. BMA 1,524/GP 31 (1947–8).

76   MH 80/30, Harvey to Rucker, 15 Feb. 1946; report of Ministry meeting with medical representatives. 5 March 1946.

77   *BMJ*, 29 May 1948, pp. 1,046–7 (Norris). See also the letters in *BMJ*, 7 Feb. 1948, pp. 271–2 (Kemp); 21 Feb. 1948, pp. 357–8 (O'Connor and Laventhal); 20 March 1948, p. 573 (Morris).

78   *BMJ*, 15 May 1948, pp. 949–50.

79   Foot (1973 and 1975) p. 215 of 1975 edition.

80   CAB 128/1 or MH 80/29, Cabinet minutes 18 Oct. 1945.

81   CAB 129/4, memo by Minister of Health on sale of practices, 23 Nov. 1945. CAB 128/2, Cabinet minutes 3 Dec. 1945.

82   MH 80/32, report of Ministry meeting with medical representatives on compensation for abolition of sale of practices, 5 March 1946.

83   MH 80/32, correspondence between George and Hale, 23 Oct., 2 and 7 Nov. 1945.

84   MH 80/32, minute to Secretary with revised draft of paper on compensation proposals, 22 Nov. 1945.

85   MH 80/32, report of Ministry meeting with medical representatives on compensation for abolition of sale of practices, 13 Dec. 1945.

86   *BMJ*, 20 June 1942, p. 749 under section headed 'Principals' in model health centre.

87   BMA 1,399/RC 37 (1943–4), representative committee minutes 7 July 1943, p. 2.

88   CAB 128/12 or PREM 8/844, Cabinet minutes 22 Jan. 1948, p. 43.

89   MH 77/176, Spens to Fass, 15 Feb. 1946.

90   MH 77/177, report of discussion by Ministry officials of paper on GP pay, 11 July 1946.

91   MH 80/30 or 80/32, 'Remuneration of GPs', no author indicated but Rucker is identified as the author in MH 80/32 paper, located in file with papers dated Jan. 1946. See also CAB 128/5, Cabinet minutes 8 Jan. 1946, pp. 22–4; and MH 77/177, report of Ministry discussion on medical pay, 3 Dec. 1946.

92   MH 80/32, 'How to pay doctors in the GP service', no author but with papers dated Feb. 1946.

93   HC Debs (Standing Committee C) 509, 6 June 1946.

94   CAB 129/5, memo by Minister of Health on NHS proposals, 13 Dec. 1945, p. 8, para. 36; CAB 128/2, Cabinet minutes 20 Dec. 1945, pp. 338–41.

95   *BMJ*, 20 April 1946, pp. 612–13. See also MH 80/32, medical negotiating committee observations on NHS proposals, no date but with papers dated Feb. 1946, p. 7, para. 21.

96   BMA 2,364/C 28 and 30, para. 408–9 (1945–6).

97   MH 80/32, medical negotiating committee observations on NHS proposals, p. 6, para. 20. See also *BMJ*, 30 March 1946, pp. 470, 472 (paras 10 and 22 of Council report), 489–91; 20 April 1946, pp. 612–13.

98   MH 80/30, report of Ministry meeting with medical representatives, 6 Feb. 1946.

99   HC Debs (422) 60–1, 30 April 1946. See also Foot (1973 and 1975) pp. 116–17, 144–5 of 1975 edition.

100   MH 80/30 or 80/32, report of Ministry meeting with AMC representatives, 26 Feb. 1946. See also GLC, LCC PH/HOSP/1/12, memo by Daley, 27 Feb. 1946.

101 GLC, LCC PH/HOSP/1/12, memos by Daley, 8 and 28 Feb. 1946. MH 80/33, report of Ministry meeting with LCC and CCA representatives, 27 Feb. 1946.

102 MH 80/33, Rucker to Secretary, 18 April 19465. MH 80/41, Lord Chancellor to Bevan, 26 Oct. 1946. HC Debs (Standing Committee C) 466, 5 June 1946. HC Debs (425) 1,819–42, 22 July 1946.

103 MH 80/30 or 80/33, report of Ministry meeting with AMC representatives, 26 Feb. 1946.

104 MH 77/119 or 80/28, report of Jameson and Rucker meeting with medical representatives, 20 Feb. 1945, pp. 5–6, para. 16.

105 MH 77/82, handwritten note to CMO and Secretary, 2 March 1946, author not clear but possibly Rucker.

106 HC Debs (422) 57, 30 April 1946.

107 BMA 2,364/C 10 (1945–6), Council agenda 30 Jan. 1946, para. 19 (8). *BMJ*, 3 Aug. 1946, Supp. p. 40; 2 Aug. 1947, Supp. p. 37. MH 80/57, report of Ministry meeting with BMA representatives, 17 Dec. 1948, para. 11.

108 HC Debs (449) 1,156–7, 15 April 1948.

109 CAB 21/2,032 or 128/5, Cabinet minutes 8 Jan. 1946, pp. 22–4.

110 For Bevan's earlier objection to a basic salary of £300 because it would not satisfy his Cabinet colleagues, see MH 77/177, Ministry discussion on GP pay, 3 Dec. 1946.

111 PREM 8/844, note by LMF? (initials not clear) on conversation with Douglas, 17 Feb. 1948.

112 RCP 1/78, Moran to Bevan, 4 April 1948.

113 *BMJ*, 3 April 1948, Supp. pp. 64–6. For the second reading debate, see the separate collection of Parliamentary Debates (Northern Ireland) volume 1,990, cols 1,453–780, Sept. and Oct. 1947, on file in the Official Publications Department of the British Library.

114 MH 80/57, note on points arising out of meeting with BMA, 7 May 1948, para. III. BMA 2,459, Douglas to Hill, 26 May 1948; BMA 1,521/NC GP 47, agenda 16 July 1948, para. 12 (4).

115 This was the result of a recommendation by the CHSC: MH 80/57, extract from CHSC meeting, 21 June 1949.

116 BMA 1,400/NC 92 (1945–6), opinion of Cecil Havers, KC, on NHS Bill, 16 April 1946, pp. 5–6. BMA 1,513/NC 174 (1947–8), opinion on partnerships by Sir Cyril Radcliffe, KC, and J.H. Stamp, 19 Nov. 1947.

117 BMA 1,513/NC 178 (1947–8), report of Bevan's meeting with medical negotiating committee, 2 and 3 Dec. 1947, pp. 5–7.

118 PREM 8/844, Brook to Prime Minister, 21 Jan. 1948.

119 HC Debs (Standing Committee C) 774–5, 26 June 1946.

120 For a clear indication of obstetrician interest in this restriction, see RCOG A4/5/1, Holland to Mrs Churchill, 29 April 1946. See also pages 131 and 138.

121 Honigsbaum (1979) pp. 139–40, 155.

122 *BMJ*, 2 Aug. 1947, Supp. pp. 30–1; 27 March 1948, Supp. p. 55.

123 MH 80/57, report of Ministry meetings with BMA representatives, 7, 10, 13 May, and 23 June 1948. BMA 1,521/NC GP 43, para. 17, letter from Minister, 11 June 1948.

124 Goodman (1970) p. 127.

125 MH 77/177, correspondence George and Hale, 20 Jan. 4 and 5 Feb. 1948.

126 MH 80/57, report of Ministry meeting with BMA representatives, 23 June and 17 Dec. 1948.

127 RCOG A2, Council minutes 29 Jan. 1949, pp. 181–2.

Chapter 10 Moran organizes consultants

In the notes listed here, Charles Wilson is referred to as Moran before he became a peer in January 1943. Many letters in the RCP files contain no signature, but Moran can be identified as the author from the contents or from the indication that it was sent by the president. Letters from Boldero always had the word 'Registrar' on them.

1 BEV VIII/31, Wetenhall to Beveridge, 15 June 1941.
2 For this whole development, see Honigsbaum (1979). However, it should be noted that the wrong term is used there to describe GP-specialists: they were known as 'consultoids', not 'consultands'. The term is first used on p. 141.
3 RCP 16/2/22, note on voluntary and municipal hospitals by Cohen, no date but with papers of the Younger Fellows Club for 1941.
4 RCP 16/2/SP9, MPC, Special Practice Committee Minutes 3 March 1942, remarks by Platt and Walton.
5 Titmuss (1950) pp. 191–2.
6 Abel-Smith (1964) pp. 424–39.
7 RCOG A3/4, pp. 154–5, report of meeting with Ministry on Emergency Maternity Service, 25 March 1942.
8 *BMJ*, 7 Feb. 1948, Supp. p. 265 (Horder reporting on a study made by Eric Steeler).
9 RCP 11/3/30, memo by Sheldon on non-teaching provincial hospitals, Aug. 1941.
10 HC Debs (338) 3,372–3, 28 July 1938 (Elliot). See also Rivett (1986) pp. 226, 238–42.
11 RCP, oral history recording of Moran's conversation, 25 June 1970.
12 RCP 22/1/1, notes of joint meeting of college representatives, 25 Oct. 1940, p. 4 (Lett).
13 Watson (1950) p. 256.
14 Stevens (1966) p. 69.
15 Cooke (1972) p. 1,046., See also the review of Cooke's history by Dr Charles Newman in *Lancet*, 19 Feb. 1972, pp. 429–30.
16 RCOG A4/4/10, Fletcher Shaw to Maclean, 14 May 1941.
17 Cooke (1972) p. 1,096, from Moran's 1945 presidential address.
18 RCP 22/1/1, notes of joint meeting of college representatives, 25 Oct. 1940, p. 1.
19 RCOG B2/14, Anderson to Fletcher Shaw, 1 May 1941.
20 RCOG B2/14, summary of points made at meeting of college presidents with Anderson, 16 Oct. 1940.
21 RCOG B2/14, Fletcher Shaw to Maclean, 14 May 1941.
22 RCP 7/2/155, Moran to Watson, 23 April 1943.
23 RCP 7/3/74, Moran to Stopford, 24 Aug. 1943.
24 RCP 7/3/43, Moran to Nattrass, 30 July 1943. This honorary appointment aroused the ire of the TUC's medical adviser, Dr Morgan. For his concern about its implications, see MH 55/895, Morgan to Brown, 16 Sept. 1943.
25 RCP 7/2/136, Moran to Hardy, 3 May 1943.
26 RCP 7/4/17, Moran to Parsons, 9 Feb. 1941. RCP 1/45, note on meeting of college presidents with Hill, no date but contents suggest it was written by Moran on 4 Dec. 1947.
27 RCP 7/4/17, Moran to Parsons, 9 Feb. 1944. RCP 7/4/64, Moran to Sheldon, 6 May 1944. RCP 2/1/18, Moran to Boldero, 8 Feb. 1945.
28 Wheeler-Bennett (1968) pp. 110–12, from a memoir by Churchill's private secretary, Sir John Colville. See also Colville (1985 and 1987) pp. 183, 424 of 1987 edition. I am indebted to Professor Ben Pimlott for making me aware of Moran's interest in a Minister of Health appointment.
29 RCP 7/5/10, Moran to Charles, 22 Jan. 1944.
30 For recognition of this by Moran's colleagues, see RCP 7/4/24, Parsons to Moran,

17 Feb. 1944; and RCP 11/1/5, note by Moncrieff on interview with Hill, 12 Jan. 1944.

31 RCP 22/1/21, draft statement by Moran on MPC Report, 30 July 1942.

32 RCP 21/1/30, 'The representation of consultants and specialists — the case for a joint committee', no author but contents suggest it was written by Moran about July, 1948.

33 Hill (1964) pp. 96–7. For an exchange between one BMA leader (Peter Macdonald, a specialist) and the college presidents on this issue, see BMA 1,399/RC 11 (1943–4) representative committee minutes 15 April 1943, para. 14. Though Moran defended his action, he was aware of the danger. RCP 9/1/11, Moran to Oliver, 11 March 1943; and RCP 7/2/136, Moran to Hardy, 3 May 1943.

34 RCOG B2/14, summary of points made at meeting of college presidents with Anderson, 19 Oct. 1940, and Anderson to Fletcher Shaw, 1 May 1941. See also RCP 7/2/124, Moran to Barber, 26 April 1943.

35 Honigsbaum (1979) p. 146.

36 Moran did not consider Macdonald a worthy representative of consultants because of his GP-specialist background. Macdonald acquired specialist skills through experience rather than by earning college qualifications. For Moran's criticism, see RCP 7/3/32, Moran to Sheldon, 23 Aug. 1943. For a profile of Macdonald, see Honigsbaum (1979) pp. 333–4, and his obituary notice in BMJ, 10 Sept. 1960, pp. 809–10.

37 RCP 31/2/11, Moncrieff to Moran, 3 Sept. 1948.

38 RCP 21/1/21, consultant services committee minutes 14 June 1948, p. 17.

39 RCP 4/1/58 or BMA 1,400/NC 48 (1945–6), negotiating committee minutes 4 Dec. 1945, para. 10.

40 For an example of Cohen's deference to Moran, see RCP 7/2/39, Cohen to Moran, 27 Feb. 1943.

41 RCP 7/2/13, Moran to Stopford, 9 Feb. 1943; RCP 17/3/14, Moran to Daley, 13 Nov. 1946.

42 RCP 7/4/51, Moran to Platt, 6 April 1944.

43 RCOG B2/15A, memo from Murray, 18 June 1936, pp. 2–3. Due to the dispute, Murray resigned as division secretary after having held that office for seven years.

44 RCP 7/4/64, Moran to Sheldon, 6 May 1944.

45 RCP 7/4/65, Moran to Webb-Johnson, 12 May 1944.

46 Stevens (1966) p. 18.

47 In 1944 Moran indicated that the RCP had 700 fellows, whereas 2,755 was cited as the number in the RCS by 1948. RCP 9/2/25, Moran to Oliver, 13 June 1944; RCS, 'Proceedings at a meeting of fellows, 28 April 1948', p. 20 (Payne), copy in writer's possession and also on file in RCS library.

48 RCP 7/2/122, Moran to Hardy, 22 April 1943; RCP 7/4/51, Moran to Platt, 6 April 1944; RCP 21/1/21, consultant services committee minutes 14 June 1948, pp. 12–13. Listen also to the tape in the RCP library of Moran's conversation, 25 June 1970.

49 For an appreciation of Webb-Johnson's role in NHS negotiations, see his obituary notice in BMJ, 7 Aug. 1958, pp. 1,357–9.

50 Cope (1959) pp. 207–26; Stevens (1966) pp. 121, 340.

51 RCOG A3/6, p. 164, finance and executive committee minutes 11 June 1948 (Wyatt).

52 RCP 7/3/71, Fletcher Shaw to Moran, 18 Aug. 1943; RCP 17/4/18, Moran to Boon, 15 Oct. 1947.

53 RCOG A2, pp. 159–61, Council papers, statement by president, 26 Oct. 1940; RCP 7/2/139, Fletcher Shaw to Moran, 4 May 1943.

54 Shaw (1954) p. 163.

55 RCOG A3/5, p. 218, finance and executive committee minutes 14 Dec. 1945.

56 RCOG A4/4/10, Fletcher Shaw to Maclean, 14 May 1941; RCOG A3/3, pp. 43–4, finance and executive committee minutes 18 June 1943; RCOG C1, p. 51, colleges'

joint committee minutes Oct. 1944.
57 RCP 5/1/18, Hill to Moran, 19 Oct. 1945.
58 Stevens (1966) p. 63.
59 RCP 11/3/3–5, RCP planning committee and colleges' joint committee minutes, Aug, Oct. and Nov. 1941. Also on file in RCOG C1, pp. 1–2, 3–5.
60 Cooke (1972) pp. 1,095–101.
61 RCP 7/2/122, Moran to Hardy, 22 April 1943.
62 RCP 7/2/101, 103, 108, and 109, correspondence between Moran and Charles, March and April 1943.
63 For a profile of the elder Charles, see his obituary notice in *BMJ*, 15 Nov. 1947, pp. 798–9.
64 This was noted by a Ministry colleague in the obituary notice for Charles in *Lancet*, 17 April 1971, p. 182.
65 RCP 7/2/103, Charles to Moran, 31 March 1943.
66 RCP 7/2/128, Hardy to Moran, 30 April 1943. See also correspondence numbered 133 and 140 in same file.
67 RCP 7/2/136, Moran to Hardy, 3 May 1943.
68 RCP 7/2/139, Fletcher Shaw to Moran, 4 May 1943.
69 Wilson (1966) p. 197.
70 RCP 7/4/51, Moran to Platt, 6 April 1944.
71 For a profile of McCurrich, see his obituary notice in *BMJ*, 30 July 1955, pp. 328–9.
72 RCP 8/3/29, Moran to Sheldon, 6 April 1943.
73 These figures are based on data supplied by McCurrich in 1947. He cited only 406 consultants in teaching hospitals as opposed to 3,550 in the non-teaching sector, but the 406 figure was challenged by the RCP Registrar, Dr (later Sir) Harold Boldero, who said it should be at least twice that number. RCP 20/1/47 and 48, McCurrich to Ministry of Health, 7 Feb. 1947, and Boldero to McCurrich, 18 Feb. 1947. Either way, the total exceeds the 3,500 estimate made for the number of fully qualified consultants in Britain at the time. Since all in the teaching sector were no doubt fully qualified, the 3,550 figure for the non-teaching sector must have included a large number of 'consultoids'.
74 RCP 9/2/25, Moran to Oliver, 13 June 1944.
75 For the papers from Sheldon and his correspondence with Moran, see RCP 7/2/94–5, 7/3/36, 7/4/63–4, 8/3/47, 11/3/30, and 78.
76 For the members of the 'Beveridge Committee' as enlarged in 1943, see RCP 11/1/1.
77 RCP 8/7/40, Hall to Boldero, 17 May 1943.
78 The idea was suggested by Dr Esmond Rees of Swansea, but since qualified surgeons vastly outnumbered qualified physicians, Moran planned to start one through the Provincial Surgical Club with the aid of its president, Gerald Alderson. RCP 8/11/18, Moran to Rees, 27 Sept. 1943; RCP 8/3/62 and 67, Moran to Alderson, 12 Nov. 1943, and paper by Alderson on proposed association.
79 RCP 8/3/68, Alderson to Boldero, 13 Jan. 1944; RCP 7/4/12, Webb-Johnson to Moran, 4 Feb. 1944.
80 RCP 7/5/29, Hill to Moran, 6 March 1944.
81 RCP 11/1/9, consultant service committee minutes 30 March 1944. See also RCP 7/4/80, Moran to Morrison, 30 July 1944.
82 Moran chose all members of the sub-committee except for one who was added by Webb-Johnson. RCP 7/4/71, Moran to Alderson, 21 June 1944; RCP 8/3/34, Boldero to Kindersley, 10 July 1944.
83 RCP 7/4/61, Moran to Platt, 29 April 1944.
84 Initially, only eleven members were appointed to the sub-committee. Fuller and Alderson were added in June or July, Alderson as the result of pressure from Webb-Johnson.

RCP 7/5/82, Moran to Fuller, 8 May 1944; RCP 13/2/11, sub-committee minutes 14 June 1944. For a full list of sub-committee members, see RCP 7/4/79, Moran to Messer, 26 July 1944. For a full set of sub-committee minutes, see RCP 14/3.

85 Since Alderson was an RCS fellow, a profile did appear in Robinson and Le Fanu (1970) p.7. However, the notice said nothing about the Provincial Surgical Club or Alderson's work on the sub-committee of the 'Beveridge Committee'.

86 RCP 8/7/9 and 64, correspondence between McCurrich and Boldero, 31 May and 11 July 1944. McCurrich also complained about his failure to receive the minutes of the 'Beveridge Committee' — which were sent after he protested. RCP 8/7/56 and 57, corespondence with McCurrich, 8 and 12 May 1944.

87 RCP 8/7/71, circular letter by McCurrich, 14 Sept. 1944. For the relevant section of the White Paper, see Ministry of Health and Department of Health for Scotland (1944a) p. 24.

88 RCP 13/2/9 for the March circular; RCP 8/7/63 and 71 for the June and Sept. circulars.

89 RCP 7/5/61, Moran to Hardy, 13 April 1944.

90 RCP 13/2/22, Kinderlsey to Moran, 4 July 1944; RCP 8/5/34, 36, 37, 39, and 40, correspondence with Kindersley, July to Nov. 1944; RCP 11/1/24, consultant services committee minutes, 22 Nov. 1944.

91 RCP 8/3/53, Urwick to Hinds-Howell, 27 July 1944. See also RCP 7/5/107, Alderson to Moran, 23 June 1944.

92 RCP 12/2/10, McCurrich to Moran, 9 June 1944.

93 RCP 8/12/11, Moran to Woodward, 26 June 1944; RCP 8/10/41 and 42, correspondence between Moran and Cohen, 5 and 9 July 1944; RCP 13/2/23, Moran to non-teaching hospital staff, 13 July 1944; RCP 13/2/36–8, correspondence between Moran and Boldero, 15 and 18 Sept. 1944.

94 RCP 13/4, whole file of letters sent by Moran in 1944, arranging meetings in the provinces to stop McCurrich.

95 RCP 8/1/54, Moran to Edgecombe, 16 June 1944.

96 RCP 8/7/72, McCurrich to Moran, 7 Nov. 1944; RCP 17/2/2, circular letter from Beddington of McCurrich's association, 24 March 1945.

97 RCP 8/8/28, Jones to Moran, 12 June 1944; RCP 8/10/45, Dewhurst to Moran, 13 July 1944; RCP 8/12/10, Beatty to Moran, 26 June 1944; RCP 9/2/40, Fuller to Moran, 28 July 1944.

98 RCP 9/1/8–11, correspondence regarding Provincial Teaching Hospital Association demand for separate representation, March 1943. See also RCP 13/2/13, Moran to Rees, 4 July 1944.

99 RCP 9/12/18–25, correspondence regarding Oliver demand, May and June 1944.

100 RCP 9/2/26, Moran to Watkins, 1 May 1944. See also RCP 9/2/39, Hill to Moran, 26 June 1944.

101 RCP 11/1/19, C. to D.M. [Moran to ?], 24 Aug. 1944.

102 RCP 13/5/32, Rowland Hill to Moran, 19 June 1944; RCP 11/1/25, minutes of meeting of non-teachers in London, 31 July 1944.

103 RCP 13/5/39, Rowland Hill to Moran, 24 Aug. 1944; RCP 7/4/107 and 14/1/16, correspondence between Moran and Tanner, 9 and 25 Nov. 1944.

104 RCP 7/4/114, Moran to Stebbing, 24 Nov. 1944.

105 RCP 13/3/13, Reddington to Moran, 26 March 1945. See also RCP 8/8/37, Reid to Jones, 20 July 1944.

106 RCP 9/2/39A, Moran to Alderson, 19 July 1944.

107 Colville (1987) p. 183.

108 RCP 21/1/21, report of meeting on consultant organization, 14 June 1948, p. 19.

109 RCP 17/2/2, letter from Reddington sent on behalf of McCurrich's association, 24 March 1945.

110 RCP 17/1/8, Hill to Moran, 2 March 1945.
111 RCP 7/4/107, 111, and 113, correspondence between Moran and Tanner, Nov. 1944.
112 RCP 13/5/46, Rowland Hill to Moran, 24 May 1945.

Chapter 11 Who is a consultant? Who should decide?

1 MH 77/173, RCP testimony, 3 Oct 1945, p. 1, italics added.
2 Honigsbaum (1979) p. 151.
3 Stevens (1966) pp. 19–20.
4 RCP 7/4/88–9, comments by Moran on paper from Medley to Boldero, 30 Aug. 1944.
5 RCOG B2/13, memo by RCOG president on register for consultants, July 1943.
6 MH 55/895 or RCP 11/3/17, Fraser to Moran, 5 Feb. 1942.
7 RCP 11/3/15, conference on survey of consultant services, 27 March 1942.
8 MH 55/895, Heseltine to Maude, 18 Feb. 1943.
9 MH 55/895, memo for file by Pater, 14 May 1943.
10 RCP 11/3/32 or RCOG B2/15A, CMAC minutes 22 March 1943; RCOG C1, pp. 27–34, colleges' joint committee minutes 18 Feb., 2 March, and 1 June 1943.
11 MH 55/895, see Jameson's handwritten comments on a minute from Hawton, 24 and 25 June 1943.
12 MH 55/895, Heseltine to Maude, 4 June 1943.
13 RCP 7/3/20 or MH 55/895, Percy to Moran, 28 June 1943.
14 MH 55/895, Hawton to Maude, 18 June 1943.
15 MH 55/895 or RCP 7/3/21, Moran to Brown, 29 June 1943.
16 MH 55/895, report of Ministry meeting with GMC representatives, 30 June 1943.
17 MH 55/895, report of Ministry meeting with GMC representatives, 30 June 1943.
18 MH 55/895, Brown to Moran, 21 July 1943; college presidents to Brown, 4 Aug. 1943.
19 MH 55/895, note on meeting between Maude, Eason, and Heseltine, 31 Aug. 1943. See also documents from Eason to Stopford and university representatives in same file, 8 Sept. 1943.
20 RCP 7/4/88–9, comments by Moran on paper from Medley to Boldero, 30 Aug. 1944.
21 RCOG C1, colleges' joint committee minutes 18 Feb. 1943.
22 RCP 11/3/32 or RCOG B2/15A, CMAC minutes 22 March 1943.
23 RCP 7/3/43, Moran to Nattrass, 30 July 1943. See also the angry comments by the TUC's medical adviser in MH 55/895, Morgan to Brown, 16 Sept. 1943.
24 RCP 14/5 or RCOG B2/15A, CMAC minutes 8 Feb. 1944. For a letter from McCurrich expressing concern about the way consultants were being selected, see *BMJ*, 29 Jan. 1944, p. 158.
25 For an indication of Hill's attitude here, see his testimony to the Spens Committee on GP Remuneration in MH 77/173, BMA testimony, 16 Oct. 1945, p. 1, and 28 Nov. 1945, pp. 16–17.
26 RCP 11/1/5, note by Moncrieff on interview with Hill, 12 Jan. 1944.
27 RCP 7/4/17, Moran to Parsons, 9 Feb. 1944. Exception might have been taken to the BMA lists because of their tendency to exclude those who were not BMA members; in one area, twelve locally-recognized specialists had been omitted for this reason. RCP 8/3/11, Shore to Moran, 22 March 1944. But Moran's concern lay in the opposite direction: he feared the BMA lists would contain too many names, not too few.
28 MH 55/895, Morgan to Brown, 9 Aug. 1944.
29 MH 55/895, Heseltine to Jameson, 20 Jan. 1944. For Willink's response, see HC Debs (396) 1,387–8, 3 Feb. 1944.
30 MH 55/895, correspondence between Jameson and Percy, 22 and 23 Feb. 1944.
31 MH 55/895, Reed to Martin, 29 Feb. 1944. In the speech Churchill delivered he only briefly expressed Moran's concern about the need to uphold consultant standards

while the number expanded: *BMJ*, 11 March 1944, p. 368.
32 RCP 7/4/17, Moran to Parsons, 9 Feb. 1944.
33 RCP, recording of Moran's conversation, 25 June 1970.
34 RCOG A2, pp. 60-1, Council minutes 27 Jan. 1945; RCOG A3/5, pp. 145, 159, 163, finance and executive committee minutes 13 Oct. 1944, 19 Jan. and 9 March 1945.
35 MH 77/173, RCOG testimony, 8 Nov. 1945, pp. 15-16.
36 RCOG A3/5, pp. 8-9, finance and executive committee minutes 22 Jan. 1943; RCOG A2, pp. 231-2, Council minutes 30 Jan. 1943.
37 RCOG A4/4/11, Fletcher Shaw to Mallon, 24 March 1944.
38 RCOG A2, between pp. 75 and 76, memo by Claye, 'Obstetric training of medical students', 27 Jan. 1945. For the report of the Goodenough Committee, see Ministry of Health and Department of Health for Scotland (1944b).
39 RCOG B7, p. 10, maternal and infant health services committee minutes 29 Jan. 1944; RCOG A2, pp. 67-8, Council minutes 24 March 1945.
40 RCOG A2, pp. 71-2, Council minutes 24 March 1945; RCOG B2/13, external affairs committee, 'The question of a statutory register', March 1945; and in same file, Holland to Boldero, 29 March 1945.
41 RCOG C1, pp. 56-7, colleges' joint committee minutes 12 June 1945 (Boldero). For an adverse legal opinion on the college lists, see RCP 7/4/88, Medley to Boldero, 30 Aug. 1944. Moran himself stressed the subjective nature of the lists so that the GMC would not use them to buttress its case for a statutory register. RCP 7/4/88-9, comments by Moran on paper from Medley to Boldero, 30 Aug. 1944.
42 RCOG B2/13, external affairs committee, 'The question of a statutory register', March 1945, p. 5.
43 BMA 1,400/NC 106 (1945-6), report of special sub-committee, May 1946, p. 7.

Chapter 12 The struggle for regional control

1 For a review of all regionalization proposals from the 1920 Dawson Report, see BMA 2,075/GP 10, 18 Sept. 1941. This theme assumes a key role in a comparative study by an American historian: Fox (1986).
2 BMA 2,075/H4, Appendix, 'Hospital services — the objects of a medical service', 16 July 1941, p. 3.
3 RCP 15/3, 'A consultant service for the nation', 1 Feb. 1946, Appendix I by Rock Carling, p. 26.
4 *BMJ*, 20 June 1942, p. 749, paras 55-60.
5 BMA 1,660/32, Health Services Committee agenda 16 June 1937, para. 5. See also Ministry of Health and Department of Health for Scotland (1944a) p. 78.
6 RCP 26/3 Admin. 6, para. 57-8, MPC Administrative Committee, Appendix — revised paragraph of draft report, 9 Feb. 1943; BMA 1,399/NHS 9, office notes on administration, 5 April 1943.
7 MH 77/173, RCP testimony, 3 Oct. 1945, p. 3.
8 Wilson (1966) p. 252, entry for 20 May 1945.
9 RCP 2/6/11, Moran to Willink, 29 Jan. 1945. See also MH 80/32, Ministry meeting with medical representatives, 23 Jan. 1945.
10 RCP 2/1/16, report by Boldero on 6 Feb. 1945 meeting with Ministry, and Moran to Boldero, 8 Feb. 1945.
11 RCP 2/1/18, Moran to Boldero, 8 Feb. 1945. For the report of the subsequent meeting with the Ministry, see MH 80/32, report of Ministry meeting with medical representatives, 20 Feb. 1945.
12 RCP 8/3/50, Moran to Dyke, 12 June 1943.
13 BMA 1,489/NC 12 (1945-6), negotiating committee minutes 12 Jan. 1945, para. 9.

14 BMA, 1,489/NC 31 (1945–6), negotiating committee minutes 23 May 1945, para.
   6. For municipal insistence on the same points, see MH 80/28, report of Ministry
   meeting with local authority representatives, 8 May 1945.
15 MH 80/32, report of Ministry and Scottish Department meeting with medical representatives, 24 May 1945.
16 RCP 15/3, 'A consultant service for the nation', 1 Feb. 1946, pp. 9–10.
17 *The Times*, 16 Sept. 1944, p. 5.
18 Honigsbaum (1979) pp. 9–21.
19 Note in particular the article by the paper's health correspondent, Hugh Ferguson,
   'Plotters against the nation's health', in *Tribune*, 29 June 1945, pp. 5–6.
20 Abel-Smith (1964) p. 486.
21 BMA 1,400/NC 61 (1945–6) or RCP 2/3, negotiating committee minutes 17 Jan.
   1946, para. 88.
22 RCP 2/3/34, consultant service committee minutes 28 March 1946.
23 RCP 3/3/28, Ives to Moran, 8 Feb. 1946.
24 RCP 2/3/34, consultant service committee minutes, 28 March 1946.
25 BMA 1,400/NC 81 (1945–6) or RCP 4, third meeting between negotiating committee and BHA, 7 Feb. 1946.
26 RCP 20/1/3, Wetenhall, to RCP fellows, 10 April 1946.
27 RCP 3/1/7, meeting of RCP members, 24 April 1946.
28 RCP 17/2/39, Reddington to Moran, 4 May 1946.
29 For an indication of McCurrich's loss of control, see RCP 9/3/30, Andrews to Moran,
   6 March 1947.
30 RCP 17/2/40, 44, and 45, Moran to fellows, 6 and 13 May 1946.
31 RCP 20/1/7, Moran to Nixon, 3 May 1946.
32 *BMJ*, 11 May 1946, Supp. p. 123. For more detail, see BMA, 2,424, Special Representative Meeting, 1–2 May 1946, para. 48.
33 RCP 1/68 and 72, Moran to fellows, March 1946.
34 RCP library, recording of Moran's conversation, 25 June 1970.
35 RCOG A2, pp. 136–8, Council minutes 12 April 1946.
36 RCOG A2, p. 125, Council minutes 26 Jan. 1946; RCOG B7, p. 17, maternal and
   infant health services committee minutes 30 March 1946; BMA 1,400/NC 87 (1945–6)
   or RCP 4, memo on maternity services, 10 April 1946.
37 RCOG A3/4, pp. 111–12, finance and executive committee, memo to Ministry on
   appointment of regional consultant advisers, Sept. 1941. See also Shaw (1954) pp.
   140–1.
38 RCOG B2/7/11 and B2/13, external affairs committee, memo by Fletcher Shaw on
   regional advisers, July 1943; RCOG A3/5, pp. 64–5, finance and executive committee minutes 16 July 1943. See also Shaw (1954) p. 143.
39 RCOG A4/4/18, Fletcher Shaw to Gibberd, 28 Aug. 1939.
40 For Jameson's support, see RCOG B2/15, Inter-departmental Committee on Medical
   Schools, MP Paper 221, notes of interview with RCOG Representatives, 17 Feb. 1943.
41 RCOG A2, pp. 93–6, 124, 127–8, Council minutes on reports of meetings with BMA,
   21 June and 5 Dec. 1945.
42 RCOG A2, pp. 45–7, 59–60, Council minutes 26 July and 4 Oct. 1946.
43 BMA, 1,521/NC GP 8, 11, and 12, April and May 1947.
44 RCOG A3/6, pp. 155–6, finance and executive committee minutes 14 May and 11
   June 1948.
45 Ministry of Health (1959) p. 52, para. 184.
46 *The Times*, 9 July 1948, p. 5.
47 RCOG, A2, pp. 125, 139–41, Council minutes 24 July 1948.
48 *BMJ*, 7 Dec. 1946, pp, 869–71; *Lancet*, 23 Nov. and 7 Dec. 1948, pp. 765, 840, 854.

49 RCS, Council minutes 1948, p. 317. See also Payne's privately published 'An address to the Right Honourable Lord Moran of Manton', 1949, on file in British Library. For a profile of Payne, see his obituary notice in *Lancet*, 28 Oct 1968, p. 241; and in Ross and LeFanu (1981) pp. 286–8.

50 *BMJ*, 12 July 1958, Supp. p. 34 (Rowland Hill).

51 BMA 1,400/NC 81 (1945–6) or RCP 4, third conference between negotiating committee and BHA, 7 Feb, 1946, p. 3; RCS, Council minutes 1946, pp. 237–8, 262–3.

52 NHS Act 1946, 9 & 10 George 6, Chapter 81, Part II, section 7.

53 *BMJ*, 17 March 1948, Supp. pp. 85–7.

54 MH 77/173, Spens Committee on GP Remuneration, RCP testimony, 3 Oct. 1945, p. 2.

55 Same reference as in note 54. See also Nuffield Provincial Hospitals Trust (1946) pp. 12–13.

56 RCP 9/1/19, Roberts to Moran, 13 April 1943.

57 RCP 15/3, 'A consultant service for the nation', 1 Feb. 1946. Carling's views are set forth in Appendix I, pp. 23–7. See also Moran's letter to the *The Times*, 22 April 1946, pp. 10–11.

58 RCP 14/4/27, paper by Carling, 14 Dec. 1945; RCP 20/1/13, statement by Carling as chairman of Nuffield Trust medical advisory committee; RCP 17/2/30, Moran to Carling, 25 April 1946.

59 RCP 2/3/34, consultant service committee minutes 28 March 1946.

60 *The Times*, 24 April 1946, p. 13 (Webb-Johnson).

61 *Lancet*, 19 June 1948, p. 963 (Payne and other RCS fellows); 3 and 24 July 1948, pp. 32 (Webb-Johnson), 161 (Payne and other RCS fellows). See also the leaderette in *BMJ*, 4 May 1948, p. 888.

62 RCS, Council minutes 1948, p. 317.

63 MH 77/179, ? to Charles, Jameson, and Rucker, 14 Feb. 1947, and see note added by Rucker, 19 Feb. 1947; Smith to Secretary, 16 Sept. 1947; Robertson to Firth, 18 Sept. 1947. See also Stevens (1966) p. 214.

64 *BMJ*, 12 June 1948, pp. 1,140–1.

65 Stevens (1966) p. 89.

66 *BMJ*, 10 April 1948, Supp. p. 77; 22 May 1948, pp. 985–6.

67 RCP 21/1/21, consultant service committee minutes, 14 June 1948, pp. 12–13.

68 RCP 21/1/30, paper by Moran, 'The representation of consultants and specialists — the case for a joint committee', no date, but with papers Sept. 1948; RCOG A2, pp. 125–7, Council minutes 24 July 1948.

69 Stevens (1966) pp. 89–94, 277–8.

70 Stevens (1966) p. 217.

71 Mh 80/57, reports of Ministry meetings with joint consultants committee, 10 March and 3 May 1949.

72 Stevens (1966) pp. 97–9.

73 BMA 1,514, compensation/sub-committee rules governing compensation, 1948–50.

74 For a full acount of this exchange, see BMA 1,246, 1,485, and 1,509.

75 MH 77/180, Spens Committee on Consultant Remuneration, fourth meeting, 4–5 Feb. 1948, pp. 3 and 11, paras 3 and 43.

76 FAB K 10/5, 'Principles of a comprehensive health service', no author but probably by Dr Brian Thompson of the medical service group, end of 1943.

77 FAB C 64/2/10, lecture by Taylor to Fabian Society at Central Hall, Westminster, 18 Dec. 1946.

78 Royal Commission on Doctors' and Dentists' Remuneration (1958). Minutes of Evidence, Days 3–4, Q. 1,023.

79 HL Debs (210) 469, 2 July 1958. See also Honigsbaum (1979) p. 319.

Chapter 13 Bevan's concessions — more to consultants or GPs?

1 Abel-Smith (1964) p. 480.
2 See the verbatim transcript of the meeting of RCS fellows, 28 April 1948, p. 30 (Northfield), copy in writer's possession and also on file in RCS library.
3 Ministry of Health and Department of Health for Scotland (1956) p. 155, para. 444.
4 RCP 2/3/4, Daley to Boldero, 4 Feb. 1946.
5 MH 80/30, report of Ministry meeting with LCC and other local authority representatives, 26 April 1946.
6 MH 80/34, 'Regionalisation of London Area', no author but with papers dated April 1946.
7 Abel-Smith (1964) p. 490.
8 MH 77/180, Spens Committee on Consultant Remuneration, first meeting, 11 Dec. 1947, testimony of Bradford Hill, p. 3. See also the paper by Bradford Hill in *Journal of Royal Statistical Society*, vol. CXIV, 1951, pp. 26–7.
9 MH 80/27, Godber, 'An attempt to estimate the number of consultants required', no date but with papers dated May 1944.
10 For a detailed description of the 'firm', see Goldman (1957) pp. 8–20.
11 Abel-Smith (1964) pp. 493–500. Honigsbaum (1979) pp. 70–1.
12 HC Debs (Standing Committee C) 133, 16 May 1946.
13 MH 77/180, Spens Committee on Consultant Remuneration, fourth meeting, 4–5 Feb. 1948.
14 MH 77/180, Spens Committee on Consultant Remuneration, sixth and ninth meetings, 3 and 18–19 March, 14 April, 4 May 1948. For the report, see Ministry of Health and Department of Health for Scotland (1948).
15 MH 80/31, 'Specialists and consultants', no author but with papers dated April 1943.
16 See the paper by Bradford Hill in *Journal of Royal Statistical Society*, vol. CXIV, 1951, pp. 26–34.
17 HC Debs (Standing Committee C) 177–9 (Strauss), 21 May 1946. *BMJ*, 3 Jan. 1948, pp. 17–18.
18 *Journal of Chartered Society of Physiotherapy*, Feb. 1946, pp. 85–9.
19 CAB 129–5 or MH 80/32, memo by Minister of Health on NHS proposals, 13 Dec. 1945, p. 19, para. 14. HC Debs (Standing Committee C) 145, 164–5, 21 May 1946.
20 MH 80/32, report of Ministry and Scottish Department meeting with medical representatives, 10 Jan. 1946.
21 Foot (1973 and 1975) p. 138 of 1975 edition. The rest of this chapter draws heavily on Foot's account of NHS negotiations, pp. 100–215.
22 BMA, 2,364/C 17, supplementary agenda for Council meeting 20 Feb. 1946.
23 BEV III/45, Advisory Panel on Home Affairs, fifth meeting, 30 Nov. 1942; HL Debs (130) 215–18, 9 Dec. 1943. See also Honigsbaum (1979) pp. 296–7.
24 *BMJ*, 17 March 1945, pp. 357–60.
25 HL Debs (140) 852–4, 16 April 1946.
26 *BMJ*, 14 Dec. 1946, pp. 947–8, 956.
27 MH 77/177, Douglas to Hill, 20 Dec. 1946; Bevan to college presidents, 6 Jan. 1947.
28 MH 80/28, report of Ministry meeting with medical representatives, 20 Feb. and 24 April 1941. BMA 1,521/NC GP 5 (1947–8), report of discussion with Ministry representatives, 27 March 1947, p. 4.
29 BMA 1,481/NC 161B (1946–7), negotiating committee agenda, 21 July 1947, para. 9.
30 *BMJ*, 2 Aug. 1947, Supp. pp. 26–7.
31 *BMJ*, 20 Dec. 1947, Supp. pp. 141–64.
32 Foot (1973 and 1975) p. 167 of 1975 edition. *BMJ*, 3 Jan. 1948, pp. 17–18.

33 CAB 129/3, memo by Minister of Health, 'NHS: attitude of medical profession', 19 Jan. 1948.

34 *Surrey Times*, 31 March 1944, p. 4. *Truth*, 28 April 1944, pp. 338–9. See also the letter from Charles Hill, defending the way the BMA conducted the poll, in Social Creditor, 29 April 1944, p. 7. No record of this letter appears in the BMA Registry file, but it shows how sensitive Hill was to criticism from social credit or MPA quarters.

35 HC Debs (446) 1,203–5, 29 Jan. 1948.

36 BMA 2,362/C25 (1947–8), agenda for Council meeting, 18 Feb. 1948, pp. 6–7. BMA 2,361/C5 (1948–9), agenda for Council meeting, 30 June 1948, p. 45.

37 Graham-Little stressed this point in HC Debs (446) 91–3, 9 Feb. 1948.

38 BMA 2461, Special Representative Meeting, 8 Jan. 1948, paras 16 and 21. See also *BMJ*, 17 Jan. 1948, Supp. pp. 9–11.

39 For the concern shown by the BMA over this possibility, see the minutes of the Financial Hardship Committee it created in 1946. BMA 1,447, full file but note in particular FH5, agenda for meeting, 17 Feb. 1948.

40 HC Debs (447) 35–160, 9 Feb. 1948.

41 *BMJ*, 21 Feb. 1948, pp. 352–3.

42 *BMJ*, 27 March 1948, Supp. p. 50.

43 BMA 2362/C28 (15(3) and C28B 10(3), agenda for Council meeting, 24 March 1948.

44 MH 77/179, Moran to Bevan, 24 March 1948.

45 HC Debs (449) 164–9, 7 April 1948. For Moran's response when the announcement was made in the House of Lords, see HL Debs (154) 1,194–8, 7 April 1948.

46 Foot (1973 and 1975) p. 197 of 1975 edition.

47 RCP 1/81, Clegg to Moran, 13 April 1948. For the full text of this letter, see the Appendix on page 219.

48 For Butler's half-hearted support, see HC Debs (447) 61–2, 9 Feb. 1948.

49 Foot (1973 and 1975) p. 200 of 1975 edition.

50 *BMJ*, 24 April 1948, pp. 848–50.

51 A verbatim transcript of these proceedings is in the writer's possession and on file in the RCS library. For a summary, see the paper by Sir Reginald Murley in *BMJ*, 22–29 Dec. 1984, pp. 1,782–3.

52 *BMJ*, 8 May 1948, p. 888.

53 See the exchange of letters between Webb-Johnson and the group led by Payne in *Lancet*, 19 June 1948, p. 963; 3 and 24 July 1948, pp. 32 and 161.

54 *BMJ*, 7 Dec. 1946, pp. 869–71.

55 *BMJ*, 15 May 1948, pp. 949–50.

56 Foot (1973 and 1975) p. 202 of 1975 edition. *BMJ*, 5 June 1948, Supp. pp. 159–60.

57 *BMJ*, 8 May 1948, Supp. pp. 119–20.

58 MH 80/57, report of Ministry meeting with BMA representatives, 7 May to 23 June 1948. For the Second Reading debate on the 1949 Amending Act, see HC debs (465) 1,066–180 , 24 May 1959.

59 For the acceptance by Watson-Jones, see *BMJ*, 1 May 1948, p. 849. For more on the orthopaedic radicals, see Honigsbaum (1979) p. 240. For a somewhat different interpretation of their role, see Cooter (1987) pp. 306–32.

60 *BMJ*, 5 June 1948, Supp. p. 154. For the leader that stirred criticism of Clegg, see *BMJ*, 17 April 1948, pp. 737–8.

61 For the founding meeting, see *BMJ*, 26 Nov. 1949, Supp. pp. 180–1.

62 Helme stood for the Surrey Group in which the Guildford Division was located and lost by the vote of 461 to 256. He died a year and a half later at the tender age of 49. *BMJ*, 5 June 1948, Supp. p. 157; 4 March 1950, pp. 554–5.

63 For Arthur Helme's opposition to NHI, see *BMJ*, 13 July 1911, p. 139; 16 and 23 Dec. 1911, Supp. pp. 610–11, 657–9. Donald Whitaker lost his place as division

representative at BMA meetings in 1944 and did not regain it until June 1948: BMA 2,427, 2,428, 2,458.
64 Hill (1964) pp. 92–3.
65 This proportion applies to consultants and specialists not holding whole-time salaried posts: 2,345 of 3,926 opposed service, as compared with 9,588 of 18,227 GPs. Again, the consultant total must have included a number of 'consultoids'. BMA 2459/SRM2, plebiscite on the NHS Acts, replies to 3 May 1948.,
66 *BMJ*, 1 May 1948, Supp. pp. 848–50.
67 See the quotation from the Manchester *Guardian* in Association of Jewish Refugees Information, Feb. 1946, p. 11. See also Bevan's statement in *Medical World*, 23 Nov. 1945, p. 455; BMA 1,423/11 (1945), agenda for meeting of aliens committee, 26 Sept. 1945, para. 9; BMA 1,423/6 (1946), aliens committee minutes 10 Dec. 1946, statement by Dr Murchie of Ministry of Health. See also Honigsbaum (1979) pp. 312–14.
68 MH 76/514, Weiler to Roffey, 30 Dec. 1949.
69 *BMJ*, 1 May 1948, pp. 848–50 (Dr E.C. Warner).

Chapter 14 No charge for hospital care

1 MH 77/25, Maude to Barlow, 23 Sept. 1941.
2 MH 80/34, report of Ministry meeting with voluntary hospital representatives, 30 March 1943 (Maude).
3 MH 77/25, Maude to Barlow, 26 Sept. 1941.
4 Department of Health for Scotland (1936) pp. 291–311. See also MH 80/26, report of Scottish Department meeting with voluntary hospital representatives, 25 May 1943 (Henderson).
5 MH 77/25, Menzies, 'Memorandum on hospital policy in London', Aug. 1941.
6 MH 80/34, report of Ministry meeting with voluntary hospital representatives, 30 March 1943.
7 MH 80/24, Secretary [Chrystal], comments on Forber memo on regional organization of hospital services, 18 Dec. 1940, p. 2.
8 MH 80/34, sheet listing answers to Minister's questionnaire, 7 Aug. 1945.
9 MH 77/22, Daley to Rucker, 4 March 1941, enclosing memo on hospital policy, 28 Feb. 1941.
10 MH 77/22, Brock to Maude, 4 Sept. 1941.
11 HO 186/92, report of meeting at Ministry of Health on establishment of EMS, 27 June 1939.
12 MH 77/22, Brock to Maude, 4 Sept. 1941.
13 MH 77/25, Menzies, 'Memorandum on hospital policy in London', Aug. 1941. p. 6.
14 MH 80/34, reports of Ministry meetings and papers on hospital policy, April and May 1942.
15 Beveridge (1942) pp. 158–9, para. 427.
16 Beveridge (1942) pp. 160–1, paras 432–3.
17 MH 80/31, report of meeting between Beveridge, Maude, Jameson, and others, 17 Feb. 1942.
18 Beveridge (1942) p. 161, para. 434.
19 MH 80/34, Pater and McNicholl, 'Hospital contributory schemes and the Beveridge plan', 31 Dec. 1942.
20 MH 80/31, memo to Minister for meeting with Docker, April 1943, no author. For Pater's attitude to voluntary hospitals, see MH 80/24, note on hospital policy, 14 Nov. 1940; and MH 80/26 or 80/31, 'BHA and KF paper and hospital services', 18 May 1943.

21 MH 80/26, draft letter to Chancellor of Exchequer on hotel charge, no author but with papers dated Nov. 1943.
22 CAB 87/5, RC minutes 10 Jan. 1944. pp. 1–2.
23 MH 80/26, draft letter to Chancellor of Exchequer on hotel charge, no author but with papers dated Nov. 1943.
24 MH 80/26, report of Ministry meeting with local authority representatives, 27 July 1943; Maude to Minister, 28 July 1943.
25 HC Debs (223) 2,845–906, 18 Dec. 1928. See also LP, Public Health Sub-Committee, R.D.R. 16, paper by Somerville Hastings, 'A scheme for a state medical service', Nov. 1941.
26 MH 77/27, Pater to Wetenhall, 14 Feb. 1944.
27 MH 79/287, Maclachlan to Maude, 11 June 1936; Highton to Maude, 26 June 1936.
28 MH 77/27, Scottish Branch of BHA, scheme for Scottish NHS, Sept. 1943. MH 80/34, report of Scottish Department meeting with BHA, 5 Nov. 1943.
29 MH 80/26, 'Maintenance of patients in hospital', no author but probably written Oct. 1943. CAB 87/13 or MH 80/34, RC, memo by Minister of Health and Scottish Secretary, 'Sources of income of voluntary hospitals', 29 Oct. 1943.
30 MH 80/26, Maude, 'Payment by patients in hospital', 11 Dec. 1943.
31 CAB 87/9 or MH 80/27, RC, memo by Scottish Secretary on NHS, 27 Sept. 1944, p. 2, para. 6.
32 Department of Health for Scotland (1943) paras 65–77.
33 CAB 87/13, RC, memo by Scottish Secretary, 12 Oct. 1943, p. 1, paras 1–3.
34 MH 77/26, Maude to Fraser, 21 April 1942.
35 MH 80/26, 'Maintenance of patients in hospital', no author but with papers dated Aug. 1943; 'Charges for maintenance while in hospital', no author but with papers dated Sept. 1943; Maude, 'Payments by patients in hospital', 11 Dec. 1943, para. 6.
36 MH 80/34, Pater and McNicholl, 'Hospital contributory schemes and the Beveridge Plan', 31 Dec. 1942. For Maude's rebuttal, see MH 80/25, 'Should hospital treatment be free of charge?', 28 Feb. 1943.
37 MH 80/25 or 80/31, notes on general administrative structure for discussion with voluntary hospital representatives, March 1943, p. 3, para. 7.
38 MH 80/26 or 80/34, report of informal conference on role of hospital contributory schemes, 2 July 1943. See also CAB 87/13 or MH 80/26, RPC, memo by Minister of Health on NHS, 28 July 1943, paras 42–3.
39 MH 80/26, 'Maintenance of patients in hospital', no author but with papers dated Sept. 1943. For the papers presented to the RC, see CAB 87/13, MH 80/26 or 80/34, memos by Minister of Health and Scottish Secretary, 9, 12, and 29 Oct. 1943.
40 CAB 87/12, MH 80/26 or 80/34, RC minutes 15 Oct. 1943.
41 CAB 87/12, MH 80/26 or 80/34, RC minutes 1 Nov. 1943. For Brown's reaction, see MH 77/27, Brown to Anderson, 8 Nov. 1943.
42 CAB 87/7, MH 80/27 or 80/34, RC, memo by Minister of Health and Scottish Secretary,'Draft White Paper on the new health service', 3 Jan. 1944, pp. 4–5. CAB 87/5, MH 80/27 or 80/34, RC minutes 10 Jan. 1944. For Maude's brief to the new Minister on this issue, see MH 80/26, 'Payments by patients in hospital', 11 Dec. 1943.
43 CAB 124/442, report of Ministers' meeting with voluntary hospital representatives, 18 Jan. 1944; Woolton to Willink, 18 Jan. 1944 (latter also in MH 80/27).
44 Ministry of Health and Department of Health for Scotland (1944a) p. 46.
45 For the details here, see relevant papers in CAB 87/5, 87/7, 87/8, 87/11; MH 80/27; PIN 21/67.
46 MH 80/26, Hawton, 'NHS — Summary of main happenings of the year', Nov. 1944, p. 10.
47 The Hospital, Nov. 1943, pp. 336–8. This was cited by Johnston in CAB 87/5 or

MH 80/27 or 80/34, RC, minutes 10 Jan. 1944.
48 CAB 124/442, report of Ministers' meeting with voluntary hospital representatives, 18 Jan. 1944.
49 MH 80/27 or 80/34, BHA statement on White Paper, 21 Feb. 1944. However, much concern was expressed behind the closed doors of the BHA's Executive Committee, minutes, 29 Feb. 1944.
50 MH 80/27, notes by Vallance, March 1944. For Vallance's role as adviser to the BMA, see p. 63.
51 MH 80/26, Pater, 'Voluntary Hospitals and Cost of Maintenance of In-patients', 7 pp. typescript, no date but with papers dated Sept. 1943.
52 RCP 11/3/35, 'Beveridge Committee', minutes 30 March 1944, p. 17.

Chapter 15 Deadlock in negotiations

1 MH 80/24, Maude to Barlow, 18 Nov. 1942.
2 MH 80/34, Rucker to Wetenhall, 24 Oct. 1944; Rucker to Minister, 5 Sept. 1945. See also 80/27, note to answer criticisms of White Paper, no author but with papers dated March 1944.
3 Ministry of Health and Department of Health for Scotland (1944a) p. 23.
4 CAB 87/13 or MH 80/26, RPC, memo by Minister of Health on NHS, 28 July 1943, para. 44.
5 MH 80/27, report of Ministry meeting with BHA representatives, 5 Oct. 1944; report of Ministry meeting with KF representatives, 17 Oct. 1944.
6 Ministry of Health and Department of Health for Scotland (1944a) pp. 80–5.
7 MH 80/25 or 80/31, note on administrative structure for discussion with local authority representatives, 12 and 23 March 1943; note on administrative structure for discussion with voluntary hospital representatives, March 1943 (latter also in MH 80/34).
8 For early recognition, see MH 55/571, 'Combinations of local authorities for provision of hospital accommodation', no author, 22 Nov. 1934. See also MH 80/24, Maude, note for file, 1 Sept. 1942.
9 MH 77/26 or 80/34, 'Outline of proposals, paper A', June 1942, no author, but elsewhere indicated that Maude wrote it.
10 MH 80/25 or 80/31, note for meeting with local authority representatives or organization of local authority committees, and report of meeting, 16 April 1943.
11 For a defence of in-breeding at Guy's and St Thomas' Hospitals by a leading physician, Dr Geoffrey Evans, see GLC KF A/KE/106, co-ordination of hospital services sub-committee minutes 24 Feb. 1942.
12 MH 80/26, 80/31 or 80/34, BHA and KF, 'A national hospital service', 14 May 1943.
13 MH 80/26 or 80/31, Pater, comments on BHA and KF paper, 18 May 1943. For Maude's objections, see MH 80/25, Maude to Minister, 12 April 1943; and MH 80/26, Maude on BHA paper, 18 May 1943. See also pages 57 and 61–2.
14 MH 80/26 or 80/31, report of Ministry meeting with voluntary hospital representatives, 26 May 1943.
15 For the Nuffield plan, see MH 80/25 or 80/31, 'Comprehensive health service — notes on the outline of a plan for the administrative structure of a national hospital service', May 1943.
16 Ministry of Health and Department of Health for Scotland (1944a) pp. 14–16, 77–9.
17 Ministry of Health and Department of Health for Scotland (1944a) pp. 19–20. See also MH 80/26, A.N.R. (Rucker) to Secretary and Minister, 23 Dec. 1943; CAB 87/7 or MH 30/27, RC, memo by Minister of Health and Scottish Secretary, 3 Jan. 1944, pp. 3–4.
18 Ministry of Health and Department of Health for Scotland (1944a) p. 24. Inspection

as always seen as a key issue. For early views on the subject, see the exchange of minutes between Maude and Dalrymple-Champneys, Deputy CMO, in MH 77/25, 28 Oct. and 8 Nov. 1941.

19 Ministry of Health and Department of Health for Scotland (1944a) p. 23.
20 Ministry of Health and Department of Health for Scotland (1944a) pp. 14–15.
21 Note in particular the BHA's nation-wide campaign against the White Paper in MH 80/34, 18 May 1944. The Nuffield Trust and KF joined the attack.
22 HC Debs (398) 540–1, 17 March 1944.
23 GLC, KF A/KE/63/3, voluntary hospital committee minutes 1 March 1944.
24 MH 77/30B or 80/27, report of Ministry meeting with CCA and LCC representatives, 18 June 1944.
25 MH 77/30B or 80/27, report of Ministry meeting with AMC representatives, 20 June 1944.
26 MH 80/27 or 80/34, reports of Ministry meetings with BHA representatives, 3 Aug. 1, and 18 Oct. 1944.
27 CAB 87/6 or MH 80/27, RC minutes 2 Oct. 1944.
28 MH 80/28 or 80/34, note by Hawton outlining proposals for Ministry meeting with voluntary hospital representatives, 5 Feb. 1945; report of Ministry meeting with BHA representatives, 22 Feb. 1945.
29 MH 80/28 or 80/34, note for Ministry meeting with KF and minutes of meeting 16 March 1945.
30 MH 80/34, Wetenhall to Rucker, 12 April 1945.
31 MH 80/28 or 80/34, report of Ministry meeting with BHA representatives, 17 April 1945.
32 PREM 4/36/3, Lord President (Woolton), memo to Cabinet on NHS, 4 June 1945. For Moran's criticism of Willink's plan, see the exchange of letters between them in the *The Times*, 18 and 22 April 1946, p. 5 (both days).
33 MH 80/28 or 80/33, reports of Ministry meetings with various local authority representatives, 9, 12, 23 March, and 8 May 1943. For an LCC report on the 8 May meeting, see GLC, LCC PH/GEN/1/16, memo by Daley, 10 May 1945.
34 GLC, LCC PH/HOSP/1/7, 'Second (supplementary) memorandum to Daley from medical superintendents', Jan. 1944, p. 25, para. 105, italics added.
35 GLC, LCC PH/GEN/1/16, memos from Daley to Salmon and Scott, 21 April, 17 May, 15 June 1945. For the same demand from Lord Donoughmore of KF, see MH 80/28 or 80/34, report of Ministry meeting with KF representatives, 16 March 1945. For the medical view, see RCP 1/1/19, Hill to Moran, 25 Oct. 1945.
36 RCP 2/2/14, report of second conference between medical negotiating committee and BHA, 14 Sept. 1945, paras 30–2.
37 GLC, LCC PH/GEN/1/16, Daley to Latham, 15 June 1945.
38 GLC, KF A/KE/355, Docker to Donoughmore, 26 July 1945. See also RCP 2/2/12 and 14, reports of conferences between medical negotiating committee and BHA, 20 July and 14 Sept. 1944.
39 RCP 1/28, Ives to Moran, 8 Feb. 1946.

Chapter 16 The hospitals are nationalized

1 GLC, KF A/KE355, ? to Peacock, 9 Nov. 1945.
2 MH 77/19, cited by Souttar in his statement of resignation as president of the BMA, 1946.
3 Nuffield Provincial Hospitals Trust (1946) pp. 13–15.
4 HC Debs (422) 229, 1 May 1946.
5 MH 80/27, Conservative Health Committee report on NHS proposals, 25 May 1944,

pp. 9–10, paras 22–3. See also the Ministry's comments on the report which follows in the file.

6 MH 80/27, report of Scottish Department meeting with BHA representatives, 22 Aug. 1944.

7 HC Debs (398) 551, 17 March 1944.

8 *Daily Herald*, 22 Dec. 1945, p. 1. See also Campbell (1987) pp. 152–3.

9 Claim made by Dorothy White, then an Assistant Principal in the hospital section of the Ministry. No documents are available in the Public Record Office.

10 FAB, K 10/5, 'Principles of a comprehensive health service', no author but probably by Dr Brian Thompson of Medical Services Group, end of 1943.

11 Pater (1981) p. 178.

12 Interview with Pater, 16 Feb. 1988.

13 Interview with Godber, 8 Feb. 1988.

14 Interview with Hill, 1 March 1983.

15 Interview with Godber, 8 Feb. 1988.

16 Foot (1973 and 1975) p. 131 of 1975 edition.

17 Letter from Foot, 24 Sept. 1987.

18 HL Debs (140) 824, 16 April 1946.

19 Interview with Marre, 30 Oct. 1987.

20 MH 80/34, Minister's questionnaire with sheet of answers, 7 Aug. 1945; sources of income of voluntary hopsitals, 11 and 21 Aug. 1945.

21 MH 80/34, Rucker to Minister, 5 Sept. 1945.

22 MH 80/34, 'NHS — proposed system of payment to voluntary hospitals', 8 pp. typescript appended to Rucker minute of 5 Sept. 1945, p. 7, para. 15.

23 MH 80/34, Buzzard statement to press, 'The voluntary hospital is dead: long live the voluntary hospitals', 29 Nov. 1944.

24 For the draft, see MH 80/34, Rucker, 'NHS hospitals scheme', no date; for the submitted minute, see MH 80/29, same title, 7 pp. typescript.

25 CAB 21/2,032 or 129/3, MH 80/29 or 80/34, memo by Minister of Health, 'Future of hospital service', 5 Oct. 1945.

26 CAB 21/2,032 or 129/3, MH 80/29 or 80/34, memo by Joint Parliamentary Under-Secretary of State for Scotland 'NHS', 5 Oct. 1945.

27 CAB 21/2,032 or 128/1, Cabinet minutes 11 Oct. 1945.

28 Abel-Smith (1964) p. 479.

29 Allen Daley, 'The British NHS', *American Journal of Public Health*, Oct. 1952, p. 1,233.

30 CAB 21/2,032 or 129/3, MH 80/29 or 80/34, memo by Lord President of Council 'Future of hospital service', 12 Oct. 1945.

31 Ministry of Health and Department of Health for Scotland (1956) pp. 274–86.

32 CAB 21/2,032 or 128/1, MH 80/29 or 80/34, memo by Minister of Health, 'Hospital service', 16 Oct. 1945.

33 HC Debs (379) 531 (Messer), 21 April 1942.

34 CAB 21/2,032 or 128/1, Cabinet minutes 11, 18, and 25 Oct. 1945. The quotation here is from the meeting on 18 Oct.

35 Morgan (1984) pp. 51, 174–5.

36 Morgan (1984) p. 54.

37 CAB 87/12, RPC minutes, 30 July 1943.

38 CAB 21/2,032 or 128/2, MH 80/29 or 80/34, Cabinet minutes, 20 Dec. 1945, pp. 338–41.

39 CAB 21/2,032 or 128/5, Cabinet minutes 8 Jan. 1946, pp. 22–4.

40 HC Debs (413) 257–9, 17 Aug. 1945.

41 CAB 21/2,032 or 129/7, joint memo of Lord President and Lord Privy Seal, 6 March

1946. For earlier indications of Greenwood's concern, see CB 21/2,032 or 128/1 and 128/2, Cabinet minutes 11 Oct. and 20 Dec. 1945.

42 CAB 21/2,032 or 128/5, Cabinet minutes 8 March 1946, pp. 182–4.

43 Morgan (1984) pp. 51, 54–5, 354–5.

44 HC Debs (391) 1,580–3, 28 July 1943; (392) 1,591–7, 21 Oct. 1943.

45 CAB 21/2,032 or MH 80/30, correspondence between Morrison and Bevan, 19 and 30 March, 8, 17, and 24 April 1946.

46 MH 80/30, J.E.P. [Pater] to Hawton, 13 April 1946.

47 CAB 21/2,035, A.S. [?] A.R.W. Bavin, 27 Jan. 1949; Morrison to Attlee, 29 Sept. 1949. See also Morgan (1984) pp. 400–1.

48 *Manchester Guardian*, 18 Sept. 1958, p. 14.

49 *The Times*, 8 March 1965, p. 15.

50 Foot (1973 and 1975) p. 208 in 1975 edition. For the wider MOH reaction, see Mackintosh (1953) pp. 90, 139, 161, 174–91.

51 Menzies, F. 'Memorandum on LCC hospital service', 22 Aug. 1941, p. 29, in HAS Box 5.

52 Daley, A. 'Health and municipal hospital services of London', *BMJ*, 3 July 1948, pp. 19–22.

53 MH 77/82 or 80/33, report of Ministry meeting with LCC and CCA representatives, 26 Feb. 1946.

54 MH 80/30, report of Ministry meeting with LCC and local authority representatives, 26 April 1946. Note also Daley's failure to persuade Rucker during meetings of the 'London Syndicate', a body created to deal with London's problems as a whole. MH 99/40, minutes 26 April and 16 May 1946; Daley to Rucker, 20 Nov. 1946.

55 MH 80/33, Rucker to Secretary, 18 April 1946.

56 HC Debs (425) 1,819–42, 22 July 1946.

57 Daley in *American Journal of Public Health*, Oct. 1952, p. 1,238. *Manchester Guardian*, 13 Feb. 1961, p. 7.

58 MH 80/30 or 80/33, reports of Ministry meetings with various local authority representatives, 26 and 27 Feb. 1946.

59 BHA, executive committee minutes, correspondence between Hill and Wetenhall, 28 Nov. and 4 Dec. 1945.

60 RCP 4 or BMA 1,400, NC 81 (1945–6), report of third conference between negotiating committee and BHA with KF representatives, 7 Feb. 1946.

61 HL Debs (140) 836–9, 16 April 1946. See also MH 80/30 or 80/34, report of Ministry meeting with KF representatives, 7 Feb. 1946.

62 *The Times*, 6 April, 1946, p. 5.

63 RCP 4 or BMA 1,400 NC 81 (1945–6), report of third conference between negotiating committee and BHA with KF representatives, 7 Feb. 1946. See also the *The Times*, 24 April 1946, p. 5 (Webb-Johnson).

64 Daley in *American Journal of Public Health*, Oct. 1952, p. 1,233.

65 MH 80/30 or 80/34, report of Ministry meeting with BHA representatives, 11 Feb. 1946. See also BHA, correspondence between Bevan and Wetenhall, 14 Feb. 1946; and nine-page statement setting forth BHA objections to NHS Bill, April 1946.

66 Abel-Smith (1964) pp. 410–14, 443.

67 BHA, Sankey Commission proceedings, 25 March and 8 April 1936.

68 Abel-Smith (1964) pp. 472–3, 486, 489.

69 For Graham-Little's fierce opposition to the Bill, see HC Debs (422) 372–6, 2 May 1946; (426) 438–44, 26 July 1946; (446) 91–8, 9 Feb. 1948.

70 MH 80/32 or BMA 1,400, NC 76 (1945–6), negotiating committee observations on Minister's proposals, 6 Feb. 1946, pp. 5–6, para. 18.

71 MH 77/119 or 80/32, BMA 1,400/NC 77 (1945–6), report of Ministry meeting with

negotiating committee, 6 Feb. 1946.
72 Abel-Smith (1964) p. 490.
73 *BMJ*, 3 April 1948, Supp. pp. 64–6.
74 *BMJ*, 20 April 1946, pp. 612–13; 11 May 1946, Supp. p. 123.
75 HC Debs (422) 64–76 (Law), 222–42 (Willink).
76 HL Debs (143) 431–4, 21 Oct. 1946.
77 *BMJ*, 20 Dec. 1947, Supp. pp. 141–64.
78 *BMJ*, 3 Jan. 1948, pp. 17–18.
79 *BMJ*, 7 Feb. 1948, pp. 264–7.
80 MH 77/64, Cardew to Bruce, 3 Nov. 1948. MH 80/32, 'Enlarging scope for specialist appointments', no author, no date but near end of file.
81 MH 99/18, memo from Newstead of British Hospital Contributory Schemes Association, 22 July 1947; report of Ministry meeting with Association, 11 March 1948. For the aftermath, see Dodd (1961) pp. 9–13.
82 WILL 2/236, privately printed memoir by Willink, 'As I remember', Dec. 1968, p. 81.

Chapter 17 Financial constraints

1 FAB K10/3. memo by health service sub-committee, National Health Insurance', 14 March 1939.
2 PREM, 4/36/3, Cherwell to Prime Minister, no date but with papers dated Feb. 1944.
3 MH 80/24, S. (?) to Minister on post-war hospital policy, 19 Nov. 1940. See also Ministry of Health and Department of Health for Scotland (1944a) p. 81.
4 Abel-Smith (1964) pp. 309, 414–15, 443–4.
5 MH 58/321, medical advisory committee, memo by secretary (prepared by Neville) on scheme setting forth relations between doctors, voluntary hospitals, and local authorities, no date but with papers dated Jan. 1938.
6 MH 79/409. CMO, 'Memorandum on provision of specialist services, 15 March 1937, p. 1.
7 MH 80/34, 'Sources of income of voluntary hospitals', 21 Aug. 1945, no author but data taken from *Hospitals Yearbook*.
8 MH 79/409, Hudson to Secretary and Minister, 27 Jan. 1937.
9 MH 79/409, CMO, 'Memorandum on provision of specialist services', 15 March 1937, p. 13.
10 MH 79/409, Neville, 'Consultant and specialist service for insured persons', 14 March 1938.
11 MH 79/409, MacNalty to Wilkinson, 11 Jan. 1938.
12 MH 79/409, report of office policy conference, 6 April 1938.
13 MH 79/409, reports of office policy conferences, 31 May and 27 June 1938.
14 MH 79/409, 'Outline of scheme for medical benefit for dependants of insured persons', 14 March 1938, no author but possibly by Neville.
15 MH 79/409, report of office policy conference, 7 Feb. 1938.
16 MH 58/235, note by Maude for file, 13 March 1941.
17 Titmuss (1950) pp. 110–36, 506–8.
18 MH 80/24, George, estimate of cost of extension of medical benefit to dependants, 11 March 1941, with note from Maddex, 28 Feb. 1941. For the heated negotiations over the increase in panel pay, see MH 62/243.
19 MH 77/22, Ritson to Rucker, 24 Jan. 1941. MH 77/25 or 80/24, Rucker, 'Office committee on post-war hospital policy', 6 Feb. 1941.
20 *National Insurance Gazette*, 30 Oct. 1941, p. 520; 1 and 8 Oct. 1942, pp. 472, 485.
21 CAB 87/29, Beveridge Committee, memo by National Conference of Industrial Assurance Approved Societies, 20 March 1942, para. 56.

22 MH 80/24, E.J.M. [Maude], 'Office committee on post-war hospital policy', 9 Jan. 1941.
23 MH 80/24, Maude, 'Suggestions for a post-war hospital policy', Aug. 1941, paras 7–8.
24 MH 80/26, George, 'Cost of a comprehensive health service', 21 May 1943.
25 For a clear indication of this, see the amounts spent on additional benefits from 1928 to 1947 as compiled by the Canadian Department of National Health and Welfare (1952) pp. 54–5, 151. Hospital benefit never exceeded 7 per cent of the total and from 1936 to 1947 amounted to less than 2 per cent.

Chapter 18 Beveridge pressure

1 Beveridge (1953) p. 317.
2 Honigsbaum (1979) pp. 217–57.
3 Harris (1977) pp. 346–61.
4 CAB 87/77, Beveridge Committee, TUC evidence, 14 Jan. 1942, Q. 316–46, 397–463.
5 PIN 8/85, note of conclusions on terms of reference for Beveridge Committee, 24 April 1941.
6 CAB 21/1,588, Chester to Anderson, 17 Aug. 1943.
7 Government Actuary (1943) p. 12.
8 ACT 1/684 Beveridge, 'Heads of a scheme for social security', 9 Dec. 1941, p. 18.
9 Beveridge (1942) p. 159, para. 430.
10 ACT 1/684, Beveridge, 'Heads of a scheme for social security', 9 Dec. 1941. See also MH 77/26, Maude to Fraser, 21 April 1942.
11 Beveridge (1942) pp. 160–1, para. 433.
12 Honigsbaum (1979) p. 282.
13 MH 80/24, first draft of Beveridge report, 10 July 1942, part IV, pp. 4–5.
14 Beveridge (1942) pp. 159–60, para. 431.
15 MH 80/31 or BEV VIII/31/4, Beveridge, 'Some problems of medical treatment', enclosed with letter to Maude, 2 Feb. 1942.
16 MH 77/26 or 80/24, 'Post-war medical policy. General practitioner service', no author, March 1942, p. 5, para. 13.
17 Beveridge (1942) pp. 151 (para. 434), 162 (para. 437), 201 (para. 63).
18 MH 80/31, Maude to Brock, 22 May 1943.
19 MH 77/124, recommendations from the Teviot Committee, 24 Oct. 1944. See also Ministry of Health and Department of Health for Scotland (1944c).
20 MH 80/24, official committee on Beveridge Report, response of health departments, 28 Dec. 1942, Q. 9, para. 5.
21 Foot (1962 and 1966) pp. 37, 138 of 1966 edition.
22 Foot (1962 and 1966) p. 354 of 1966 edition. Foot (1973 and 1975) p. 136 of 1975 edition. See also Bevan (1961) pp. 98–121.
23 Honigsbaum (1979) p. 288.
24 MH 80/31, Maude to 'Demo', 9 Feb. 1942.
25 MH 80/28, report of Ministry meeting with GP representatives, 24 April 1945.
26 MH 80/27, note on deputation from Christian Scientists, no author but with papers dated Dec. 1944.

Chapter 19 NHS costs

1 MH 80/24, Maude to Beveridge, 21 March 1942. For the PEP estimate, see PEP (1937) pp. 387–91.
2 MH 77/26 or 80/24, 'Post-war medical policy. General practitioner service', no author, March 1942, pp. 6–7.

3 ACT 1/708, correspondence between Epps and Maude, 23 and 24 March 1942. For biographical data about Epps, see his obituary notice in the *The Times*, 12 Feb. 1951, p. 6.
4 MH 80/26, report of Ministry meeting with local authority representatives, 27 July 1943.
5 MH 80/24, estimates of cost of comprehensive health service, 21 and 29 July 1942. See also the document sent to Beveridge, 'Public medical service (England and Wales)', 13 Aug. 1942 (copy also in BEV VIII/43).
6 ACT 1/708, note for file from Epps, 'Total cost of health services', 27 July 1943, based on information over the phone supplied by George of the Ministry of Health.
7 ACT 1/708, note by Epps of two talks with George, 20 and 21 Aug. 1942. MH 80/25, George to Hale, 2 March 1943. Beveridge (1942) p. 201, paras 61–4.
8 ACT 1/708, paper by Buckatzsch, E.J., 'Reform of the health services', in *Oxford Institute of Statistics Bulletin*, 8 April 1944.
9 Beveridge (1942) p. 105, para. 270 (3).
10 CAB 87/82, note by Epps on finance, 10 Oct. 1942.
11 Beveridge (1942) p. 183, para. 22.
12 CAB 21/2,032 or 129/5, memo by Minister of Health on NHS proposals, 13 Dec. 1945, p. 20.
13 HC Debs (461) 1,452, 17 Feb. 1949.
14 Abel-Smith and Titmuss (1956) p. 2.
15 Beveridge (1942) p. 201.
16 Ministry of Health (1966) p. 7.
17 Abel-Smith and Titmuss (1956) pp. 60–1. See also the way this data was presented by the Guillebaud Committee: Ministry of Health and Department of Health for Scotland (1956) pp. 9–10.
18 Organization for European Co-operation and Development (1985).
19 Abel-Smith and Titmuss (1956) pp. 24–35.
20 Abel-Smith and Titmuss (1956) pp. 137–8.
21 Ministry of Health and Department of Health for Scotland (1956) pp. 33–4, para. 66.
22 Department of Health and Social Security (1979) p. 46, para. 99.
23 *The Times*, 8 June 1980, p. 3.
24 Honigsbaum (1979) p. 340.
25 PREM 4/89/2, K.W. [Kingsley Wood], 'The Beveridge social security plan', 17 Nov. 1942.
26 BEV VIII/27, Meade to Chester, 28 Aug. 1941. CAB 87/80, memo from Economic Section of War Cabinet Secretariat, 16 June 1942.
27 PREM 4/89/2, memo by Cherwell on Beveridge report, 25 Nov. 1942.
28 PREM 4/88/2, memo by Churchill on Beveridge Report, 14 Feb. 1943.
29 MH 80/24, Maude to Fraser, 13 Aug. 1942.
30 MH 80/27, Gilbert to Maude, 14 Jan. 1944.
31 MH 77/27, Brown to Anderson, 8 Nov. 1943; Woolton to Willink, 10 Dec. 1943. CAB 87/13, memo by Chancellor Exchequer (Anderson), 'New services and commitments after the war', 9 Nov. 1943.
32 PREM 4/36/3, Cherwell to Prime Minister, no date but with papers dated Feb. 1944.
33 Note the reference to Anderson's role on the Royal Commission on NHI by Dr Brodie at the BMA's representative meeting in Dec. 1944: *BMJ*, 16 Dec. 1944, Supp. p. 164.
34 Royal Commission on National Health Insurance (1928) p. 65, para. 138.
35 PREM 4/36/3, Churchill to Foreign Secretary (Eden), 10 Feb. 1944.
36 PREM 4/36/3, A.E. (Anthony Eden) to Prime Minister, 10 Feb. 1944.
37 PREM 4/36/3, Cabinet minutes 15 Feb. 1944.
38 PREM 4/36/3, Churchill to Willink, 18 June 1945.
39 PREM 4/36/3, Cherwell to Prime Minister, 5 June 1945.

40 CAB 21/2,019, memo on financial implications of NHS Bill, comments at end by B.W.G. (Bernard Gilbert), 5 Jan. 1946.
41 HC Debs (431) 1,058–9 (Carmichael), 10 Dec. 1946.
42 HC Debs (422) 224–5, 1 May 1946.
43 Quoted in *Public Health*, Dec. 1942, pp. 27–8. The report, which was titled 'Health for the people', was prepared by a committee headed by Sir John Stewart-Willane and Lady Rhys-Williams, a leading figure in the movement to reduce maternal mortality. Frank Byers reaffirmed the Liberal Party's support for the report during the debate on the NHS Bill, and his words are worth quoting: 'I am no socialist. I disagree with a great deal that the Government has done and intend to do, but in matters of social reform and health services I am with them the whole of the time' (HC Debs (446) 66–72, 9 Feb. 1948).
44 *Lancet*, 13 Dec. 1947, pp. 876–7.

Chapter 20 Medical movement toward universal coverage

1 *BMJ*, 6 June 1936, Supp. pp. 301–3.
2 *Medical Press and Circular*, 23 June 1943, p. 385.
3 For a detailed description of this prolonged battle and its aftermath, see the brilliant series of articles in the *Lancet* from 1895 to 1915 by its special commissioner, Dr Adolphe Smith.
4 HC Debs (26) 296–7, 1 Aug. 1911.
5 Interview with Dain, 7 Feb. 1959.
6 *BMJ*, 7 April 1923, Supp. pp. 105–6.
7 MH 62/242, Hackforth to Secretary, 15 Jan. 1937. *BMJ*, 5 and 26 June 1937, Supp. pp. 355, 416–17 (letter from Beauchamp).
8 MH 58/238, Cox to Robinson, 23 April 1930.
9 MH 58/238, Newman to Secretary, 6 Aug. 1930.
10 MH 58/238, Anderson to Secretary, 30 Jan. 1933.
11 MH 58/238, Young to Macdonald, 20 Feb. 1934.
12 MH 58/238, memo on 'General medical service for the nation', Kinnear identified as author at office conference, 4 July 1934.
13 *Medical World*, 12 Oct. 1934, pp. 205–12.
14 Labour Party, *Annual Conference Reports*: 1932, pp. 269–70; 1934, pp. 214–15, 256–8.
15 FAB J41/3/5, underlining in original.
16 MH 58/238, Robinson to Minister, 10 July 1934.
17 MH 58/238, report of office conference, 4 July 1934.
18 MH 58/238, Robinson to Minister, 17 Nov. 1934.
19 MH 58/238, Robinson to Minister, 10 July 1934.
20 MH 58/238, Robinson to Minister, 17 Nov. 1934.
21 MH 58/238, report of office conference, 31 Oct. 1934.
22 MH 58/238, Young to Robinson, 30 July and 29 Nov. 1934.
23 Honigsbaum (1979) p. 157.
24 MH 58/338, A.W.N. [Neville] to Hill, 1 Aug. 1936.
25 Honigsbaum (1979) pp. 184–5.

Chapter 21 Civil servants and doctors: their influence compared

1 Honigsbaum (1979) p. 194.
2 See the obituary notice by Godber in *BMJ*, 10 Jan. 1981, p. 159. Additional infor-

mation based on interviews with Godber, Marre, and Pater.

3 RCP 11/3/47, report of Ministry meeting with medical representatives, 14 July 1943, p. 2.

4 RCP 1/45, no author but contents indicate it was written by Moran, 5 Dec. 1947.

5 Honigsbaum (1979) pp. 51–63.

6 *Pulse*, 28 Nov. 1981, p. 14.

7 Interview with Dr Harvey Flack, 31 March 1965. Flack was intimately involved with BMA affairs from the 1930s, serving on the *BMJ* editorial staff 1935–9 and 1946–51.

8 RCP 7/4/17 and 24, correspondence between Moran and Parsons, 9 and 17 Feb. 1944. The issue at hand was the GMC attempt to create a statutory register of consultants, a move which Moran strongly opposed. See page 127.

9 Letter from Godber to Honigsbaum, 18 Feb. 1988.

10 RCP 21/1/30, 'The representation of consultants and specialists — the case for a joint committee', no author but contents indicate it was written by Moran about July 1948.

11 WILL, memoir by Willink, 'As I remember', p. 80.

12 Interview with Baron Bruce of Donnington, 1 Feb. 1988.

13 For this and other qualities in Bevan, see the tribute by Stephen Taylor in *Update Review*, 1 March 1979, p. 632.

14 Interview with Pater, 16 Feb. 1988.

15 Interview with Godber, 8 Feb. 1988.

16 Godber was among those who expected costs to be higher than estimated. Interview with Godber, 8 Feb. 1988.

17 From Disraeli's famous 'Sanitas, sanitatum, omnia sanitas' speech delivered at Manchester, 3 April 1872. The full text appeared in Kebbel (1882) pp. 511–12.

Bibliography

Detailed references are given in the notes. I propose to indicate here the main material on which the study is based and list other sources which have provided background material.

Most important were the papers of the Ministry of Health (particularly the MH 80 series) at the Public Record Office in Kew, and the papers kept by the leading medical organizations — BMA (BMA Registry collection), Royal College of Physicians (boxes dealing with health planning and NHS negotiations), Royal College of Obstetricians and Gynaecologists (NHS and related files).

All of this needs to be supplemented by a close reading of the medical journals, particularly the *British Medical Journal* and *The Lancet*, which appeared weekly throughout the period. Most of this ground was covered in my earlier study, *The Division in British Medicine* (Honigsbaum, 1979), and many notes relate to data given there.

The main gap in medical material deals with the internal debates of the Royal College of Surgeons. Minutes of council meetings are available in the college library, as well as a verbatim transcript of an important meeting of fellows held in April 1948. The president's part in negotiations can be seen in the papers held by the BMA and the other colleges, and much can be learned from a close reading of the medical press. But the papers and minutes of the college committee dealing with the NHS affairs are not available.

At Cabinet level, most of the material dealing with the planning of the health service before July 1945 will be found in the papers of the Reconstruction Priorities Committee and its successor, the Reconstruction Committee (CAB 87 series). After Labour came to power, the main exchanges took place in the proceedings of the Cabinet itself (CAB 128 and 129 series). Throughout the whole period, Parliamentary debates were a fruitful source and this applied to both Houses, since some of the leading medical figures — Dawson, Moran, and Horder — spoke frequently in the House of Lords.

The Beveridge Report played a crucial role in health planning and the papers of the official committee that produced it will be found in the records of the Cabinet (CAB 21 and 87 series), Ministry of Pensions and National Insurance (PIN 8, 12, and 21 series), Government Actuary's Department (ACT 1 series), and the Prime Minister's Office (PREM 1 series). The Beveridge collection at the British Library of Political and Economic Science provides a useful supplement, but the papers of the committee's secretary, Sir Norman Chester (available at Nuffield College, Oxford), did not contain material that could be used in this study.

Only limited biographical details of leading civil servants are available in the MH 107 series and because of the thirty-year rule, all are not yet open to the public. Some like Maude and Hawton have been the subject of obituary notices in *The Times*, or listings in *Who's Who*. Jameson has even had a full-scale biography devoted to him, but the careers of many civil servants (particularly those below the grade of assistant secretary) can only be traced by a detailed study of the yearly *Imperial Calendars* (available on open shelves at the Public Record Office in Kew).

Where medical leaders are concerned, biographical material is easier to collect. Charles Hill has published an autobiography, Dawson has been the subject of a biography, and much can be learned from obituary notices in the *British Medical Journal* and *The Lancet*. For those who were fellows of the royal colleges, profiles are given in the series covering the lives of physicians (*Munk's Roll*) and surgeons (*Plarr's Lives*).

Papers in the Public Record office, Kew

Actuary's Department	ACT 1
Cabinet	CAB 21, 24, 65, 87, 102, 117, 124, 128, 129, 134
Home Office	HO 186
Ministry of Health	MH 55, 58, 62, 71, 77, 79, 80, 99, 102, 107
Ministry of Labour	LAB 14
Ministry of Pensions and National Insurance	PIN 4, 5, 8, 12, 21
Prime Minister's Office	PREM 4, 8
Treasury	T 172

Papers in the Great London Record Office, London

King Edward's Hospital Fund for London
London County Council

Private papers

Beveridge, William — British Library of Political and Economic Science
British Hospitals Association — British Library of Political and Economic Science
British Medical Association Registry — BMA Library, London
D. Norman Chester — Nuffield College, Oxford.
Fabian Society — Nuffield College, Oxford.
Hastings, Somerville — Brynmor Jones Library, University of Hull
Labour Party — Labour Party headquarters, London
Political and Economic Planning — British Library of Political and Economic Science
Royal College of Obstetricians and Gynaecologists — RCOG, London
Royal College of Physicians — RCP, London
Socialist Medical Association — Brynmor Jones Library, University of Hull
Trades Union Congress — TUC headquarters, London
Willink, Henry — Churchill College, Cambridge

Official publications

This list excludes official histories which are covered in the general bibliography below.

Hansard, Parliamentary Debates: House of Commons, Fifth Series
House of Commons, Standing Committee C on NHS, 1946
House of Commons (Northern Ireland), 1947
House of Lords, Fifth Series

Imperial Calendar, 1913–48
National Health Service Act, 1946, 9 & 10 Geo. 6, Ch. 81
National Health Service (Scotland) Act, 1947, 10 & 11 Geo. 6, Ch. 27
Annual Reports of Ministry of Health, 1936–48 and 1966
Annual Reports of Chief Medical Officer of Ministry of Health, 1936–8

Periodicals

American Journal of Public Health
Animals's Defender
Association of Jewish Refugees Information
British Medical Journal
Hospital
Journal of Chartered Society of Physiotherapy
Journal of Royal Statistical Society
Journal of Social Policy
Lancet
Maternity and Child Welfare
Medical History
Medical Officer
Medical Press and Circular
Medical World
National Health
National Insurance Gazette
Nursing Notes
Patriot
Proceedings of Royal Society of Medicine
Pulse
Spectator
Truth
Update
World Medicine

Newspapers

Barnet Press
Daily Express
Daily Herald
Daily Telegraph
Evening Standard
Manchester Guardian
Surrey Times
The Times
Tribune

Reports of organizations

British Medical Association
Labour Party
Medical Policy Association
Medical Practitioners' Union

National Conference of Labour Women
Royal College of Obstetricians and Gynaecologists
Royal College of Physicians
Royal College of Surgeons
Trades Union Congress

Bibliography

Abel-Smith, B. (1964) *The Hospitals 1800–1948*, London: Heinemann.
Abel-Smith, B. and Titmuss, R.M. (1956) *The Cost of the National Health Service in England and Wales*, Cambridge: Cambridge University Press.
Acton Society Trust (1955) *Hospitals and the State — Hospital Organisation and Administration Under the National Health Service*, London: Acton Society Trust.
Addison, P. (1975) *The Road to 1945, British Politics and the Second World War*, London Jonathan Cape.
Baldwin, A.W. (1955) *My Father: The True Story*, London: Allen & Unwin.
Bevan, A. (1961) *In Place of Fear*, London: MacGibbon & Kee.
Beveridge, W. (1942) *Social Insurance and Allied Services*, London: HMSO, Cmnd 6,404.
Beveridge, W. (1953) *Power and Influence*, London: Hodder & Stoughton.
Brackenbury, H.B. (1935) *Patient and Doctor*, London: Hodder & Stoughton.
Brand, J.L. (1965) *Doctors and the State: The British Medical Association and Government Action in Public Health, 1870–1912*, Baltimore, Md.: Johns Hopkins Press.
British Medical Journal (1978) Six doctors recall the birth of the NHS — interviews with Godber, Hill, Stevenson, Taylor, Thwaites, and Wand, *British Medical Journal*, 1 July: 28–33.
Bullock, A. (1960) *The Life and Times of Ernest Bevin, Volume 1, Trade Union Leader, 1881–1940*, London: Heinemann.
Bullock, A. (1967) *The Life and Times of Ernest Bevin, Volume 2, Minister of Labour, 1940–1945*, London: Heinemann.
Bullock, A. (1983) *Ernest Bevin: Foreign Secretary*, London, Heinemann.
Bunbury, H.N. (ed.) (1957) *Lloyd George's Ambulance Wagon, the Memoirs of William J. Braithwaite, 1911–1912*, London: Methuen.
Burridge, T. (1985) *Clement Attlee: A Political Biography*, London: Jonathan Cape.
Campbell, J. (1987) *Nye Bevan and the Mirage of British Socialism*, London: Weidenfeld & Nicolson.
Canadian Department of National Health and Welfare (1952) *Health Insurance in Great Britain 1911–1948*, Ottawa: Research Division, Department of National Health and Welfare; Social Security Series, Memo. 11, March.
Chester, D.N. (ed.) and Willson, F.M.G. (1957) *The Organization of British Central Government 1914–1956*, London: Allen & Unwin.
Colville, J. (1985 and 1986) *The Fringes of Power, Downing Street Diaries, Volume 1: 1939–October 1941*, London: Hodder & Stoughton and Sceptre.
Colville, J. (1985 and 1987) *The Fringes of Power, Downing Street Diaries, Volume 2: 1941–April 1955*, London: Hodder & Stoughton and Sceptre.
Cooke, A.M. (1972) *A History of the Royal College of Physicians of London, Volume 3*, Oxford: Clarendon Press for the RCP.
Cooter, R. (1987) 'The meaning of fractures: orthopaedics and reform of British hospitals in the inter-war period', *Medical History* July: 306–32. This is part of a larger study to be published under the title, *Medical Specialisation in Peace and War: The Making of Modern Orthopaedics 1880–1945*, Manchester: Manchester University Press.
Cope, Z. (1959) *The History of the Royal College of Surgeons of England*, London: Anthony Blond.

Cox, A. (1950) *Among the Doctors*, London: Christopher Johnson.

Cronin, A.J. (1937) *The Citadel*, London: Gollancz.

Crosby, T.L. (1986) *The Impact of Civilian Evacuation in the Second World War*, London: Croom Helm.

Dale, H.E. (1941) *The Higher Civil Service of Great Britain*, Oxford: Oxford University Press.

Department of Health for Scotland (1936) *Report of the Committee on Scottish Health Services* (Cathcart Report), Edinburgh: HMSO, Cmnd 5,204.

Department of Health for Scotland (1943) *Report of the Committee on Post-War Hospital Problems for Scotland* (Hetherington Report), Edinburgh, HMSO, Cmnd 6,472.

Department of Health and Social Security (1979) *Review of Health Capital*, London: DHSS Library.

Dilks, D. (1984) *Neville Chamberlain: Volume 1, Pioneering and Reform, 1869–1929*, Cambridge: Cambridge University Press.

Dodd, J. (1961) *Hospitals and Health Services in Britain and America*, Bristol: British Hospitals Contributory Schemes Association.

Donnison, J. (1977) *Midwives and Medical Men*, London: Heinemann.

Donoghue, B. and Jones, G.W. (1973) *Herbert Morrison: Portrait of a Politician*, London: Weidenfeld & Nicolson.

Dunn, C.L. (1952) *The Emergency Medical Services*, London: HMSO.

Eckstein, H. (1958) *The English Health Service*, Cambridge, Mass.: Harvard University Press.

Eckstein, H. (1960) *Pressure Group Politics, The Case of the British Medical Association*, London: Allen & Unwin.

Feiling, K. (1946) *The Life of Neville Chamberlain*, London: Macmillan.

Foot, M. (1962 and 1964) *Aneurin Bevan — Volume 1: 1897–1945*, London: MacGibbon & Kee and Four Square.

Foot, M. (1966) *Aneurin Bevan — Volume 2: 1945–1960*, London: Davis-Poynter and Granada.

Forsyth, G. (1966) *Doctors and State Medicine*, London: Pitman.

Fox, D.M. (1986) *Health Policies and Health Politics, The British and American Experience 1911–1965*, Princeton: NJ: Princeton University Press.

Frazer, W.M. (1950) *A History of English Public Health, 1834–1939*, London: Ballière, Tindall & Cox.

Gilbert, B.B. (1966) *The Evolution of National Insurance in Britain*, London: Michael Joseph.

Gilbert, B.B. (1970) *British Social Policy 1914–1939*, London: Batsford.

Goldman, L. (1957) *Angry Young Doctor*, London: Hamish Hamilton.

Goodman, N.M. (1970) *Wilson Jameson*, London: Allen & Unwin.

Gordon, A. (1924) *Social Insurance, What It Is and What It Might Be*, London: Allen & Unwin for the Fabian Society.

Government Actuary (1943) *Fifth Valuation of the Assets and Liabilities of Approved Societies*, London: HMSO, Cmnd 6,455.

Gray, A. (1923) *Some Aspects of National Health Insurance*, London: P.S. King.

Gray, F. (1981) articles on the formation of the NHS in *Pulse*, 14, 21, and 28 Nov.

Grey-Turner, E. and Sutherland, F.M. (1982) *History of the British Medical Association, Volume 2 1932–1981*, London: British Medical Association.

Harris, J. (1977) *William Beveridge, a Biography*, Oxford: Clarendon Press.

Harris, K. (1982) *Attlee*, London: Weidenfeld & Nicolson.

Harris, R.W. (1946) *National Health Insurance in Great Britain 1911–1946*, London: Allen & Unwin.

Hennessy, P. (1986) *Cabinet*, Oxford: Basil Blackwell.

Hill, C. (1964) *Both Sides of the Hill*, London: Heinemann.

Hodgkinson, R.G. (1967) *The Origins of the National Health Service: The Medical Services of the New Poor Law, 1834–1871*, London: Wellcome Historical Medical Library, Monograph No. 11.

Honigsbaum, F. (1968) 'Unity in British public health administration: the failure of reform, 1926–9', *Medical History*, April: 109–21.

Honigsbaum, F. (1970) *The Struggle for the Ministry of Health*, Occasional Papers on Social Administration No. 37, London: G. Bell.

Honigsbaum, F. (1979) *The Division in British Medicine: A History of the Separation of General Practice from Hospital Care, 1911–1968*, London: Kogan Page and Jessica Kingsley; New York: St Martin's Press.

Honigsbaum, F. (1983) 'The interwar health insurance scheme: a rejoinder', *Journal of Social Policy*, Oct.: 515–24.

Jewkes, J. and S. (1961) *The Genesis of the British National Health Service*, Oxford: Basil Blackwell.

Johnson, D. McI. (1962) *The British National Health Service*, London: Johnson.

Joint Committee of Royal College of Obstetricians and Gynaecologists and Population Investigation Committee (1948) *Maternity in Great Britain*, Oxford: Oxford University Press.

Jones, K. (1972) *A History of the Mental Health Services*, London: Routledge & Kegan Paul.

Kebbel, T.E. (ed.) (1882) *Selected Speeches of the Late Earl of Beaconsfield*, Volume 2, London: Longman.

Kellner, P. and Crowther-Hunt, B. (1980) *Civil Servant: An Inquiry into Britain's Ruling Class*, London: Macdonald

Kelsall, R.K. (1955) *Higher Civil Servants in Britain*, London: Routledge & Kegan Paul.

Klein, R. (1983) *The Politics of the National Health Service*, London: Longman.

Labour Party (1943) *National Service for Health*, London: Labour Party.

Lee, J.M. (1980) *The Churchill Coalition 1940–1945*, London: Batsford.

Levy, H. (1944) *National Health Insurance, A Critical Study*, Cambridge: Cambridge University Press.

Lewis, Jane (1980) *The Politics of Motherhood, Child and Maternal Welfare in England, 1900–1939*, London: Croom Helm.

Lewis, Jane (1986) *What Price Community Medicine? The Philosophy, Practice and Politics of Public Health Since 1919*, London: Wheatsheaf.

Lindsey, A. (1962) *Socialized Medicine in England and Wales, The National Health Service, 1948–1961*, Chapel Hill and Oxford: North Carolina University Press and Oxford University Press.

Little, E.M. (ed.) (1932) *History of the British Medical Association, 1832–1932*, London: British Medical Association.

McCleary, G.F. (1932) *National Health Insurance*, London: H.K. Lewis.

McCleary, G.F. (1933) *The Early History of the Infant Welfare Movement*, London: H.K. Lewis.

McCleary, G.F. (1935) *The Maternity and Child Welfare Movement*, London: P.S. King.

Mackenzie, W.J.M. and Grove, J.W. (1957) *Central Administration in Britain*, London: Longman.

Mackintosh, J.M. (1953) *Trends of Opinion About the Public Health, 1901–51*, Oxford: Oxford University Press.

Mackintosh, J.P. (1962) *The British Cabinet*, London: Stevens.

McLachlan, G. (ed.) (1987) *Improving the Common Weal: Aspects of Scottish Health Services 1900–1984*, Edinburgh: Edinburgh University Press for Nuffield Trust.

Middlemass, K. and Barnes, J. (1969) *Baldwin*, London: Weidenfeld & Nicolson.

Ministry of Health (1959) *Report of Maternity Services Committee*, London: HMSO.

Ministry of Health (1966) *Annual Report of the Ministry of Health for 1965*, London: HMSO, Cmnd 3,039.

Ministry of Health, Consultative Council on Medical and Allied Services (1920) *Interim Report on the Future Provision of Medical and Allied Services* (Dawson Report), London: HMSO, Cmnd 693.

Ministry of Health and Department of Health for Scotland (1944a) *A National Health Service* (White Paper), London: HMSO, Cmnd 6,502.

Ministry of Health and Department of Health for Scotland (1944b) *Report of the Inter-departmental Committee on Medical Schools* (Goodenough Report), London: HMSO.

Ministry of Health and Department of Health for Scotland (1944c) *Interim Report of the Inter-departmental Committee on Dentistry* (Chairman, Lord Teviot), London: HMSO, Cmnd 6,565.

Ministry of Health and Department of Health for Scotland (1946) *Report of the Inter-departmental Committee on Remuneration of General Practitioners* (Spens Report on GP pay), London: HMSO, Cmnd 6,810.

Ministry of Health and Department of Health for Scotland(1948) *Report of the Inter-departmental Committee on Remuneration of Consultants and Specialists* (Spens Report on consultant pay), London: HMSO, Cmnd 7,420.

Ministry of Health and Department of Health for Scotland (1956) *Report of the Committee of Enquiry into the Cost of the National Health Service* (Chairman, C.W. Guillebaud), London: HMSO, Cmnd 9,663.

Morgan, K. and Morgan, J. (1980) *Portrait of a Progressive, the Political Career of Christopher, Viscount Addison*, Oxford: Clarendon Press.

Morgan, K.O. (1984) *Labour in Power, 1945-1951*, Oxford: Clarendon Press.

Morrison, H. (1960) *Herbert Morrison, An Autobiography*, London: Odhams.

Murray, D.S. (1942) *Health for All*, London: Gollancz.

Murray, D.S. (1971) *Why a National Health Service?* London: Pemberton.

Newman, G. (1939) *The Building of a Nation's Health*, London: Macmillan.

Newsholme, A. (1932) *Medicine and the State*, London: Allen & Unwin.

Nuffield Provincial Hospitals Trust (1941) *A National Hospital Service*, London: Nuffield Trust.

Nuffield Provincial Hospitals Trust (1946) *The Hospital Surveys — The Domesday Book of the Hospital Services*, Oxford: Oxford University Press.

Nuffield Provincial Hospitals Trust (1949) *A Report on the Purpose and Activities of the Trust, 1939-1948*, Oxford: Oxford University Press.

Oakley, A. (1984) *The Captured Womb, A History of the Medical Care of Pregnant Women*, Oxford: Basil Blackwell.

Organization for European Co-operation and Development (1985) *Measuring Health Care, 1980-1983*, Paris: OECD.

Orr, D.W. and Orr, J.W. (1938) *Health Insurance with Medical Care, the British Experience*, London: Macmillan.

Parry, N. and Parry J. (1976) *The Rise of the Medical Profession*, London: Croom Helm.

Pater, J. (1981) *The Making of the National Health Service*, London: King's Fund.

Pelling, H. (1984) *The Labour Governments, 1945-51*, London: Macmillan.

Pimlott, B. (1985) *Hugh Dalton*, London: Macmillan.

Pinker, R. (1966) *English Hospital Statistics 1861-1938*, London: Heinemann.

Political and Economic Planning (1937) *Report on the British Health Services*, London: PEP.

Rivett, G. (1986) *The Development of the London Hospital System 1823-1982*, London: King's Fund.

Roberts, F. (1952) *The Cost of Health*, London: Turnstile Press.

Robinson, R.H.O.B. and Le Fanu, W.R. (1970) *Lives of the Fellows of the Royal College of Surgeons of England 1952-1964*, London: E. & S. Livingstone.

Rogers, A.T. 'Looking forward with hindsight', *Proceedings of the Royal Society of Medicine*, 65: 109–18.

Ross, J.P. and Le Fanu, W.R. (1981) *Lives of the Fellows of the Royal College of Surgeons, 1965–1973*, London: Pitman.

Ross, J.S. (1952) *The National Health Service in Great Britain*, Oxford: Oxford University Press.

Royal College of Obstetricians and Gynaecologists (1944) *Report on a National Maternity Service*, London: Royal College of Obstetricians and Gynaecologists.

Royal Commission on Doctors' and Dentists' Remuneration (1958) *Minutes of Evidence, Days 3–4*, London: HMSO.

Royal Commission on National Health Insurance (issued 1926, published 1928) *Report*, London: HMSO, Cmd 2,596.

Shaw, W.F. (1954) *Twenty Five Years, The Story of the Royal College of Obstetricians and Gynaecologists, 1929–1954*, London: J. & A. Churchill.

Smith, H.L. (ed.) (1986) *War and Social Change, British Society in the Second World War*, Manchester: Manchester University Press.

Stevens, R. (1966) *Medical Practice in Modern England. The Impact of Specialization and State Medicine*, Yale University Press.

Taylor, A.J.P. (1965) *English History 1914–1945*, Oxford: Clarendon Press.

Taylor, S. (1978, 1979, 1980) articles on the birth of the NHS, *Update Review*, 15 Nov. 1978; 15 Jan., 1 Feb., 1 Mar., 15 Jun., 15 Oct. 1979; 15 Feb. 1980.

Titmuss, R.M. (1950) *Problems of Social Policy*, London: Longman, for HMSO, UK Civil History Series.

Titmuss, R.M. (1958) *Essays on 'The Welfare State'*, London: Allen & Unwin.

Titmuss, R.M. (1959) 'Health', in Ginsberg, M. (ed.) *Law and Opinion in the Twentieth Century*, London: Stevens.

Vaughan, P. (1959) *Doctors' Commons, A Short History of the British Medical Association*, London: Heinemann.

Watson, F. (1950) *Dawson of Penn*, London, Chatto & Windus.

Webb, S. and Webb, B. (1910) *The State and the Doctor*, London: Longman.

Webster, C. (1988) *The Health Service Since the War. Volume 1: Problems of Health Care, the National Health Service Before 1957*, London: HMSO (an official history).

Wheeler-Bennett, J.W. (1962) *John Anderson, Viscount Waverley*, London: Macmillan.

Wheeler-Bennett, J.W. (ed.) (1968) *Action This Day — Working with Churchill*, London: Macmillan.

Willcocks, A.J. (1967) *The Creation of the National Health Service*, London: Routledge & Kegan Paul.

Wilson, C.M. (1966) *Winston Churchill — The Struggle for Survival 1940–1965*, London: Constable.

Wilson, N. (1946) *Municipal Health Services*, London: Allen & Unwin.

Name index

Abel, Lawrence 117, 125, 148, 181
Abel-Smith, Brian 199, 200
Addison, Christopher (later Lord) 4, 15, 177, 178
Alderson, Gerald 123
Alexander, A.V. 177
Anderson, George 44, 56, 57, 58, 70, 74-5, 115-16, 118, 216, 217
Anderson, Sir John (later Lord Waverley) 68, 70, 104, 163, 164, 201
Attlee, Clement 33, 67, 94, 177-8
Aylwen, Sir George 169, 180

Baldwin, Stanley 6
Bannatyne, Robert (later Sir) 35
Barlow, Sir Alan 47, 200
Beaverbrook, Lord 201, 202
Beckett, J.N. 41
Beddow Bayly, Maurice 98
Bevan, Aneurin 94-5, 204; and basic salary 147, 149; and BMA 148-50; and capitation 95-6, 107, 153; and Civil Service 217; and concessions 95, 96-7; and consultants 142-3, 148, 151, 152-3, 182; and disciplinary bodies 97; exploits doctors' divisions 148-50, 152-3; and GPs 152-3; and Hawton 173; and health centres 95, 105; hospitals, nationalization 95, 97, 98, 103, 136, 172; and maternity services 108-9; and medical aid societies 95; and Moran 216; and Morrison 176-7; as negotiator 147-8, 216-17, 218; and pay beds 181, 182; and private practice 145; representation, changes in 96-7; and Rucker 175; and salaried service

95-6, 97, 99-100, 149; and sale of practices 96, 100-3, 103-4; and Spens Committee 101, 102; and teaching hospitals 176; and universal coverage 195; and workers' control 97
Beveridge, Sir William (later Lord) 35, 44, 217; and approved societies 192; and costs, increase in 198; and health care 192-3; and insurance principle 193; and unemployment insurance 192; and universal service 192, 193-4, 195; see also Beveridge Committee in Subject Index
Bevin, Ernest 67, 91, 94, 163, 178
Blair Bell, William 119
Boldero, Harold 134, 143
Bone, J.W. 130
Bourne, Geoffrey 55
Bracken, Brendan 201, 202
Brackenbury, Sir Henry 8-9, 84
Bradford Hill, Professor 101
Brock, Sir Laurence 25-6, 28, 40, 158
Brodie, F. Martin 83
Brook, Norman 108
Brooke, Henry 78, 79
Brown, Ernest 27, 34, 65, 67, 70, 129, 215, 217; and GP services 52, 57, 58; and hospital service 27, 28, 33, 163; joint board plan 143; and Nuffield 27; and TUC 35
Buchan, J.J. 29
Buchanan, George 104
Burnet, James 98
Butler, Rab 150
Buzzard, Sir Farquhar 175

Cathcart, Edward P. 10
Chamberlain, Neville 6, 173

Champneys, Sir Francis 214
Charles, John (later Sir) 121, 123
Cherwell, Lord 82, 200, 201, 202
Chester, D.N. (later Sir Norman) 37, 192
Chrystal, Sir George 13, 14, 15, 22-3,
    27, 33
Churchill, Winston 170; and Beveridge
    Report 200; and Moran 116, 125,
    132, 216; and NHS 201-2
Chuter Ede, James 177
Clarke, Joan 84-5
Claye, Andrew 131
Clegg, Hugh 150, 151, 152, 219-21
Cockshut, Roland W. 88, 145-6, 148
Cohen, Henry (later Lord) 78, 114, 118
Cox, Alfred 49-50, 98, 99, 100, 103,
    117, 146, 151, 206, 207
Craik, Sir Henry 205
Cronin, A.J. 94

Dain, Guy (later Sir) 53, 58, 74, 76,
    102, 116, 120, 130, 134, 150, 151
Daley, Allen (later Sir) 18, 29, 143, 158
Dalrymple-Champneys, Sir Weldon 49, 214
Dalton, Hugh 104, 177
Danckwerts, Justice 101
Davies, Rhys 22
Dawson, Sir Bertrand (later Lord) 4,
    215; and central control 135; and
    CHSC 88; influence 115; and London
    hospitals 17; on medical representation
    55, 78; and municipal control 133;
    and SMA 82; on White Paper 72-3, 75
Demo see De Montmorency
De Montmorency, Harvey (later Sir
    Angus) 27; as adviser 214; and
    dependent coverage 189; and GP
    service 37-8, 41; on mental hospitals
    28; on NHI finance 25; and
    regionalization 25; and salaried
    service 15
Dickson Wright, Arthur 117, 148, 181
Disraeli, Benjamin 218
Docker, Sir Bernard 136, 160, 171, 180
Doll, Richard (later Sir) 137
Donoughmore, Lord 180
Douglas, Major Clifford 73
Douglas, Sir William 99, 107, 150, 173

Eason, Sir Herbert 129
Eden, Anthony 201
Elliot, Walter (later Sir) 10, 11, 15, 17,
18, 217
Epps, George (later Sir) 197, 198, 217

Fairfield, Letitia 73
Farquhar Murray, E. 118
Farrell, Hamilton 36
Fletcher Shaw, William (later Sir) 115,
    116, 119, 121, 131, 138
Foot, Michael 174
Forber, Sir Edward 18, 19-20, 25, 28, 41
Fraser, Sir Francis 128
Fuller, C.J. 123

Gask, George 172
George, H.H. 41, 197, 198
Gilbert, Sir Bernard 164, 200-1, 202
Gilliatt, William 119, 138
Godber, G.E. (later Sir George) 174,
    214, 216, 217
Goodenough, Sir William 26, 60; and
    Medical schools 33; and municipal
    control 27, 29; and nationalization
    180; and voluntary hospitals 160
Goodman, Harold 147
Gowers, Sir Ernest 140
Graham-Little, Sir Ernest 75, 148, 181,
    183
Grant, William 107
Gray, Frank 75, 141, 215
Gray, Sir Henry 172
Greenwood, Arthur (later Lord) 6, 7,
    23, 33, 34-5, 36, 95, 178
Gregg, Edward 78

Hackforth, Edgar 34
Haden Guest, Leslie (later Lord) 18
Hale, Edward (later Sir) 103-4, 109
Hardy, T.L. 121
Harris, R.W. 50, 204
Hastings, Somerville 91, 95, 96, 149, 207
Havers, Cecil 146
Hawton, J.M.K. (later Sir John) 64, 67,
    169, 170
Helme, Arthur C de B. 98. 152
Helme, T. Arthur 152
Henderson, G.H. 42, 55-6, 64-5
Heseltine, Michael 128, 129, 130, 132
Hetherington, Sir Hector 20, 35
Hill, Charles (later Lord) 62; and Bevan
    148, 150; as BMA leader 74-5; and
    consultant lists 130; and GP service
    56, 57, 58, 73, 89; GPs and

health insurance 36-7; as leader 74-5, 216; and Moran 116, 117; and MPA 82; and MPC 47, 49; and municipal control 214, 215, 216; and nationalization 136, 172, 173; and NHS Act 146, 150; and non-teachers 125; and RCOG 119-20; and regional powers 134; and Royal Colleges 123, 124; and salaried service 99, 104, 214; and sale of practices 90, 99, 102; on White Paper 76

Hogan, E.A. 44

Holland, Eardley 119, 131, 137, 138

Horder, Lord 22, 99, 137, 216; and Bevan's Bill 146; as consultant spokesman 117; Fellowship for Freedom in Medicine 139, 152; and honorary status 114; and London sectors 171; and NHS Act 149, 150, 151-2; opposes nationalization 181-3; on White Paper 75-6

Horsbrugh, Florence 169, 173

Hudson, Robert Spear (later Lord) 15, 188

Hutchison, Sir Robert 115, 116

Hyde, William 26, 160, 189

Ives, A.G.L. 171

Jameson, Sir Wilson 22, 29, 42, 121, 217; as adviser 214; and basic salary 104; and CMSC demands 56; and consultant list 128, 130-1; and free entry 109; and health centres 44, 45; and hospital service 24; and Medical Advisory Committee 53, 55; on Ministry role 114; and municipal control 106; as negotiator 76, 77, 218; and sale of practices 69

Johnston, T. 60-1; and compensation for practices 90; and GP service 65; and health centres 67, 68; and hospital service 87; 'hotel' charge 162, 163; and joint boards 66, 170; and municipal control 173; and sale of practices 91; and two-tier plan 80-1

Jowitt, Sir William (later Lord) 67, 177, 178

Kershaw, Fred (later Lord) 6, 7

Kindersley, Charles 124

Kinnear, Sir Walter 207

Latham, Charles (later Lord) 27; and

concessions 91; and health centres 106; and nationalization 136, 179; and sectors 179; and voluntary hospitals 171, 172, 179

Law, Richard 182

Le Fleming, Kaye (later Sir) 11

Lloyd George, David 4, 99, 204, 206, 217

McCurrich, H.J. 117, 122-5, 136, 137, 216; provincial hospitals association 123-5

Macdonald, Malcolm 22, 27, 217

Macdonald, Peter 117

Macdonald, Ramsay 207

MacGregor, Alexander (later Sir) 11

MacGregor, E.D. 23, 26, 27, 42, 64

MacNalty, Sir Arthur 22, 42; and central control 20, 23; and specialist services 13, 14-15, 16, 188; and unification 14-15; and voluntary hospitals 18

McNicholl, Niven S. 10, 48, 64, 160, 162

MacWilliam, E.U. 83

Marchbank, F.F. 42, 70-1

Marre, Sir Alan 174

Maude, Sir John 23, 36; and BHA plan 167-8; on Boundary Commission 176; and CMB 56-7; and competition 58; dental and optical care 190; dependent coverage 15; and direct representation 56, 70; and disciplinary procedure 57; and GP reform 26, 37-43, 51-3, 64; and group practice 59; health service costs 197-8; and Hetherington Committee 162; and Hill 214, 215; and hospital service 22, 27-9; influence 217, 218; and joint boards 60, 78; and medical politics 214-15; and mental hospitals 190; and municipal control 41-3, 47-8, 59-62, 64, 166, 173, 213-14; pressures on 160-1; and private practice 68; radicalism 49; and regional organization 24, 25, 26; and salaried service 64, 215; and sale of practices 69; and Scottish situation 161; sensitivity to criticism 77-8; and superannuation 102; and teaching hospitals 157; universal coverage 193, 194, 195; and voluntary hospital administrators 55; and voluntary

hospitals 19, 28, 29, 157-8, 159, 165-6, 190-1
Meade, James 200
Menzies, Sir Frederick 16, 29, 157, 179
Miller, J.B. 120, 213
Mitchell, Sir Miles 106
Moran (Charles MacMoran Wilson), Lord 17, 73; and Bevan 136, 149-50, 216; and Bevan's Bill 146; and BMA dominance 115, 116, 133-5; and Churchill 116, 121, 125, 132, 216; and Clegg 219-21; and Cohen 118; and consultant salaries 144; consultant unity, attempts 120-1; and 'consultoids' 113, 127; and EMS 115; and GP service 134; and health centres 134; and Hill 116-17, 215; and Jameson 131; London sectors 171; and medical hierarchy 141, 142; and municipal control 120-1, 133; and nationalization 172, 174; as negotiator 216; and NHS Act 149-50, 151; and non-teaching consultants 122-6; personality 116; and regional councils 88; on representation 55; on salaried service 99, 100, 107; two-tier plan, rejects 135; on White Paper 75, 76
Morgan, H.B.W. 22, 92, 130, 142
Morrison, Herbert 16-17, 65, 66, 67, 70, 103, 148, 152, 176
Murley, Reginald 152

Neville, Arthur W. 13, 18-19, 33, 188, 209
Newman, Sir George 22, 207, 208, 213
Nuffield, Lord 26

Oliver, T.H. 124

Pater, John 27, 51, 52, 53, 60, 160, 162, 164, 173
Payne, Reginald 139, 150, 152
Percy, Lord 128-9, 130
Pooley, Sir Ernest 55, 160

Reed, Michael 130
Ritson, Muriel 36
Roberts, Ffrangon 140
Robinson, Sir Arthur 207
Rock Carling, Ernest (later Sir) 128, 140
Rose, F.M. 102
Rucker, Arthur (later Sir) 24, 217, 218; and Chamberlain 173; grant-in-aid of

private practice 196; and hospital service 25, 67; and Moran 140; as negotiator 76; resists nationalization 173, 174-5; and sale of practices 69; and sectors 144; and two-tier plan 86, 175; and voluntary hospitals 173
Ryle, John 62, 82

Sheldon, H.J. 122, 123
Smyth, J.L. 92
Souttar, Henry 49, 74, 117, 120, 130, 136, 146, 216
Spens, Sir William 92, 140
Stark Murray, David 74

Talbot Rogers, A. 62, 82, 84, 90, 141
Taylor, Stephen (later Lord) 19, 82-3, 105, 141-2
Titmuss, Richard 199, 200
Tribe, Sir Frank 158

Vallance, J.W. 63, 164
Vaughan Jones, J.A.L. 84

Watson-Jones, Sir Reginald 151
Waverley, Lord, see Anderson, Sir John
Webb, Beatrice 6
Webb, Sidney 6
Webb-Johnson, Sir Alfred (later Lord) 58, 118, 119-20; and Bevan's Bill 146; and nationalization 136; and NHS 139, 140; and non-teacher organization 122; and RCP 'Beveridge Committee' 121; and voluntary hospitals 84, 180; and White Paper 82
Wetenhall, J.P. 136, 137, 180-1
Whitaker, Donald 152
Whitaker, Sir James 152
Wilkie Millar, A.F. 83
Wilkinson, Ellen 177
Willink, Henry (later Sir) 70, 76, 78, 182; and CHSC 69; and consultant lists 130; and GP service 87; and health centres 68; and 'hotel' charge 163; and nationalization 172-3, 183; negotiations with GPs 89, 90, 91, 92, 217; representation, changes in 96-7; and sale of practices 90; two-tier plan 78, 79-81, 86, 169-70, 177
Wilson, Charles McMoran see Moran, Lord

Wilson, M.U. 45
Wood, Sir Kingsley 13, 15, 23, 35-6, 200
Woolton, Lord 67, 68, 90, 163, 170, 171, 201
Wrigley, John (later Sir) 23-4, 42, 61

Wyatt, James 131

Young, E. Hilton (later Lord Kennet) 207
Young, James 11, 131

Subject index

administration, medical influence over 206

administration, medical representation in 55-6, 69-70, 86; Bevan's proposals 96-7; BMA on 73, 75, 76, 78, 81, 84; consultants 144; in health centres 78

administration, two-tier 79-81

ante-natal care: expansion 7; by GPs 6, 10-11

apprenticeship period 69

approved societies 4; abolition 39; and doctors 5, 62; funds 190; influence 206, 209; and local authorities 14; and maternity benefits 6, 7; and the medical profession 83; opposition to 192-3; and panel system 8-9; surplus funds 4-5; and voluntary hospitals 158, 159, 191

area authority, municipal majority 170; powers 134, 135; and voluntary hospitals 170

Association of Municipal Corporations (AMC), and area powers 135; and GP service 54; and hospital planning group 171; and nationalization 180; and White paper 169

assurance societies, and comprehensive service 190; and doctors 9, 206; and maternity benefits 6, 7, 9

basic salary 96, 97, 99, 104, 107-8, 147, 149

'Beveridge Committee' (RCP) see Royal College of Physicians

Beveridge Report (1942) 23; costs, increase in 198; debate on 68; and GP service 38; and health matters 36, 37, 57; health service costs 197-8; and hospital benefit 158; and hospital service 194; 'hotel charge' 159-60; insurance matters 57; and MPC 37; and municipal control 42; and NHS 192, 194; and salaried service 42; and trade unions 34-6, 192; and universal coverage 165

BMA see British Medical Association

Bradford, salaried experiments 43

British Hospitals Association (BHA) 120; and Central Hospital Board 180-1; and honorary service 180; McCurrich on 122; and municipal control 55; and nationalization 136, 180-1; and regionalization 20; and voluntary hospitals 160, 167; weakness 180-1; White Paper, attacks 169

British Institute of Public Opinion 75

British Medical Association (BMA), and administration, medical representation in 73, 75, 76, 78, 81, 84; alliance with TUC 9-10, 34, 91-2, 108; and Bevan 148-50; and Beveridge Report 57; and BHA 120; Central Consultant Committee 140; and central control 98; conflict within over NHS Act 150-1; constitution 82; and consultants 117-18; and 'consultoids' 127, 128; General Medical Service scheme (1929) 36, 44, 206-7; GP influence in 116; Guildford Division 74, 82; and health centres 44-5, 73, 75, 77, 81; and Health Ministry 77-8; and honorary service 180; hospital service, negotiations 120; independence fund 149; Insurance Acts Committee 215; and medical aid societies 94; Medical Planning Commission (MPC) *see* Medical Planning Commission; medical politics, dominance 115-17; and MPA 74, 81-5 and municipal control 56, 206-8; and municipal domiciliary services 7; and municipal maternity services 6; national maternity policy 8; and nationalization 137; opposes Bevan's plan 146-7; and PEP 82; plebiscites 107, 148-9, 152, 182; and RCP 'Beveridge Committee' 124, 125; regional consultant committee 140; and regional organization 133, 134-5; Royal Commission, demands 57; and sale of practices 75, 76-7, 81, 90, 98-9, 100, 102, 103; SMA role in 74, 82; and split in profession 117; and two-tier plan 170; and universal coverage 73, 193, 209; and White Paper 72-4, 75-6, 81-5

Cabinet, and health centres 67-9; and nationalization 175-9; White Paper, debating 65-9, 70
Cancer Act (1939) 14, 28, 48, 133, 157, 166, 189
cancer treatment 15
capital expenditure 199
capitation 68; Bevan on 95, 96, 99-100, 107; disadvantages of 48-9; doctors' preference for 45; and independent status 45; levels 39, 59, 153; NHS increase in 147
Cathcart Committee (1936) 10-11, 13, 15, 157, 208, 209
CCA *see* County Councils Association
Central Health Services Council (CHSC) 53; BMA on 76; and direct representation 78; doctors on 69, 81, 88; and joint authority 168; splitting 88; and voluntary hospitals 168; and White Paper 169
Central Hospital Services Council 56
Central Hospitals Council 60
Central Medical Academic Council (CMAC) 128, 130
Central Medical Board (CMB) 42-3, 46; BMA on 76; contracts, termination 56; and disciplinary procedure 57; and doctors 42, 80, 89, 91; duties

87; GP intake, regulation 42; as GPs' employer 68, 69; power 56-7, 75, 89; and promotions 43
Central Medical Services Council (CMSC) 56
certification of sickness benefits, and free access to GPs 40; and GP service 52; and medical boards 59; and salaried service 42
child welfare services, metropolitan 179
Christian Scientists 196
Chrystal Committee (1939) 18
CHSC *see* Central Health Services Council
Civil Service, and doctors 213; influence 97; and municipal control 213-14; NHS, planning 213, 216-17, 217-18
clinics, linked with hospitals 24 municipal 66
Clyde Basin Experiment 66
CMAC *see* Central Medical Academic Council
CMSC *see* Central Medical Services Council
collective responsibility 147
compensation, midwives 189; for practices 40, 75, 100-3, 104, 202; workmen's 9, 192
competition, disadvantages of 39, 45; and medical profession 89; minimizing 104-5; as problem 48-9, 58
Conservative Party, on medical representation 78, 79; and nationalization 172-3 and NHS Bill 137; and voluntary hospitals 80
consultant service, charges for 14; and 'consultoids' 113, 114; importance in planning 52; municipal provision 13, 14, 15; under NHI 5, 8, 13, 14; planning 51-2, 73, 134
consultants, appointment 182; Bevan's concessions to 143-5; on BMA 117-18; control of 80; direct representation 144; distinction awards 140; divisions among 117-18; earnings 144-5; influence on policy 125; local recognition 128, 129; Moran's list of 127-32; and municipal control 121, 125-6, 133; and nationalization 81-3, 143, 145; non-teaching 122-5; pay beds 181, 182;

private practice 147, 148; regional advisers 114; regional powers, loss 93; and regional tier 88; resist NHS Act 151-3; salaries 51, 63, 182; scarcity 52, 113, 114; as team leaders 144; training 134; *see also* specialist service
Consultative Council on Approved Societies Work 6
'consultoids', abolition 127, 183; and EMS 114; increasing use of 113, 114; oppose nationalization 181, 182; phasing out 141-2; and provincial consultants 118
contracts, part-time 145; termination 43, 47, 56-7, 108
contributory schemes, voluntary hospitals 159, 160
cottage hospitals, 'consultoids' 113-14; finances 114; incompetence 109; surgery in 18, 113-14, 139
County Councils Association (CCA), and area powers 135; and direct representation 78; and GP plan 54; and hospital planning group 171; and nationalization 179-80; and Nuffield 27; and White Paper 169

Dawson Report (1920) 53; and group practice 36, 44; medical consultative council 70; teamwork principle 44
dental care 195; charge for 198
dependent coverage 44, 84, 165; cost 14, 15; and maternity services 15; under NHI 5, 7, 8
direct representation *see* administration
disability benefit 13-14, 37; and 'hotel' charge 162
disciplinary bodies, and appeals 97-8; Bevan's proposals 97
disciplinary procedure 39, 57, 59; and municipal control 72
dismissal, appeal against 108; *see also* contracts, termination
distinction awards 140
district councils, powers 61
doctors *see* British Medical Association; consultants; GPs; medical profession domiciliary service, municipal 7-8, 20-1 double standards of treatment 43, 49

Education Act (1918) 7
Emergency Medical Service (EMS) 17-18; and consultants 114; hospital management 114; maternity services 137-8; private practice in 115; regional perspective 133; sector organization 115; voluntary hospitals 158
England and Wales, joint boards 67; medical representation 86
equipment, allowance for 40, 44; cost 197

Fabian Society, and GPs 141; and municipal control 173
Fellowship for Freedom in Medicine 139, 152
free entry to practice 42, 46; abolition 47; controls over 59
friendly societies, conditions of work 205; and doctors 9; freedom from 205-6

General Medical Council (GMC), blocks Moran's plan 127-9; general register 127; membership 127; specialists' register 128-9, 132
General Medical Service scheme (BMA, 1929) 36, 44, 206-7
general practice, separation from hospital work 113; *see also* GPs
Glasgow, salaried service 11
GMC *see* General Medical Council
Goodenough Committee 123, 131
GP-consultants *see* 'consultoids'
GP service, access to hospital service 107; apprenticeship period 69; basic salary 96, 97, 99, 104, 107-8, 147; bed provision 53; and certification 52; and 'consultoids' 113-14; control of 55, 80; cost 39-40, 42, 44, 54, 197; impasse in discussions 56-8; importance in planning 51-3; integration 26; maternity service 108-10; minor surgery 109; municipal control, 41-3, 53-6, 59-62, 86-7; negotiations 89-93; planning 37-43; remuneration 68; salaries *see* salaried service; separate practice 86
GPs, and Bevan's proposals 97-100, 146; financing 37; free entry to practice 42, 46, 47, 59; group

practice 36; in health centres 36; income 39, 47, 62-3, 101-2; join NHS 151; midwifery 131, 138; and MOHs 213; oppose NHS Act 152; pensions 59, 101, 102; and private practice 145; selection 42; superannuation 101, 102; surgery, inferior 109, 113-14, 139; and universal coverage 205; *see also* salaried service

gross national product, costs related to 199, 200

group practice 36, 44, 45; control of 45; importance 59; salaried service 64; *see also* health centres

Guillebaud Committee 176

health authorities, formation 61

health care, finance 187, 188, 189-90; and insurance principle 7, 8, 10, 187; spending 199

health centres 36, 44, 45; administration, representation in 78; advantages 59; area control 88; Bevan on 95-6, 105; BMA on 73, 75, 77, 81; Cabinet debate 67-9; 'consultoids' in 141; cost 58, 197; deferred 105-7; as diagnostic facility 107; equipment 40, 44, 197; experimental 58, 59, 67; hopes for 64; landlord-tenant relationship 87, 91; municipal control 47, 56, 66, 81, 86-7, 105-6; and NHS 179; planning 53; private patients 108, 145; and regional hospital boards 106; salaried service in 45, 59, 68, 89; Scotland 68, 81; statutory 47

health committees, representation on 96-7

Health, Ministry of, and Beveridge Committee 34-5; and BMA 77-8; and CHSC 88; and competition 104; and dependent coverage 14, 15, 189-90; disagreement with doctors 45-8; and EMS 189; and health centres 105; health service planning 33; hospital plan (1943) 166-7; hospital policy statement (1941) 189; and hospital service 16, 33, 188-9, 190; hospital survey 29, 33, 127, 128, 129; housing role 87-8; and insurance principle 187, 190; joint boards

78-81; Medical Advisory Committee (1943) 53; and medical profession 55; and medical representation on Boards 46-7; municipal control 20-1, 166, 167, 171, 173, 190; and nationalization 172-4; and NHI 5; and Nuffield Trust 27; and obstetric list 138; powers, increased 97-8; and regionalization 46, 79; and specialist services 13-15, 188, 189; and teaching hospitals 16; and unification 13, 15; and universal coverage 195; and voluntary hospitals 17, 18, 21, 159, 166-7, 173

health service, and Beveridge 36; BMA Commission (1940-42) 36; cost, estimated 40, 197; dependant coverage 44; funding 83-4; regional organization 133; universal coverage 44

Hetherington Committee (1941-3) 20, 161-2, 163; and hospital service 162, 166; and municipal control 173; and regional advisory councils 79

Highlands and Islands medical service 66

hospital building programme 199

hospital doctors, increase in 144; salaried 52; shortage 73

Hospital Endowments Fund 139

hospital management committees (HMC) 182

hospital planning group, Labour majority 171

Hospital Savings Association 127

hospital service, advisory boards 23; area tier 92-3; central control 135; and community care, split 106-7; cost 177; finance 24, 37, 39, 40; free provision 163-4; GP access 107; and GP service, separation 113-14; 'hotel' charge 40, 68, 159-60, 162, 198; insurance basis 19; joint authority 166-7, 168; nationalization 95, 97, 98, 103, 136-7; negotiations 92-3; planning 24; post-war policy 157-8; regional organization 92-3; state aid 114; White Paper 168-9

'hotel' charge 40, 68, 159-60, 198; dropped 162; voluntary hospitals 159-60

housing 87-8; and local government reform 61

independence fund (BMA) 149
industrial insurance 35
industrial medicine 130
Information, Ministry of 82
Insurance Act (1911) 115, 204, 205
Insurance Acts Committee 141
insurance committees, abolition 14; and
    medical benefit 5; membership 13;
    municipal control 13; representation
    on 91; recast 96, 97; and specialist
    services 15
Insurance Fund 193, 194, 195
insurance principle 187; abandoned 187;
    and medical care 7, 8, 10

joint boards 48; concessions on 65-7;
    conflict over 60-1; disadvantages 176,
    177; England and Wales 67; and
    Health, Ministry of 78-81; and local
    authorities 54, 78; medical
    representation on 46-7, 78; Scotland
    67, 80

Kent County Council 27
King's College Hospital 16
King's Fund 167; and nationalization
    136, 180; and voluntary hospitals
    160; White Paper, attacks 169

Labour Party, and competition 104;
    concessions to doctors 91-2; and
    hospital planning group 171; and
    hospital service 95; and joint boards
    61; and municipal control 173; and
    municipal maternity service 6; and
    nationalization 173; and outside
    representation 171; and salaried
    service 94; and sale of practices 90
LCC see London County Council
Let Us Face the Future 176
Liberal Party, and insurance principle
    202
life expectancy 203
local authorities, and area powers 135;
    and Bevan's concessions 106; conflict
    with doctors 45-8, 53-6, 59-62; and
    'consultoids' 139; and disciplinary
    procedures 72; and health centres 56,
    81, 105-6; hospital service 20, 175-6;
    and joint boards 60-1, 78; landlord
    role 87, 91; and medical
    representation 86; and nationalized

hospitals 143-4, 176, 179-80; and
    salaried service 89; and voluntary
    hospitals 20, 60, 161
Local Government Act (1929) 7, 8, 13,
    16, 21, 27, 54, 161, 177, 188, 189,
    207
Local Government Board 41-2
local government reorganization 133
Local Health Services Council 78, 168
location of practices, controls over 59,
    108
London, Emergency Medical Service
    17-18; hospitals, financial difficulties
    16-17, 144; sectors 144, 171, 176,
    179; war damage 179
London County Council (LCC) 7, 54; as
    area body 93, 171; and concessions
    to doctors 91; consultant salaries 116;
    and direct representation 55, 78; and
    EMS 17-18; health centres 106, 179;
    hospital service 65; and metropolitan
    boroughs 106; and nationalization
    136, 180; and Nuffield Trust 27; and
    regional organization 29; and sectors
    144; and teaching hospitals 16-17;
    and voluntary hospitals 17, 19; war
    damage 179; and White Paper 169
Lords, House of, and NHS Bill 99

Machinery of Government Committee 70
management see administration
maternal mortality rate 7; fall 11
Maternity Act (1937) 161
maternity benefit, and assurance societies
    6, 7, 9; and doctors 9
Maternity and Child Welfare Act (1918)
    7
maternity services, Bevan on 108-9;
    division of 137; GPs 108-10;
    metropolitan 179; municipal control
    6, 7-9, 72; national, plans for 6-7
means test 3, 9, 10; distaste for 161;
    and voluntary hospitals 158
Medical Act (1950) 119
medical clubs, and BMA 94
Medical Officers of Health (MOH),
    control by 54; doctors' objection to
    9, 208; domiciliary care 8; and health
    centres 105; and maternity services 6;
    and municipal control 121;
    supervisory role 9, 42, 86-7, 208
Medical Planning Commission (MPC)

36-7, 44, 45, 47, 146; and Hill 214; report (1942) 133; Royal Colleges on 115, 116; Teaching Hospital Committee 115, 116; and universal coverage 193, 209

Medical Planning Research and national health service 82

Medical Policy Association (MPA) 73-4; and central control 98; dies out 152; and PEP 82, 84; and sale of practices 98-9; and White Paper 81-5

Medical Practitioners' Union (MPU) 98, 207, 208, 209

medical profession, acquiescence in NHS 204; administration, representation in 46-7, 55-6, 69-70; and approved societies 62, 83, 106, 109; and assurance offices 9, 206; as businessmen 49; and CHSC 88; and Civil Service 215-16; collective responsibility 147; conflict with local authorities 53-6, 59-62; demands 87-8; and friendly societies 9, 205; and group practice 36, 44, 45; and health centres 36; and Health Ministry 55; hierarchy 113, 141, 142; influence on administration 206; influence on policy 215-16, 218; and joint boards 54; and local authorities 9, 43, 46-8, 53-6, 59-62, 87, 105-6, 206-8, 209, 213; and nationalization 136; negotiations with Bevan 147-8; and panel system 205-6; and regional organization 46, 79; and remuneration 45; and salaried service 48, 49-50, 90, 205, 209; socialism 77; and two-tier plan 81; and universal coverage 91, 204-5, 209

medical school organization 33

mental health service 195, 209; exclusion 40, 197; reform 40

metropolitan boroughs and LCC 106

middle classes and GP service 38

midwifery, GP 108-9, 110, 131, 138; payment 108, 109; pre-registration experience 131

Midwives Act (1936) 10, 102, 137

midwives, compensation 189; municipal control 8; salaried 8

MOH see Medical Officers of Health

MPA see Medical Policy Association

MPU see Medical Practitioners Union

municipal control, conflict over 45-8, 53-6, 59-62; diluting 41-3

municipal hospitals and NPHT 27

National Federation of Rural Workers' Approved Society 26

National Health Insurance (NHI), double standards 49; as hospital funding 24; and NHS 149; reform 34

National Health Service (NHS), costs 198-9; free entry 108, 182; and qualifications 209-10

National Health Service Bill, GPs, remuneration 99; opposition to 136

National Health Services Act (1948), opposition to 149-52

National Insurance Act (1911) 3-4, 115, 204, 205

National Insurance, Ministry, and health service 88

nationalization, Cabinet debate 175-9; and local government 176; as proposal 172-4; resistance to 174-5

New Zealand refund scheme 83

non-teaching consultants see consultants

Northern Ireland, basic salary 107; dismissal, appeals 108; free entry to NHS 182; GP midwifery 109; NHS Act (1948) 99, 108

Nuffield Provincial Hospitals Trust (NPHT) 23, 25, 26-9, 167; and BHA 180-1; hospital policy 157, 158; and hospital surveys (1945) 29, 172; influence 33; and joint boards 61; and municipal hospitals 27; nationalization 180; provident insurance scheme 120; standard service payments 168; and voluntary hospitals 160, 188; White Paper, attacks 169

obstetricians, and GP midwifery 109-10; list 138

optical service 195; charge 198

panel system, advantages 38; approved society influence 8-9; care standards 10, 43; competition with 39; disadvantages 5, 39, 41, 48; extension 4, 7, 8; free entry 39; income 39; reforms needed 59; retreat to 91

partnership agreements 108

part-time contracts 145
past service credits, and compensation 103, 104
patients join NHS 151
pay beds, access to 181, 182
pensions, GPs 59
PEP see Political and Economic Planning
planning bodies, conflict over 88
plebiscites (BMA) 107, 147, 148-9, 152, 182
Political and Economic Planning (PEP), and BMA 82; health care report (1937) 15; and MPA 82, 84; on medical representation 78
Poor Law 3, 6, 7, 9-10; and hospitals 177
Post-War Hospital Problems, Committee for Scotland on see Hetherington Committee
practice allowance 104; see also salaried service
practices, free entry to 42, 46, 47, 59 vacancies, appointment to 47
practices, sale of 39, 75, 76-7, 81; abolition 47, 59; Bevan on 96, 100-3, 103-4; and BMA 75, 76-7, 81; compensation for 100-3, 202; negotiations 90-1; and property rights 98-9; retaining 69; value 43
private practice 38; debate on 68-9; and double standards 58; in health centres 108; and list size 59; in NHS 145; restricting 58; retaining 57-8; surgeons 118; universal coverage 118-19; see also pay beds
prontosil 11
provincial hospitals 161; association of 123-5
Provincial Surgical Club 123
Public Health Act (1875) 16
Public Health Act (1936) 46, 161, 188
public health service 179; salaries 39

RCOG see Royal College of Obstetricians and Gynaecologists
RCP see Royal College of Physicians
RCS see Royal College of Surgeons
Reconstruction Committee 168; on CHSC 81; and direct representation 78; and health centres 67-9; and 'hotel' charge 161, 162-3; private practice rights 68-9; and represent-ation 69-70, 81; and sale of practices 69, 90-1; and White Paper 201
Reconstruction Priorities Committee, amalgamation 67; and joint boards 65-7; White Paper, debating 65-9, 70
Reconstruction Problems Committee 23, 67; and GP service 33; and workmen's compensation 34
regional hospital boards (RHB) and health centres 106
regional organization 20, 22; and consultants 88; debating 23-4, 25, 29; directly elected 46; dismissal of 48; doctors' role in 24; and Health Ministry 79; and medical profession 79; powers 92, 134; voluntary hospitals 19-20, 170
representation, medical see administration
revenue costs 199
Royal College of General Practice 142
Royal College of Obstetricians and Gynaecologists (RCOG), and consultant lists 131-2; and 'consultoids' 131; financial difficulties 119; manpower needs 131; and nationalization 137-8; and standing committee 120; status 119-20
Royal College of Physicians (RCP), 'Beveridge Committee' 120, 121, 122-3, 124, 125, 136; Comitia 118, 121, 122, 136, 137; constitution 116; elitism 118; financial resources 119; influence 115; and nationalization 137; non-teaching consultants 122; and regional powers 134; role 119
Royal College of Surgeons (RCS): elitism 118; financial affairs 118-19, 140, 141; and nationalization 139-41; and NHS Act 150-1; non-teaching consultants 122; and private practice 58; records 118; tax-free status 119
Royal Colleges, and BMA opposition to NHS Bill 147; differences between 118-20; and provinces 123-4; and regionalization 134; standing committee (1933) 120; unity, attempts at 120-1; and the universities 128
Royal Commission, demand for 57
Royal Commission on Doctors' and Dentists' Remuneration 142
Royal Commission on National Health

Insurance (1926) 5
Royal Commission on Workmen's
Compensation (1939-40) 34-5
Rushcliffe Committee (1943) 167

salaried service 24; basic salary 96, 97,
99, 104, 107-8; Bevan on 95, 96, 97,
99-100, 104, 219-21; Beveridge on
37; central control 47; consultants 51;
debate on 38-9, 40; experiments 43;
GP fears of 97; group practice 64;
health centres 68; hospital doctors 52;
hostility towards 41; levels of pay
62-3; medical profession 48, 49, 90;
political differences on 201; and
restriction of choice 45; and sale of
practices 98-9; support for 49-50; and
training 59; Treasury pressure 104
Sankey Commission (1937) 19, 23,
26-7, 181
Scotland, beds, shortage 161; central
control 65, 66; GP maternity services
10-11, 109; health centres 68, 81;
'hotel' charge, rejection 161-2; joint
boards 67, 80, 170; maternity policy
10-11; and medical representation
64-5; municipal control 61; municipal
domiciliary care 7-8; municipal
maternity services 10-11; teaching
hospitals 176; voluntary hospitals
161-2
Scottish Committee (1943) 20
Scottish Department, and EMS hospitals
161; and teaching hospitals 176; and
voluntary hospitals 157
Social Security League 84-5
Social Security Ministry, Insurance Fund
193, 194, 195
Socialist Medical Association (SMA) 18,
49; and concessions to doctors 91;
and municipal control 173, 209; and
nationalization 173, 176; and salaried
service 74; and universal state service
207-8, 209
specialist service see consultant service
specialists see consultants
Spens Committee on Consultant
Remuneration 144, 151, 182
Spens Committee on GP Remuneration
101, 102, 104, 127, 131, 134, 140,
142
superannuation 101, 102

surgeons, private practice 118, 205;
resist nationalization 139-41; training
139

TB treatment 14, 15
teaching hospitals, financial problems
16, 158; funds 157; GP-consultants
113; honorary status 114; and
nationalization 176; special status
176; state aid 16
Teviot Committee 195
trade unions, and Beveridge Report
(1942) 34-6; and disability benefit
13-14; and insurance industry 9; NHI
reform 34; and unificiation 13; and
workmens' compensation 34
Trades Union Congress (TUC), and
assurance societies 192; BMA,
alliance with 9-10, 34, 91-2, 108;
and CHSC 92; and nationalization
192; and workmen's compensation
192
training, post-graduate 59
Treasury, and compensation for practices
202; and free hospital service 164;
and health service costs 188, 200-1,
202-3; and hospital service 166, 187,
188, 189, 190; and maternity service
202; and midwifery payments 109;
and salaried service 92, 104; and sale
of practices 92, 103-4
treatment, double standards 43, 49, 58
TUC see Trades Union Congress

UGC see University Grants Committee
unemployment benefit 14
unification, and extension 13-15
unit grant 60
universal coverage 44; and BMA 73;
and medical profession 91; and
private practice 118-19
university faculties and consultant lists
127-8, 129
University Grants Committee (UGC) 16,
157, 188
Urban District Councils Association, and
joint boards 61

Volims Committee 124-5
voluntary hospitals, and Beveridge
165-6; and 'consultoids' 113, 139-40;
contributory schemes 159, 160;

control of 80; and cottage hospitals
114; and EMS 17-18, 158; end of
183; finance 28, 29, 60, 188;
financial dependence 165, 169-70,
172, 175; financial problems 114,
158; Health Ministry dislike of 160;
honorary service 52, 114, 180; 'hotel
charge' 159-60; isolation 23; and
joint authority 168-9; and LCC 17,
157; and Local Health Services
Committee 168; and means tests 158;
and municipal control 55, 60, 157
nationalization 18-21, 136, 180-1;
private finance 158, 160, 165, 169;
and private patients 158; regional
organization 19-20, 170; regional
powers, loss 93; Scottish 161-2; and
the state 16, 18; trust funds 180; and
White Paper 168-9
Voluntary Hospitals Commission (1937)
see Sankey Commission

White Paper on the NHS (Feb. 1944)
53, 120; alterations to 70; and BMA
81-5; Cabinet debate 65-9, 70;
criticism of 75-6; and health centres
64; on hospital service 168-9; and
'hotel' charge 163; medical reaction
to 72-4; and Moran 121; and
municipal control 171; negotiations
following 127; parliamentary debate
75-6; and teaching hospitals 123; and
voluntary hospitals 168-9
White Paper, second (1945) 92, 93
Woodberry Down 179
workers' control, principle of 98
workmen's compensation 9, 34, 192
Workmen's Compensation Bill (1943)
178

Yalta, Moran at 134